THE CLASSICS
OF WESTERN
SPIRITUALITY

# Nicholas of Cusa

## SELECTED SPIRITUAL WRITINGS

TRANSLATED AND INTRODUCED BY
**H. LAWRENCE BOND**

PREFACE BY
**MORIMICHI WATANABE**

PAULIST PRESS
NEW YORK • MAHWAH

*Cover art:* This representation of Nicholas of Cusa is taken from *Nikolaus von Kues, 1401–1464, Leben und Werk im Bild,* edited by Helmut Gestrich, p. 5, Mainz, Hermann Schmidt, 1990. Photo: Landesbildsteele Rheinland-Pfalz. The photo is cropped from a triptych painting dating from 1460 that now resides over the altar at the chapel in the St.-Nikolaus-Hospital in Kues.

The publisher and translator are grateful for permission to translate *Nicolai de Cusa, De apice theoriae* from *Nicolai de Cusa Opera omnia.* Vol. XII. *De venatione sapientiae.—De apice theoriae.* Ediderunt commentariisque illustraverunt Raymundus Klibansky et Iohannes Gerhardus Senger. © Felix Meiner Verlag. Hamburg, 1981.

The translator is in debt to other volumes in this opera upon which translations were also derived.

Library of Congress Cataloging-in-Publication Data

Nicholas, of Cusa, Cardinal, 1401–1464.
   [Selections. English. 1997]
   Selected spiritual writings / Nicholas of Cusa; translated and introduced by H. Lawerence Bond.
     p.  cm. — (The classics of Western spirituality; #89)
   Includes bibliographical references (p.   ) and indexes.
   Contents: On learned ignorance—Dialogue on the hidden God—On seeking God—On the vision of God—On the summit of contemplation.
    ISBN 0-8091-3698-8 — ISBN 0-8091-0482-2 (alk. paper).
   1. Spiritual life—Catholic Church.  2. Catholic Church—Doctrines.  I. Bond, H. Lawrence.  II. Title.  III. Series.
BX2349.N49213   1997
248 — DC21                                     96-44466
                                                          CIP

Published by Paulist Press
997 Macarthur Boulevard
Mahwah, New Jersey 07430

Printed and bound in the United States of America

# CONTENTS

FOREWORD                                                                     xi
PREFACE                                                                      xiii
ABBREVIATIONS                                                                xix


## INTRODUCTION

  I. LIFE AND TIMES                                                3
 II. IMPORTANCE                                                         13
III. THE COINCIDENCE OF OPPOSITES:
    *ON LEARNED IGNORANCE*                                19
    *On Learned Ignorance* and Cusa's Earliest Use of the
      Coincidence of Opposites                   21
    Book One: God as Absolute Maximum                     23
    Book Two: The World as Contracted Maximum             23
    Book Three: Christ as Absolute and Contracted Maximum 24
    Theological Application of Coincidence                27
      A Proper Consideration                    27
      A Proper Application                      32
 IV. THE SPIRITUALITY OF IGNORANCE: *DIALOGUE
    ON THE HIDDEN GOD* AND
    *ON SEEKING GOD*                                      36
    Ignorance and the Knowledge of God in *Dialogue on the
      Hidden God*                               37
    Ignorance and the Spirituality of Seeing in *On Seeking God*  39
  V. MYSTICAL THEOLOGY AND COINCIDENCE:
    *ON THE VISION OF GOD*                                43
    Reappropriation of Coincidence in *On the Vision of God*  44

# CONTENTS

| | |
|---|---|
| Application of Coincidence to Mystical Theology | 48 |
| The Evocative Function | 49 |
| The Descriptive Function | 50 |
| VI. CONTEMPLATION AND THEOLOGY: *ON THE SUMMIT OF CONTEMPLATION* | 56 |
| Sight as Gift | 61 |
| Sight as Ascent | 63 |
| Sight as Fulfillment | 67 |
| A Note About Capitalization of Terms | 70 |
| NOTES TO INTRODUCTION | 71 |

*ON LEARNED IGNORANCE*    85

*DIALOGUE ON THE HIDDEN GOD*    207

*ON SEEKING GOD*    215

*ON THE VISION OF GOD*    233

*ON THE SUMMIT OF CONTEMPLATION*    291

| | |
|---|---|
| NOTES TO TEXTS | 304 |
| A BRIEF GLOSSARY OF CUSAN TERMS | 335 |
| SELECT BIBLIOGRAPHY | 341 |
| INDEXES | 357 |

Translator of This Volume

HUGH LAWRENCE BOND was born in Memphis, Tennessee, and received an A.B. degree from Lambuth College (Jackson, Tenn.) and B.D. and Ph.D. degrees from Duke University. He has published articles on medieval intellectual and ecclesiastical history and a book, with James Biechler, entitled *Nicholas of Cusa on Interreligious Harmony*, which includes a translation of Cusa's *De pace fidei*. Professor of medieval history at Appalachian State University, where from 1979 to 1981 he was named I. G. Greer Distinguished Professor of History, he is past president of the American Cusanus Society. He is also an ordained minister in the United Methodist Church. Currently he is writing a book on the mystical theology of Nicholas of Cusa.

Author of the Preface

MORIMICHI WATANABE received his Ph.D. in political theory and comparative government from Columbia University in 1961, following an LL.B. from the University of Tokyo. He is presently professor of history and political science at Long Island University — C. W. Post Campus. He has also taught at Meiji Gakuin University, Keio University, Himeji Dokkyo University and Seigakuin University in Japan. His monograph *The Political Ideas of Nicholas of Cusa, with Special Reference to His "De concordantia catholica"* (1963) was one of the earliest books on Cusanus in English published after World War II. Currently he serves not only as president of the American Cusanus Society but also as editor of the *American Cusanus Society Newsletter*. In addition, he is a member of the Scholarly Advisory Board of the Cusanus-Gesellschaft in Germany and honorary advisor to the Japanese Cusanus Society.

*For my wife, Shelly,*
*and*
*my daughter, Stephanie,*
*whose gifts of love and grace*
*gladden my heart*
*and deepened this book.*

# FOREWORD

$B$ehind every book there is a story, and behind a long book, especially one that has occupied years in the making, there is a long
story and an equally long list of indebtedness. What is of value in
the following volume owes much to the assistance and encouragement of several individuals and to the support of grants and insti-
tutions, although they in no way bear responsibility for any of its
shortcomings.

I am especially grateful for the support of the libraries of Duke
University and of Donn Michael Farris, formerly head librarian of
Duke Divinity School; Thomas Izbicki of the Eisenhower Library
at Johns Hopkins University; the Cusanus-Bibliothek at the St.-
Nikolaus-Hospital in Bernkastel-Kues; and the Institut für Cusanus-
Forschung at Trier. I bear an enduring personal and professional debt
to the Institute's late director, Professor Dr. Rudolf Haubst. Grants
from the National Endowment of Humanities and from the Board
of Trustees, the Graduate Research Council, and the International
Studies Program at Appalachian State University made much of the
research possible. Specific research assistance from Peter Robbins,
Philip Kielty, and particularly Donna Spivey Ellington importantly
facilitated the work, as did secretarial support from Brenda Green,
Lorraine Childers, and Kathy Issacs. Many thanks also to colleagues
and friends who read all or part of the manuscript and offered valuable
suggestions: Charles Blanck, Maria Lichtmann, William Strickland,
Karen Lohr, and especially my wife and soulful colleague, Shelly Wil-
son. I am grateful also to members of the American Cusanus Society,
who, over the years, have patiently listened to and offered kind cri-
tique of sections of this work, especially F. Edward Cranz, Thomas
McTighe, Donald Duclow, and Clyde Lee Miller. An older debt be-

longs to my late mentors and dear friends Ray C. Petry, of Duke University, and Martin Schmidt, of the University of Heidelberg. Also, a special word of appreciation belongs to Maria L. Maggi, the insightful and resourceful editor at Paulist Press. Finally, this work would never have been started or completed without, at different stages, the encouragement of Richard Payne, Ewert Cousins, and Bernard McGinn. I pray this work does credit to all these and to the powerful contemplative theology of that remarkable *idiota* Nicholas of Cusa.

Memorial of St. John Chrysostom                    Deep Gap, N. C.
Holy Cross Eve

# PREFACE

The present selection of the spiritual writings of Nicholas of Cusa (1401–1464) in English translation will certainly contribute to the enhancement of the already considerable reputation he has as one of the most original thinkers of the fifteenth century and also to the diffusion of his name, which is not so well known in the English-speaking countries as in Europe and elsewhere. A few words on the origins of the fame and contemporary significance of his ideas are in order.

Although there were always some writers in his own period and after his death in 1464 who were influenced by Cusanus, it cannot be said that his works were widely read and studied in the following centuries. To be sure, the first edition of many of his works was published in Strasbourg in 1488 by Martin Flach, the second edition, which is usually known as the Milan edition, was printed by Benedetto Dolcibelli at Cortemaggiore in 1502, the third edition was issued in Paris in 1514 by the famous humanist Jacques Lefèvre d'Étaples, and the fourth edition was published in Basel in 1565, edited by Heinrich Petri. But it was after the beginning of the romantic movement in the middle of the eighteenth century that more attention began to be paid to this rather obscure, if not completely forgotten, thinker of the fifteenth century. A large number of books and articles on Cusanus were produced after the nineteenth century, and Cusanus studies reached a milestone when the *Nicolai de Cusa Opera omnia*, the complete works of Nicholas of Cusa, were initiated in 1932 by the Heidelberg Academy of Sciences under the editorship of Ernst Hoffmann (1880–1952) and Raymond Klibansky (1905– ).

What especially promoted and facilitated Cusanus research after a period of difficulties and unproductivity due to World War II was the five-hundredth anniversary of his death in 1964. In preparation for the occasion, the Cusanus-Gesellschaft was established in Germany in 1960 and started to organize commemorative events and to publish scholarly and popular literature on Cusanus. There was even talk of the Cusanus Renaissance in this connection. The Cusanus-Gesellschaft held its first symposium in 1964 and has sponsored ten symposia since then. Its chief organ, the *Mitteilungen und Forschungsbeiträge der Cusanus-Gesellschaft*, which began publication in 1961, has reached volume 22 in 1995. As part of the *Opera omnia*, Cusanus' sermons began to be edited and published in 1970. In parallel with the *Opera omnia*, a new series, called the *Acta Cusana*, was launched in 1976 by Erich Meuthen and Hermann Hallauer. It was designed to publish all extant documents, letters, deeds, and other materials in which Cusanus or his activities are mentioned. The *Acta Cusana*, vol. 1, no. 1 (1401–May 17, 1437) and no. 2 (May 17, 1437–December 31, 1450) were published in 1976 and 1983, respectively, and vol. 1, no. 3 (January 1451–March 1452), which will contain more than fifteen hundred entries, is scheduled to appear in the fall of 1996. Perhaps no other medieval thinker's life has been studied so carefully and minutely.

Stimulated by these new developments, in 1971 a small group of Japanese scholars organized the Cusanus Association of Japan, which, after a period of inactivity, was reorganized as the Japanese Cusanus Society in 1982. The Society has published its *Annual Reports* and the *Studia Cusana*, vols. 1–3 (1991, 1993, 1995) and has held a Cusanus conference almost every year. In the United States, in 1981 Professor H. Lawrence Bond and a few other scholars were instrumental in organizing the Cusanus Society of America, which was expanded and developed into the American Cusanus Society in 1983. The society has sponsored three sessions at the International Congress on Medieval Studies in Kalamazoo, Michigan, every year since 1983 and has held five biennial conferences on the works of Nicholas of Cusa in Gettysburg, Pennsylvania, since 1986. The *American Cusanus Society Newsletter*, the latest issue being vol. 13, no. 1 (June 1996), has served as a means of communication and research for its members and supporters.

Although they have no formal organizations as in Germany, Japan, and the United States, a fairly large number of Cusanus scholars and researchers can be found these days in the Scandinavian countries, the Netherlands, and such eastern European countries as Russia and Poland. Thus, thanks to the activities of the Cusanus societies and independent scholars in many countries, great progress in Cusanus research has already been made in the past thirty to forty years. It is quite possible that the forthcoming celebration in 2001 of the six-hundredth anniversary of Cusanus' birth will bring further attention to the life and works of the man from Bernkastel-Kues in Germany.

How can one account for the fame of Nicholas of Cusa not only in Europe and the United States but also in an east Asian country like Japan? Does he offer ideas that are interesting, attractive, and stimulating not only to the Western mind but also to the Oriental one? Do some of his spiritual and metaphysical ideas, especially mystical and religious ones, engage the minds of people anywhere in the world who seek answers to many perennial problems we face today? In this connection, there are three aspects of Cusanus' life and thought that are worth discussing here briefly.

The first is the question of Cusanus' influence on later thinkers. Various claims or overinterpretations have been made for Cusanus' influence on later thinkers. He is said to have influenced Ficino, da Vinci, Pico, Campanella, Bruno, Copernicus, Kepler, Spinoza, Leibniz, Kant, Lessing, Hegel, Schelling, and others. He himself was partly responsible for this development because he often used ambiguous terminologies and unclear concepts. But many of the assertions of his presumed influence on later thinkers are difficult to prove clearly. Since the writer's significance in the history of ideas does not depend solely on his influence on other thinkers, the paucity of Cusanus' influence on others should not detain us here unduly.

More important, secondly, are Nicholas of Cusa's own personality and the kind of life he lived. He lived a fully engaged, busy, and active life as a conciliarist thinker at the council of Basel from 1432 to 1437; a papal champion against the neutrality of German princes from 1438 to 1449; a papal *legatus a latere* to reform religious life, to mediate disputes, and to dispense jubilee indulgences in Germany and the Low Countries between 1451 and 1452; a tragic reform-minded bishop of Brixen against Sigismund, Duke of Austria and Count of the Tyrol, from 1452 to 1459; and a papal vicar-general in Rome after 1459, still anxious to bring about reform in the church. Almost a *homo politicus*, as a recent blurb on his works characterized him, he still managed to produce his brilliant spiritual, mystical, and contemplative writings. His *vita activa* was fascinatingly intertwined with his *vita contemplativa*. According to Karl Jaspers, he was "the only one of the great philosophers to have led a busy life." His sense of responsibility was strong; his devotion to the ideal of reform was steadfast. Yet he managed to produce about twenty-five philosophical and spiritual works. The total number of his works is more than fifty.

As is indicated in Professor Bond's Introduction that follows, because his life was threatened by the soldiers of Duke Sigismund after his visit to Wilten near Innsbruck on 26 and 27 June 1457, Bishop Cusanus left his episcopal city of Brixen and, wandering through the wilderness of the Dolomites, finally reached Castle Andraz with the help of Archangel Raphael, as he himself wrote later. The grateful bishop called the castle St. Raphaelsburg. Anyone who visits the isolated, forlorn castle at Andraz in the remote region of Buchenstein in the Diocese of Brixen today will wonder how Cusanus could concentrate on writing the *De beryllo* (1458), that book of meditation, in the lonely castle after so great a humiliation in his active life. He also completed the *Caesarea circuli quadratura* (1457) at Castle Andraz, and possibly the *De possest* (1460). Although many of his reform attempts in the Tyrol, Orvieto, and Rome failed in the last years of his life, his intellectual powers did not show any sign of decline. What kind of man was he? How could he sustain himself intellectually under so much pressure? This mystery contributes much to contemporary fascination with Cusanus.

Thirdly, the most important factor to be considered in assessing any thinker's importance is, no doubt, his own ideas. Although there are scholars who maintain that even in his later works Cusanus did not deviate from the philosophical and metaphysical ideas he expressed in his earliest and best known philosophical work, the *De docta ignorantia* (1440), Professor Bond takes the position that Cusanus' philosophical position developed and changed. Starting with the negative theology of the *De docta ignorantia* that God is beyond the reach of the human reason and intellect and that there is no proportion between the finite and the Infinite, Cusanus moved on, in the *De visione Dei* (1453), to the concept of the wall of paradise or contradictions, beyond which God can be found, and at Easter in 1464 reached his final metaphysical position that God is best designated as the *Posse Ipsum* (Possibility Itself). This implies that the truth, instead of being found in the darkness, *in obscuro*, of the *De docta ignorantia*, can be easily seen everywhere. Although Cusanus seems to stress continuity in his thought, the enthusiasm with which he speaks of the Possibility Itself is apparent. As a result, the name for God is now much more positive. These new discoveries in the Easter season of 1464 made him beam with joy.

This "progressive" interpretation of Cusanus' views on God and the *Quiddity* or *Whatness* began to be stressed only relatively recently by some Cusanus scholars. It is only when the reader of the present collection studies the works of Cusanus carefully that the validity of the above interpretation can be grasped and appreciated. Cusanus himself was a relentless seeker after truth. Our task is to let him speak for himself. More than his influence on other thinkers and his life and personality, his ideas—metaphysical, spiritual, and religious—are finding repercussions not only in the West but also in other parts of the world. As the recent publication of the French (1977), German (1982—fifth German translation), Swedish (1983), English (two in 1990), Japanese (1992), Dutch (1993), and English (1993—fourth English translation) translations of his *De pace fidei* (1453) demonstrates, there is a great deal of interest in Cusanus' ideas about religious pluralism and harmony as well.

Some of Cusanus' commentators and critics have pointed out that although his speculative and metaphysical ideas are magnificent and full of creative imaginativeness, they are often paradoxical, cryptic, and even impenetrable. His terminology is said to be loose, and his definitions imprecise. It is rather well known that his Latin is rough and never simple. There are more serious charges against him. Some critics have said that he had no sense of sin, that he experienced no change of heart, and that he was scarcely aware of the problem of evil. To separate his philosophy from his religious context, it is said, is to destroy his philosophical ideas. Compared with these grave criticisms, the comment that he made no attempt to prove the existence of God sounds almost academic.

How true or well-founded are these criticisms? Again, the best way to know the answer is to turn to Cusanus' writings in the present selection and read and study them carefully. In the course of engagement with Cusanus' works, the reader will be able to find out what kind of thinker Cusanus was and to know why there has been so much interest recently in the works of Nicholas of Cusa. And let us hope that like one of the human beings in Plato's allegory of the cave, the reader can ascend from the darkness of the cave and, going through various philosophical and metaphysical stages and barriers, finally reach the Light that shines forth brightly. It was this ascent and discovery that brought Cusanus great joy in the Easter season of 1464.

# ABBREVIATIONS

BGPThM =     *Beiträge zur Geschichte der Philosophie und Theologie des Mittelalters*

CCSL =     *Corpus Christianorum, Series Latina.* Turnhout, 1954ff.

*Dionysiaca* =     Philippe Chevalier. *Dionysiaca: Recueil donnant l'ensemble des traditions latines des ouvrages attribués au Denys de l'Aréopage.* 2 vols. (Paris, 1937–1950)

DDI =     *De docta ignorantia*

Eckhart LW =     *Die lateinischen Werke,* edited by J. Koch (Stuttgart-Berlin, 1936– )

h =     *Nicolai de Cusa Opera omnia iussu et auctoritate Academiae Litterarum Heidelbergensis* (Leipzig-Hamburg, 1932– )

    Individual works are cited by book, chapter, section number; the *Opera* by volume, page, and line. For example, DDI I.6.15 (h I.13, 1–2) refers to *De docta ignorantia,* Book One, Chapter Six, Section 15 (Heidelberg edition, Volume One, page 13, lines 1–2).

HSB =     *Sitzungsberichte der Heidelberger Akademie der Wissenschaften.* Philosophisch-historische Klasse (Heidelberg)

# ABBREVIATIONS

MFCG =       *Mitteilungen und Forschungsbeiträge der Cusa-nus-Gesellschaft*

P =       *Nicolai Cusae Cardinalis Operae*, ed. Faber Stapulensis (Paris, 1514) (reprinted Frankfurt/M., 1962)

PL =       J. P. Migne (ed.), *Patrologia cursus completus . . . Series Latina*

*Schriften* =       *Schriften des Nikolaus von Kues in deutscher Übersetzung hg. im Auftrag der Heidelberger Akademie der Wissenschaften* (Leipzig, 1936ff., and Hamburg 1949ff.)

---

The following is a list of the works cited in this book from the edition of the Heidelberg Academy (h):

I.       *De docta ignorantia*, ed. E. Hoffmann and R. Klibansky (1932)

II.       *Apologia doctae ignorantiae*, ed. R. Klibansky (1932)

III.       *De coniecturis*, ed. I. Koch and K. Bormann with I. G. Senger (1972)

IV.       *Opuscula* I, ed. P. Wilpert (1959): *De Deo abscondito; De quaerendo Deum; De filiatione Dei; De dato patris luminum; Coniectura de ultimis diebus; De genesi*

V.       *Idiota de sapientia. Idiota de mente*, ed. L. Baur (1937); *Idiota de staticis experimentis*, ed. L. Baur (1937)

$V^2$.       *Idiota de sapientia. Idiota de mente*, ed. R. Steiger (1983). *Idiota de staticis experimentis*, ed. L. Baur (1983)

# ABBREVIATIONS

VII.  *De pace fidei cum epistula ad Ioannem de Segobia,* ed. R. Klibansky and H. Bascour (1959)

VII².  *De pace fidei cum epistula ad Ioannem de Segobia,* ed. R. Klibansky and H. Bascour (1970)

VIII.  *Cribratio Alkorani,* ed. L. Hagemann (1986)

X,2a.  *Opuscula* II: Fasc. 2a. *De theologicis complementis,* ed. A. D. Riemann and C. Bormann (1994)

X,2b.  *Opuscula* II: Fasc. 2b. *De deo unitrino principio. Tu quis es (De principio),* ed. C. Bormann and A. D. Riemann (1988)

XI,1.  *De beryllo,* ed. L. Baur (1940)

XI,1².  *De beryllo,* ed. I. G. Senger and C. Bormann (1988)

XI,2.  *Trialogus de possest,* ed. R. Steiger (1973)

XI,3.  *Compendium,* ed. B. Decker and C. Bormann (1964)

XII.  *De venatione sapientiae; De apice theoriae,* ed. R. Klibansky and I. G. Senger (1981)

XIII.  *Directio speculantis seu de non aliud,* ed. L. Baur and P. Wilpert (1944)

XVI, 1, 2, 3, 4.  *Sermones* (1430–1441), ed. R. Haubst, M. Bodewig, and W. Krämer (1970–1985)

XVII.  *Sermones* II (1443–1452), fasc. I–II, ed. R. Haubst and H. Schnarr (1983, 1991)

XVIII.  *Sermones* III (1452–1455), fasc. I, ed. R. Haubst and H. Pauli (1995)

# Introduction

# I. LIFE AND TIMES

Nicholas of Cusa was one of the most remarkable thinkers of the fifteenth century and at the same time actively engaged in his era's most critical ecclesiastical disputes in Italy and the Holy Roman Empire. His life (1401–1464) spans the first six decades of the fifteenth century, which represents the demarcation of the Middle Ages from the Renaissance in northern Europe and simultaneously the crowning point of Renaissance culture in Italy and southern Europe.

Specific issues preoccupying ecclesiastical and secular leadership during his youth would one day critically shape his public life. England and France were still embroiled in the Hundred Years' War (1338–1453); the papacy suffered the humiliation of a triple schism with Alexander V (1409–1410) added by the council of Pisa to the list of rival claimants that included Gregory XII (1406–1416) of the Roman line and Benedict XIII (1394–1423) of the Avignonese line; conciliarism enjoyed a short-lived triumph and dominated the deliberations at the councils of Pisa (1409) and Constance (1414–1417); the newly elected Pope Martin V (1417–1431) successfully ended the schism, recovered the papal states, but disdained the conciliar and reform movements that brought him to power; Venice was at war with the Turks over activity in the Aegean; Sigismund of Luxembourg (1410–1437), Holy Roman Emperor as well as king of Bohemia and king of Hungary, called the council of Constance and advocated unity and reform; yet John of Hus was burned at the stake at Constance notwithstanding the emperor's promise of safe passage; and nationalism and the Hussite wars (1420–1433) were increasingly dominating Bohemia.

Cusa was born in Germany at Kues just across the Mosel River from its twin village Bernkastel.[1] He was the child of Katherina Roemer and Johan Cryfftz (or Krebs), a prospering boatman and merchant with an impressive house along the river. His siblings included a younger sister, Klara, and a younger brother, Johannes, a priest who received the parish church of Bernkastel and supervised the construction of the St. Nicholas hospice that Nicholas founded at Kues.[2] As a student, he referred to himself as Nycolaus Cancer de Coesse, later as Nicolaus de Cusa. Italian humanists first knew him as Nicolaus

3

# INTRODUCTION

Treverensis, but Aeneas Sylvius Piccolomini preferred the name Nicolaus Cusanus.[3]

In 1416 he entered the University of Heidelberg, rich in scholastic tradition and then dominated by conciliarism and the nominalism of the *via moderna*. He went on to study at the University of Padua, where he completed the degree of Doctor of Decretals by 1423. He studied with Giuliano Cesarini, the canonist, later cardinal and a president of the council of Basel, who became a lifelong friend and mentor.[4] He also befriended the mathematician and physician Paolo del Pozzo Toscanelli, who in 1443 sent Cusa Ambrogio Traversari's translation of Pseudo-Dionysius' *The Mystical Theology.*[5] Cusa's work in Italy enabled him later to acquire a reputation for himself as collector of classical manuscripts, particularly the lost comedies of Plautus.[6]

In 1425 he enrolled at the University of Cologne and lectured in canon law. He also studied theology and philosophy there under the tutelage of his friend Heymeric van den Velde (de Campo)[7] at which time he probably came in contact with the theology of Pseudo-Dionysius,[8] Ramon Lull,[9] and Thierry of Chartres[10] as well as Heymeric's version of Albertus Magnus.[11]

Though not yet a priest, he received several benefices near his birthplace and by 1432 represented Ulrich of Manderscheid's claim to the archbishopric of Trier at the council of Basel.[12] During its deliberations he became engaged with the larger questions of church reform and of harmony and concord among differing rites and factions within Western Christendom. Cusa was incorporated into the council and made a member of the committee on faith and quickly rose within the structure of the council's leadership. He wrote his first works on its behalf: (1) a reconciliatory opusculum to enable the Hussites to rejoin the Catholic communion (1433);[13] (2) a proposal for resolving the question of presidency over the council's deliberations, *De auctoritate praesidendi in concilio generali* (1434);[14] (3) an elaborate treatise on ecclesiology and conciliarism, entitled *De concordantia catholica* (1434);[15] and (4) a plan for reforming the church's calendar, *Reparatio kalendarii* (1434/1435).[16]

Cusa undoubtedly would have been remembered in ecclesiastical history exclusively as an effective ecclesiastical lawyer and a major spokesman for conciliarism had it not been for a radical turn of events at the council that caused him to depart Basel and join Pope Eugene

IV, who was in the process of transferring the council to Ferrara in Italy, against the wishes of the majority leadership at Basel.[17]

Cusa had earlier been a vigorous advocate of conciliarism and had opposed Pope Eugene IV's effort to dissolve the council. But in late 1436 he voted with the minority to support Eugene's choice for the location of the new council. On May 7, 1437, the council formally split into two factions in the disagreement over the site for a union council with the Greeks. Cusa joined the papal party, and on May 20, together with the bishops of Digne and Oporto, he departed with the minority faction's decree to Bologna.[18] In July, Eugene sent Cusa and the two bishops as his official delegates to Constantinople to help secure Greek approval for a joint East-West council in Italy.[19] The trip to the East and return journey home left a profound impression on him. His career and his thought were never again the same.

He therefore experienced two major shifts following his entry into conciliar work: The first, the break with Basel, brought him into the papal camp, to an ideology of collegiality under papal authority in the spatial and temporal church; and the second, the journey eastward, which turned out to be a spiritual pilgrimage, provided him with a fresh vision of unity and difference coexisting not only within the church but also in the soul's experience of God and world.

The lengthy return voyage to Venice provided interesting company. The Greek traveling companions apparently included Bessarion, the Archbishop of Nicaea, who became a lasting friend and corrected a copy of Aristotle's *Metaphysics* for him; Georgius Gemistus Plethon, a vigorous and effective advocate of Platonism; and the theologian Marcus Eugenicus, Archbishop of Ephesus.[20] Cusa, however, tells us nothing of his conversations during the two months' journey, but he does record a profound experience. A revelation of some sort, which he describes as a divine gift, brought him to a vision of the "incomprehensible" and a way of speaking about the ineffable for which he says he had for years struggled unsuccessfully before receiving this illumination.[21] He returned apparently with a number of Greek manuscripts, including codices of early councils and patristic writings for resolving differences in the negotiations at the union council and perhaps with a Greek text of the *Platonic Theology* of Proclus.[22]

The council of Ferrara opened in January of 1438 before the Greeks arrived and was transferred in 1439 to Florence, where later in the year it ended with a fragile union agreement between the Greek and Latin churches. Cusa may have attended the council but only briefly. He rapidly became occupied with negotiations at successive German imperial diets on behalf of the papal cause against that of the council of Basel.

After Cusa's break with Basel and his work as papal emissary to Constantinople, his career falls into four rather distinct stages: (1) papal advocate before the imperial diets, 1438–1449; (2) cardinal-legate to Germany and the Netherlands, 1450–1452; (3) bishop at Brixen, 1450/1452–1460; and (4) papal adviser, vicar-general, and *camerarius* 1459/1460–1464.

In the fall of 1437 the pope had transferred the council of Basel to Ferrara against the wishes of the conciliar majority. The German princes and the emperor, in March 1438, declared their neutrality in the resultant conflict between council and pope. The council in turn pronounced the pope a heretic and in June 1439 proceeded to depose him. In November Duke Amadeus VIII of Savoy was elected antipope Felix V. Both the papal and conciliar sides now devoted their attention to winning support from the monarchs and princes of Europe. From 1438 until 1447 Cusa became an important figure in successive papal legations to the imperial diets. Among his colleagues were Tommaso Parentucelli, the future Nicholas V, and Aeneas Sylvius Piccolomini, later Pope Pius II, who had dubbed Cusa "the Hercules of the Eugenians."[23] The particular work of Cusa, Aeneas Sylvius, and Juan de Carvajal reached definitive success when in July 1447, the German princes at the diet of Aschaffenburg declared an end to their official neutrality and formally sided with Pope Eugene. The matter was finalized when the emperor Frederick III signed the Concordat of Vienna in 1448 and Felix resigned in 1449.

Cusa was ordained priest between 1436 and 1440.[24] Eugene IV made him subdeacon of the pope and archdeacon of Brabant and at the end of 1446 nominated him cardinal, *in petto*, but died before publication. Nicholas V ordained him cardinal in 1448 and assigned him San Pietro in Vincoli as his titular church.[25]

The decade of his activities at the imperial diets corresponds to perhaps the most fruitful literary period of his life. Cusa continued to pursue the vital theological and philosophical inquiry inspired by the revelatory experience on shipboard en route from Constantinople. Cusa later makes clear in his *Apologia doctae ignorantiae* (1449) that he received the concept of learned ignorance "from on high" as a divine gift and not from Dionysius or those whom he calls other "true theologians."[26] Yet among the writers he said he eagerly investigated following this experience, the list must have included Meister Eckhart[27] as well as Pseudo-Dionysius, Augustine, Bonaventure,[28] and Thierry of Chartres. Out of his private studies and speculation he wrote his most famous work, *De docta ignorantia* (1440),[29] and supplemented it later with *De coniecturis* (c. 1442),[30] which together can be said to provide the nearest to a complete system of thought offered by Cusa. He also composed ecclesiological explanations of his papal advocacy in the *Dialogus concludens Amedistarum errorem* (1441)[31] and in his letter to Rodrigo Sánchez de Arévalo (1442).[32] In 1445–1446 he completed an interesting series of theological and philosophical inquiries into the limits of human knowing and the search for God: *De Deo abscondito* (1444/1445), *De quaerendo Deum* and *De filiatione Dei* (1445), and *De dato patris luminum* (1445/1446).[33] In the *De genesi* (1447)[34] he employed a broadened hermeneutic in the effort to reconcile the biblical account of creation with a newly emerging cosmology, and in his *Apologia doctae ignorantiae* (1449)[35] he defended his views against charges of heresy and pantheism from the Heidelberg scholastic Johannes Wenck.[36] In addition he completed his first mathematical writings: *De transmutationibus geometricis* and *De arithmeticis complementis* (1445).[37]

In 1450, after the resignation of the antipope Felix V and the end of schism, Pope Nicholas V announced a Jubilee year. The start of the year also marked the break of Cusa's ties with his Mosel homeland, which he had often visited during his work at the German diets and regional ecclesiastical duties. Following his ordination as cardinal in January, he was named by Nicholas V, in March, to fill the vacant prince-episcopacy in Brixen, today Bressanone, in the Tyrolean Alps. This was an ecclesiastical principality within the archiepiscopal province of Salzburg but in temporal powers under the authority of the emperor. Serious complications arose immediately because the local chapter, with the urging of Archduke Sigismund of Habsburg, count of the Tyrol, had elected Leonard Wismayer bishop. In October a papal bull nullified Wismayer's claims, and the matter was finally settled in March 1451 with Cusa's recognition by Emperor Frederick III.[38]

Before Cusa took up residence in his bishopric, the pope in 1450 named him *legatus a latere* to dispense the Jubilee indulgences throughout Germany and the Low Countries. Cusa was given authority over all ecclesiastics except archbishops and bishops and empowered to hold local and provincial synods, to carry out censures, to render absolution in cases reserved to the Holy See, to visit and to reform monasteries, to investigate abuses, especially of simony and concubinage, and to impose reform. In the summer before assuming this enormous task, he composed the four dialogues entitled *Idiota* (*De sapientia* I-II; *De mente* III; and *De staticis experimentis* IV),[39] set in the city of Rome in the multitude of the Jubilee year.

He left Rome at the end of December 1450 to undertake the arduous journey that would cause him to traverse the ecclesiastical provinces of Salzburg, Magdeburg, Cologne, Utrecht, Mainz, and Trier in a circular trek that would end a year and a quarter later in Brixen on Good Friday, 1452.[40] He anticipated resistance by promising a return of part of the indulgence revenue to assist local parishes and charities. He also undertook responsibility for reform of both clergy and laity and in his preaching insisted on the regularization of liturgy, sound doctrinal instruction, and the end to abuses of relic worship and to various superstitious practices.[41]

By late October he was in Trier and remained in the region for two weeks. By November he was in Mainz, and from there he traveled to Cologne and after Christmas to Brussels. In January 1452, he met with Philip of Burgundy and returned to Cologne. He entered Brixen as the new bishop just before Easter. In May, he began to initiate reform measures within his own diocese. He was determined both to restore the full secular authority historically and legally enjoyed by the bishop of Brixen over his diocese and to reform the clergy and the monasteries. He called for an annual synod and the regulation of liturgy, and he posted the reform decrees of the Salzburg provincial synod that he had personally presided over at the start of his legation journey. He emphasized monastic reform and the strict enclosure of convents. He quickly met resistance from several houses, including the convent at Sonnenberg, which opposed the bishop's reform demands for seven years.[42]

In some ways 1453 proved to be Cusa's most successful year as bishop. In February he summoned his first diocesan synod, which attempted to regulate, with special rigor, the daily life of priests as well as to require liturgical conformity, instruction of laity, and a concentrated attack on superstition. It was Cusa's hope to provide annual synods, and accordingly he divided the clergy into three separate chapters, each—presided over by a canon—to convene annually. This was also the year in which he composed two of his most enduring works. In a remarkably irenic response to the fall of Constantinople to the Turks, he wrote the dialogue *De pace fidei*,[43] and as a special favor to the monks at the Benedictine cloister of Tegernsee,[44] he completed his eloquent work on spirituality, *De visione Dei*.[45] He also composed the *De theologicis complementis*,[46] in which he pursued his continuing fascination with theological applications of mathematical models.

In 1454 and 1455 Cusa worked hard to stabilize the diocesan financial situation and to visit the entire diocese of Brixen in order to apply in miniature the reform measures he had attempted in his larger legation journey. But in 1456 he faced another serious conflict, this time over the benefices controlled by Leonard Wismayer, his former rival, who had just been elected bishop of nearby Chur. Cusa had forced the chapter at Brixen to transfer them to his nephew Simon von Wehlen. The gravest strife of Cusa's career, however, began at the turn of the year 1457 with the initiation of a struggle with Duke Sigismund that would last until the end of Cusa's life.

Opposition of the nobility to Cusa's consolidation of the bishopric and to the severity of his reforms together with the duke's persistent ambition to dominate the dioceses within his territory drove the duke to change his peaceful relationship with the bishop. In an effort to reduce the increasing tension, Cusa traveled to meet Sigismund at Innsbruck in June 1457. Near Witten, on the outskirts of Innsbruck, Cusa was intimidated by threats and on the return journey was the subject of a feigned ambush and attempted murder.[47] He fled from Brixen to his castle at Andraz in Buchenstein on the edge of the diocese and remained there until September 1458. In response to his complaints, Pope Calixtus III pronounced an interdict against the ducal territories.

Sigismund became conciliatory and promised to arrange the abdication of a major antagonist, Verena von Stuben, the abbess of the Benedictine convent at Sonnenberg. However, the situation became perhaps more complicated when in May of 1458 Sigismund employed Gregory Heimburg, a conciliarist opponent from Cusa's days at Basel and the imperial diets.[48] In August, Aeneas Sylvius Piccolomini, the humanist and Cusa's longtime friend, became Pope Pius II and encouraged Cusa to join him. Subsequently, Cusa left his castle in September and arrived at Rome by the end of the month. But before his departure and while still at Brixen, in the midst of his seemingly interminable struggle against the duke, he composed *De beryllo*,[49] a brief but important epistemological treatise using a beryl or transparent stone as the crucial analogy. By the end of the year he drew up a document for the present-day foundation at Kues, providing residence for thirty-three elderly men, one for each year of Christ's life. The institution still operates today and is one of the oldest private foundations in Europe. The structure would eventually house Cusa's remarkable personal library, which now comprises perhaps the largest private collection of manuscripts in Germany.

Cusa was diverted from the struggles at Brixen in January 1459. Pius, frustrated in his efforts to initiate a new crusade against the Turks, left Rome to promote his case at the congress of princes at Mantua and appointed Cusa *legatus urbis* or legate and vicar-general in temporalities over papal territories. He was given charge of the governance of both Rome and the provinces on the west side of the Apennines, and he became the first vicar-general of the papal states to be commissioned with the power to reform the Roman clergy. He began with reform of the chapter of St. Peter's, called for a reform synod of Roman clergy, and followed with reform of the chapters of St. John Lateran and St. Mary Major. By June, perhaps after having scrutinized Proclus' commentary on Parmenides, Cusa wrote two brief philosophical treatises, *De aequalitate*[50] and *De principio*,[51] on what it means to speak of God as "Oneness," as "Equality," and as "Beginning." By the end of the 1459 he had, at the pope's request, submitted a reform proposal, *Reformatio generalis.*[52]

At the beginning of 1460, he made a final and disastrous return to Brixen. He found Brixen filled with armed men and quickly withdrew to Bruneck and from there once again to his castle at Andraz. Cusa prepared for the worst, although in February he managed to write *De possest*,[53] in which he coins a new name for God by conflating *posse est* (can-is). He also penned a warning to Duke Sigismund that if the intimidation did not cease, Cusa would return all the fiefs of the church of Brixen to the emperor. He went back to Bruneck and awaited reply. Sigismund declared war and on April 12 sent troops to surround the town and besiege the castle. Cusa was forced to surrender and to submit to a humiliating treaty. However, five days after his release, Cusa fled to the safety of Ampezzo in Italy and renounced the document.

After the assault at Bruneck, the conflict broadened to include both pope and emperor, the Swiss cantons, the emperor's brother Albrecht, the King of Bohemia, the archbishop of Salzburg, the bishops of Trent, Augsburg, and Constance, the French court, the dukes of Milan and Bavaria, and the republic of Venice. By August of 1460 the pope took the diocese under his own administration, placed Sigismund's dominions under an interdict, and began a series of severe censures against the duke that lasted until 1464. The emperor condemned Sigismund's actions and promised military aid. After an invasion of the Tyrol by Swiss cantons, Sigismund was forced to sign a peace in December 1460. However, Pope Pius II demanded further action to protect the bishopric. The situation was made more difficult when the emperor's territories were invaded by his brother, the Archduke Albrecht.

Nicholas of Cusa had returned to Rome and in the winter of 1460/1461, at the request of Pope Pius, wrote *Cribratio Alkorani*,[54] a Christocentric evaluation of the Koran based on the twelfth-century translation of Robert of Ketton. Cusa may subsequently have been caught up in the curia's occupation with the war over succession to the crown of Naples. In June 1461, he experienced the start of serious health problems. He drew up the first of his wills and spent the summer recuperating at Orvieto. His lingering interest in reform and his growing frustration with the curia[55] led him to offer to resign with these impassioned words addressed to Pope Pius:

> You are preparing to create new Cardinals without any pressing reason merely at your own whim, and you have no regard for the oath you swore to the Sacred College in the Conclave before and after your election: namely that you would on no account create Cardinals unless with the consent of the majority of the College and according to the decrees of the Council of Constance. Now you ignore the ordinance of the Synod and do not ask the consent of the College, and you wish to make me a tool of your ambition. I cannot do it. I do not know how to flatter. I hate adulation. If you can bear to hear the truth, I like nothing which goes on in this Curia. Everything is corrupt. No one does his duty. Neither you nor the Cardinals have any care for the Church. What observance of the canons is there? What reverence for laws? What assiduity in divine worship? All are bent on ambition and avarice. If I ever speak in a Consistory about reform, I am laughed at. I do no good here. Allow me to withdraw. I cannot endure these ways. I am an

old man and need rest. I will return into seclusion, and since
I cannot live for the commonweal, I live for myself.

Pius recorded this in his commentaries adding "with these words
[Nicholas of Cusa] burst into tears."[56]

Nevertheless, Pius dissuaded him, and Cusa spent the last years
of his life in and around Rome and devoted himself increasingly to
literary production.[57] In 1462 he completed one of his most speculative works, *De non aliud*,[58] stressing the total otherness of God in
relation to human conception, and *De venatione Dei*,[59] a searching
recapitulation of what he calls his "hunts after Wisdom." In 1463 he
added *De ludo globi*,[60] which uses a game of a curiously shaped ball or
sphere as model for understanding the relationship of God to the
world and to the individual soul, and the *Compendium*,[61] an important
and final abridgement of his epistemological theory. He also composed *De mathematicis complementis*[62] and a letter to the novices at
the Benedictine abbey of Monteoliveto, near Umbria, that serves as a
kind of spiritual testament. At Easter 1464, several months before his
death, he wrote his last work, *De apice theoriae*,[63] in which he analyzes
the contemplation of God to which he has at last come, the contemplation of God as "Possibility Itself."

His official tasks, however, continued to the end. At the turn of
1463 a controversy developed at Rome between the Dominicans and
Franciscans, and in response Cusa drew up for Pius II a thesis and
fourteen questions regarding the hypostatic union and the blood of
Christ.[64] The pope made him visitor and reformer of the city and
diocese of Orvieto. He also intervened in the feud between the Mo-
naldeschi and the Cervara.

In June 1464, Cusa received word that the Sigismund affair had
finally been settled after negotiations at the emperor's court. Cusa
was to remain as bishop and to exercise that office through a substi-
tute. The emperor ordered the duke to return all diocesan property
that he had seized after the Bruneck attack and the bishop to restore
to the duke all fiefs of the church invested to him. The documents of
settlement, however, would not be signed until August 25, two weeks
after Cusa's death.

In the summer of 1464, Pius's crusade was supposed to begin.
He left Rome for Ancona to direct personally what would prove to be
a failed, last effort to retake the Holy Land. A Venetian fleet was to
transport the crusaders. Cusa was commissioned to collect the dwin-

dling remnant of what had been more than five thousand knights, now dispersed between Ancona and Rome. In addition, Cusa had been asked to serve as a judge in the question of papal approval for the return of the city of Breslau to the Bohemian king Podiebrad. Cusa was to deliver to Pius at Ancona a final version of a document citing the king to appear. On July 16, en route to Ancona, he became seriously ill at Todi in Umbria. Attending him during his last days were his long-time friend Paolo del Pozzo Toscanelli; his physician, Ferdinand Martins; Giovanni Andrea Bussi, once Cusa's secretary and now bishop of Accia; Johann Römer, a relative and later rector of the St. Nicholas hospice at Kues; and Peter von Erkelenz, his notary. On August 6 he made his last will, and he died on August 11, 1464.

It was his intent that his body be buried at his titular church of San Pietro in Vincoli and his heart in the chapel at the hospice that he founded at Kues. Andrea Bregno designed the monument, which stands at the opposite corner of the church from Michelangelo's famous statue of the "horned" Moses. His heart was transported to Kues and eventually placed in the floor of the chapel. He had used his income from benefices to construct and maintain the institution, which was completed in 1458 but which he was never able to visit. He had also established a *Bursa Cusana* for twenty poor clerical students at Deventer. With the consent of his sister Klara and his brother Johannes, Cusa had used his inheritance as the basis for the foundation and had also bequeathed it his altar service, his library, and his scientific instruments. The basic structures—the chapel, cloister, refectory, and library—remain in use to the present day.

Cusa left to the library at the hospice approximately three hundred manuscripts, a number with his own notations.[65] Some thirty of them are now in Oxford, London, and Brussels.[66] The largest part of the collection is devoted to theology, philosophy, and civil and ecclesiastical law, although the range of his holdings included the sciences, history, and literature. Included with his library is the collection of many of his writings in manuscript that he had commissioned and personally edited and a large portion of his sermons. About three hundred of his sermons survive in manuscript, some in his own handwriting.[67] They provide an additional rich resource for a knowledge of his theology and spirituality.[68]

## II. IMPORTANCE

Nicholas of Cusa led a full and vigorous intellectual life in a fifteenth-century Europe so diffuse and expansive that only a thoroughgoing visionary could pretend to comprehend its needs in his body of thought. Cusa was just such an ecumenist whose concordizing impulse left his scholarly efforts omnidirectional and reconciling. Both a new vitality in learning and a determination to rehearse the apostolic tradition in a modern civilization contributed to Cusa's urgency to refashion the nature and method of medieval theology. As reformer and humanist, sharply critical of scholastic systems, he found it necessary to construct a new synthesis of the ways of God, being, and the world.[69] He deplored the inheritance of a feckless handling of the mysteries of the faith and a succession of impotent schemes for political and ecclesiastical harmony, and he endeavored throughout his life to repair the ineffectuality of paths of discursive reasoning and to restore the freshness of the Christian proclamation for the church.

*Concordantia catholica, unitrinitas universi, coincidentia oppositorum, pax fidei,* and *complicatio-explicatio* were central titles and themes that pervaded and directed major writings in his voluminous corpus. Moreover, these were healing notions that Cusa prescribed for a fragmented and dissident age. He extended them to such a multiplicity of problems that he has been treated in the histories of almost all the traditional academic disciplines.

The diversity of his interests and activities makes it difficult to treat Cusa fairly from any one point of view, and has given rise to multiple and often contradictory representations. Scholars have described his life with both idealized and captious treatments; they have delineated his political theory; they have pointed to his role in the natural sciences and mathematics, in conciliarism and papal politics, and in the humanist collection of manuscripts; they have atomized his philosophy and have assessed him in contrast with movements and personalities before and after his time; they have analyzed his mysticism and relativism; they have debated his influence on the Roman Catholic, Protestant, and Left-Wing reform movements; and they have celebrated his relevance for present ecumenical discussions. The result has reduced to straits any endeavor to view Cusa's experience as an ecclesiastic and scholar from his own angle of vision. Furthermore, he so thoroughly engaged himself in the church and thought of the Quattrocento that the quest for the historical Cusa has produced an incredibly malleable personality, able to be shaped by whatever vested interest a historian might bring to him. He has been equally subject to the biases of nationalism, ideology, and religion and to the changing emphases that have directed the historiography of the late Middle Ages and the Renaissance. He has been characterized simultaneously as a humanist and a counter-Renaissance figure; as a heretic and a conservative; as a gnostic and an agnostic; as a scientist and a pseudo-scientist; as a papal monarchist and a conciliarist; as a reformer and an opportunist in need of reforming; as a peacemaker and a belligerent; as a politician and a pastor; and as a philosopher and a theologian.

It is equally problematic to determine what direct influence Cusa had on later writers. Certainly he inspired no schools devoted to the extension of his thought. Yet, at the time and soon after, Bernard de Waging (d. 1472), Jacques LeFèvre d'Étaples (Faber Stapulensis) (d. 1536), Charles de Bovelles (d. 1567), and Giordano Bruno (d. 1600), among others, were indebted to his work, and four printed editions of his *opera* appeared within a hundred years following his death.[70] Stephan Meier-Oeser has recently documented the continued citations to Cusa's writings through the eighteenth century,[71] and Morimichi Watanabe has traced the start of modern Cusa scholarship at the universities at Tübingen, Marburg, and Heidelberg that has generated a kind of "Cusa renaissance."[72]

It is also difficult to gauge the contributions of Nicholas of Cusa. The attempts to measure his influence and significance often reveal more about the measurers than the measured. Even fifty years ago it seemed a simple task to link Cusa, at least as precursor, to many important European intellectual endeavors from constitutionalism and humanism to religious reform and the search for quantification and infinity in the sciences and modern philosophy. Reacting to excesses, especially in nationalistic scholarship, more recently, revisionists have pared down the rhetoric and acknowledge very little direct influence.

Emphasis is placed less on Cusa's originality and more on his extension of received notions—for example, from Nicole Oresme, that the infinite is not subject to comparisons of greater or lesser;[73] from Ramon Lull, the joining of beginning, middle, end; from Thierry of Chartres and other Chartrians, the trinity of unity, equality, connection and the *complicatio-explicatio* motif; and from Anselm, the notion of God as maximum.[74] The truth, however, may lie somewhere in between, for Cusa modifies and shapes these notions to his own design and purpose. Of greatest importance is whether he will say something to us in the twenty-first century, whether he will continue to communicate fresh things in an increasingly complex age.

Moreover, the dynamics of Cusa's historical and intellectual participation in the full maturation of his century are reflected both in the scope of his writings and in the continuing stream of literature concerned with Cusa and with his creatively disjunctive era. A newcomer to Cusa's life and writings may be surprised at the broad range of his interests and at the far-reaching extent of scholarship that has maintained an interest in his accomplishments.[75] A few examples suggest the breadth of interest in Cusa's thought. The term "Middle Ages," referring to a distinct period in European history, may first have occurred in a phrase Giovanni Bussi, his secretary, used in a eulogy commemorating Cusa's life.[76] Thomas Merton translated Cusa's dialogue *On the Hidden God* with special interest;[77] C. S. Lewis wrote a poem dedicated to a single passage from *On Learned Ignorance;*[78] national and international societies, in Germany, the United States, Japan, and elsewhere, have been established to research and discuss his works; the Cusanus-Gesellschaft sponsors three series of Cusanus studies and translations; and the Heidelberg Academy supports the *Cusanus-Studien* and the *Cusanus-Texte* subseries in its *Sitzungsberichte* (Phil./his. Kl.) and, most notably, a critical edition of Cusa's *opera*, which since 1932 has provided a new standard for the editing of medieval theological and philosophical literature.

What did Nicholas of Cusa accomplish? It may be helpful to begin with a random sample of some comments about his contributions, especially to theology and Christian philosophy. Heiko Oberman numbers Cusa among those vitally connecting reform and peace.[79] Charles Lohr cites his crucial role in the revival of Platonism in the fifteenth century and the early development of modern metaphysics.[80] Wolfhart Pannenberg credits him with having produced a Christian humanism of the active life and having constructed a bridge from medieval to modern Christian thought, renewing rather than betraying the Christian tradition.[81] Hans Küng cites the daring character of his thought,[82] while Hans-Georg Gadamer specifically attributes to him a revolutionary challenge to traditional metaphysics and as well the development of a critical new stage in discerning the problem of language and its relationship to epistemology.[83] Martin Buber assigns Cusa a key role in the new, modern "earnestness" about the human being as human being in which the person could boast that "he carried all things in himself and thus that he could know all things."[84]

16

# INTRODUCTION

Paul Tillich links him with Meister Eckhart, who inspired Tillich's notion of God beyond God, and credits Cusa's idea of the coincidence of opposites, along with Luther's doctrine of justification of the sinner, for breaking the power of "the hierarchical principle."[85]

> When Luther said that the "right hand of God" is not on a *locus circumscriptus* but everywhere, since God's power and creativity act at every place, he destroyed the traditional interpretation of God's omnipresence and expressed the doctrine of Nicolaus Cusandus [*sic*] that God is in everything, in that which is central as well as in that which is peripheral.[86]

Ernst Cassirer calls him "the first modern philosopher," pointing to "a completely new *total intellectual orientation*,"[87] and Karl Jaspers names him "one of the 'original metaphysicians,' " an indispensable link in the chain of great metaphysicians, and vitally important to modern thought for his anthropology: "Perhaps no earlier thinker so compellingly placed at the core of things an image of man's greatness and limitations in respect of his creative intellectual powers."[88]

Given the difficulties of measuring his influence and the lack of a Cusan school or tradition, why, therefore, has Cusa continued to be the subject of curiosity and interest now almost into the twenty-first century? It would appear that in those both past and present who cite him with enthusiasm, there is vigorous interest in issues that kept arising in his life and keep emerging in ours.

First, there is the interestingly universal and paradoxical figure of Cusa himself. On the one hand, he presents himself to us as *idiota*,[89] posing as a philosopher, but his writings are always filled more with wonder than a *théologie dogmatique et systématique*. He writes philosophy but more as *therapeia* and as *cura animarum* than as *logica*, and yet he fulfilled his episcopal duties as if he would have been far better suited to *theoria* and the lecture hall. On the other hand, he also presents himself as a remarkably imaginative and gifted philosopher, posing as a pastoral administrator, who was at the same time laboring outside the academy and quietly extending the limits of human thought.

Second, there is a common curiosity. Many share Cusa's mystification. We are commonly intrigued with issues that kept mystifying him. For all his intellectual power, he never closes his thought into a

system. He is a significator and a conjecturer. He keeps pointing beyond his own words and beyond even his most prized formula and
labels, including *docta ignorantia* and *coincidentia oppositorum.* He
persistently lacked either the opportunity or the inclination to provide intellectual closure. Cusa never has to warn us, as did Thomas,
that "it was all straw."

Third, there are the perennial gauntlets that keep confronting
Cusa's readers. We continue to be challenged because he defined
problems that still pose challenges to contemporary church and society. He raised questions in ways that have remained fresh, especially
in the context of the absolute, the infinite, the uncertain, and the un-
fathomable. He anticipated, in a sometimes comparatively modern idiom, issues that remain with us yet, such as questions of ecumenicity
and pluralism, empowerment and reconciliation, and tolerance and
individuality.

Finally, there is Cusa's spirituality and ours. Mystical theology,
to be authentic, must be rooted in experience. For all his insecurities,
fears, and conflicts, and notwithstanding ours, Cusa's writings have
communicated to us his experience of a very large God that jostles us
out of our parochialism, compels us to disclose ourselves, and, to bor-
row a favorite word of Gerard Manley Hopkins, "bids" us to leap
across our finitudes. This is nowhere better stated in Cusa's work
than in the *De visione Dei:*

> [O God] ... no one can approach you because you are
> unapproachable.... How will my prayer reach you, who
> are unapproachable by every means? How will I beseech
> you, for what would be more absurd than to ask that you
> give yourself to me, you who are all in all? And how will
> you give yourself to me if you do not at the same time give
> me heaven and earth and all that are in them? And, even
> more, how will you give me yourself if you do not also give
> me myself?
>
> And when I thus rest in the silence of contemplation,
> you, Lord, answer me within my heart, saying: "Be yours
> and I too will be yours."
>
> O Lord, the Sweetness of every delight, you have
> placed within my freedom to be my own if I am willing.
> Hence, unless I am my own, you are not mine, for you
> would constrain my freedom since you cannot be mine un-

less I also am mine. And since you have placed this in my freedom, you do not constrain me, but you wait for me to choose to be my own. This depends on me and not on you, O Lord, for you do not limit your maximum goodness but lavish it on all who are able to receive it.[90]

## III. THE COINCIDENCE OF OPPOSITES: *ON LEARNED IGNORANCE*

Nicholas of Cusa attributes the inspiration for *De docta ignorantia* to a profound experience during his journey back from Constantinople in the winter of 1437/1438.[91] A revelation of some sort, which he describes as a divine gift, brought him to an "embrace" of what is incomprehensible and a way of speaking about what is ineffable for which he had struggled unsuccessfully for years before receiving this illumination. The composition it invoked is surely Cusa's most famous treatise, with its rich unitive themes of learned ignorance and other coincidences of opposites, the contraction of the universal to the particular, and the unfolding of the infinite in the finite and the enfolding of the finite in the infinite.

Early in the work, he outlines his plan for analyzing what he feels sure the reader will find to be a surprising subject: All three sections or books are to deal with ignorance as the greatest learning, as *maxima doctrina*. They will strive to develop this principle along two lines—the conditions and limits of knowledge and the coincidence of opposites. He begins by defining the nature of the *maximum* itself as that than which nothing greater can exist.

Book One of *On Learned Ignorance* sets forth his concept of the "absolute maximum" (*maximum absolutum*), which is the God of all being, the ultimate term of all. Book Two describes the "contracted maximum" (*maximum contractum*), which is the universe, the maximum effect of the absolute and the sum of all contracted (i.e., derived) things. Book Three treats the "absolute and contracted maximum" (*maximum contractum pariter et absolutum*), which is Jesus Christ, simultaneously the maximum in the universe united with the absolute, the perfection of the universe, and the center and circumference of all intellectual nature. The entire study, however, rests on the premise that absolute truth is humanly incomprehensible and that the truest knowledge—the highest learning that the human being by oneself can obtain—is to know that one is ignorant. Knowledge of one's own ignorance, however, is able to be the occasion for reaching beyond both knowledge and ignorance to a coincidence of knowing and not-knowing.

The impelling vision of *On Learned Ignorance* is the coincidence of opposites. It is a frequent *Leitwort* here and in important theological writings after 1440. "Coincidence of opposites" (*coincidentia oppositorum*) and "learned ignorance" (*docta ignorantia*) are generally recognized as the most important notions that Cusa has contributed to the history of European thought. However, there is considerable debate over what these terms mean and how Cusa intends that they be applied. How Cusa came upon the idea of the coincidence of opposites and how he developed it into a major treatise are especially troublesome questions. The history of his use of coincidence from its inception to its formulation in *On Learned Ignorance* covers slightly more than two years, from around December 1437 to February 1440. In a covering letter to Cardinal Cesarini, he explains the source as a divine illumination: "a celestial gift of the Father of Lights."[92] He describes its conception as a discovery to which he was led.

The theme can be found in writers before him. Cusa never denies this, although he will subsequently disclaim that he had knowingly borrowed the idea. This, therefore, is what he wishes his mentor to understand regarding the origin of learned ignorance and the coincidence of opposites:

> Accept now, Reverend Father, what for so long I desired to attain by different paths of learning but previously could not until returning by sea from Greece when by what I believe was a celestial gift from the Father of Lights, from whom comes every perfect gift, I was led to embrace incomprehensibles incomprehensibly in learned ignorance, by transcending those incorruptible truths that can be humanly known. This learned ignorance I have, in the one who is the Truth, now set loose in these books, which on the basis of this same principle can be compressed or expanded.[93]

In the same passage he precisely locates coincidence within the divine *simplicitas*, "that simplicity where contradictories coincide."[94]

Later, when defending himself against accusations of heresy,

Cusa insists that he had not invented the idea. He claims that it was inspired of God and that it was not a dangerous novelty but could be found throughout the Christian contemplative tradition. He also adds that he himself had confirmed its authenticity in studies after his illuminative experience. At that very point in his own life-story, it was, to be sure, an idea novel to his previous experience, but he vigorously maintains that it was novel neither to the history of the church nor to its theology.[95] He views the coincidence of opposites as a revealed notion and as an orthodox "learning" that may also be characterized as ignorance, or better, sacred ignorance. In short, Cusa wishes us to consider it as something he had long sought for in his own searching but came to at last as a gift, unearned.

The idea's development over a two-year period until the completion of *On Learned Ignorance* is unclear.[96] Within that time there are no specific written references either to learned ignorance or to the coincidence of opposites, except for the treatise itself. In the preface, also addressed to Cesarini, he expresses regret that his style might lead the cardinal to think that his work was too hastily written or his ideas rashly conceived. He assures his mentor that the book was a work of considerable labor.[97] Given the heavy ecclesiastical responsibilities and full schedule that he assumed on his return from Greece, it is difficult to account for his composing such a work. From 1438 to 1446, Eugene IV commissioned him to win over the various imperial diets to the papal position, and he had time for little else. It seems most likely that he formulated the arguments of the treatise's three books in stages, especially during short interludes of rest between appearances before the diets and other assignments, and that he finished the final copy during the winter of 1439/1440 at Kues.

### On Learned Ignorance *and Cusa's Earliest Use of the Coincidence of Opposites*

The themes of *ignorantia* and *negatio* appear in advance of the treatise in three of Cusa's sermons, delivered in the winter of 1438/1439.[98] They provide the only available evidence of Cusa's development of thought from his illuminative experience on shipboard to the composition of *On Learned Ignorance.* They alone indicate, however obliquely, his readiness to treat the notion of learned ignorance in a formal and systematic fashion. The sermons seem to record a heightened attention to the infinity of God and the ineffability of divine truth and to their implications for both preacher and hearer. He bids his hearers to glory in the grace of the holy truth that, apart from human incapacities, makes known its own truthfulness. Paradoxically, silence furnishes the most effective articulation of the Word and ignorance the most effective learning.

The sermons essentially supply the crucial theological presentiments for fundamental themes worked out later in Cusa's system: the gulf between infinite and finite; the necessity of ignorance; the dilemma of divine names; the suitability of negative theology and of paradox; the transcendence of an intellectual vision; God as maximum as well as both hidden and revealed; the work of grace in divine knowledge; and Christ's centrality. The sermons, however, lack the definition, the systematization, and especially the delineation of a theological method appropriate to Cusa's impelling earlier vision. Written a year later by February 1440, *On Learned Ignorance* completes what the sermons anticipate. The coincidence of opposites as the proper theological method is now developed for the first time; it is the logic behind the work's structure. It is not only the logic of a system, but it is also a logic emanating from a spirituality and elucidating it.

What, then, does Cusa precisely mean by coincidence? As method, it is the way of viewing and of solving problems from the standpoint of infinity. For Cusa, whenever infinity is introduced into mathematics and geometry, whenever values or figures are raised to infinity, extraordinary things happen conceptually and logically. What is otherwise ruled out reenters as possible and plausible. At infinity thoroughgoing coincidence occurs. It is Cusa's premise that there can be only one infinite, and this infinite also precedes all plurality and differentiation. Therefore, at true infinity there is one only and all are one. The coincidence of opposites provides a method that resolves contradictions without violating the integrity of the contrary elements and without diminishing the reality or the force of their contradiction. It is not a question of seeing unity where there is no real contrariety, nor is it a question of forcing harmony by synthesizing resistant parties. Coincidence as a method issues from coincidence as a fact or condition of opposition that is resolved in and by infinity. From that basis we may speak of coincidence as (1) the method of logically setting opposites into a harmony and (2) the principle of viewing opposites as reconciled. Examples from each of the three books of *On Learned Ignorance* demonstrate the different tasks to which Cusa assigns the idea. The books deal successively with God, the universe, and Christ, and in so doing they employ the coincidence of opposites in order to explicate the divine truth and unity bearing on each topic.[99]

## BOOK ONE: GOD AS ABSOLUTE MAXIMUM

The specific term *coincidence* appears seventeen times in Book One. It is used to explain the ideas of absolute maximum, the absolute infinite line, the Trinity, the maximum triangle, and infinite maximum measure. In every case by applying the logic of infinitude, coincidence, as Cusa intends it, accomplishes certain common tasks: (1) It unites opposites; (2) it transcends analogy and comparison; (3) it overcomes the limits of discursive reasoning;[100] (4) it exceeds composition and synthesis; (5) it surpasses both affirmative and negative language; (6) it frees the mind from quantitative concepts and enables it to achieve a comparatively pure abstraction; and (7) whether operating from theology, philosophy, mathematics, or geometry, it renders infinite concepts understandable and describable without violating their incomprehensibility or illimitability.

## BOOK TWO: THE WORLD AS CONTRACTED MAXIMUM

The coincidence of opposites, Cusa believes, also accommodates itself admirably to the needs of metaphysics, which is the subject of the second book. "Coincidence" occurs only seven times. It is used to make intelligible the unity and distinction between God as absolute maximum and the universe as "contracted" maximum. The "universe" is maximum because it is the whole of things, "the all." But like the particulars that comprise it, the universe is "contracted," rather than absolute, because it derives or is drawn (*contractum*) in relation to the absolute maximum. All things may be said to be differentiated or contracted within the world's unity, the *universum*, but all exist antecedently as one in God and proceed by contraction to individual and multiple existence, subject to materiality and otherness. The world, therefore, is a created, finite, and constricted maximum: The maximality of God is, so to speak, *subsequently* "contracted" and "explicated" (*explicata*) in the universe while the world and all its particulars are, as it were, *antecedently* "enfolded" (*complicata*) as infinite and one in the mind of God.

# INTRODUCTION

## BOOK THREE: CHRIST AS ABSOLUTE AND CONTRACTED MAXIMUM

Book Three is Cusa's supreme Christological statement.[101] Here we not only find coincidence rendering theological service, but we also discover the source of coincidence itself, the coincident source of every reconciliation in being and nature: the coincidence of the absolute and contracted maximum. The term *coincidence* occurs sixteen times and in every use touches on the union of opposites enfolded within or unfolding from the Christ-maximum. Four particular theological lessons are rehearsed throughout.

*First.* The coincidence of opposites does not exist apart from the infinite. Such coincidence is the property only of the absolute and infinite, whether one speaks of the maximum line or maximum being. With respect to being we may speak of only one infinite and maximum and that is God.

*Second.* In *On Learned Ignorance* God is not the coincidence of opposites but the absolute maximum in whom opposites antecedently coincide. Moreover, God provides the coincidence in the unity of nature. The universe as the limited maximum comprises degrees of difference and a necessary variety and plurality of things. God, the absolute maximum, binds together their diversity into "one continuous and perfect universe."[102] Only the absolute could be the beginning, middle, and end of the totality of every species and of every member; consequently, all may approach God. Such a maximum provides the linking between higher and lower so that they coincide, the highest species of one genus coinciding with the lowest species of the genus immediately above.

*Third.* God also works coincidence in the historical experience of human beings. In either case, whether of nature or of persons, the agent of coincidence can be only that which is both absolute and limited maximum. Cusa devotes considerable attention to this argument and weighs his words with obvious care. Such an agent must be an individual human being who is also God. The absolute maximum contracted to any actually existing species would have to realize every possible perfection of that contraction. Since no greater perfection could be conceived, this agent would be the infinite maximum encompassing the whole nature of that contraction. But the maximum contracted individual of a particular species could not itself be the God who is illimitable. Such an individual would have to be God *and* crea-

24

ture, absolute *and* limited, in whom "minimum" would coincide with the absolute maximum and in whom the contracted minimum would coincide with the contracted maximum.

The rule applied, once more, is that coincidence unites one thing with another so that it does not exclude another but rather includes all. This necessitates a species occurring in the middle, sharing the nature of the largest number of things. It is human nature, preeminent among the works of God and established a little lower than the angels, that exhibits the fullest perfection of the universe and of every particular in it. But humanity or human nature exists only by contraction in the limited existence of the individual.

> For this reason, it would not be possible for more than one true human being to be able to ascend to union with maximumness, and, certainly, this being would be a human in such a way as to be God and God in such a way as to be a human. . . . And in this human being the least, the greatest and the middle things of the nature united to absolute maximumness would so coincide that this human would be the perfection of all things, and all things, as contracted, would come to rest in this individual as in their own perfection.[103]

*Fourth.* The coincidence of the Christ-maximum is the work of God, the never-failing, perfect activity of the maximal power of God. By the hypostatic coincidence of the two natures in Christ, God provides the bond in the world structure between absolute and contracted being, God and nature; in Christ God effects the coincidence that reconciles human beings to God.

The human condition is finite and therefore distant from God, sinful and therefore helplessly removed from God's will and dispossessed of the highest good, which is eternal union with God. The Christ-maximum mediates and saves, for, in the mystery of the union of natures, the divine and the human coincide. The God-human is the supreme coincidence. He is spoken of as maximum, but he is no mere abstraction. He is real, individual, and historical and so is the coincidence he accomplishes: for here "minimum things coincide with maximum . . . maximum humiliation with exaltation; the most shameful death of a virtuous human being with the most glorious life; and so on. And all these are revealed to us in the life, passion, and crucifixion of Christ."[104]

Union with God through Christ by faith is itself a coincidence and is also an effect of the coincidence both in Christ's person and in his ministry. The unity of the faithful with Christ, moreover, results from and coincides with the union of the divine and human natures in Christ. So too, the incorporation and the unity of the members in the church are resolved through coincidence, for the Holy Spirit, which unites Christ's two natures, binds together the whole church so that we may say that the unity of the church in some fashion coincides with the hypostatic union; therefore, the union of the triumphant souls in heaven is in the Spirit of Jesus, who is in the Holy Spirit.[105] Cusa closes the treatise by extolling the "union" of differences as divine reconciliation, no longer simply as a linguistic or logical tool but as God's remedy for all human beings as well as for theologians.[106]

What, therefore, may we conclude about the uses Cusa makes of coincidence in *On Learned Ignorance?* We have seen that he assigns the idea to a variety of tasks beginning with the question of the knowledge of God as absolute maximum. He employs it in part as a metaphor most easily translatable into mathematical and geometric terms, for Cusa, reason's purest language. He offers it, in addition, as a way of viewing the convergence of all things in the infinite, whether by "infinite," one is referring to God or to an abstraction. It is also presented as fact and principle, real coincidence in the real world of actual contraries. From one's experience or knowledge of it, as for example in learned ignorance, one can then see and treat coincidence in diverse conditions and entities.

Accordingly, we may distinguish between types of coincidences as Cusa employs them throughout the treatise. First of all, we may separate *coincidence of opposites* from *coincidence of things not opposing.* Examples of the former would include the coincidence of rest and motion, past and future, diversity and identity, inequality and equality, and divisibility and simplicity. However, God and human beings, though distinct, cannot be said to be opposites, for God has no opposite. Second, we may speak of *coincidence in theory,* such as the coincidence of all polygons in the triangle, and *coincidence in fact or being,* such as the coincidence of the divine and human natures in Christ. Third, we may speak of *coincidence as derived* and *coincidence as given and formative,* from which other coincidences can be construed. An example of the former, the *complicatio-explicatio* couplet, describing the work of the divine in nature, is derived from an example of the latter, the creative activity of the Trinity, of the three persons of the Godhead acting in coincidence.

Finally, we may distinguish between *coincidence in epistemology*, as a way of viewing problems, and *coincidence in methodology*, as a way of solving them. Learned ignorance is an example of both. It is a vision beyond contradictions, above reason, a revelatory insight into the reality of things that properly lie beyond human comprehension. Through it we can see truths otherwise inaccessible and solve problems otherwise insoluble. Cusa frequently prompts the reader to see beyond apparent contrariety by reviewing the problem "in the light of learned ignorance." The phrase itself is also an example of a "coincident" method, a joining together of what otherwise seems forever removed—knowing and not knowing. The seeing, however, makes the uniting possible, for epistemology impels method, just as faith writes theology.

### Theological Application of Coincidence

What, then, would Cusa have us understand about the application of the coincidence of opposites to questions of theological method? His statements about method, which occur piecemeal, suggest several working principles, and foremostly among them that coincidence should be properly considered and that it should be properly applied. We have seen examples of Cusa as an employer of coincidence; now we turn our attention to Cusa as its commentator and analyst.

### A PROPER CONSIDERATION

Two particular matters are of extreme importance: (1) the question of coincidence as unity and (2) that of coincidence as remedy. First, is coincidence merely a synonym for unity? The coincidence of opposites obviously suggests a union of opposites. Coincidence, to be sure, accomplishes unity and may be described as a kind of uniting. To Cusa, however, not all unities are coincidence.[107] There are several possible unities through which opposition might be overcome: (1) unity through the obliteration of one party by the other; (2) unity through the obliteration of both parties and in their place the creation of a third, such as may occur in a certain kind of synthesis; (3) unity through concretion or coalescence by retaining and mingling both

27

parties; and (4) unity in convergence, that is, a "falling together," as the term *coincidentia* literally denotes. For Cusa, coincidence of opposites clearly holds the last meaning: a unity geometrically conceived, but without quantity, working as a gross metaphor for both theology and metaphysics. It is a unity of substance[108] without mingling and without obliteration of either party or substance.

Coincidence of opposites, therefore, should be considered as a distinct kind of unity, not to be confused with others. Moreover, for Cusa, it is not the sort of unity one speaks of in discursive reasoning. In theology the term *coincidence* must embrace the kind of unity by which one may speak of God. It must communicate mystery revealed.

> "Unity" . . . is not the name of God as we assign or understand the name, because just as God transcends all understanding, so God is, a fortiori, above every name. In order to distinguish between things, names are imposed by a movement of reason which is much inferior to the intellect. But since reason cannot leap over contradictories, there is, in accord with reason's movement, no name to which another is not opposed. So then according to the movement of reason, plurality or multitude is opposed to unity. Hence, it is not a unity of this sort which properly applies to God, but the unity to which neither otherness nor plurality nor multiplicity is opposed. This unity is the maximum name enfolding all things in its simplicity of unity, and this is the name which is ineffable and above all understanding.[109]

Second, coincidence is a methodological remedy because it is first a conceptual remedy. Its value as method depends on a right viewing of both problem-construction and language. In its every application, epistemology precedes method.[110] "In order to pursue this method," Cusa explains in an introductory chapter, "I have attempted, by avoiding all harshness of style, to explain to ordinary minds as clearly as I could, and at the start I show plainly that the basis of learned ignorance is the fact that the precision of truth cannot be grasped."[111] The principal remedy is the understanding or learning that fashions the method; in other words, sacred ignorance teaches us coincidence. "The precise truth shines forth incomprehensibly in the darkness of our ignorance": That is the remedy that has generated the coincidence idea.[112]

But what then of *method?* What remedy does coincidence have to offer here?

1. It views problems from the vantage point of utter *simplicity* prior to contradiction. Or we may say it traces the contradiction in logic to its origin, which always stands outside, over and above, both the given problem and its contradictory point. After citing Augustine's presumed remark on the Trinity: "When you begin to count the Trinity you depart from the truth," Cusa sets forth this principle for the theologian:

> With God we must, as far as possible, forestall contradictories and embrace them in a simple concept. In God we must not conceive of distinction and indistinction, for example, as two contradictories, but we must conceive of them as antecedently existing in their own most simple beginning, where distinction is not other than indistinction.[113]

2. Coincidence also formulates problems in terms of their relation to *infinity.* In geometry, according to Cusa, when we consider the question of the relation of the line to the point or to any geometric figure whatsoever, we encounter one set of problems, but when we interpose the idea of infinity into the question, we face a completely different set.[114] So too theology develops extraordinary capabilities using the same method. For Cusa, all the theology that we are capable of grasping comes from this principle. Through coincidence we may say that the absolute maximum, which "infinitely and completely transcends all opposition," enfolds and unfolds all and is known but not comprehended.[115] Learned ignorance sees and coincidence enunciates what otherwise fails the sciences, wisdom, and language.[116]

3. Coincidence requires, moreover, a certain symbolic use of language because it arises from a vision beyond what terms and names seem to be and toward what they become with reference to *absolutes.* Cusa calls this an intellectual vision, a transcending as opposed to a comprehending view.

A coincident logic requires elevating the intellect "above the force of words" rather than insisting on their properties, for these natural properties cannot be "suitably adapted to such great intellectual mysteries" as theology would describe. Cusa admonishes the reader to view the author's own illustrations, including drawings, from a special perspective: One must transcend them intellectually, abandoning what is sensible, so that unimpeded one might reach "simple intellectuality."[117] His two key terms of coincidence, "maximum" and "minimum," will do for an example. When not limited to quantitative concepts such as those of mass or force, they are no longer infinitely distant from one another as they have to be according to any other logic. Rather they are reconcilable through coincidence when we attribute to them an absolutely transcendent value embracing all things in their simplicity.

Treating the idea of the infinite requires "appropriate illustrations." For in theology, as in mathematics, we are dealing with what is so above and beyond all figures that we are compelled to reject all that sense, imagination, or reason with its material associations can attain, if we would reach that "most simple and most abstract understanding, where all are one."[118] Only in this manner, through a transcendent and coincident logic, may we speak of what is incomparably and infinitely above both reasoning and speech.

In theological discourse, we may use terms but only as symbols that are appropriate to the realities they suggest. The measure of the symbol in coincident logic is always the reality itself, which in the case of the absolute maximum can never be equated by any symbol. The more abstract the symbol (that is, the more contentless it is at the start, such as in mathematics), the more appropriately it signifies the reality beyond it and toward which it points. Cusa offers further explanation in the following statement about the doctrine of the Trinity:

> Therefore, because the simply maximum is the measure of all we give it those names without which we do not understand it to be able to be the measure of all. Thus, although the maximum is infinitely above all trinity, we speak of it as threefold, for otherwise we would not understand it to be the simple cause, rule, and measure of the things whose unity of being is a trinity, just as, with figures, triangular unity consists of a trinity of angles. Apart from this observation, however, in truth both the name and our concept of "trinity" never properly apply to the maximum but fall infinitely short of this maximum and incomprehensible truth.[119]

The language of coincidence should be the language that pictures without distortion, that communicates both distinction and reconciliation, and that preserves the utter transcendence and mystery of the Infinite while effectively disclosing infinite truth to the finite intellect. The question is whether any language can in fact do this — not without right delimitation and not without right grounding, Cusa answers in Book II of *On Learned Ignorance* and later in his *Apology of Learned Ignorance* (*Apologia doctae ignorantiae*).[120] The value of logic and dialectic is actually quite limited. "Even if I were the most ignorant of all human beings," the "Magister" in the *Apology* says, "I would be satisfied in having the knowledge of this ignorance." He quotes Ambrose's prayer: "Free us, O Lord, from dialecticians." "A garrulous logic," he adds, "detracts from . . . theology more than it confers."[121]

Cusa's *Apology* furnishes the best commentary on what he originally intended to accomplish in *On Learned Ignorance*, and he makes it clear that learned ignorance is experiential as well as speculative. It is a speculative or contemplative *experience*. It is the experience of seeing the truth that precedes the telling of it. Its method of theological seeing and telling differs from other ways "as sight from hearing"; it considers "by the eye of the mind the hidden things" that are given us to see. "Those who through learned ignorance are transported from hearing to the seeing of the mind rejoice that they have attained the knowledge of ignorance by a more certain experience."[122] Even the masters who specialize in the study of Scripture cannot understand their own subject without learned ignorance.[123] One cannot know God's truth, which is incomprehensible, except by leaping across the image to the incomprehensible truth incomprehensibly. Seeing the truth is seeing through and beyond the image.[124]

Theologians are to test images and similitudes as they study and as they proceed to write theology. The issue is not logic but spirituality, not skill but humility. Learned ignorance instructs us that absolute truth is not comprehensible and that no image therefore can be an adequate measure of the truth, for as image it inevitably fails before such truth.[125] Theologians, as Cusa defines their task, should take pains in presuming to declare divine truth while at the same time confessing that "God is not able to be known as God is." This acknowledgement, Cusa maintains, is "the root of learned ignorance."[126]

Learned ignorance, therefore, is the experiential source of theology. Through it one is elevated to the vision of divine things, "lifted up to the simplicity of understanding and to the greater knowing of the unknowable God."[127] It is a being-lifted-up in order to see coincidence of and from the infinite. "In that coincidence every apprehensible theology is hidden."[128] Furthermore, learned ignorance entails *admiratio*, wonder. "Not a knowledge by which someone believes one knows what is unable to be known, rather [such ignorance] is that in which knowing is knowing that one is not able to know."[129] It is learned ignorance, therefore, that invokes a theology of coincidence, a theology that neither commingles nor separates essences in the divine and a theology that regards all terms and other similitudes as bearing entirely no proportion to the infinite. To those presuming to be theologians, Cusa offers this advice: "It is necessary that everyone who desires to ascend to the divine way rise above all imaginable and intelligible ways."[130] The divine truth known in learned ignorance is the ground of a true theology.

## A PROPER APPLICATION

Cusa acknowledges clear reformative implication in his use of coincidence of opposites. He views himself as challenging certain conventional ways of constructing and solving theological problems. His use of language as well as his epistemology plainly unsettled his antagonist Johannes Wenck. Cusa's reforming hopes boldly appear at the end of the dialogue when he has his partisan, the *discipulus*, say to another:

> I am transmitting these to you . . . so that in your fervor this admirable seed may grow by which we are elevated to seeing the divine, just as I recently heard that a great fruit is about to ripen throughout Italy from this seed having been received in studious talents through your solicitous cultivating. For this speculation undoubtedly will surpass all the ways of reasoning of all the philosophers, although it is difficult to relinquish the customary.[131]

Cusa also later characterizes the theological position that he first worked out in *On Learned Ignorance* as an alternative to both negative and affirmative methods. He stresses this point in a letter to Caspar Aindorffer (1453), abbot of the Benedictine cloister at Tegernsee in Bavaria.[132] This particular letter responds to another critic, Vincent of Aggsbach, an unrelenting conciliarist who considered Cusa a turn-

coat. In a previous letter the monks had asked Cusa about the identi-
fication of mystical theology and contemplation in the writings of
Jean Gerson, whom Aggsbach accused of confusing mystical theology and prayer.[133] From the start Cusa moves to the question of negative theology and his own position regarding it. Negative and
affirmative theology, he explains, are limited in what they can say;
neither attains the divine obscurity directly.[134]

The Pseudo-Areopagite is the touchstone. Cusa acknowledges
that the idea of coincidence, as he wishes to apply it, occurs in Dionysius' *The Mystical Theology*. It is not enough to speak of the traditional "disjunctive theology," consisting alternatively of both negative and affirmative methods. A theology that penetrates the divine
obscurity must press beyond even the *via negativa*. We find in *The
Mystical Theology*, especially, the kind of theological method that
Cusa sees himself as pursuing — not disjunctive, neither affirmative
nor negative, but coincident. As "a form of absolutely simple union,"
coincidence, Cusa adds, surpasses every "ablation" and every "position" because in it "ablation" coincides with "position" and negation
with affirmation.[135]

By Cusa's own designation, his is a coincident theology able to
use the accomplishments of both the negative and positive ways and
at the same time to exceed them. For only a theology of coincidence
treats the highest mysteries of the faith — the absolutely hidden
theology — to which no philosopher has ever attained, nor can attain,
so long as one holds to the conventional philosophic principle that
opposites are mutually exclusive. By its very nature mystical theology
assumes the task of outstripping reason and intellect. It presumes to
see what reason excludes as impossible, such as the notion that the
coincidence of being and of not-being is necessity itself. So, unlike
other methods, coincidence allows us to acknowledge the darkness
and density of the idea of the Impossible while at the same time grasping the supreme Necessity itself.[136]

In the chapter on negative theology in Book One of *On Learned
Ignorance* Cusa likewise looks beyond the negative method while
praising its special usefulness. "The theology of negation is so necessary to the theology of affirmation that without it God would not be
worshiped as the infinite God but as creature; and such worship is
idolatry, for it gives to an image that which belongs only to truth
itself."[137] Negation teaches the theologian humility and reverence,
for it stresses that God is infinitely more than words can affirm. By

the process of elimination, negative propositions lead us nearer to divine truth. But *Deus absconditus* is all that the negative method can say about God.

> According to the theology of negation, nothing other than infinity is found in God. Consequently, negative theology holds that God is unknowable either in this world or in the world to come, for in this respect every creature is darkness, which cannot comprehend infinite light, but God is known to God alone.[138]

Nevertheless, the theologian *can* say more and *must* say more. There is the fact of *Deus revelatus*, the theme of Book Three. This is learned ignorance raised to the heights of divine illumination, beyond a Socratic self-knowledge and beyond the divine obscurity. This is the knowledge of the Christ-maximum, who is the model coincident. Coincidence is the corrective for other theological methods, and coincidence is the preferred alternative to the affirmative and negative ways because of the coincidence worked in Christ.

Learned ignorance operates on at least two levels: (1) as recognition of one's incapacity to know God as God is, which is the subject of the first section of *On Learned Ignorance;* and (2) as the reconciliation of human ignorance through God's self-disclosure in Christ, which is the subject of the third part. Moreover, on the first level, the Christ-maximum, the coincidence worked by Christ, furnishes us with the only true knowledge of God, which is the epistemological ground for every theological effort. On the second, the coincidence of the two natures in Christ establishes criteria and models for right theologizing.

To Cusa, the relationship between epistemology and the proper application of the coincidence of opposites is critical. Knowing precedes theologizing, just as experience precedes understanding.[139] A genuinely learned ignorance recognizes the thoroughgoing transcendence of God-in-God's-self, always infinite, absolute, and hidden to human eyes. It teaches us that what we presume to discover about the divine nature we cannot reconcile rationally. But the Christ-maximum, through coincidence, converts oblique knowledge into effective knowledge by disclosing God otherwise hidden. Learned ignorance becomes sacred ignorance when it is ignorance enlightened through Christ.[140] So too learned ignorance, as the knowledge of faith in Christ, is the necessary means by which we come to an appropriate theological method.

Consequently, both human need and Christ's person and work require that coincidence should be employed in theology. But what demonstrates how it should be properly applied? Once again Cusa appeals to Christology.[141] As the incarnate Son resolves the dilemma of the knowledge of God, so Christ the incarnate Word resolves the problem of theological discourse. The hypostatic coincidence of the divine and human natures in his person is the supreme and model coincident.

Theological method contracts the truth to terms and portrays the infinite in the language of temporality and sensibility. So too the theologian's task is incarnational, to render eternal truth into finite forms; its logical precedent is the truth of the hypostatic union. The Christ-maximum provides the epistemological foundation and the logical model for theological method. As the prime coincidence, the Incarnation establishes criteria for appropriate theological language: to disclose mystery and the knowable; to preserve the divine transcendence while proclaiming divine revelation; and to work coincidence without confounding the infinite and the finite. Cusa, therefore, would redirect contemporary efforts to theologize beyond "positive" or "negative" toward a theology of coincidence. Two points summarize his grounds: (1) The paradoxical and infinite nature of theology's subject-matter requires not merely a symbolic but a coincident language communicating both the transcendence and the self-disclosure of God, the absolute maximum; and (2) patterned after the Incarnation, the coincident method enables us to form models and terms that communicate God-as-revealed, while also preserving the mystery of God's nature.

The theology of coincidence, properly applied, is iconographic, picturing the divine work of coincidence in the Word, not God in Godself, who surpasses all language and knowing. Its subject is God's activity — by telling what God does, it tells who God is, for God is hidden except as God reveals Godself. Like the doctrine of the Incarnation, theological language should communicate God's uniting activity, the divine Word contracted to the human word without confounding the integrity of either. Coincident theology, therefore, is reconciling not reductive, and it is declarative, not discursive.

Cusa's use of coincidence of opposites is misrepresented if it is confined to negative theology and if only its contemplative or mystical features are emphasized. As Cusa demonstrates in his writing after *On Learned Ignorance,* the coincidence of opposites is applicable to a wide variety of tasks within several disciplines. In his earlier works, which we have examined, coincidence is first theologically conceived and then extended to multiple problems. Because we start with God as absolute maximum in whom maximum and minimum coincide and because we know God through God's coincident work in Christ, Cusa says, we can, in consequence, see God as the enfolder and unfolder of all reality, and we can see the world in its unity and particularity operating "coincidently." Coincident theology is an enabling theology that frees the mind to see and to say truths beyond its capacity. The idea of coincidence is extendable to metaphysics and other subjects because it is seen first as issuing from the Ground of Being Itself. This is how Cusa perceives coincidence when he first applies the idea.

## IV. THE SPIRITUALITY OF IGNORANCE: *DIALOGUE ON THE HIDDEN GOD* AND *ON SEEKING GOD*

In the sermon delivered on Christmas day (1438),[142] described above, Cusa initiates his exposition of John 1:14 "The Word was made flesh and dwelt among us" by a series of citations from Fulgentius, Pseudo-Augustine, and John Scotus Eriugena. In succession each quotation suggests a distinct kind of ignorance: (1) first, from a sermon by Fulgentius, the insufficiency of language with which to speak of the Word of God; and (2) second, from the *Soliloquies* of Pseudo-Augustine, the darkness of the human condition in which the night is so pervasive that the dark is mistaken for the light, and there is only blindness and night. But then, (3) third, as Cusa continues his exposition, apparently drawing from John Scotus Eriugena's "Homily on the Prologue of John," which he attributes to Origen, he refers to yet another ignorance, a not-knowing beyond both ignorance and knowledge, which necessitates a flight of the intellect. The text does not speak specifically of learned ignorance, nor simply of overcoming ignorance, but of an ignorance illuminated not merely by light but by union with the Light. This form of ignorance, therefore, is other than knowing: It is more being than knowing. It is an enlightenment beyond all vision. It is really another darkness occurring beyond both what is and what is not.[143] Here, and in his other sermons of the same time, the resolution of ignorance is not knowledge but another sort of ignorance, a holy ignorance that is not the opposite of knowing but its fulfillment.

Is this ignorance, described in the context of spirituality, the learned ignorance Cusa speaks of in his famous treatise? Not entirely. Just as we may speak of this as a kind of ignorance, so we may speak of it also as *one kind* of learned ignorance. It is not philosophical or even theological; it is not even conceptual. It may seem fundamentally absurd, as Cusa will acknowledge later in *On the Hidden God* (1442). Whatever kind of learned ignorance it may be, it is not merely a humble acknowledgment of the limitations of one's knowledge; and it is not the realization of the need to know and to learn more, nor is it an ignorance now merely become instructed where once it was unknowing.

### *Ignorance and the Knowledge of God in* Dialogue on the Hidden God

Two years after the completion of *On Learned Ignorance*, Cusa pressed the case for "ignorance" still further in a brief dialogue with the equally provocative title *On the Hidden God* (*De Deo abscondito*) (1444/1445). It is a theological conversation seemingly between a "Pagan" and a "Christian." The Pagan, it turns out, might be anyone, Christian or non-Christian, who presumes to "know" God. Cusa's astonishing thesis, as stated by the Christian, startled the Pagan and might be expected to surprise the Christian reader as well: *I* do not know God, *we* do not know God. "Who is the God you worship?" the Pagan asks. The Christian responds bluntly: "I do not know." The reader is left wondering which of the two is the real pagan. The Pagan of the dialogue is bemused: "How can you so earnestly worship what you do not know?" He receives this odd acknowledgment: "It is because I do not know that I worship."[144] The rest of the dialogue deciphers the meaning of such a response, of such a worship and faith. It ends with a celebration of the hiddenness of God in a benediction pronounced by the Pagan.

What does Cusa mean by ignorance here and what does ignorance have to do with the knowledge of God? No precise definition of ignorance is provided. But if we may assume ignorance to be the opposite of knowledge, we have a definition given us by default when

Cusa has the Christian say: "By knowledge I understand the apprehension of truth."[145] Ignorance, therefore, is not having apprehended truth. But the ignorance that leads to worship is more than the lack of knowledge; it seems to be a higher order of knowing, an acknowledgment of not having apprehended truth or better a knowledge of truth not acquired, being not knowing, a "being in truth"[146] beyond knowing and not-knowing. There are at least two kinds of not-knowing in the dialogue: (1) not knowing what can be known and perhaps should be known; and (2) not knowing by possessing something other than knowing, something greater and fuller and utterly transcendent.

If we may apply to the experience of *knowing* God what the "Christian," in the dialogue, says of *naming* God, then we may say that it is neither true nor false to state that we know God. We neither know nor not know God, nor do we both know and not know God.[147] For God is outside the realm of knowing; God's simplicity precedes both everything that can be known and everything that cannot. Cusa's analogy of sight and color to explain the problem of names is also applicable to the problem of knowledge, as is clear when he moves to the analogy of composite things. God, the Christian explains, is to all things what sight is to visible things.

> For color is attained in no other way than by sight, and so that sight can freely attain every color, the center of sight is without color. Therefore, because sight is without color, sight is not found in the realm of color.[148] And so to the realm of color sight is nothing rather than something. For the realm of color does not attain any being outside its realm, but it maintains that everything that exists is in its realm. But sight is not found there. Therefore, sight, because it exists without color, is unnameable within the realm of color, for no color's name corresponds to it.[149]

After hearing this, the Pagan says that he now sees. But what does he see? It is simply the hiddenness of God. In consequence, the Pagan explains that now "I clearly understand that neither God nor God's name are to be found in the realm of all creatures and that God flees from every concept rather than being asserted as something. For that which does not have the condition of a creature is not to be found in the realm of creatures."[150] Knowing that God is hidden is, as Cusa seems to be saying, the highest form of knowledge, but not the highest form of ignorance, or of not-knowing, which is higher than all forms of knowing, if we consider the Christian's words prior to the discussion of divine names. All I know of God, he says in response to the Pagan's plea for information, is "that everything I know is not God and that everything I conceive is not like God, but rather God surpasses all these."[151] But even this negative knowledge is not the cause of worship. No form of knowing, not even acknowledged not-knowing, is the cause of worship. "It is because I do not know that I worship," the Christian replies at the outset;[152] but this "not-knowing," which is the cause of worship, is neither merely knowledge nor merely ignorance. It is the highest form of not-knowing, an other-than-knowing, beyond every form of knowing; it is "being in truth," the worship of truth itself, which is "absolute, unmixed, eternal and ineffable."[153] The one who has genuine knowledge, therefore, is one who knows that one is ignorant and knows that apart from truth one can know nothing of "being or living or understanding."[154]

Therefore, according to the dialogue, ignorance and not God is the object of knowledge; it is a true knowing as opposed to an illusory one, for it is the acknowledgment of the human incapacity to grasp truth itself. Moreover, it is reverent, expectant, and submissive. A vulnerable and adoring ignorance is the only mediating condition we can bring to a knowing of God. The effects of such an ignorance are the desire to worship and therefore to be in truth, a dependency on truth, which is its own access to itself, and a receptivity to being caught up in the truth, which is utterly transcendent. Why rejoice in the hiddenness of God? Because this means we are *to be in God* rather than merely *to know God*. To have an apprehensible "god" is not to have God, who is before the beginning of things and above all things, but it is to have a finite god that the human mind can comprehend and exhaust. Only the God who remains hidden continues to reveal Godself and is worthy of wonder and praise.

### Ignorance and the Spirituality of Seeing in On Seeking God

In 1445 Cusa treated ignorance further in a more contemplative treatise briefly titled *On Seeking God* (*De quaerendo Deum*). He offers the work to satisfy a request for an explanation of the meaning of the name of God, which he had discussed in the sermon "Dies sanctificatus" delivered on Epiphany in the same year.[155]

The question of naming God once again offers the essential clue in the search for the hidden God: *Theos* from its Greek origin, according to Cusa, means both "I see" and also "I run forth."[156] "Seeing" provides a paradigm for the way along which the wayfarer ought to proceed in one's search. In an analysis of the nature of sight, Cusa outlines a "ladder of ascent" embracing the kinds of seeing.[157] Ignorance encompasses both blindness and sight at several levels of experience.

This treatise suggests different forms of ignorance occurring at what we may speak of as several levels of being and knowing.

1. First, there is a smug and specious "knowing," which in fact is the hard and irresponsive ignorance of those who trust in their own intelligence and shut themselves off from the way to Wisdom by not seeing there is any other way than that which they can measure by their own understanding. Such an ignorance has a distinct and personal cause: They "fell short and embraced the tree of knowledge but did not apprehend the tree of life."[158]

2. There is another ignorance that is simply the condition of every finite thing before the transcendence and boundlessness of God: the inability of all to conceive, name, or even imagine God. Again, Cusa appeals to the analogy of sight and color, in which the knowledge of color is described as limited to the domain of color alone and therefore blind to sight, which, though colorless, is the only source and sovereign of all color. At every level and throughout all the senses, knowledge is contained within one's own realm or species of reality and utterly restricted to knowing only those things that bear some comparison or proportion to what is present in one's own realm. At each level the respective order of reality is entirely ignorant of its perfection and sovereign source, which lies outside its domain at the next higher level. This is also true of the highest nature, the intellectual, whose sovereign is called *Theos*, which Cusa likens to contemplation or intuition itself.

> Yet in the whole region of intellectual powers, nothing is found to which the king himself is similar; nor in all the intellectual region is there anywhere hidden a concept of his likeness. But above all that is conceived and understood is the one whose name is not intelligible, although it is the name that names and discerns all intelligible things. And his nature infinitely precedes all intellectual wisdom in loftiness, simplicity, strength, power, beauty, and goodness,

since compared with his nature everything inhabiting the intellectual nature is a shadow, an empty space without power, a grossness and paucity of wisdom.[159]

3. Finally, there is also a kind of illumined ignorance,[160] not simply learned (the expression "learned ignorance" does not occur here), but brightened within by a knowing entering in, like light. It is an ignorance remaining ignorant in itself, still not knowing, but obtaining and using the sight of another. Here again Cusa appeals to sight in another analogy. An exterior light and an interior light provide the mind with sight and color. The first light source causes the image of an object to penetrate the eye, and the second, from within, discriminates among perceived things and conveys distinct impressions. So also light, of one kind or another, insinuates itself at each level of discernment and makes a variety of seeing possible. At the most elementary level the light of reason brings discrimination to the sensory process; at the next level the light of the intellect brings understanding to the rational process; and at the highest level the light of the divine Spirit brings illumination to the intellectual process. So we may say that, in some fashion, God is present in every being in the same way that the discriminating light is present in the senses and the intellectual light is in reasoning. Moreover, as Cusa explains,

In God's light is all our knowledge, so that it is not we ourselves who know, but rather it is God who knows in us. When we ascend to the knowledge of God, although God is unknown to us, yet we are moved only in God's light, which transmits itself into our spirit, so that we proceed toward God in God's light. Therefore, just as being depends on God so does being known.[161]

But illumination is not the exclusion of ignorance. However we may share in God's light and however illumined our ignorance may become, ignorance is still our enduring property and not the opposite of illumination. Illumined ignorance, therefore, is not so much a knowing that is ours or even a knowledge given us; it is more a knowing that is within us, something that is not our knowing, in the sense that it is not from us or by us, but it is God's knowing within us. We know God as God knows Godself in us.

This, therefore, is how the light of God is present in us and how

41

we participate it. Yet God, Cusa continues to remind us, is imparticipable and unmixable. Cusa returns to the analogy of sight. Color does not become visible through itself, but by its sovereign spirit, sight, which color cannot comprehend because sight lies outside all the boundaries of color. Yet even sight does not see in and of itself, but the discriminative spirit of reason, which sight does not know, sees in it and for it; nor does our intellect understand or live except as the divine Spirit understands and lives within us, though the Spirit remains unbounded by the constraints of our intellect.

There is, therefore, a "spirituality" in all the kinds of seeing at whatever level. Each level of sight is raised to a higher discernment by what Cusa calls the "spirit" of the next order, which, in a kind of ministry, penetrates into the lower and lifts sight to the higher order without a mingling of orders or spirits. Just as the spirit of sensory sight reaches down into the domain of color and makes it visible, the rational spirit lifts sensation to a distinct perception; the intellectual spirit brings rational sight to comprehension; and the divine Spirit, utterly obscure to the intellect, elevates understanding to illumination. Each higher order ministers as "spirit" to the lower without violating the distinction among the levels.

In consequence, there is a kind of unknowing ascent in which a lower level of discernment is elevated into a higher level beyond itself and all its capacity. The ascent is unknowing because both the agent, which interpenetrates and works the ascent of the lower level of seeing, and the ascent itself exceed each level's own capacity to grasp. But in this ascent there is no confusion or intermingling; each remains itself and ministers to each. In the irony of such ministry the higher remains unknown to the lower, which can discern only what lies within the limits of its own domain. Each, therefore, remains ignorant of the higher spirit that is its source of sight and its sovereign.

So too the unknown God "can be known only if God discloses Godself"[162] and draws us by grace into God's light. God wishes to be sought and to be found; however, God gives knowledge not to those who seek it but to those who seek God, who "seek life," not just the experience of God but God Godself. The soul's unquenchable thirst for God, human love pursuing divine Love, Itself in pursuit of the soul, equips us not merely to seek but to race after God from an ardent wondering, from an intellect on fire. "For our intellectual spirit has the power of fire within it. It has been sent by God to earth for no other end than to glow and to spring up in flame. It increases when it is excited by wonder, as if wind blowing on fire excites its potency to actuality."[163]

How far, then, can Cusa stretch the concept of ignorance? Its application seems as limitless as the infinity of God to which he so often refers. The treatise, however, suggests that ignorance comes to its end not in knowledge of any kind but at some utterly simple center within one's own being, really within all being. A kind of severe simplicity and renunciation is required. Among all the ways we may seek God, the deepest yearning and wonder relentlessly drive us past all else toward God alone. The point is to seek God, not the knowledge of God. An enlightened ignorance "rejects" every limited and contracted thing when such ignorance conceives that God is superior to every concept that we can form.[164]

Cusa describes the journey toward God as more of a rush, pushing beyond the senses, common sense, reason, the intellect, and even the most inward self. None of these are God or are similar to God. Where is God to be found? Again, not in knowing, but as Cusa concludes, farther on even beyond all "interiority." It is to God "you turn yourself . . . by entering each day more deeply within yourself, forsaking everything that lies outside in order that you be found on that path on which God is met so that after this you can apprehend God in truth."[165] Perhaps, then, being "in truth" the desire for which, according to On the Hidden God, brought the Christian to worship is the same as this being "in truth" the knowledge of which is the end of ignorance; and this being "in truth" is in fact no different than saying that "God knows in us."[166]

Although it is tempting to see ignorance as Cusa's main consideration, in fact, as Cusa discusses spirituality, ignorance, for him, is not end but way and mediation, access and entry. It is the way of wonder, and like contemplation it is receptivity to mystery, and the end remains forever unspeakable and incomprehensible: beyond knowing and not knowing, God and not God, never merely God.

# V. MYSTICAL THEOLOGY AND COINCIDENCE: ON THE VISION OF GOD

Cusa completed his devotional classic On the Vision of God (De visione Dei) in 1453 at the request of the monks of the Benedictine abbey at Tegernsee. He was then the bishop of Bressanone-Brixen and was responding to the monks' interest in his notion of the coincidence of opposites. He concentrated on its significance for spirituality, sending them this long-delayed work and adding a surprise gift, an amazing portrait of an omnivoyant face, probably Christ's.

We know nothing about the original icon except from the theological inferences Cusa makes throughout the treatise. For example, the icon would have had to have possessed qualities apt for the Divine Face on which Cusa is focusing the contemplation of the reader.

> [God's] true face is absolute from every contraction. It has neither quality nor quantity, nor is it of time or place, for it is the absolute form, which is the face of faces.
>
> When, therefore, I consider how this face is the truth and the most adequate measure of all faces, I am numbed with astonishment. For this face which is the truth of all faces has no quantity.[167]

In conformity with Cusa's theology, the icon, in overall effect, would probably have presented a relentlessly capturing gaze with nothing to release the viewer from a mysterious confrontation with it but only a vacancy or negation, that is, with nothing included in the icon to let the viewer off.[168]

At the start of the treatise he directs his monastic readers to place the painting on a north wall. By observing it carefully, two of the brothers can readily confirm the truly amazing experience of being seen by an all-seeing face who simultaneously regards each, whether moving or still, as if it cared only for him. The entire treatise considers, from one angle of view and then from others, the theological significance of the gaze of God represented by the icon.[169]

### Reappropriation of Coincidence in On the Vision of God

The work represents a fresh application of coincidence, taking the concept to the depths of personal experience with God. The specific term *coincidence* occurs forty-six times and in nine of the twenty-five chapters. In every case Cusa employs it to explain either God's vision of the human or the human's vision of God. Chapter 2 first introduces it to explain the capacity of absolute sight to embrace every mode of seeing. Chapter 9 describes the omnivoyant gaze, seeing all and each, for in God's faculty of sight the universal coincides with the particular.

What does it mean to say that God sees at the same time all things and each thing? And what does it mean to say that the human can see and know God, the absolute and infinite Simplicity? Each successive chapter in which the term appears suggests coincidence, rightly understood, as the device by which finite knowing and saying can grasp the incomprehensible and speak the ineffable. Though the term surfaces here and there throughout the treatise rather unsystematically, with multiple applications, it has a precise and proper meaning, one that Cusa intends that the reader not misconstrue. The coincidence of opposites is a certain kind of unity perceived as coincidence, a unity of contrarieties overcoming opposition by convergence without destroying or merely blending the constituent elements. It is a fact or principle and therefore discoverable, but not merely invented or contrived as we might use comparisons, metaphors, or analogies in ordinary language. As in *On Learned Ignorance*, coincidence does not really describe God. Rather it sets forth the way God works, the order of things in relation to God and to each other, and the manner by which humans may approach and abide in God.

In *On the Vision of God*, Cusa makes use of the coincidence of opposites first as the way of perceiving the truth of God as the absolute and thereby as the way of logically and linguistically treating the truth perceived. He employs several types of coincidence here: (1) *coincidence in nature*, that is, among finite things; (2) *coincidence in the relationship between nature and God*, that is, both the Word's unfolding-enfolding activity in the world and God's self-disclosure in human experience; and (3) *coincidence beyond nature*, that is within God, as triune and as the absolute form of forms.

One instance of the first, *coincidence in nature*, is the coincidence of the faculties of lower species and their perfection with the faculties of species having a higher nature.[170] God and nature, however, do not coincide, if by coincidence we mean equality or identity. There is this second type, *coincidence in the relationship between nature and God*, but God is not in any one thing nor is any one thing in God. The Word, as agent and nexus of coincidence, mediates the coincident relationship of God and creation. Creatures exist not only by God's seeing but also by seeing God.[171] The human, nevertheless, possesses a special vocation and capacity to see God that is unique among all creatures. Nevertheless, what we can see is not God, at least not altogether God, nor even fully God in that small portion we may see. Creatures see God as if God were what they are. The human seeing God sees only the human.[172] The Word, however, mediates the knowledge of God as sacred or informed ignorance. God acts on human knowledge as a self-disclosing subject and effects reconciliation through Christ in whose person and work all contradictions are reconciled.[173]

Coincidence also occurs on the other side, in God, who is not composite but in whom all attributes coincide.[174] *Coincidence beyond nature* is the most of God the human can hope to see, and this one can see only by a transcendent vision beyond sensibility and discursus. We may accordingly distinguish two principal features of the coincidence that is beyond nature: (1) coincidence as *the condition and activity or process of enfolding opposites;* and (2) coincidence as *the transcendent place* on the other side of which God dwells beyond human knowledge. Pursuing the metaphor of "place" further, Cusa describes it both as a doorway and as an encircling wall beyond which God exists unveiled. Moreover, it is a wall of absurdity and of contradiction beyond contradictions. It is the wall of paradise.[175] After the icon itself, the wall is the next most important metaphor in the treatise.

What does Cusa mean that the coincidence of opposites is a wall beyond which is God? First, he means that God is beyond the realm of contradictories. Although the absolute is not subject to contrariety, differentiation, otherness, or proportion, human sensible and intellectual capacities require them; consequently, there exists an impenetrable barrier to human vision and reason. Second, he intends that the reader understand not so much that God is the coincidence of opposites, but rather that opposites coincide in God. Third, he is insisting that the notion of opposites coinciding requires a transcendent vision—a seeing beyond particularity and sensibility, a seeing through and beyond the image or symbol, and an antecedent seeing, considering problems in their infinitely simple principle prior to contradiction. Finally, he means that seeing God, the utterly transcendent absolute, is a logical impossibility and an epistemological impossibility on the grounds of any other logic or epistemology than learned ignorance.

In *On the Vision of God* Cusa takes the notion of coincidence to its limits, beyond itself and beyond his previous discussion in *On Learned Ignorance.* To see coincidence is still not to see God. God, the object of the human's effort to see, however, acts on our seeing as subject so that the searcher and observer discovers oneself searched out, observed, measured, defined. This is one of the more interesting features of Cusa's treatise — the human as *figura*, the theologian discovering oneself as symbol; the searcher after the meaning behind symbols becomes oneself a symbol.

In *On the Vision of God*, as in other writings, Cusa is the tutor of coincidence as well as its advocate. Here he endeavors more to clarify and to instruct in the doctrine than to establish it. Coincidence as fact and principle — given, disclosed, unfolded — is the controlling concept that justifies, shapes, and requires the use of a coincident method in theologizing. In this treatise Cusa stresses that the theological starting-point is the God who acts as the active subject of theology and not simply as its object. The theologian studies first not what God is, but what God does. The theologian appropriates the Word effecting coincidence. All being and all truth spring from what Cusa calls God's "unique concept," the divine Word, enfolding "all things and each single thing."[176]

In several passages, Cusa instructs the reader to comprehend rightly the precise set of relationships suggested by coincidence. He refers to infinity with equal vigor as in *On Learned Ignorance*. A favored metaphor in this regard is still mathematical, but the context now is more emphatically spirituality. To say God enfolds all is to say that all concepts are embraced by the concept of infinity, as all numbers are encompassed by infinite unity and all points by an infinite line. The infinite line, for example, is not precisely a line but a line at infinity.[177] We may say elements coincide in the infinite, but since nothing can be added to the infinite, we may *not* say the infinite can be limited to any one so as to become another. All good things and all quantities coincide in infinite goodness and infinite quantity, but together or separately they also can be nothing other than infinity.

Coincidence, therefore, means union without one constituent "passing over" into the other.[178] The union of two natures in Christ is a union without mixing, compounding, or commingling of the infinite and the finite.[179] Coincidence does not make one thing to be another.

These three things require the theologian to apply a coincident formula and logic: (1) the fact that God is infinite; (2) the principle that the infinite God is absolute Simplicity, to whom there is no other, that is, without opposition; and (3) the historical experience that the chasm between infinite and finite is overcome by the activity of the infinite itself in finitude. How else, Cusa asks, can we speak of the intellect's knowledge of the Infinite except through learned ignorance?

The coincidence of opposites is epistemologically and methodologically necessary. I see God, Cusa explains, "to be infinity itself" wherefore nothing is alien, nothing differing, nothing opposed to God.[180] Coincidence of opposites as theological method proceeds from coincidence as "seeing," that is, as viewing opposites reconciled in infinity. In *On the Vision of God* this is fundamentally a spiritual experience. Cusa calls this "seeing"—scaling "the wall of invisible vision," where God is found.[181] Not just finitude but also human incapacity through sin obscures this vision.[182] Contradictions are finally overcome, not simply in a theory of the infinite, but in history, in the phenomenon of the Christ as God-human. Theology as vision through union and reconciliation precedes theology as discourse, however coincident the logic may be. The theology of coincidence issues from experience, from wonder and from grace. It is, Cusa argues, especially well suited for mystical theology.

### *Application of Coincidence to Mystical Theology*

Mystical theology makes special demands on the theologian, both affective and didactic. The ministry of such a theology requires a coincident method and an iconographic language, acknowledging the utter transcendence and mystery of God and communicating the paradoxical truth that God is known, and seen, as made known.

In a brief digression in Chapter 17, Cusa explains the approach to mystical theology he has taken in this particular work: to present by a similitude some kind of foretaste and to image forth the unimaginable savor of experience with God. The special capacities that coincidence brings to the task of mystical theology are several. First, it enables the theologian to rise above the literal sense of words and to describe the dialectic and process of knowing God. Second, it allows one to communicate the mystery of the vision of God while preserving the divine transcendence. Third, it sanctions the use of an image or figure to stimulate the mind to see beyond itself and to evoke wonder. Using the method I have sent to you, Cusa repeats to the brothers, "You will marvel."[183]

# INTRODUCTION

The coincident method in service to mystical theology, therefore, performs both an evocative and a descriptive function.

## THE EVOCATIVE FUNCTION

It evokes the vision of God — as *the knowledge of God* and as *the experience of God*. *The knowledge of God* called forth by this method includes the following properties: (1) right images of God in the realm of the purest possible abstraction, beyond the material sense of words and imagery; (2) effective mediation through equipping the intellect with right consideration, for example, the multiple consideration of the icon at different levels and angles of perception; (3) the enlightenment of ignorance through divine self-disclosure by which the mind can see what otherwise is unseeable; and (4) proper self-knowledge, that is, God's vision of us, for in seeing God's seeing, we see God.

This last is perhaps one of the most striking conclusions of Cusa's treatment, namely, that while searching for traces and images of God we discover ourselves in God and thereby God. Commenting on the difficulty of his effort to picture God, Cusa remarks that God as imagined seems to receive the form of whoever looks on God.[184] But through the coincident method, we are permitted to see that God raises us up so that we may perceive how we who look on God do not give God form but see ourselves in God, because from God we receive that which God is. Whatever we seem to project into the form of God is in fact God's gift to us. If, for example, one speaks of God as "the living mirror of eternity,"[185] one looks into the mirror and appears to see one's own form there as in a material mirror. Yet the contrary is true, for in this mirror what one sees is not a figure, but the truth of which the beholder's own self is a figure. In God, the coincidence of opposites permits us to say "the figure is the truth,"[186] and the human figure is the object searching after the subject.

Coincidence also evokes the vision of God — as *the experience of God*. Illumination, encounter, and filiation are three concomitant ways of experiencing God in the coincidence accomplished by God's grace.

1. Learned or illumined ignorance provides an intellectual ascent into the obscurity where God resides. God as infinite can be approached only by one who has experienced oneself as ignorant of God. It is, therefore, the vocation of the intellect to become ignorant and to abide in darkness if it would see God.

2. The vision of God as experience through coincidence is encounter or dialogue. The knowledge of God proceeds from the experience of God as object and subject—the one seen is also the one who is present in the seeing itself. Thus, the object of faith is the one present in the faith, and the object of knowledge is the subject knowing and disclosing. God confronts us conformably to our condition, so that the more God offers Godself to the human being like a human being the more we can receive and love God. As God presents Godself, God draws us into God by figures, as if God were our creature. Here coincidence signifies that God so adapts Godself to the human situation that in God "being created coincides with creating, for the likeness which seems to be created by me is the Truth which creates me."[187]

3. Coincidence also engenders filiation. God unites us to Godself in knowledge and love by filiation. True knowledge of God is actual knowing, experiencing God, as loved and loving children of the lovable Parent. We receive God through the bond of filiation, a name used because it is the most close-knit bond in human experience. We are made children through the most perfect sonship of Christ, enfolding all filiations. Jesus, the divine Child, moreover, is the model coincident, the most perfect union.

## THE DESCRIPTIVE FUNCTION

Mystical theology describes the process and the content of *theoria* and seeing. Through the coincident method, the vision of God, seeing God, embraces (*a*) seeing God's seeing, that is, God's gaze; (*b*) seeing God being seen, that is, in the Incarnation; and (*c*) seeing God beyond seeing. So in the same manner the theology of coincidence unfolds (*a*) telling God's own telling, God's omnipresent and ongoing disclosure by the Spirit in act and the Word; (*b*) telling God being told, that is, in the incarnate Concept of God; and (*c*) telling God beyond telling, through symbolic language drawing the mind beyond itself.

There is, however, a dialectic or crisis in theological language as in knowledge. The finite mind requires sensate images and comparisons for knowledge and for speech, but God abides utterly beyond analogy and similitude. The awesome truth of God's simplicity and infinity and the limitations of human language bid the wise theologian to keep silent, though it is the theologian's vocation to communicate, if not at length. Language, by its very nature, delimits, encapsulates, confines. Theological discourse is a contradiction, for what word or term can demonstrate or describe the ineffable, transcendent God?

What word, indeed? The answer is the same as that given to the question of what knowledge can grasp the Unknowable — the *coincident* Word and concept. As in *On Learned Ignorance*, Cusa draws distinct reformative inferences from spirituality for theology. Ignorance and incapacity are resolved through Christ, who provides the coincident solution to the problem of theological language. It is by going in and out the door of coincidence's wall, Cusa says, that one encounters God.[188] The door of the wall of coincidence is the divine Word and Concept. Coincidence means that only as subject does God become object, that God becomes the object of knowledge only by first being its subject. Just as the intellect understands by not understanding and ignorance grasps what exceeds all knowing, so, through coincidence, language describes by not describing and says what exceeds saying.

The dilemma for the theologian of divine mystery is twofold: One must comprehend the incomprehensible and communicate the indescribable. The divinely provided resolution is coincidence. The coincident solution uniquely performs two descriptive functions within mystical theology: One is *declarative* and the other *iconographic*. First, coincident theological language describes what God does, not God's essence. It depicts not only what God *has* done but what God *is* doing. This method theologizes out of the process of knowing; it employs a coincident language borne out of a coincident knowledge that is still knowing and becoming. Cusa uses the analogy of an insatiable hunger satisfied only by food that is within reach but that though continuously eaten, yet can never be utterly consumed or diminished.[189]

Knowing proceeds, but God does not change. The human's perspective, one's perception of truth, changes, as does the place and angle from which one sees God. We only *perceive* truth to change. While staying the same, God seems to move where we are — through God's omnivoyance, seeing all and each, and through God's omnipresence, being everywhere and nowhere in particular. God is known in motion, in process, though God in Godself is not subject to succession. Rest and motion, place and process, coincide in God's vision of the human and in the human's experience of seeing God seeing. Coincidence, therefore, describes the knowledge of God as present, proceeding and experiential, as well as orthodox, "traditioned," and formulated. By declaring what God does, it describes who God is.

Second, there is the iconographic function of the coincidence notion. With what language may the theologian speak of the divine union with the human soul or of God at all? Human reasoning is unable of itself to invent appropriate terms and phrases that communicate God effectively to other finite minds without distortion. The problems of epistemology and language once again are closely related. While (a) discursive reasoning is informed by concrete images and particular experience and (b) the human intellect best comprehends through a kind of abstraction, yet (c) God is utterly beyond both sensation and comprehension. What is required is a coincident language urging reason to defer to a higher vision of pure abstraction and impelling the intellect through and beyond the literal and theoretical meaning of words to a communion with God that exceeds the human's highest capacity to conceptualize and to name—into the realm of God's knowing and love, where opposites are reconciled. There God informs the mind with the understanding and vision it needs. Coincident language, following the model of divinely illumined ignorance, is God-informed language, *symbolic* as God gives comparisons in the experience of the world, and *incarnational*, the idea contracted to word, as the divine to flesh in Christ, the icon of icons and model coincident.

1. *Symbolic language.* Cusa's language in *On the Vision of God* is purposefully iconographic. He employs a succession of metaphors to communicate, not God in Godself, but coincidence in and from God. Here the problem of symbol or image arises. With Cusa, theology cannot describe God's essence, and the theologian searching after symbol and imagery is oneself symbol and image. The theologian is living symbol.

We may deduce the following principles concerning symbolic language from the series of comments Cusa makes on language throughout his treatment of mystical theology:

1. God is beyond all comparison and sight; images and comparisons evoking abstract concepts, nevertheless, more closely approximate the nature of God as absolute.
2. The human comprehends things only by a likeness. The frailty of our corruptible and finite nature requires the "milk" of comparisons in preparation for receiving "more solid food."[190]

3. Symbols and images, such as Cusa's icon, require perception in "the mind's eye" of the invisible truth signified under the form of quantity and quality, yet a truth possessing neither.[191]
4. A right consideration of examples requires passing beyond and through the image, as from the individuated nature to the exemplar.
5. Terms and symbols, rightly used, point and show without presumption of exact replica or comprehensiveness, as the icon demonstrates God's gaze as unmoving, yet seeming to move.
6. God's mental word or concept communicates itself through the experience of "things" and suggests to the mind acceptable comparisons so that, for example, the concept of a simple clock may represent or suggest the succession of time enfolded in the mind of God.[192]
7. Theological language and symbols picture the "figure" of infinity, linguistically and in the mind, not infinity itself. By seeing through the figure, the eye may penetrate the wall separating the human and God and experience "a kind of foretaste" of God's nature, as Cusa says he has set forth.[193]
8. The utility of an image is measurable by its effect on the intellect and the senses, its ability, not to perfect the intellect, but to stir up an inquiry after the truth of the exemplar.

What then of the capacities and utility of analogy and metaphor? We may say that both are kinds of similitude, performing a symbolic function as signs drawing the mind beyond itself to another. Metaphor is used here to denote a linguistic similitude, that is, a single term or phrase to which another is likened; and analogy denotes a logical similitude, that is, a comparison drawn out in logic. In both cases the author constructs similitude by intellectually and linguistically moving from immaterial to material reality that stands for the immaterial. But with image, as a kind of iconic similitude, the mind moves from material to immaterial reality that is seen in the material as vestige or reflection. An image is a reflection disclosing another, partly contained or mirrored in it, in some sense as exemplar. Images may be devised by humans or given by God in nature, history, and revelation.

But God as absolute stands beyond all conceptualizing, imagining, being proportioned, and naming. God is not simply immaterial but infinite as well. In this treatise particularly, the point of departure for theological language is divine reality, neither the material nor the immaterial, transcending but embracing both. Cusa emphatically rejects the analogy of proportion, for he considers it a process of misapplied and feckless discursive reasoning. However, he does employ a series of examples, appealing to the characteristics of creatures to enhance the understanding of God's way and work: the human's vision and face; an acorn and its tree; a clock; a mirror; the being of Socrates, that is, any individual; the parent-child relationship; a student and a teacher; and the joining of the sun's light to a candle's. Are these not analogies? Perhaps, but they are not to be understood as proportional, and they are analogies only if by analogy we mean literally *ana* + *logia*, the placing of a known term or concept alongside an unknown to make it comprehensible, or in the case of the infinite, more luminous to the understanding. We may, for example, liken God's relationship to the individual soul to that of a parent to a child, but the one relationship is not proportionate to the other, nor does God stand in a proportional relationship to the human or anything else. The troublesome word seems to be *proportio*. *Nulla proportio* remains a relentless truth for Cusa so that analogy better remains in the realm of figure and metaphor (*figura* and *translatio*) rather than in that of attribution or proportionality.

Cusa's own principle of signification is that of a coincident language using symbols: (*a*) which picture without distorting or exhausting, that is, appropriately though not comprehensively or untruthfully, producing an apt but always incomplete and imperfect picture; (*b*) which picture so that the similitude might induce beyond itself a transcendent, intellective vision—perhaps through a succession of abstract images—the more abstract the nearer to the truth; and (*c*) which picture truthfully, though not exhaustively, uniting truth and image, without obliterating either and without mixing.

2. *Incarnational theology*. Christ is the final and entirely perfect image of God for knowing and theologizing, the model of models and icon of icons. As the incarnate absolute, he unites ignorance and knowing and resolves the problem of theological knowledge in his person and work. As the incarnate Word, he renders discourse about God possible and appropriate. Jesus is the Word "humanified" in whom likeliness is united to truth, to the exemplar, in perfect union.[194] The hypostatic union of the two natures of his person is the perfect coincident, without mixture, composition, or proportion between the two parts—a coincident union without transference of

either component. Coincidence on this model embraces distinction and unity.

In the last chapters of *On the Vision of God,* Cusa again concludes that the coincidence of the Incarnation is the basis and validation for the human word, for discourse about God. He stresses that Christ's reconciling work itself verifies the meaning of creatureliness, which is the source and limit of language. The Incarnation makes possible the discernment of the real value of the created order and the validation of creaturely models or iconography in theological language. Theological method, therefore, is incarnational; it gives a certain incarnation to the word and takes its point of departure from the Christ-event.

Cusa, therefore, employs coincidence of opposites in *On the Vision of God* to generate an iconic and a mystical theology. He proposes this as his alternative to the apophasis and silence of the *via negativa,* as well as to the less worthy descriptions of predication and analogy. Coincidence is the rudimentary model of disclosure. It is the parent metaphor in establishing other serviceable models. Cusa offers the coincidence of opposites as the central and unifying logical model in order to depict an appropriate likeness between metaphors and the divine reality. In this way, coincidence of opposites as theological method steers appropriate theological understanding and speech. Avoiding scale models, the theologian instead is to apply coincident models that cause the mind to leap across to divine mystery.

The function of language in mystical theology, therefore, is to do more than to depict; it is to rouse, to kindle, to stir the soul, not to grasp knowledge, but to receive the presence of God in the rapture of the intellect by submission to the Word. This, once more, is the extraordinary capacity of a coincident language and method in theology: to "window" the closest possible intimacy with God; to reconcile contraries; and to mediate between the infinite and finite while rendering the intellect receptive and submissive in learned, sacred ignorance.

> The end of desire is infinite. You, therefore, O God, are infinity itself, which alone I desire in every desiring. But I cannot approach the knowledge of this infinity more closely than to know that it is infinity. The more I comprehend you, my God, to be incomprehensible, the more I attain you, because the more I attain the end of my desire.[195]

## VI. CONTEMPLATION AND THEOLOGY:
## *ON THE SUMMIT OF CONTEMPLATION*

The work *On the Summit of Contemplation*[196] is a dialogue between Cusa, now designated Cardinal of St. Peter,[197] and his last secretary, Peter of Erkelenz, canon in Aachen. The conversation takes place soon after Easter in April 1464. Peter remarks that he had hesitated to disturb the cardinal during the Easter holidays because he seemed engaged in a profound meditation. Now, however, Peter finds him relaxed and open to conversation, beaming with joy as if he had just uncovered something of great importance.[198]

Peter provokes the dialogue that follows with the comment that he thought Cusa had already finished every speculation in the many different books he had composed. What possible new insight could he have reached during his most recent meditation?[199] Cusa chides him that not even the apostle Paul following his rapture could "comprehend the incomprehensible." He stuns Peter in verbal play by announcing the object of his searchings as simply *Quid*, the "What," the great What of things, the What Itself. Cusa presents himself as still the relentless seeker, in quest of the "What" that he believes every authentic seeker is driven ultimately to pursue, the self-subsistent What or Quiddity of, beyond and within all things.[200] He will designate it by that which, for Cusa, is a new divine name, *Posse Ipsum*, *Posse* Itself.

Peter asks the obvious question: What are you doing beyond what others have done? Cusa's answer provides interesting insight about a new turn in his own thought. First, he lists a series of simple declarations about the What and its seekers. (*a*) It is not entirely unseen, unseeable, or indescribable. "In some way or other many have seen it." (*b*) "Visions" of it have been left behind in the writings of its pursuers. (*c*) It is recognizable and known but obliquely, from a distance.[201] Second, Cusa then offers a brief, yet still explicit, reflection on the development of his thought since his letter to Cardinal Cesarini (1440) and the *Apologia* (1449), which explained his composition of *On Learned Ignorance*.

The dialogue *On the Summit of Contemplation* and its central theme of God as *Posse* Itself clearly issue from Cusa's recent insights. His remarks indicate a distinct development in his thinking and not just in his use of terminology. He believes he is now seeing God as he has never before, and he has found a more appropriate name. God is more than being. God is the *Posse*, the Possibility, the "Can" before, behind, and present in all that "is."

Cusa's treatise a year earlier, the *Compendium* (1463), indicates his further examining of the idea of *posse*, which appeared so significantly in his dialogue *On Can-Is* [*De possest*] (1460). Already anticipating his extension of the notion in *On the Summit of Contemplation*, the epilogue to his *Compendium* speaks of a *posse* that is Itself *the Posse*.

> There is one object of mental sight and of sensory sight; it is the object of mental sight as the object is in itself and of sensory sight as the object is in signs, and this object is itself the *Posse*, than which nothing is more powerful. . . . Therefore, since itself the *Posse*, than which nothing is more powerful, wishes to be seen as *posse*, this is the reason why all things are.[202]

In *On the Summit of Contemplation* Cusa successively lists the changes that have occurred in his thinking as he reconsidered the concept of quiddity[203] as subsisting in itself. He describes two stages of development in his own understanding and pursuit of the What: an earlier and a later. *Earlier*, "for many years," he had seen that this quiddity had to be sought beyond all power of knowing and prior to every diversity and opposition. Nevertheless, Cusa reveals that he had not yet perceived three critical points. (1) Whatness-subsisting-in-itself is also the invariable subsistence of all substances. In other words it is that which has its own reality from itself alone, never changes, and is the undergirding reality out of which all other reality proceeds and in which all other quiddities first exist as possible. (2) Consequently, it is unable to be increased or multiplied. (3) Therefore, there is one and the same hypostasis for all and not a different whatness for each entity.

*Later*, in the last stage of Cusa's thought, he says he came to several linked observations. (1) One is compelled to acknowledge that this common "hypostasis or substance" for all things "can be." (2) Since this *What* "can be," it "cannot be" without *Posse* Itself, "Can Itself." (3) Nothing can be more subsistent than *Posse* Itself, which for Cusa is now the preferred name for God, and without it nothing at all can be. Therefore, he views his contemplation over Easter as having unlocked for him the mystery of the self-subsistent What or Quiddity that is continuously being sought: *Posse* Itself is the quiddity itself without which nothing can be. This, Cusa explains, is the What or Whatness Itself that has been sought, and this was the focus of contemplation that "occupied [his] thoughts with great delight during these holy days."[204]

Cusa seems aware of the newness of this approach for he pictures his secretary as highly surprised. Peter says he understood why *posse* is called quiddity. But he reminds the cardinal of the term *Possest*, which Cusa had coined earlier in a "trialogue" (1460) of the same name.[205] Cusa, as author, thus alerts the reader to expect an important change of direction by having Peter, as a character in the dialogue, put forward the question of the continued usefulness of *Possest* as an appropriate title for God. The term Cusa had invented earlier, *Possest*, is one of the most positive names that he had cited before composing *On the Summit of Contemplation* (1464). It is itself a play on words, a coincidence of *posse* ("can") and *est* ("is"), the Can, the Possibility that at the same time Is, the Can-Is, which only God can be.[206]

Cusa, thereupon, describes another change in his thinking, this time having to do with predication. He states that he now believes that *Posse* Itself signifies more appropriately than any other term the quiddity without which nothing can be anything or can live or can understand. It does so because "Can Itself" designates that beyond which nothing can be anything else, namely, more powerful, prior, better, more perfect, and so forth.[207] Therefore, *Posse* Itself is that than which nothing whatsoever "can" be or "can" do anything.

He also indicates that he had once believed that the truth could best be found in darkness, *in obscuro*. But now he believes it to be easily seen everywhere for "of great power is truth, and in it *Posse* Itself shines brightly."[208] By Cusa's own estimation, in each of the writings after 1440, by whatever divine name Cusa may have preferred, he had usually emphasized negativity: the obscurity of divine reality, and with it, the utter transcendence, the maximity, and the infinity. But now he maintains, with enthusiasm, that the divine reveals itself clearly and directly through a positive name, *Posse* Itself. It seems almost self-evident that "without *Posse* nothing can be or can have, can do, or can experience anything." Not even a child would find surprising that every "can" presupposes "Can Itself."[209] Further on, he adds a crucial, final point. He is prepared now to present a "facility" that he had not discussed before and had considered "most secret": the highest contemplation is of *Posse* Itself and its appearances. All who have contemplated in the right manner have expressed this point in one way or another. They have all beheld either *Posse* Itself or a variation of its appearing.[210]

At the end of the dialogue, Cusa bids Peter to reexamine Cusa's writings and those of others from this perspective, looking for *Posse* Itself. He will find what Cusa is saying in their conversation already present in his books and sermons if they are properly understood, especially in the tract *De dato patris luminum* (*On the Gift of the Father of Lights* [1445/1446]). He also commends reading his *De visione Dei* (*On the Vision of God* [1453]) and *De quaerendo Deum* (*On Seeking God* [1445]).[211] Cusa, however, does not indicate specific differences from his earlier views. He seems to stress continuity. Yet he does not explicitly say that the notion of *Posse* Itself can be found in any one or all of his previous writings. He may mean that some of his own work is clearer to him now following his recent meditation. It is uncertain how long he had kept secret this "facility" that he had not expressed before. Had he been thinking along these lines prior to Easter of 1464 as the *Compendium* suggests? His reference to previous works, while stressing fresh developments in his thought, suggests both continuity and an evolving of his thought toward the notion of God seen in all things as *Posse* Itself.

It is interesting that as late as 1464 Cusa is still speaking of his own search as progressive. The dialogue communicates a sense of journey that Cusa, just months before his death, continues to see himself as experiencing: the incompleteness of his speculations; the search for the Incomprehensible; the perennial quest for the very *What* of things; and searching as a *motus* not given in vain.[212]

As usual with Cusa, the problem of naming and the problem of knowing go hand in hand. In his earlier efforts he often spoke of knowing and naming God by means of negation or a negative theology. He also developed a coincident theology by which one might behold negation and affirmation before opposition, tracing opposites back antecedently to God, in whom all is one. But now in *On the Summit of Contemplation* Cusa seems to be moving to another kind of positive theology or to a theology superseding not only negation and affirmation but also the coincidence of opposites. Cusa may provide an important clue in the terse remark cited above that *at one time* he had believed that the truth was to be found in a better way in darkness. But, in contrast, he immediately touts his work *Idiota*

59

(1450), in which he says he eventually came to explicate the notion that "truth shouts in the streets." *Now* he sees that truth shows itself everywhere and is easily found. "The clearer the truth is," he says, the easier it is to find.[213] What can be clearer or easier than *Posse* Itself, Can Itself? The search is for the What without which nothing can be anything or live or understand. Consequently, in his last work, this dialogue of 1464, he prefers the name *Posse* Itself, which he describes as so utterly "Can" that it is altogether antecedent to being and act.

What is the nature of seeing that Cusa characterizes in *On the Summit of Contemplation?* Here again Cusa seems to be developing a more positive theology. Seeing in this dialogue is not quite the paradoxical seeing/not seeing or knowing/not knowing of *On the Hidden God* and other earlier writings. In *On the Summit of Contemplation* the name for God is more positive and so is the nature of sight. It is not sight so inverted that it is really a kind of blindness or blindness so illuminative that it becomes sight. The contemplation of God in Cusa's final work is emphatically the work of grace, interiority, and ascent.

The dialogue propounds a final lesson in *theoria* or *contemplatio*. It is the lesson of *introspicere*, of "seeing within," of paying careful attention to what and how the mind sees *in variis entibus*, what and how it sees as it sees *in* the various beings.[214] This is not a simple transcendent vision, although it is a simple vision. This is introspection. The mind sees *intra* what is invisible to sensory sight; it sees the invisible *in* the visible and sees the *posse in* the *esse;* it sees *in* various beings that which they can be and that which they can have only in *Posse* Itself. In so doing the mind sees the various modes of appearance of *Posse* Itself and not *Posse* Itself as visible. As the Whatness of things, *Posse* Itself cannot be various, so what the mind sees is *Posse* Itself appearing variously.

But does the mind through *introspicere* or contemplation see *Posse* Itself? No and yes. It does not see *Posse* Itself as itself, but neither does the mind see *Posse* Itself only in an image or in an enigma or darkness. What does the mind see at the pinnacle of sight? It sees *Posse* Itself but only as it manifests itself, only as it appears *in* things, or in beings or in powers or in "*posse*," and only when the mind sees *in* them *only Posse* Itself, that is, only when the mind sees in them nothing except *Posse* Itself.

Cusa carefully draws several distinctions in the contemplation of things and their *posse*. (1) Nothing is whatever it is unless it *can be*, unless there is a *can*, a *posse*, preceding and underlying it as its *substantia* or *hypostasis*. (2) The *posse* in each thing that is or lives or understands is, therefore, the "what," the quiddity of each thing, but such a *posse* is *posse* with something added. (3) However, *in* every such *posse* there is the one *Posse* of every power, which is *Posse* Itself. Consequently, the *apex theoriae*, the highest point of contemplation, is to see *in* all things nothing except *Posse* Itself. For at the summit of sight nothing can be seen except *Posse* Itself.

### Sight as Gift

The dialogue suggests three concurrent paths: sight as gift; sight as ascent; and sight as fulfillment. The first originates from the fact that we see *Posse* Itself only because it shows itself, that is, because of the power of its manifestation, for it shines intensely everywhere. This absolute, one, divine *Posse* is graciously and purposefully self-evident in every *posse*. The logic is pure and simple: Everything that "is" presumes "can"; every "can" be or "can" do requires a simple "can"; and every "can" presupposes, as necessary, a single "Can" with nothing added, a *Posse* behind all *posse*, or *Posse* Itself. Nothing, therefore, "can be" more anything, that is, more known, easier, more certain, and so forth, than Can Itself.

Why should this be so? Cusa takes pains that his companion understand what the cardinal means by *Posse* Itself and how it manifests itself so readily. When we genuinely see the truth in and through all things, we see the *posse* of the first cause, or the principle, of each kind and of the species of things. But every such *posse* is originated and holds its power from one, original *Posse*, "the absolute, uncontracted, and completely omnipotent *Posse* Itself."[215] Without it there could be nothing else: It is the quiddity in and of itself than which there is nothing prior, more perfect, or more powerful. Cusa describes it as "the whatness and the hypostasis of all things."[216]

Cusa appeals to the analogy of light. Some holy writers spoke of this *Posse* as light, "the light of all that can emit light."[217] Cusa draws on the metaphor of the *posse* of sensible light in relation to the absolute *Posse* and the being of color in relation to simple being.[218] First, he examines the nature of sensible light, which makes all sensible sight possible. Light is the single hypostasis in the domain of sight and of visible things: It in itself is not visible but appears variously in the various modes of being of color, and without it there would not be color, a visible object, or sight. The brightness of such light subsisting in itself surpasses all visual power. How, therefore, can light itself be seen? It is never seen as it is, but it reveals itself in visibles in varying degrees, more brightly in one thing than in another. Since its brightness cannot be grasped in visible things, it reveals itself in visibles in order to reveal itself as invisible, that is, as the invisible *posse* in and behind all color, visibility, and sight. We see light's brightness more truly when we see it to be invisible in visible things.

Next, Cusa enjoins Peter to transfer these "sensibles" to "intelligibles."[219] He develops his metaphor very carefully because *Posse* Itself stands beyond simple comparison or proportion. *Posse* simply, that is, *Posse* Itself as absolute, is to simple being what light's *posse* is to color's being. If the equation were that the *posse* of light is in relation to the being of color what $x$ is to simple being, then *Posse* Itself would be $x$. When sensible sight occurs at its summit, the eyes see the invisible light or *posse* in the being of color or visible things. But what is seen when intelligible sight reaches its summit? Cusa directs Peter to examine carefully what the mind sees in simple being. The comparison is interesting. When you make this transference, Cusa tells Peter, you will see: (1) Various beings are that which they can be and have that which they can have only from *Posse* Itself; (2) various beings are only various modes of appearance of *Posse* Itself; (3) quiddity is not various, because it is *Posse* Itself appearing variously; (4) no other quiddity but *Posse* Itself finally can be seen in things that exist or live or understand; (5) every *posse*, that is, to be or to live or to understand, is the manifestation of *Posse* Itself; but (6) *Posse* Itself as it is cannot be perfectly grasped in all powers of being or knowing.[220]

So then what does Nicholas of Cusa mean when he speaks of the "appearance" of *Posse* Itself? And how does the mind grasp the reality in and behind its "appearance"? Cusa distinguishes between "being" and "appearing" and between "seeing" and "comprehending" and seems to contrast "seeing" and "knowing." He preserves *ignorantia*—not-knowing as the proper negative way, appropriate to what is absolute and infinite—while also juxtaposing a positive way, of sight, or *theoria*, which is not blindness or a privation of sight but is also not ignorance, that is, he embraces the negation of knowing and at the same time the affirmation of sight.

If *Posse* Itself cannot be perfectly grasped as it is in any of the powers of being and of knowing, then to what extent can it be grasped at all? Cusa says that it cannot be grasped or comprehended in them. He insists that rather than "being" in them it "appears" in them and appears variously in one more powerfully than another, for example, more in intellectual and less in sensory things. Its appearance varies more or less brightly as light does in different visible objects and in colors. *Posse* Itself appears and is seen but without either comprehension or cognition.

The mind sees *Posse* Itself but cannot be said to know it. The only way this is possible is for the mind to see beyond knowledge and beyond its own capacious sight. Cusa here is obviously not following a distinction between an affective and an intellective vision of God, about which the Tegernsee monks had inquired of him when he wrote for them his treatise *On the Vision of God.*[221] But the distinction for Cusa in the dialogue of 1464 is between seeing and knowing or between seeing and other ways of knowing. Moreover, the seeing is not from a mental calculating or from the operation of the mind in any special effort or *actus*, but from the mind's own *posse*. Here is where the highest and brightest appearing occurs—in the mind's *posse*.

### Sight as Ascent

Therefore, *Posse* Itself is seen because it keeps showing itself. Moreover, to see this *Posse* is the mind's ordained end. Although the *Posse* Itself appears in all being, nowhere does it reveal itself more than in the mind, and this showing is gift.[222] How, then, does the mind see? And with what kind of vision? A second path of sight stems from the fact that contemplation of *Posse* Itself depends on the way of seeing, as Cusa insists, on how we "attend."[223] The mind's vision of God as *Posse* Itself is sight taken to its summit.

Only the mind sees *Posse* Itself, and it sees it by means of a hierarchy of seeing. *Posse* Itself shows itself in different degrees of intensity. At the lowest level it appears in sensible *posse*, that is, in the *posse* of sensibles, and at the next level above, it appears more powerfully in intelligible *posse*, in the *posse* of mind. However, although the mind sees *Posse* Itself in and through beings by means of its own power, this is not the summit of contemplation.

In the abridgment attached to the dialogue, which Cusa calls a *Memoriale*, a memory device of twelve points,[224] he indicates that every *posse* is an image of *Posse* Itself through a kind of hierarchy of images, of greater and lesser imaging. Just as image is the appearance of truth so all things are manifestations of *Posse* Itself.[225] Cusa also appeals to another analogy: Just as Aristotle reveals the *posse* of his mind in his books, so *Posse* Itself shows itself in all things.[226] But unlike any other reality in creation, the mind looks in itself to see the intent of its Author for itself and all else. All others exist for the sake of the mind, and the mind alone exists to contemplate in itself the *Posse* Itself.[227]

What, therefore, is the highest point of sight? The pinnacle, the *apex*, occurs only when the mind sees *in* its own *posse*. Cusa calls this *posse* the "intelligible" *posse*.[228] At sight's highest level, *Posse* Itself is, by means of the intelligible *posse*, seen in itself in beings but only when *Posse* Itself alone is seen in them. But the mind contains a hierarchy of *posse* or power. The intelligible *posse*, which is above other *posse*, seems itself to possess levels. The *apex* of the intelligible *posse*, the mind's *posse*, is the *posse* of seeing, the highest peak of the intelligible *posse*. "When," Cusa explains, "the mind in its own *posse* sees that *Posse* Itself cannot be grasped because of its eminence, the mind then sees with a sight beyond its capacity." The mind's *posse* of seeing surpasses its power of comprehending and all its other faculties and powers.[229]

What is this seeing? (1) It is a *visio simplex*, not a comprehensive sight; and it is a *visio elevans* in order to see incomprehensibly from the "elevation" but not from the comprehending power of sight. (2) It is sight occurring at the *posse supremum mentis*. (3) It is sight seeing beyond every comprehensive faculty and capability. (4) It is sight directed to *Posse* Itself alone as the principle and goal of the mind's desire; nothing is desired beyond this. The mind's supreme *posse*, therefore, is the *posse*, the potential, to see beyond every faculty and power. Therefore, all these statements rest on Cusa's prior claim that *Posse* Itself most manifests itself in the mind's supreme *posse*.

Nowhere else does *Posse* Itself appear more powerfully or more incorruptibly than in the mind's *posse*. *Memorial* VIII lists successively what the mind sees as it peers at divine *Posse* within: (1) intelligibles, therefore, itself; (2) the mind's own *posse* of being, not as *Posse* Itself but as its image; (3) *Posse* Itself present in the mind's own *posse*; and (4) the mind itself as a mode of appearance of *Posse* Itself. Consequently, the mind also sees the manifestation of *Posse* Itself in everything that exists. What the mind comes to grasp, therefore, is that all that it sees are "modes of the appearance of the incorruptible *Posse* Itself."[230] Therefore, by means of its own *posse* the mind ascends beyond the seeing both of the senses and of the intellect to the highest point of appearance and sight "above every cognitive power" to behold *Posse* Itself. This occurs when the mind sees *Posse* Itself to exceed every power and capacity of even the intelligible *posse*.

For Cusa the difference in our seeing, again, is in our attention. The secret lies in the way we attend. The highest sight is the mind's sight in which it sees with a seeing beyond its capacity. Cusa's notion here appears reminiscent of "learned ignorance." But he seems to be moving a step beyond. For Cusa does not speak of a coincidence of sight and blindness but of the highest order of sight, sight brought to its summit. Moreover, the language is not oxymoronic, although his thesis does not seem entirely discontinuous with the coincident theology we found him developing in *On Learned Ignorance* and other works. But in *On the Summit of Contemplation* he is not speaking of an enlightened blindness per se or a blindness lifted to its highest realm in a dark cloud of unknowing, but rather he is describing a seeing that is not blind at all but that reaches beyond comprehensive sight as well as blindness. The *posse* to see, in the way Cusa is asserting here, stands beyond the *posse* to comprehend just as learned ignorance stands beyond comprehension, but Cusa does not appeal to coincidence. Such seeing is not designated as a seeing not-seeing above sight and its opposite; rather, it is the mind's "simple vision," the vision of elevated sight.

The vision of *Posse* Itself may not be a comprehensive seeing, but it carries with it a comprehension of all else. When we finally see *Posse* Itself in and beyond all being, we then see *Posse* Itself as the root presupposition behind every question of "can." It is the *posse* that stands alone, self-subsistent, the one quiddity prior to being and to all other *posse*. Unlike "can" be or "can" live or "can" understand, and so forth, it is the one *posse* with nothing added. It is pure and absolute *posse*, invariable, to which nothing can be added, from which nothing can be separated; it is "can" in and of itself, never diminished nor augmented.[231]

In the context of this description Cusa has Peter ask if the cardinal would now say anything further about the concept of "the First."[232] Behind this question is the larger inquiry, as Cusa sees it, occupying the whole history of philosophy. How does one explain the fundamental principle of things? It is here that Cusa shares what he calls "a facility, not openly expressed before, which I consider to be most secret": Precision of seeing, sight at its highest and clearest, is to see *Posse* Itself and its appearance. Every right seeing in the history of thought has attempted to express this. All the wise have seen either *Posse* Itself or its appearance; they have seen one or the other depending on wherever they may have trained their sight. Again, it is a question of "attention."[233] (1) Some see only *Posse* Itself, as do those who eschew many forms and see only the One as the principle of things, whereas (2) others see both *Posse* Itself and its appearances, as do those who see the One *and* the many, and (3) still others see only the appearances, such as those who look at many ideas and forms, which are the modes of being of the appearance of *Posse* Itself. But in all that is or can be there is only one thing to be seen by sight at its summit and that is *Posse* Itself.[234] The summit of contemplation, therefore, is to see *Posse* Itself, the *Posse* of all *posse*, without which nothing can be contemplated.[235]

What is the *Posse* Itself that is seen invisibly and incomprehensibly? To see *Posse* Itself is not to see being but instead it is to see *in* being the *Posse* Itself behind every *posse* and every being. Cusa explains to Peter how the question of whether *Posse* Itself exists is impertinent. The question of existence is not related to and does not reach to *Posse* Itself, and neither does doubt. The *posse* to be and the *posse* to be this or that presuppose *Posse* Itself. The very ability to doubt presupposes *Posse* Itself. In other words *Posse* Itself is *posse* without addition. Rather, to have being is to possess the appearance of *Posse* Itself.[236] Without its appearance there is no being.

God as *Posse* Itself, therefore, is God without being. Cusa now locates God, before all else, not in being, but in the realm of pure possibility. All else is not this supreme *Posse* but its appearance. Moreover, this is all there is to be seen. One sees either God or the manifestation of God. There is nothing else. God, *Posse* Itself, is the *Primum*, not the First Being, but the "First" itself without being or anything else attached. "All speculative precision is to be placed only in *Posse* Itself and its appearance."[237] This Cusa believes is borne out in the history of philosophy and theology. All who have appropriately seen tried to express this when they spoke of the First—whether they operated from affirmative or negative traditions. (1) Those who looked at both *Posse* Itself and also at its many modes of appearance emphasized a *via affirmativa*. Consequently, they spoke of One and many, of the newness of things, of God as the source of ideas and forms, and of a multiplicity of forms and ideas. (2) However, those who contemplated only *Posse* Itself practiced a *via negativa*. For this reason they spoke of the One alone, of the absence of newness, of the denial of plural forms and ideas, and of the nonexistence of death. The question of the difference between the two traditions was the question of "attention" or of contemplation, that is, the manner of beholding.

What is the relationship between *Posse* Itself and its appearances? *Posse* with an addition, such as *posse + esse, posse + vivere,* or *posse + intelligere,* is an image of *Posse* Itself. There is a hierarchy of images on a scale ascending from *posse esse,* next to *posse vivere,* and finally to *posse intelligere,* the highest image. "Just as an image is the appearance of truth so all things are nothing but appearances of *Posse* Itself."[238] The key words in the dialogue for describing created things in relation to their Creator are *imago* and *apparitio* and, unlike *De docta ignorantia,* not *contractio* or *explicatio.*

Cusa extends the notion of hierarchy further when he explains why it is that *Posse* Itself may be seen at all—whatever its character and however it may be seen. The mind is the highest of created things in the world, and among kinds of light the living and intellectual light, which the mind is, is the highest light. Further, the ordering is purposeful, directed, and ministering. "The living, intellectual light, called the mind, contemplates in itself *Posse* Itself. Therefore, all things exist for the mind, and the mind exists for the sake of seeing *Posse* Itself."[239] The mind was ordained in such a way as not only to desire *Posse* Itself but to run toward it.[240]

### Sight as Fulfillment

What is the effect of such contemplation? The answer is Cusa's third path of sight: To see *Posse* Itself is to enjoy a kind of rest and to see finally the connection and end of all things. The mind was made to see *Posse* Itself. Moreover, when the mind sees *Posse* Itself, it also sees all else in a proper and embracing view.

Cusa calls the mind's *posse* by which it can see God its supreme *posse.* It is the *posse* to see above every faculty and power of comprehension, beyond the *posse* to see by its own capacity. This highest "can" of the mind is unbounded this side of *Posse* Itself. Moreover, it is in the mind's supreme *posse* that *Posse* Itself most reveals itself and sight reaches its goal. This is the divine intent. (1) The *posse* to see is ordered only to the *Posse* Itself so that the mind may foresee that toward which it is striving, as a traveler can see beforehand one's journey's end in order to direct one's steps toward the goal. (2) All things are ordered so that the mind could journey to *Posse* Itself, which it sees from afar. The final and enduring sight, however, is eschatological. "For *Posse* Itself, when it will appear in the glory of majesty, is alone able to satisfy the mind's longing."[241]

The "What" that is sought is *Posse* Itself. But it is not arbitrarily sought. It is sought out of deepest longing. It is the "What" sought by every mind, the cause of the mind's desiring, and the end of the highest longing. It alone provides the mind with its highest satisfaction.[242]

The *Memoriale* concludes with brief trinitarian and Christological statements. The mind can see one *posse* after another in being. Behind and within all being is a *posse*, for example, the being of body or bodily being, which unlike a sensate body is visible only to the mind. Bodily being is body's *posse* of being and cannot be seen by sensible sight. Moreover, bodily being is triune, one and the same bodily being with three distinct dimensions—length, breadth, and depth. The mind, therefore, can see *Posse* Itself incorruptibly appearing in body's triune being and, on a higher scale, in nobler beings, as the *Posse* Itself appears more powerfully in an ascending order. At the top of the hierarchy it appears in the triune being of the mind.[243]

The mind also sees a triune *posse* in all works, that is, in "sensation, sight, taste, imagination, understanding, will, choice, contemplation, and in all good and virtuous deeds." The *posse*, for example, of that which makes and of that which can be made and of their union is one and the same. *Posse* Itself appears in each component *posse*, and every triune *posse* is a reflection of *Posse* Itself.[244] Each *posse* as image is triune because *Posse* Itself, the quiddity that is continuously sought, is threefold. At the end of the *Memoriale* Cusa emphasizes that the title *Posse* Itself really signifies "the three and one God, whose name is the 'Omnipotent' or the '*Posse* of all Power.' "[245] Christ, moreover, is the most perfect appearance of *Posse* Itself, and it is he who directs us "by word and example to the clear contemplation of *Posse* Itself. And this is the happiness which alone satisfies the highest longing of the mind."[246]

*On the Summit of Contemplation* presents itself in some ways as a story of Cusa's own venture in the perennial quest for what is at or lies beyond the very core of being. The work represents a kind of theological journey of ascent tracing evidences of God in things, in being, and in the mind but in the end pushing past the mind's own limits. Cusa takes sight or contemplation to its outermost limit and shows us God beyond being. Cusa moves above actuality and being to a vision of Possibility Itself. This is what sight sees of God at its highest peak.

In conclusion, what precisely does Nicholas of Cusa intend to convey about the reality of God when he presses the use of this new name *Posse* Itself? I want to suggest several descriptions: (1) *utter potency*, potency without the necessity of act; (2) *pure fecundity*, a concept bearing interesting comparisons (*a*) with Proclus' notion of *authypostaton*, or self-subsistence, but, as his "First Principle," beyond subsistence,[247] (*b*) with Bonaventure's idea of the self-diffusiveness of the Good,[248] but prior to the Good, and (*c*) with Eckhart's concept of God as a boiling-pot,[249] but, for Cusa, pure boiling itself without formal emanation; and (3) *pure quiddity and hypostasis*, but manifesting itself as trinitarian, whose highest appearance among beings is Christ.

It is in the attached *Memoriale* that Cusa, for the first time in the tract, relates the person and work of Christ to *Posse* Itself. He portrays Christ as the most perfect *apparitio* and the instrument of contemplation. By word and example Christ has led us to the clear contemplation of *Posse* Itself. Like truth shouting in the streets, the triune God appears brightly everywhere, in every mode of being, more powerfully in intelligible being but perfectly only in Christ. But like all *posse* God appears invisibly, for God is invisibly seen as the *Posse* Itself of every *posse*. God is not just present in all being, God appears in all. But Christ is the most perfect *apparitio*.

The notion of *Posse* Itself is Cusa's way of affirming God's boundlessness, utter freedom, and grace without necessity. Beings were created for no other reason than for the Creator, who is the *Posse* Itself behind being, to reveal the Creator's self and to do so freely. The *Posse* Itself is the one and only quiddity in all things, the *quidditas in se* present in all. This means that all are nothing else than the differing ways *Posse* Itself appears. Creation issues from pure grace, pure fruitfulness, and pure free choice. That in turn makes relationship with God take on a new immediacy, the immediacy available only to sight, the mind's highest *posse*, an immediacy beyond conceptualization, the immediacy of seeing with the mind, but without conceiving.

According to Edward Cranz, beginning with *On the Beryl* [*De beryllo*] (1458), Cusa wrestles more and more with the issue of immediate relationship to God of direct vision. In this treatise on the analogy of the beryl, God is thought to be reached unintelligibly and seen in the darkness. There is a vision, a sight, but *in* the darkness. By the time of *On the Summit of Contemplation* in 1464, this notion, along with that of immediacy, has developed from *On the Beryl* through *On "Possest"* (1460), *On the Not-Other* (1461/1462), *On the Hunt for Wisdom* (1462), and the *Compendium* (1463).[250] But with the composition of *On the Summit of Contemplation* following Cusa's Easter meditation, the darkness subsides; all the barriers fall away; and clearly and easily revealed, like truth in the streets, is the great *Quid, Posse* Itself, the unvarying and single hypostasis of all, available in the simple *theoria* of the mind, where the pinnacle of sight occurs. This is the last reorganization of Cusa's thought, but it is not discontinuous with what has preceded it. Cusa, by his own testimony, traces the theology of the work back to *On Seeking God* (1445) and *On the Vision of God* (1453). But he especially cites *On the Gift of the Father of Lights* [*De dato patris luminum*] (1445–1446), which he says "when properly understood in accordance with what has been said here, contains the same as this tract."[251]

What Cusa attempts to achieve in *On the Summit of Contemplation* is no mere tinkering or fine tuning of terminology. For Cusa, this work is intended to complete, to finish, and to redirect his earlier speculations, although not to contradict them. While these earlier writings may illumine issues in the dialogue, this final composition provides a hermeneutic and a key for unlocking Cusa's theology up to the last point in its development: "Consequently, my dear Peter, you should be willing to turn your mind's eye to this secret with keen attention and by means of this analysis enter our writings and your other reading and thoroughly work through our books and sermons."[252]

---

*A Note About Capitalization of Terms*

The translation makes sparing use of capitalization. With few exceptions, it capitalizes Cusan philosophical-theological terms, e.g., "trinity," "maximum," "truth," "being," and so forth, when, in a particular context, they specifically and exclusively apply to God as divine names or titles.

# NOTES TO INTRODUCTION

1. The invaluable source for tracing Cusa's life is the profuse collection of documents in the new series in process edited by Erich Meuthen and Hermann Hallauer, *Acta Cusana. Quellen zur Lebensgeschichte des Nikolaus von Kues* in the edition of the Heidelberg Academy of Sciences. So far two sections of volume one, edited by Meuthen, have been published: Bd. I, Lfg. 1: 1401-1437 Mai 17 (Hamburg, 1976) and Lfg. 2: 1437 Mai 17-1450 Dezember 31 (Hamburg, 1983).

2. On the history of the hospice, see Jakob Marx, *Geschichte des Armen-Hospitals zum h. Nikolaus zu Cues* (Trier, 1907).

3. This brief summary of Cusa's life relies heavily on the *Acta Cusana* as well as Edmond Vansteenberghe, *Le Cardinal Nicolas de Cues* (Paris, 1920), and the biographical studies of Erich Meuthen including *Nikolaus von Kues, 1401-1464: Skizze einer Biographie*, 7th ed. (Münster, 1992); *Die letzen Jahre des Nikolaus von Kues* [1458-1464] (Cologne, 1958); "Neue Schlaglichter auf das Leben des Nikolaus von Kues," MFCG 4 (1964): 37-53; and "Nikolaus von Kues in der Entscheidung zwischen Konzil und Papst," MFCG 9 (1971): 19-33.

4. Cusa would later dedicate four of his most important writings to him: *De concordantia catholica, De docta ignorantia, De coniecturis,* and *Apologia doctae ignorantiae.*

5. See Charles L. Stinger, *Humanism and the Church Fathers: Ambrogio Traversari (1386-1439) and Christian Antiquity in the Italian Renaissance* (Albany, 1977), pp. 158-162.

6. See Alois Meister, "Die humanistischen Anfänge des Nikolaus von Cues," *Annalen des historischen Vereins für den Niederrhein* 42 (1896): 5-9 and Ludwig Pralle, *Die Wiederentdeckung des Tacitus. Ein Beitrag zur Geistesgeschichte Fuldas und zur Biographie des jungen Cusanus* (Fulda, 1952), pp. 33-36. See also the documents in *Acta Cusana* I.1.*passim.*

7. Heymeric was an Albertist who emphasized a Platonist reading of Albert and was keenly interested in Raymond Lull's writings. See J. N. Hillgarth, *Ramon Lull and Lullism in Fourteenth-Century France* (Oxford, 1971), pp. 270ff., and on Albertism, consult Ruedi Imbach, "Le (Néo-)platonisme médiéval, Proclus latin

et l'école Dominicaine allemande," *Revue de théologie et de philosophie* 110 (1978): 427–428.

8. On Cusa's use of Pseudo-Dionysius, see Ludwig Baur, *Nicolaus Cusanus und Pseudo-Dionysius im Lichte der Zitate und Randbemerkungen des Cusanus, Cusanus-Texte. III. Marginalien. 1* (HSB, Jg. 1940/1941, 4. Abh.; Heidelberg, 1940/1941).

9. Cusa may have already come into contact with Lull's writings at Padua. On the influence of Lull for the development of Cusa's thought, see Eusebio Colomer, *Nikolaus von Kues und Raimund Llull* (Berlin, 1961); and Charles H. Lohr, "Ramón Lull und Nikolaus von Kues. Zu einem Strukturvergleich ihres Denkens," *Theologie und Philosophie* 56 (1981): 218–231, and his essay "Metaphysics" in *The Cambridge History of Renaissance Philosophy*, ed. Charles B. Schmitt et al. (Cambridge, 1988), pp. 548ff. On Cusa's dependence on Lull, see Theodor Pindl-Büchel, "The Relationship between the Epistemologies of Ramon Lull and Nicholas of Cusa," *American Catholic Philosophical Quarterly* 64 (1990): 73–87.

10. Pierre Duhem detected, but overstated, Cusa's later reliance on Thierry of Chartres in his "Thierry de Chartres et Nicolaus de Cues," *Revue des sciences philosophiques et théologiques* 3 (July 1909): 525–531. Moreover, Duhem seems unaware that Cusa draws largely from Thierry's Commentaries on Boethius. See Thomas P. McTighe, "Thierry of Chartres and Nicholas of Cusa's Epistemology," *Proceedings of the Patristic, Medieval and Renaissance Conference* 5 (1980): 169–176.

11. On Heymeric's influence, see Rudolf Haubst, "Zum Fortleben Alberts des Grossen bei Heymeric von Kamp und Nikolaus von Kues," *Studia Albertina*, Supplement IV BGPThM (1952): 420–447; and Eusebius Colomer, "Nikolaus von Kues und Heimeric van den Velde," MFCG 4 (1964): 198–213. On Cusa's reliance on Albert, see M. L. Führer, "Nicholas of Cusa and Albert the Great," in *Nicholas of Cusa in Search of God and Wisdom*, ed. Gerald Christianson and Thomas M. Izbicki (Leiden, 1991), pp. 45–69.

12. See Erich Meuthen, *Das Trierer Schisma von 1430 auf dem Basler Konzil: zur Lebensgeschichte des Nikolaus von Kues* (Münster, 1973).

13. Cusa's position on the issue of the Hussites appears in his *Contra bohemorum errorem de usu communionis*, which apparently assisted the temporary settlement of the Bohemian question in 1436. The work was printed as *Epistolae* II and III in p II and will occur in the Heidelberg Academy edition, *Opuscula* II (h X) as *Epistulae ad Bohemos.*

14. The treatise is edited by Gerhard Kallen in *De auctoritate presidendi in concilio generali, Cusanus-Texte. II. Traktate. 1* (HSB, Jg. 1935/1936, 3. Abh.; Heidelberg, 1935), pp. 10–35. See the translation with introduction and notes by H. Lawrence Bond, Gerald Christianson, and Thomas M. Izbicki in "Nicholas of Cusa: 'On Presidential Authority in a General Council,' " *Church History* 59 (1990): 19–34.

# NOTES TO INTRODUCTION

15. All the works of Cusa appear in the Heidelberg edition except for those otherwise cited. On Cusa's ecclesiology and political views, see Paul E. Sigmund, *Nicholas of Cusa and Medieval Political Thought* (Cambridge, Mass., 1963); and Morimichi Watanabe, *The Political Ideas of Nicholas of Cusa with Special Reference to His De concordantia catholica* (Geneva, 1963).

16. *Die Kalenderverbesserung (De correctione Kalendarii)*, ed. V. Stegemann (*Schriften*) (Heidelberg, 1955).

17. James E. Biechler, "Nicholas of Cusa and the End of the Conciliar Movement: A Humanist Crisis of Identity," *Church History* 44 (1975): 5–21.

18. On the debate regarding the motives for Cusa's change, see E. Meuthen, "Nikolaus von Kues in der Entscheidung zwischen Konzil und Papst," MFCG 9 (1971): 19–33; "Nikolaus von Kues und das Konzil von Basel," *Schweizer Rundschau* 63 (1964): 377–386; and Joachim W. Stieber, "The 'Hercules of the Eugenians' at the Crossroads: Nicholas of Cusa's Decision for the Pope and against the Council in 1436/1437—Theological, Political, and Social Aspects," in *Nicholas of Cusa in Search of God and Wisdom*, ed. Christianson and Izbicki, pp. 221–255.

19. On Cusa's trip to Constantinople, see Vansteenberghe, *Le Cardinal*, pp. 60–63, and Martin Honecker, *Nikolaus von Cues und die griechische Sprache*, *Cusanus-Studien, II.* (HSB, Jg. 1937/1938, 2. Abh.; Heidelberg, 1938).

20. On Cusa's journey to and from Constantinople, see H. Lawrence Bond, "From Constantinople to 'Learned Ignorance.' The Historical Matrix for the Formation of the *De docta ignorantia*," in *Nicholas of Cusa on Christ and the Church*, ed. Gerald Christianson and Thomas M. Izbicki (Leiden, 1996), pp. 135–165.

21. See the letter appended to his *De docta ignorantia*: III.263–264 (h I.163).

22. See Rudolf Haubst, "Die Thomas- und Proklos-Exzerpte des 'Nicolaus Treverensis' in codicillus Straßburg 84," MFCG 1 (1961): 17–51. On Cusa's contributions to the Council of Ferrara/Florence, see Werner Krämer, "Der Beitrag des Nikolaus von Kues zum Unionskonzil mit der Ostkirche," MFCG 9 (1971): 34–52.

23. See his *De gestis concilii Basiliensis commentariorum libri II*, ed. and tr. Denys Hay and W. K. Smith (Oxford, 1967), pp. 14–15.

24. On Cusa's ordination as priest and the benefices and ecclesiastical offices he held, see E. Meuthen, "Die Pfründen des Cusanus" MFCG 2 (1962): 15–66.

25. Note Cusa's autobiographical description (October 21, 1449) in *Acta Cusana* I.2.849.602–603.

26. (h II.12–13).

27. Cusa apparently had access to part of Eckhart's work before 1440. On the early influence of Eckhart and Cusa's citations from him, see Herbert Wackerzapp, *Der Einfluss Meister Eckharts auf die ertsen philosophischen Schriften*

*des Nikolaus von Kues* BGPThM 39, and the foreword to Eckhart, *Super oratione dominica,* ed. Raymund Klibansky, LW, I.ixf. Cusa's *Apologia* (1449) (h II.24–26) defends Eckhart against charges of heresy, and several sermons after 1453 may reflect Eckhart's continued importance for the development of Cusa's thought: *Vier Predigten im Geiste Eckharts,* ed. Josef Koch (*Cusanus-Texte*), HSB 1936–1937, no. 2 (Heidelberg, 1937). See also the studies of Cusa's "reading" of Eckhart in Rudolf Haubst, "Nikolaus von Kues als Interpret und Verteidiger Meister Eckharts," in *Freiheit und Gelassenheit: Meister Eckhart Heute,* ed. Udo Kern (Munich, 1980), pp. 75–96; and Donald F. Duclow's "Nicholas of Cusa in the Margins of Meister Eckhart: Codex Cusanus 21" in *Nicholas of Cusa in Search of God and Wisdom,* ed. Christianson and Izbicki, pp. 57–69.

28. Both Augustine (Letter no. 130) and Bonaventure (*Breviloquium* I.vi.7) refer to *docta ignorantia.*

29. (h I). On Cusa's thought before the completion of his *De docta ignorantia,* see H. G. Senger, *Die Philosophie des Nicolaus von Kues vor dem Jahre 1440. Untersuchungen zur Entwicklung einer Philosophie in der Frühzeit des Nikolaus (1430–1440),* BGPThM NF 3.

30. (h III).

31. Erich Meuthen, ed., "Der *Dialogus concludens Amedistarum errorem ex gestis et doctrina concilii Basiliensis,*" MFCG 8 (1970): 11–114.

32. The letter appears as an appendix to Gerhard Kallen, ed., *De auctoritate presidendi in concilio generali, Cusanus-Texte, II. Traktate. 1* (HSB, Jg. 1935/1936, 3. Abh.; Heidelberg, 1935), pp. 106–112. Also see his Letter of 1441 to a Carthusian monastery in *Acta Cusana* I.2.468.304–320.

33. All are edited in *Opuscula* I (h IV).

34. *Opuscula* I (h IV).

35. (h II).

36. The two modern printed editions of Wenck's text are found in Edmond Vansteenberghe, ed., *Le "De Ignota Litteratura" de Jean Wenck de Herrenberg contre Nicolas de Cusa* (Münster, 1912); and Jasper Hopkins's superior edition, *Nicholas of Cusa's Debate with John Wenck* (Minneapolis, 1981).

37. The mathematical works will appear in the Heidelberg edition as *Scripta mathematica* (h XV). See the edition in (p II).

38. On Cusa's episcopacy in Brixen and the conflicts with Sigismund, see Wilhelm Baum, *Nikolaus Cusanus in Tirol: Das Wirken des Philosophen und Reformators als Fürstbischof von Brixen* (Bozen, 1983); and Pardon E. Tillinghast, "Nicholas of Cusa vs. Sigismund of Habsburg: An Attempt at Post-Conciliar Church Reform," *Church History* 36 (1967): 371–390. See also Hans Hurten (ed.), *Akten zur Reform des Bistums Brixen, Cusanus-Texte V. Brixener Dokumente.* Erste Sammlung (HSB, Jg. 1960, 2. Abh.).

39. (h V²).

40. For the itinerary see J. Koch, *Nikolaus von Cues und seine Umwelt* (Heidelberg, 1948), 111–152.

# NOTES TO INTRODUCTION

41. On Cusa's reform efforts during his legation journey, see E. Meuthen, "Die deutschen Legationsreise des Nikolaus von Kues 1451/1452," *Lebenslehren und Weltentwürfe im Übergang vom Mittelalter zur Neuzeit: Politik-Bildung-Naturkunde-Theologie*, ed. Hartmut Boockmann et al., rev. Ludger Grenzmann (Göttingen, 1989), pp. 421–499; and Donald Sullivan, "Nicholas of Cusa as Reformer: The Papal Legation to the Germanies, 1451–1452," *Mediaeval Studies* 36 (1974): 382–428.

42. See Hermann Hallauer, "Eine Visitation des Nikolaus von Kues im Benediktinerinnenkloster Sonnenberg," MFCG 4 (1964): 104–119; and Morimichi Watanabe, "Nicholas of Cusa and the Tyrolese Monasteries: Reform and Resistance," *History of Political Thought* 7 (1986): 53–72.

43. (h VII$^2$).

44. He also later wrote *De beryllo* for them and expressed the desire to retreat from his public activities and to join them there. See Letter no. 9, *Autour de la "Docte ignorance,"* ed. E. Vansteenberghe BGPThM 14 (Münster, 1915), p. 122.

45. (h VI) in preparation. See the edition in Jasper Hopkins, ed. and tr., *Nicholas of Cusa's Dialectical Mysticism: Text, Translation, and Interpretative Study of De visione Dei* (Minneapolis, 1985).

46. *Opuscula* II (h X,2a.) in preparation. See the edition in (p II) as *Complementum theologicum*.

47. See Wilhelm Baum, *Nikolaus Cusanus in Tirol* (Bozen, 1983), pp. 355–374.

48. Gregory had vigorously attacked Cusa in an "invective," which charged that Cusa had vengefully turned against the council of Basel because it had denied his case in the lawsuit involving the archbishopric of Trier. His attack is reproduced in N. Goldast, *Monarchiae S. Romani imperii . . .* (3 vols.; Frankfurt, 1668), vol. II, col. 1626–1631.

49. (h XI/1$^2$).

50. *Opuscula* II (h IV) in preparation. A recent edition with German translation appears in *Nikolaus von Kues. Philosophisch-theologische Schriften* III, ed. Leo Gabriel and tr. Dietlind and Wilhelm Dupré (Vienna, 1967), pp. 357–417.

51. *Opuscula* II (h X/2b.).

52. The proposal is found in Stephan Ehses, "Der Reformentwurf des Kardinals Nikolaus Cusanus," *Historiches Jahrbuch 32* (1911): 274–297. See the English translation and introduction by Morimichi Watanabe and Thomas M. Izbicki, "Nicholas of Cusa, *A General Reform of the Church*," in *Nicholas of Cusa on Christ and the Church*, ed. Christianson and Izbicki, pp. 175–202.

53. (h XI/2).

54. (h VIII).

55. See Morimichi Watanabe, "Nicholas of Cusa and the Reform of the Roman Curia," in *Humanity and Divinity in Renaissance and Reformation: Essays*

*in Honor of Charles Trinkaus,* ed. John W. O'Malley, Thomas M. Izbicki, and Gerald Christianson (Leiden, 1993), pp. 185–203.

56. *The Commentaries of Pius II,* tr. Florence A. Gragg (bks. 6–9, *Smith College Studies in History,* vol. 35, Northhampton, Mass., 1951), p. 500.

57. For Cusa's special interests and activities during the last years of his life from 1459 to 1464, see Erich Meuthen, *Die letzten Jahre des Nikolaus von Kues: Biographische Untersuchungen nach neuen Quellen* (Cologne and Opladen, 1958).

58. (h XIII).

59. (h XII).

60. (h IX) in preparation. See the (p I) edition with translation in *Nicholas de Cusa. De ludo globi. The Game of the Spheres,* tr. Pauline Moffit Watts (New York, 1986).

61. (h XI/3).

62. (p II).

63. (h XII).

64. See "Vierzehn christologische Quaestionen (Cod. Cus. 40, 144$^r$–146$^v$)" in Rudolf Haubst, *Die Christologie des Nikolaus von Kues* (Freiburg, 1956), pp. 315–319.

65. The most thorough catalogue, though needing correction, is J. Marx, *Verzeichnis der Handschriften-Sammlung des Hospitals zu Cues bei Bernkastel a. Mosel* (Trier, 1905). For a list of the books still belonging to Cusa at the time of his death, see Giovanni Mantese, "Ein notarielles Inventar von Büchern und Wertgegenständen aus dem Nachlass des Nikolaus von Kues," MFCG 2 (1962): 85–116. His will is listed in Marx, *Geschichte,* pp. 248–253.

66. See the review series in MFCG 3 (1963): 16–108; 4 (1964): 323–335; 5 (1965): 137–161; 7 (1969): 129–145 and 146–157; 8 (1970): 199–237; 10 (1973): 58–103; 12 (1977): 15–71; 14 (1980): 182–197; 15 (1982): 43–56; and 17 (1986): 21–56.

67. The Heidelberg edition (h XVIff.) of Cusa's sermons is still in preparation.

68. See the theological descriptions of Cusa's sermons in Rudolf Haubst's careful studies: *Die Christologie des Nikolaus von Kues* (Freiburg, 1956), and *Das Bild des Einen und Dreieinen Gottes in der Welt nach Nikolaus von Kues* (Trier, 1952); and in Haubst's collected articles and papers in *Streifzüge in die cusanische Theologie.* Cf. also the introductions to the *sermones* in the *Cusanus-Texte I. Predigten,* vols. I–VI (Heidelberg, 1929ff.) and John W. O'Malley, *Praise and Blame in Renaissance Rome. Rhetoric, Doctrine, and Reform in the Sacred Orators of the Papal Court, c. 1450–1521* (Durham, N.C., 1979), pp. 94–101 and 142–144.

69. Interesting treatments of Cusa's anthropology and the "newness" of his disjunctive theology can be found in F. Edward Cranz, "Cusanus, Luther, and the Mystical Tradition," in *The Pursuit of Holiness,* ed. Charles Trinkaus and Heiko A. Oberman (Leiden, 1974), pp. 93–102, and "1100 A.D.: A Crisis for

Us?," *De Litteris. Occasional Papers in the Humanities* (New London, 1978); and Pauline Moffitt Watts, *Nicolaus Cusanus. A Fifteenth Century Vision of Man* (Leiden, 1982).

70. They are the editions published by: Martin Flach (Strasbourg, 1488); Benedictus Dolcibelli (Corte Maggiore, 1502), Rolando Pallavicini, ed.; Jodocus Badius Ascensius (Paris, 1514), Jacques LeFèvre d'Étaples, ed.; and Henricus Petri (Basel, 1565).

71. *Die Präsenz des Vergessenen. Zur Rezeption der Philosophie des Nicolaus Cusanus vom 15. bis zum 18. Jahrhundert* (Buchreihe der Cusanus-Gesellschaft, X) (Münster, 1989).

72. "The Origins of Modern Cusanus Research in Germany and the Foundation of the Heidelberg *Opera omnia*," in *Nicholas of Cusa in Search of God and Wisdom*, ed. Christianson and Izbicki, pp. 17–42.

73. John E. Murdoch, "Infinity and Continuity," in *The Cambridge History of Later Medieval Philosophy* (Cambridge, 1982), p. 570, n. 17.

74. Charles H. Lohr, "Metaphysics," in *The Cambridge History of Renaissance Philosophy* (Cambridge, 1988), pp. 548 and 550.

75. Current bibliographies of Cusa research can be found in various issues of the *Mitteilungen und Forschungsbeiträge der Cusanus-Gesellschaft* and in Thomas M. Izbicki, "Nicholas of Cusa: The Literature in English through 1988," in *Nicholas of Cusa in Search of God and Wisdom*, ed. Christianson and Izbicki, pp. 259–281. The latter and a companion volume, *Nicholas of Cusa on Christ and the Church*, also sponsored by the American Cusanus Society and edited by Christianson and Izbicki, and an entire issue of the *American Catholic Quarterly* (64, no. 1 [Winter 1990]), edited by Louis Dupré, devoted to Cusa, provide a useful introduction to his thought as well as a glimpse of the continued lively interest among American scholars.

76. The term used is *media tempestas*. See the text in the appendix to Martin Honecker, *Nikolaus von Cues und die griechische Sprache, Cusanus-Studien. II.* (HSB, Jg., 1937-1938, 2. Abh.; Heidelberg, 1938), p. 71 and n. 203.

77. *Dialogue about the Hidden God. Nicholas of Cusa. A Translation by Thomas Merton* (New York, 1989). This limited edition, published by Dim Gray Bar Press, is taken from Merton's translation as it appeared in the summer 1966 issue of *The Lugano Review*.

78. "On a Theme from Nicholas of Cusa (*De Docta Ignorantia*, III.ix.)," in *Poems*, ed. Walter Hooper (New York, 1964), p. 70.

79. *The Dawn of the Reformation* (Edinburg, 1986), p. 29.

80. Lohr, "Metaphysics," in *The Cambridge History of Renaissance Philosophy*, pp. 556–557.

81. *Jesus-God and Man*, tr. Lewis L. Wilkins and Duane A. Priebe (Philadelphia, 1968), pp. 203 and 346, fn. 44.

82. *On Being a Christian*, tr. Edward Quinn (New York, 1978), p. 128.

83. *Truth and Method*, 2nd rev. ed., tr. Joel Weinsheimer and Donald G.

Marshall (New York, 1989), pp. 434–435; "Nikolaus von Kues in modernen Denken," in *Nicolò Cusanus agli inizi del mondo moderno* (Florence, 1970), p. 48; and "Nicolaus von Cues in der Geschichte des Erkenntnisproblems," MFCG 11 (1975): 275–280.

84. *Between Man and Man*, tr. Ronald Gregor Smith (Boston, 1955), p. 131.

85. *Systematic Theology*, vol. III (Chicago, 1963), p. 13.

86. *Systematic Theology*, vol. I (Chicago, 1951), p. 277.

87. *The Individual and the Cosmos in Renaissance Philosophy*, tr. Mario Domandi (Philadelphia, 1972), p. 10.

88. *Anselm and Nicholas of Cusa* from *The Great Philosophers*, vol. II, ed. Hannah Arendt and tr. Ralph Manheim (New York, 1966), p. 181.

89. That is, the Socratic and perennial "amateur," the enlightened fool, as the protagonist in Cusa's dialogues on the *Idiota*, who professes his own ignorance as his greatest learning and knows what he knows less by the precepts and methods of the academy than by direct experience.

90. *De visione Dei* 7.25.

91. Marjorie O'Rourke Boyle, "Cusanus at Sea: The Topicality of Illuminative Discourse," *Journal of Religion* 71 (Nov.–Apr. 1991): 180–201, argues that Cusa's reference may be more a metaphorical allusion than a historical account.

92. Jas 1:17.

93. "Epistola," DDI III.263 (h I, 163).

94. "Epistola," DDI III.264 (h I, 163).

95. *Apologia doctae ignorantiae* (h II.6, 17, 28 and 31).

96. See H. Lawrence Bond, "Nicolaus Cusanus from Constantinople to 'Learned Ignorance.' The Historical Matrix for the Formation of the *De docta ignorantia*," in *Nicholas of Cusa on Christ and the Church*, ed. Christianson and Izbicki, pp. 135–163.

97. Prol., DDI I.1 (h I, 1–2).

98. "Verbum caro factum est" [December 25, 1438] Sermo XIX (h XVI/3, 291–300); "Nomen eius Jesus" [January 1, 1439] Sermo XX (h XVI/3, 301–317); and "Intrantes domum" [January 8, 1439] Sermo XXI (h XVI/3, 318–331). See also Peter J. Casarella, *"His Name Is Jesus:* Negative Theology and Christology in Two Writings of Nicholas of Cusa from 1440" in *Nicholas of Cusa on Christ and the Church*, ed. Christianson and Izbicki, pp. 281–308.

99. See Cusa's outline of the work in his explanation to Cesarini: "Epistola," DDI III.264 (h I, 163).

100. Cusa often uses the word *discursus* to designate an activity of reasoning as, in a syllogism, when proceeding from a premise to a conclusion, contrary to an intuitive or immediate apprehension.

101. For the most useful and thorough study of Cusa's Christology as it is developed throughout his entire *opera* see R. Haubst, *Die Christologie des Nikolaus von Kues* (Freiburg, 1956).

102. DDI III.1.185 (h I.120).

103. DDI III.3.199 (h I.126–127).

104. DDI III.6.220 (h I.139).

105. DDI III.12.262 (h I.162).

106. DDI III.12.261 (h I.162).

107. Nor do all unities harmonize opposites. For an extended treatment of unity, see DDI I.7–10.18ff. (h I.14ff.).

108. That is, *substantia* as the nature or essence of something, as opposed to its *accidentia,* the accessory or nonessential qualities of a thing not belonging to its substance or essence.

109. DDI I.24.76 (h I.49).

110. With reference to method and understanding, chapters 2 and 3 of Book One provide an interesting description of the plan of Cusa's treatise and how he intends the reader to grasp its content and language.

111. DDI I.2.8 (h I.8).

112. DDI I.26.86 and 89 (h I.54 and 56).

113. DDI I.19.57 (h I.38–39).

114. All figures, for example, proceed from an infinite figure and only one figure, for there can be only one infinite. This figure behind all figures is the infinite straight line, which is a kind of geometric "infinity itself." All figures are enfolded and coincide in the infinite straight line: the triangle, the circle, the sphere, etc.

115. DDI I.16.43 (h I.30).

116. DDI I.16.44 (h I.31).

117. DDI I.2.8 (h I.8).

118. DDI I.10.27 (h I.20).

119. DDI I.20.61 (h I.41).

120. Cusa's *Apologia* (1449) is written in the form of a recollection of a conversation between a *magister* and his *discipulus.* The work was intended to refute the attack by Johannes Wenck of Heidelberg in *De ignota litteratura.*

121. *Apologia doctae ignorantiae* (h II.21). Cusa on p. 29 lists examples of theological errors to which the misuse of logic can lead. According to Klibansky's accompanying documentation, the prayer is attributed to Ambrose by Ps.-Bede, *Comment. in Boethii De Trinitate* (PL 95.394).

122. *Apologia doctae ignorantiae* (h II.3).

123. *Apologia doctae ignorantiae* (h II.4).

124. *Apologia doctae ignorantiae* (h II.11).

125. *Apologia doctae ignorantiae* (h II.12).

126. *Apologia doctae ignorantiae* (h II.21).

127. *Apologia doctae ignorantiae* (h II.35).

128. *Apologia doctae ignorantiae* (h II.31).

129. *Apologia doctae ignorantiae* (h II.27).

130. *Apologia doctae ignorantiae* (h II.24).

# NOTES TO INTRODUCTION

131. *Apologia doctae ignorantiae* (h II.36). Cusa's "Defense," like *On Learned Ignorance*, was also intended for Cesarini, and it was apparently to him that these words were directed.

132. Letter no. 5, *Autour de la docte ignorance. Une controverse sur la théologie mystique au XVe siécle*, ed. E. Vansteenberghe BGPThM 14 (Münster, 1915): 113–117.

133. The treatise against Gerson and other writings of Aggsbach are contained in the appendix to *Autour*, pp. 189–218. His role in the rather extended debate on learned ignorance and mystical theology is treated in chs. 1 and 4–6. See Jasper Hopkins's interpretation of the controversy in *Nicholas of Cusa's Dialectical Mysticism*, pp. 3–14.

134. *Autour*, p. 114.

135. *Autour*, pp. 114–115. Here *ablatio*, "denial," is a synonym for *negatio* and *positio*, as "positing" is a synonym for *affirmatio*.

136. *Autour*, p. 115.

137. DDI I.26.86 (h I.54).

138. DDI I.26.88 (h I.55–56).

139. On the relationship between experience and understanding and applying coincidence, see *Apologia doctae ignorantiae* (h II.1).

140. The conversion of reason through Christ is explained in DDI III.9.

141. For a more detailed study of the importance of Christology to the Cusan theological method, see H. Lawrence Bond, "Nicholas of Cusa and the Reconstruction of Theology: The Centrality of Christology in the Coincidence of Opposites," in *Contemporary Reflections on the Medieval Christian Tradition*, ed. G. H. Shriver (Durham, N.C., 1974), pp. 81–94; and Ulrich Offermann, *Christus-Wahrheit des Denkens. Eine Untersuchung zur Schrift "De docta ignorantia" des Nikolaus von Kues* (Münster, 1991).

142. "Verbum caro factum est" Sermo XIX (h XVI/3, 291–300).

143. "Verbum caro factum est" Sermo XIX 1–3 and 5 (h XVI/3, 291–292 and 294). Note the documentation of R. Haubst and M. Bodewig on p. 291, 3–21; p. 292, 9–26; and p. 294, 1–58. The quotations may stem from Peter Roger (Clement VI).

144. *De Deo abscondito* 1 (h IV/1.3).

145. *De Deo abscondito* 3 (h IV/1.4).

146. *De Deo abscondito* 6 (h IV/1.6).

147. *De Deo abscondito* 10 (h IV/1.8).

148. Cf. *De quaerendo Deum* I.20 (h IV/1.25).

149. *De Deo abscondito* 14 (h IV/1.9).

150. *De Deo abscondito* 15 (h IV/1.10).

151. *De Deo abscondito* 8 (h IV/1.6–7).

152. *De Deo abscondito* 1 (h IV/1.1).

153. *De Deo abscondito* 7 (h IV/1.6).

154. *De Deo abscondito* 6 (h IV/1.5).

# NOTES TO INTRODUCTION

155. *De quaerendo Deum* 16 (h IV/1.13). See "Dies sanctificatus illuxit nobis" [January 6, 1445, at Mainz] Sermo XLVIII (p II.52ʳ-54ʳ). See E. Hoffmann and R. Klibansky, eds., *Cusanus-Texte I. Predigten 1. "Dies Sanctificatus" vom Jahre 1439.* (HSB, Jg. 1928/1929, 3. Abh.; Heidelberg, 1928/1929).

156. *De quaerendo Deum* 19 (h IV/1.15). Cf. John Scotus Eriugena, *Periphyseon (De divisione naturae)* I.12 in *Scriptores Latini Hiberniae*, ed. I. P. Sheldon-Williams, VII.60, 16–25 (Dublin, 1968).

157. *De quaerendo Deum* 19 f. (h IV/1.15 f.).

158. *De quaerendo Deum* 40 (h IV/1.28).

159. *De quaerendo Deum* 26 (h IV/1.18).

160. *De quaerendo Deum* 38 and 41 (h IV/1.27 and 28–29).

161. *De quaerendo Deum* 36 (h IV/1.26).

162. *De quaerendo Deum* 39 (h IV/1.27).

163. *De quaerendo Deum* 43 (h IV/1.30).

164. *De quaerendo Deum* 49 (h IV/1.34).

165. *De quaerendo Deum* 50 (h IV/1.35).

166. *De quaerendo Deum* 36 (h IV/1.26).

167. *De visione Dei* 6.17–18. All translation of the treatise here is from the version in Cus. Cod. 219, fo. 1ʳ–24ʳ of c. 1460. The references to the text are cited by chapter and then section number according to the divisions of the critical edition prepared by the late Martin Bodewig for the forthcoming vol. VI of the Heidelberg Academy's *Nicolai de Cusa Opera Omnia*. See Rudolf Haubst's foreword to Helmut Pfeiffer's translation, Nikolaus von Kues, *De visione Dei. Das Sehen Gottes* (Trier, 1985), p. 4.

168. This sounds very much like the icon known in the West as the "Holy Visage." In the East it is called the "icon 'made without hands' (ἀχειροποίητος) or 'the icon of the Lord on the cloth' (μανδήλιον)." See Vladmir Lossky, "Icons of Christ," in Leonid Ouspensky and Vladmir Lossky, *The Meaning of Icons*, tr. G. E. H. Palmer and E. Kadloubovsky (Crestwood, NY, 1989), pp. 69–72.

169. For especially insightful although differing interpretations of the theology in the *De visione Dei* see: Werner Beierwaltes "Visio facialis—Sehen ins Angesicht. Zur Coincidenz des endlichen und unendlichen Blicks bei Cusanus," MFCG 18 (1989): 91–124; H. G. Senger, "Mystik als Theorie bei Nikolaus von Kues," in *Gnosis und Mystik in der Geschichte der Philosophie*, ed. Peter Koslowski (Zürich, 1988), pp. 111–134; Clyde Lee Miller, "Nicholas of Cusa's *The Vision of God*," in *An Introduction to the Medieval Mystics of Europe*, ed. Paul Szarmach (Albany, 1984), pp. 293–312; Michel de Certeau, "The Gaze of Nicholas of Cusa," *Diacritics* 17 (1987): 2–38; and Louis Dupré, "The Mystical Theology of Nicholas of Cusa's *De visione dei*," in *Nicholas of Cusa on Christ and the Church*, ed. Christianson and Izbicki, pp. 205–220.

170. *De visione Dei* 22.99.

171. *De visione Dei* 10.40.

172. *De visione Dei* 6.18–19.

# NOTES TO INTRODUCTION

173. *De visione Dei* 19 and *passim*.

174. *De visione Dei* 3.8.

175. See Peter Casarella, "Neues zu den Quellen der Cusanischen Mauer-Symbolik," MFCG 19 (1991): 273–286.

176. *De visione Dei* 10.41.

177. *De visione Dei* 13.57.

178. *De visione Dei* 23.101.

179. *De visione Dei* 20.

180. *De visione Dei* 13.55.

181. *De visione Dei* 12.47.

182. *De visione Dei* 8.28.

183. *De visione Dei* pref. 3.

184. *De visione Dei* 6.18.

185. *De visione Dei* 15.63.

186. *De visione Dei* 15.63 and 66, and 20.89

187. *De visione Dei* 15.66.

188. *De visione Dei* 11.46.

189. *De visione Dei* 16.70 and also DDI III.12.259 (h I.160–161). Cf. Eckhart, *Sermones et lectiones super Ecclesiastici* 42–43 (LW II 271–272). This text is translated in *Meister Eckhart. Teacher and Preacher* (Classics of Western Spirituality) (New York, 1986), pp. 174–175.

190. *De visione Dei* 11.45.

191. *De visione Dei* 6.17–19 and 22.94.

192. *De visione Dei* 11.43–45.

193. *De visione Dei* ¶1 and 17.76 and 78.

194. *De visione Dei* 23.101.

195. *De visione Dei* 16.68–69.

196. The Latin title of the work is *De apice theoriae*, that is, regarding the *apex theoriae*, the apex or highest point of "theory," which from the Latin rendering of the Greek *theorein* means contemplation or sight. On the history of the phrase *apex theoriae* and its concept, see the introductory remarks of H. G. Senger to *Nicolai de Cusa. De apice theoriae. Die höchste Stufe der Betrachtung,* pp. xvi-xxiii.

197. That is, San Pietro in Vincoli in Rome.

198. *De apice theoriae* ¶1 (h XII.117).

199. *De apice theoriae* ¶2 (h XII.117).

200. *De apice theoriae* ¶2 (h XII.118).

201. *De apice theoriae* ¶3 (h XII.119).

202. Epilogus ¶45 and 47.

203. The Latin term *quidditas,* quiddity or whatness, means "what" a thing is, i.e., its essence. In the dialogue Cusa speaks of it also as *hypostasis* and *substantia.*

204. *De apice theoriae* ¶4 (h XII.119).

205. *De apice theoriae* ¶4 (h XII.120).

206. On the significance and application of this notion in Cusa's thought, see Jasper Hopkins's introduction to his translation of *De Possest* in *A Concise Introduction to the Philosophy* of *Nicholas of Cusa*, 2nd ed. (Minneapolis, 1980), pp. 18–19; Alfons Brüntrup, *Können und Sein. Der Zusammenhang der Spätschriften des Niklaus von Kues* (*Epimeleia. Beiträge zur Philosophie*, 23.) (München, 1973); Klaus Jacobi, *Die Methode der Cusanischen Philosophie* (Freiburg-München, 1969); Siegfried Dangelmayr, *Gotteserkenntnis und Gottesbegriff in den philosphischen Schriften des Nikoluas von Kues* (Meisenheim am Glan, 1969); and Peter Casarella, "Power of the Possible," *American Catholic Philosophical Quarterly* 64 (1990): 7–34.

207. *De apice theoriae* ¶5 (h XII.120).

208. *De apice theoriae* ¶5 (h XII.120).

209. *De apice theoriae* ¶6 (h XII.120).

210. *De apice theoriae* ¶14 & 15 (h XII.127–129).

211. *De apice theoriae* ¶16 (h XII.130).

212. *De apice theoriae* ¶2 (h XII.118).

213. *De apice theoriae* ¶5 (h XII.120).

214. *De apice theoriae* ¶9 (h XII.123).

215. *De apice theoriae* ¶7 (h XII.122).

216. *De apice theoriae* ¶8 (h XII.122).

217. *De apice theoriae* ¶8 (h XII.122).

218. *De apice theoriae* ¶9 (h XII.123).

219. *De apice theoriae* ¶9 (h XII.123).

220. *De apice theoriae* ¶9 (h XII.123).

221. See Cusa's correspondence with the monastery at Tegernsee, especially Letter 5 of September 22, 1452, and Letter 6 of September 15, 1453, in the appendix to E. Vansteenberghe, *Autour de la Docte Ignorance* BGPThM 14 (Münster, 1915): 111ff.

222. *De apice theoriae* ¶10–11 (h XII.124–125).

223. *De apice theoriae* ¶7, 9, 13, and 16.

224. *De apice theoriae* ¶17–28.

225. *De apice theoriae* ¶20 (h XII.131–132).

226. *De apice theoriae* ¶21 (h XII.132).

227. *De apice theoriae* ¶22 (h XII.132).

228. *De apice theoriae* ¶10 and 24 (h XII.124 and 133).

229. *De apice theoriae* ¶10 (h XII.124).

230. *De apice theoriae* ¶24 (h XII.133).

231. *De apice theoriae* ¶13 (h XII.126).

232. *De apice theoriae* ¶14 (h XII.126).

233. *De apice theoriae* ¶14 (h XII.126–127).

234. *De apice theoriae* ¶14-15 (h XII.128–129).

235. *De apice theoriae* ¶17 (h XII.130).

236. *De apice theoriae* ¶27 (h XII.136).
237. *De apice theoriae* ¶14 (h XII.127).
238. *De apice theoriae* ¶20 (h XII.132).
239. *De apice theoriae* ¶22 (h XII.132).
240. *De apice theoriae* ¶11 (h XII.125).
241. *De apice theoriae* ¶11 (h XII.125).
242. *De apice theoriae* ¶11 (h XII.125).
243. *De apice theoriae* ¶25 (h XII.134–135).
244. *De apice theoriae* ¶26 (h XII.135).
245. *De apice theoriae* ¶28 (h XII.136).
246. *De apice theoriae* ¶28 (h XII.136).
247. *The Elements of Theology,* Proposition 40ff. See F. Edward Cranz's discussion of Cusa's deviation from Proclus in "The Late Works of Nicholas of Cusa," in *Nicholas of Cusa in Search of God and Wisdom,* ed. Christianson and Izbicki, p. 147.
248. *Itinerarium mentis in deum* c. 6.
249. *Expositio Sancti Evangelii Secundum Ioannem* ¶342 (LW III.291) and *Expositio Libri Exodi* ¶16 (LW II.21–22). See Bernard McGinn's discussion of these and related passages in "Introduction. 2.Theological Summary," *Meister Eckhart. The Essential Sermons, Commentaries, Treatises and Defense* (New York, 1981), pp. 37ff.
250. This section is indebted to Cranz's insights into the unique place of Cusa's *De apice theoriae* among his other works. See Cranz, "The Late Works of Nicholas of Cusa," pp. 141–160.
251. *De apice theoriae* ¶16 (h XII.130).
252. *De apice theoriae* ¶16 (h XII.130).

# On Learned Ignorance (De docta ignorantia *1440*)[1]

# BOOK ONE

*Prologue:*
*Nicholas of Cusa to His Venerable Master and Very Reverend Father,*
*Beloved of God, Lord Julian,[2] Very Worthy Cardinal of the Holy*
*Apostolic See*

Your very great and, indeed, well proved intelligence will justifiably wonder why I am choosing you as judge in the rash attempt to set forth these barbarous ineptitudes of mine. It is not as if some leisure were remaining to you, occupied as you are with public matters of greatest importance in your cardinal's duties at the Apostolic See. Nor could the novel title of this probably very unsuitable work of mine attract you, with your extraordinary knowledge of all the Latin writers who have thus far become famous, and now also of the Greek authors. Indeed, you have known me for a long time, and you are already well acquainted with the sort of ability I may possess. But I hope that your wonder, not at the thought that something previously unknown is to be found here, but rather at the boldness with which I have been led to treat learned ignorance,[3] will entice your inquisitive mind to examine this work.

The natural sciences tell us that an unpleasant sensation in the stomach's opening precedes appetite so that stimulated in this way nature, which strives to preserve itself, will be replenished.[4] So I think it consistent that wondering, the cause of philosophy,[5] precedes the desire to know in order that the intellect, whose understanding is its being, will be perfected by the pursuit of truth. The unusual, even if monstrous, typically provokes our interest. Therefore, incomparable Teacher, would that out of your kindness you decide that something of worth may lie hidden here and accept from a German a method of reasoning in theological matters which the enormous labor involved has made most pleasing to me.

**2.**

*Chapter One*
*How Knowing Is Not Knowing*

We see that by a divine gift there is within all things a certain natural desire to exist in the best manner in which the condition of each thing's nature permits. Toward this end all things work and possess the appropriate instruments. They also have an inborn judgment agreeing with the purpose of their knowledge so that their desire may not be frustrated but may be able to attain rest in that object which the inclination of each thing's own nature desires. If at some time this is not the case, it is necessarily the result of an accident, as when sickness deceives taste or opinion misleads reason.

Therefore, we say that the sound and free intellect knows as true that which, from an innate searching, it insatiably longs to attain and apprehends in a loving embrace. For we are convinced that no sound mind can reject what is most true. But all who investigate judge the uncertain proportionally by comparing it to what is presupposed as certain. Therefore, every inquiry is comparative and uses the method of proportion. As long as the objects of inquiry can be compared by a close proportional reaching back to what is presupposed as certain, our judgment understands easily, but when we need many intermediaries, then we are faced with difficulty and hard work. This is acknowledged in mathematics, where earlier propositions are more easily led back to the first and most evident principles, but subsequent propositions give more difficulty since they are led back to the first principles only by means of the earlier propositions.

3.     Every inquiry, therefore, consists in a comparative proportion that is either easy or difficult. Because the infinite escapes all proportion, the infinite as infinite is unknown.[6] But since proportion expresses agreement in some one point and also expresses otherness, it cannot be understood apart from number. Number, therefore, includes all that is capable of proportion. Hence, number, which effects proportion, does not consist in quantity only but also in all those things which in any way can agree or differ substantially or accidentally.[7] Perhaps this is why Pythagoras insisted that all things are constituted and understood through the power of numbers.[8]

4.     However, the precise combinations in corporeal things and the congruent application of known to unknown so far exceed human reason that Socrates believed he knew nothing except that he did not know.[9] The very wise Solomon declared that all things are difficult and cannot be explained in words,[10] and another thinker of divine spirit says that wisdom and the seat of understanding lie hidden "from the eyes of all the living."[11] Likewise, the very profound Aristotle, in the First Philosophy, asserts that with things most evident by nature we encounter the same difficulty as a night owl trying to look at the

sun.[12] If all this is true, since the desire in us for knowledge is not in vain, surely then it is our desire to know that we do not know. If we can attain this completely, we will attain learned ignorance. For nothing more perfect comes to a person, even the most zealous in learning, than to be found most learned in the ignorance that is uniquely one's own. One will be the more learned, the more one knows that one is ignorant. It is toward this end that I have undertaken the task of writing a few words on learned ignorance.

**5.**

*Chapter Two*
*A Preliminary Explanation of What Is to Follow*

Before treating the maximum learning of ignorance, it is necessary that I discuss the nature of maximumness[13] itself. I call "maximum" that beyond which there can be nothing greater.[14] Fullness, of course, is fitting and proper to what is one. Thus, unity, which is also being, coincides with maximumness, and if such unity is completely free from all relation and contraction, it is clear that because it is absolute maximumness, nothing is opposed to it. Accordingly, the maximum is the absolute one that is all things, and all things are in this maximum, for it is the maximum. And because the maximum has no opposite, the minimum coincides with it as well, and therefore the maximum is also in all things. Because it is absolute, it is actually all possible being and contracts nothing from things, for all things come from it. This maximum, which also the indubitable faith of all nations believes to be God, I will, in the First Book, endeavor to investigate incomprehensibly above human reason by the guidance of the one "who alone dwells in inapproachable light."[15]

**6.**

In the second place, just as absolute maximumness is absolute being, by which all things are what they are, so also from absolute being there is a universal unity of being that is called "the maximum from the absolute." This universal unity exists in a contracted way as universe, and its unity is contracted in plurality, without which it cannot exist.[16] Even though this maximum embraces all things in its universal unity so that all that are from the absolute maximum are in this maximum, and it is in all things, nevertheless, it does not exist outside the plurality in which it is found, because it does not exist apart from contraction, from which it cannot be freed. About this maximum, that is, the universe, I will make some additional remarks in the Second Book.

**7.**     Finally, a maximum of a third kind will be disclosed. For since the universe exists in plurality only in a contracted way, we will seek in the many things themselves the one maximum in which the universe actually exists most greatly and most perfectly as in its end. This maximum is united with the absolute maximum, which is the universal goal, for it is the most perfect end beyond all our capacity. About this maximum, which is both contracted and also absolute,[17] and which we name Jesus, forever blessed, I will add several things, as Jesus himself will inspire me.

**8.**     But whoever wishes to attain the meaning must elevate one's intellect above the force of words and not insist on the properties of words that cannot be suitably adapted to such great intellectual mysteries. It is also necessary to use examples as guides in a transcendent way and to abandon sensible things so that the reader may readily ascend to simple intellectuality. In order to pursue this method, I have attempted, by avoiding all harshness of style, to explain to ordinary minds as clearly as I could, and at the start I show plainly that the basis of learned ignorance is the fact that the precision of truth cannot be grasped.

**9.**
*Chapter Three*
*That the Precise Truth Is Incomprehensible*

Because it is evident that there is no proportion between the infinite and the finite,[18] it is very clear that where we encounter a greater and a lesser, we do not reach the simply maximum.[19] For things that are greater and lesser are finite, but such a maximum has to be infinite. Obviously, therefore, if anything is given that is not the simply maximum, something greater can be given, and we find equality occurring in degrees so that one thing is more equal to another than to a third, according to agreement and difference in gender, species, place, influence, and time among things that are similar.[20] Clearly, therefore, two or more objects cannot be so similar and equal that they could not still be more similar ad infinitum. Consequently, however equal the measure and the thing measured may be, they will always remain different.

**10.**     A finite intellect, therefore, cannot precisely attain the truth of things by means of a likeness. For truth is neither more nor less but indivisible. Nothing not itself true is incapable of precisely measuring what is true, just as a non-circle cannot measure a circle, for the being of a circle is indivisible. So the intellect, which is not truth, never comprehends truth so precisely but that it could always be comprehended with infinitely more precision. The intellect is related to truth as a polygon to a circle. The inscribed polygon grows more like a circle the more angles it has. Yet even though the multiplication of its angles were infinite, nothing will make the polygon equal the circle unless the polygon is resolved into identity with the circle.

Clearly, therefore, we know of the truth only that we know that it cannot be comprehended precisely as it is. Truth is like the most absolute necessity, which can be neither more nor less than it is, while our intellect is like possibility. Therefore, the quiddity of things, which is the truth of beings, is unattainable in its purity, and although it is pursued by all philosophers, none has found it as it is.[21] The more profoundly learned we are in this ignorance, the more closely we draw near truth itself.

**11.**

*Chapter Four*
*The Absolute Maximum with Which the Minimum Coincides Is*
*Incomprehensibly Understood*

The simply and absolutely maximum, than which there cannot be anything greater, is greater than we can comprehend, for it is infinite truth; therefore, we can attain it only incomprehensibly. Because it is not of the nature of those things that admit a greater and a lesser, it is above all that we can conceive. Moreover, all that can be apprehended by the senses, reason, or intellect are so different in themselves and from each other that there is no precise equality among them. Therefore, maximum equality, which is neither other than nor different from anything, surpasses all understanding. Since the absolutely maximum is all that can be,[22] it is completely actual. And just as there cannot be a greater, so for the same reason there cannot be a lesser, since it is all that can be. But the minimum is that than which there cannot be a lesser. Because the maximum is also of this sort, it is obvious that the minimum coincides with the maximum.

This becomes clearer if you contract maximum and minimum to quantity. Maximum quantity is maximally large, while minimum quantity is maximally small. Therefore, if you free maximum and minimum from quantity by intellectually removing "large" and "small," you will clearly see that maximum and minimum coincide. For both maximum and minimum are superlatives. Therefore, abso-

91

lute quantity is not maximum quantity more than it is minimum quantity, because in it the minimum is the maximum in a coincident way.

12.     Oppositions, therefore, apply only to those things that admit a greater and a lesser, and they apply in different ways, but never to the absolutely maximum, for it is above all opposition. Therefore, because the absolutely maximum is absolutely and actually all that can be, and it is without opposition to such an extent that the minimum coincides with the maximum, it is above all affirmation and all negation. It both is and is not all that is conceived to be, and it both is and is not all that is conceived not to be.[23] But it is a "this" in such a way that it is all things, and it is all things in such a way that it is none of them, and it is a "this" maximally in such a way that it is also a "this" minimally. For the assertion that "God, who is absolute maximumness itself, is light" is no different than the assertion that "God is maximally light in such a way that God is minimally light." Absolute maximumness could not be actually all possible things, unless it were infinite and the limit of all things and unable to be limited by any of them, as, by God's mercy, we shall explain in the following pages.

But the absolutely maximum transcends all our understanding, which is unable by the path of reason to combine contradictories in their source, for we proceed by means of the things made evident to us by nature, and reason, falling far short of this infinite power, cannot join together contradictories, which are infinitely distant. Therefore, we see incomprehensibly, above every act of reasoning, that the absolute maximumness, to which nothing is opposed and with which the minimum coincides, is infinite. However, "maximum" and "minimum," as they are employed in this book, are transcendent terms of absolute signification, so that, above all contraction to quantity of mass or of power, they, in their absolute simplicity, embrace all things.

13.     

*Chapter Five*
*The Maximum Is One*

It is very clearly established from what has been said that the absolutely maximum is both incomprehensibly understandable and ineffably nameable; we shall offer an even clearer explanation of this later on.[24]

Nothing may be named that is not subject to more or less, for by reason's motion names are assigned to things that, in a certain proportion, admit a greater or a lesser. And since all things exist in the best way that they can, there can be no plurality of beings apart from number. For if number is withdrawn, distinction, order, proportion, and harmony cease, and so does the very plurality of beings. If number itself were infinite—since then it would be actually maximum and with it the minimum would coincide—all these would also cease. For being infinite number and being minimally number are the same thing. If, therefore, by ascending the scale of numbers one actually reaches a maximum number, nevertheless, because number is finite, one does not arrive at a maximum number beyond which there cannot be a greater number, for this number would be infinite. Clearly, therefore, the ascending numerical scale is actually finite, and this maximum number would stand potentially in relation to another, still higher number.

If this were equally true of number in descent, so that, whatever small number might be given, a smaller would always be possible by subtraction, just as in ascent a higher number is always possible by addition, the result would be the same as before with the assumption of infinite number. For then there would be no distinction between things; nor would order or plurality or greater and lesser be found in numbers; indeed, number itself would not exist. Consequently, it is necessary, with number, to arrive at a minimum beyond which there cannot be anything less, and this is unity. And because nothing can be less than unity, unity will be the simply minimum, which, as we just showed, coincides with the maximum.

**14.**     Unity, however, cannot be number, for number, which admits a greater, can in no way be either simply minimum or simply maximum; but because unity is minimum, it is the beginning of all number, and because it is maximum, it is the end of all number. Therefore, absolute unity, which has no opposite, is absolute maximumness itself, which is the blessed God. This unity, because it is maximum, cannot be multiplied for it is all that can be. It cannot, therefore, become number.

Number, as you see, has led us to the understanding that "absolute unity" more properly applies to the unnameable God and that God is so one that God is actually all that is possible. Consequently, absolute unity admits neither a greater nor a lesser; nor can it be multiplied. Thus, deity is infinite unity. Whoever has said: "Hear, O Israel," your God "is one"[25] and "Your Master" and "your Father in heaven is one"[26] could not have spoken more truly. And whoever

93

might say that there are many gods would deny most falsely that God and all the universe existed, as we shall demonstrate later. Number, which is a being of reason fashioned by our power of comparative discrimination, necessarily presupposes unity as such a beginning of number that without this beginning number could not exist. In the same way the pluralities of things, which descend from infinite unity, are so related to this unity that without it they cannot exist. For how could they exist apart from being? Absolute unity is being, as we shall see later.

15.

*Chapter Six*
*The Maximum Is Absolute Necessity*

Our discussion has shown that except the one simply maximum all else is, in relation to it, finite and limited. Now, that which is finite and limited has a boundary from which it begins and at which it ends. It cannot be said that something finite is greater than another finite thing in such a way that there would be an infinite progression of greater and greater finite things, for with things subject to greater or lesser there cannot be an actual progression into infinity; otherwise the maximum would have the nature of finite things. Therefore, the actually maximum must be the beginning and end of all finite things.

Moreover, if the simply maximum did not exist, nothing could exist. Since every non-maximum is finite, it is also originated; it will necessarily derive from another; otherwise, if it were from itself, it would have existed when it did not. It is impossible, as the rule plainly shows,[27] to proceed to infinity in beginnings and causes. Therefore, there must be a simply maximum without which nothing can exist.

16. Furthermore, if we contract maximum to being and say that nothing is opposed to maximum being, then neither non-being nor minimum being would be its opposite. And because minimum being is maximum being, how, therefore, is it possible to think that the maximum cannot exist? Without being nothing can be thought to exist. But absolute being cannot be other than the absolutely maximum. Nothing, therefore, can be thought to exist apart from the maximum.

In addition, the greatest truth is the absolutely maximum. Therefore, it is most greatly true that either the simply maximum exists or it does not exist; or that it both exists and does not exist; or that neither does it exist nor does it not exist. Nothing more can be stated or thought. No matter which of these you say is most greatly true, I have made my case; for I have the maximum truth, which is the simply maximum.

**17.** Although it is evident from the preceding that "being" or any other name is not the precise name of the maximum, which is above every name,[28] however, it is necessary that being correspond to it maximally, yet in a way unnameable by the name "maximum" and above every nameable being. On these grounds and an infinite number of similar ones, learned ignorance sees most plainly, from the above, that the simply maximum so necessarily exists that it is absolute necessity. But it has been shown that the simply maximum can exist only as one. Therefore, it is most true that the maximum is one.

**18.**
### Chapter Seven
### On the Three and One Eternity

There never was a people who did not worship God and believe that God was the absolutely maximum. We find that Marcus Varro, in his book *Antiquities,* observed that the Sissennii had worshiped unity as the maximum,[29] while Pythagoras, a man of great renown and undisputed authority in his day, affirmed that this unity is threefold.[30] As we investigate the truth of this and elevate our minds higher, we may declare, in accord with our premises, that no one doubts that what precedes all otherness is eternal. Otherness is the same as mutability, but everything that naturally precedes mutability is immutable and is, therefore, eternal. However, otherness consists of one thing plus another. Consequently, otherness, like number, comes after unity. Therefore, unity by nature is prior to otherness, and because unity naturally precedes otherness, it is eternal.

**19.** Furthermore, every inequality is composed of an equal plus something greater. So inequality by nature comes after equality, and this can be convincingly proved by resolution. Every inequality is resolved into an equality; for the equal lies between the greater and the lesser. If, therefore, you remove that which is greater, you will obtain an equal, but if there is a lesser, remove from the other that which is greater, and again you will have an equal. And this process can go on until by removing you come to the simple. So then, it is evident that, by remotion, every inequality is reduced to equality. Equality, therefore, naturally precedes inequality.

But inequality and otherness by nature occur together. For

where there is inequality, there is necessarily otherness, and conversely. Between two things there will at least be otherness; since there are two things, one of the two is a second; and, consequently, there will be inequality. Therefore, otherness and inequality by nature will occur together, especially since the number two is the first otherness and the first inequality. But it has been proved that equality by nature precedes inequality and thus also otherness. Equality, therefore, is eternal.

20.     Moreover, if one of two causes is by nature prior to the other, the effect of the first will be by nature prior to the effect of the second. But unity is either the connection or the cause of the connection, and it is because things are united that we say that they are connected. The number two is either separation or the cause of separation, for two is the first separation. If, therefore, unity is the cause of connection and the number two the cause of separation, then, as unity by nature is prior to duality, so connection by nature is prior to separation. But separation and otherness by nature occur together, and so connection like unity is eternal, for it is prior to otherness.

21.     It has been proved, therefore, that unity is eternal, equality eternal, and connection also eternal. But more than one eternal is not possible;[31] for if there were more than one eternal, then since unity precedes all plurality, something would exist that by nature would be prior to eternity, which is impossible. Further, if there were more than one eternal, one eternal thing would lack the other, and so none of them would be perfect, and thus there would be something eternal that would not be eternal, because it would not be perfect. Since this is impossible, there cannot be more than one eternal. But because unity is eternal, equality eternal, and connection also eternal, therefore, unity, equality, and connection are one. This is the threefold unity that Pythagoras, the first of all the philosophers and the glory of Italy and Greece, taught ought to be worshiped.[32] But let us add, more expressly, further explanation about the generation of equality from unity.

22.

### Chapter Eight
### On Eternal Generation

Let us now show very briefly that equality of unity is begotten from unity but that connection proceeds from unity and from equality of unity. Unity, or ὤντας so to speak, comes from the Greek ὤν, which in Latin is called *ens*, and unity is, as it were, being.[33] In fact, God is the being of things, for God is the form of being and therefore is being. Equality of unity is, so to speak, equality of entity, that is, the equality of being or of existing. Equality of being is that which is in a thing as neither more nor less, as nothing too much and as nothing too little. If it is too much in a thing, the thing is monstrous; if it is there too little, the thing does not exist.

23.     When we consider what generation is, we clearly perceive the generation of equality from unity. For generation is the repetition of unity or the multiplication of the same nature proceeding from a parent to a child, and this generation is found only in transitory things. But the generation of unity from unity is a single repetition of unity, that is, it is unity only once, but if unity is multiplied two or three more times, unity will generate from itself another, that is, two or three or another number. But unity repeated once begets only equality of unity, and this cannot be understood otherwise than that unity begets unity. And this generation is eternal.

24.

*Chapter Nine*
*On Eternal Procession of the Connection*

As the generation of unity from unity is a single repetition of unity, so the procession from both is the unity of the repetition of this unity or, if you prefer, the unity of unity and of the equality of this unity. However, "procession" indicates a sort of extension from one thing to another; for example, when two things are equal, then a certain equality, which in some way joins and connects them, is, so to speak, extended from the one to the other. Therefore, it is correct to say that connection proceeds from unity and from equality of unity, for the connection is not of one of these only, but it proceeds from unity to equality of unity and from equality of unity to unity. Therefore, because the connection is, so to speak, extended from one to the other, it is rightly said to proceed from one to the other.

25.     But we are not saying that the connection is begotten from unity or from equality of unity, for the connection does not arise from unity through either repetition or multiplication. Although the equality of unity is begotten from unity and the connection proceeds from them both, nevertheless, unity, equality of unity, and the connection proceeding from both are one and the same: It is as if we used the words "this" [*hoc*], "it" [*id*], and "the same" [*idem*] to refer to the same

thing. What we name "it" is related to a first thing, but what we call "the same" connects and joins the related object to the first thing. If, therefore, from the pronoun "it" we should form the word "itness" [*iditas*], we could speak of "unity," "itness," and "sameness" [*unitas, iditas, identitas*],[34] which would closely enough apply to the Trinity: "Itness" would bear a relation to "unity," while "sameness" would designate the connection of "itness" and "unity."

26.　　　Our very holy doctors called Unity "Father," Equality "Son," and Connection "Holy Spirit" because of a certain likeness to these transitory things.[35] For in a father and a son there is a common nature, which is one, so that in this nature the son is equal to the father. There is no more or no less humanity in the son than in the father, and between them there is a certain connection. For a natural love joins one with the other because of the likeness of the same nature in them, which descends from the father to the son, and for this reason the father loves the son more than any other who shares humanity with him.

It is from such a likeness, although a very distant one, that Unity was called "Father," Equality "Son," and Connection "Love" or "Holy Spirit," but these are names applied only with reference to creatures, as later we will show more clearly in the appropriate place.[36] And this is, in my judgment, a very revealing investigation, in keeping with the Pythagorean investigation,[37] of the ever to be adored Trinity in unity and Unity in trinity.

27.

*Chapter Ten*
*How an Understanding of Trinity in Unity Transcends All Things*

Let us now examine what Martianus means when he says that philosophy, in desiring to ascend to the knowledge of this Trinity, has rejected circles and spheres.[38]

In previous discussions[39] we have disclosed the singular and most simple maximum, and we have demonstrated that it would not be a figure such as the most perfect corporeal figure, as is the sphere, or the most perfect surface, as is the circle, or the most perfect rectilinear figure, as is the triangle, or the most perfect figure of simple straightness, as is the line. But the maximum is so beyond all these that it is necessary to reject things that, along with their material accessories, are attained through the senses, the imagination, or reason, in order to reach the most simple and most abstract understanding, where all things are one; where the line is a triangle, a circle, and a sphere; where unity is trinity and trinity is unity; where accident is substance; where body is spirit and motion is rest, and so on. Understanding occurs when each thing in the one is understood as the one and the one as all things and, consequently, each thing in the one is understood as all things. You have not properly rejected the sphere, the circle, and the others if you do not understand that maximum unity is necessarily three. For unless maximum unity is understood as three, it can in no way be rightly understood.

28.      To use appropriate examples, we see that unity of understanding is not other than what understands, what is understandable, and the act of understanding. And if, now, you want to pass from what understands to the maximum and to say that the maximum is most greatly what understands, unless you added that the maximum is also most greatly what is understandable and most greatly the act of maximum understanding, you would not rightly conceive of the maximum and most perfect unity. For if unity is the maximum and most perfect understanding, without which these three correlations could be neither understanding nor the most perfect understanding, whoever does not attain to the trinity of this unity does not have a correct concept of unity.

Unity, in fact, is only trinity, for it signifies indivision, distinction, and connection. Indivision as well as distinction and union, that is, connection, are from unity. The maximum unity, therefore, is not other than indivision, distinction, and connection. And because maximum unity is indivision, it is eternity, that is, without beginning, as the eternal is not divided by anything. Because maximum unity is distinction, it is from immutable eternity. And because maximum unity is connection, or union, it proceeds from both indivision and distinction.

29.      Furthermore, when I say that "unity is maximum," I am saying trinity. For when I say "unity" I am speaking of a beginning without a beginning; when I say "maximum," I am speaking of a beginning from a beginning; and when I join and unite them by the verb "is," I am speaking of a procession from both. If, therefore, we have already most clearly established[40] that the one is maximum, because the minimum, the maximum, and their connection are one, so that unity is minimum unity, maximum unity, and their connection, obviously, then, philosophy, which wants to comprehend by a very simple un-

derstanding that the maximum unity is not other than three, must reject all imaginable and rational things.

Yet you may wonder at what we have said: that one who wishes to grasp the maximum by a simple understanding must leap beyond the differences and varieties of things and beyond all mathematical figures, for we have said that in the maximum the line is a surface and a circle and a sphere. And so, to make your understanding keener, I will attempt to direct you more readily and surely to find these statements to be necessary and most true. And if, by interpreting the words transumptively,[41] you will lift yourself from the sign to the truth, they will, not improperly, bring you to a wondrous delight. For on this path you will advance in learned ignorance, so that as far as it is possible to the ardent searcher who is elevated in accord with the powers of human intelligence, you will be able to see the one incomprehensible maximum, the one and three, ever-blessed God.[42]

**30.**

*Chapter Eleven*
*That Mathematics Greatly Helps Us to Apprehend Different*
*Divine Truths*

All our wisest and most divine doctors concur that visible things are truly images of invisible things and that from creatures the Creator can be seen in a recognizable way[43] as if in a mirror or in an enigma.[44] But the fact that spiritual things, unattainable by us in themselves, may be symbolically investigated rests on what we have already stated. For all things in relation to each other stand in a certain proportion that is hidden and incomprehensible to us so that from all things one universe arises and in this one maximum all are this one. Although every image seems to be a likeness of its exemplar, yet, apart from the maximum image, which in unity of nature is that which its exemplar is, there is no image so similar or so equal to its exemplar but that it could be infinitely more similar and more equal. These observations have already been made known from earlier statements.

**31.**          Now, when an inquiry proceeds from an image, there must be no doubt about the image in transumptive proportion to which the unknown is investigated; for the way to the uncertain is possible only by means of what is presupposed and certain. But all sensible things are in a continual instability because of the material possibility abounding in them. However, where such things are considered, we perceive that those things, such as mathematicals, which are more abstract than sensible, are very fixed and very certain to us, although they do not entirely lack material associations, without which no image of them could be formed, and they are not completely subject to fluctuating possibility. And so in mathematics the wise ingeniously sought examples of things that the intellect was to investigate, and none of the ancients who are regarded as great undertook difficult questions by any other than mathematical likenesses. Thus, Boethius, the most learned of the Romans, maintained that without some training in mathematics no one could attain a knowledge of divine things.[45]

**32.** Did not Pythagoras, the first philosopher in name and deed, locate every investigation of truth in the study of numbers?[46] The Platonists and also our own major thinkers have followed him to such a degree that our Augustine, and later Boethius, declared that of the things to be created number was undoubtedly "the principal exemplar in the mind of the Creator."[47] And in his *Metaphysics* how could Aristotle, who refuted his predecessors in order to appear unique, transmit to us the difference of species otherwise than by comparing them to numbers?[48] And when he wanted to transmit a knowledge of natural forms, that one form is in the other, he had to turn to mathematical figures: "Just as a triangle is in a tetragon," so the lower form is found in the higher.[49] I will not speak of innumerable similar examples of his. Also the Platonist Aurelius Augustine turned to mathematics for assistance when he investigated the quantity of the soul and its immortality and other very profound subjects.[50] Our Boethius seemed to be so pleased with this method that he constantly asserted that all true doctrine is contained in the doctrines of plurality and magnitude.[51] And if you would wish me to be more concise, did not the mathematical demonstration of the Pythagoreans and the Peripatetics[52] refute the opinion of the Epicureans about atoms and the void, an opinion which denies God and dashes against all truth? For the Pythagoreans and the Peripatetics showed that it is not possible to arrive at indivisible and simple atoms, which destroyed the principle that Epicurus had assumed.[53]

Proceeding in this way of the ancients, we agree with them in saying that since our only approach to divine things is through symbols, we can appropriately use mathematical signs because of their incorruptible certitude.

**33.**
*Chapter Twelve*
*How Mathematical Signs Should Be Used for Our Purpose*

It is evident from what has been previously stated that the simply maximum cannot be any of the things which we know or of which we have any concept. When, therefore, we propose to investigate this maximum by means of symbols, we must leap beyond simple likeness. For all mathematicals are finite; otherwise they could not even be imagined. Therefore, if we want to use finite things as a method of ascending to the simply maximum, we must first consider finite mathematical figures along with their attributes and relations; then we must transfer these relations to corresponding infinite figures; and finally we must, at a still higher level, apply the relations of the infinite figures to the infinite simple, which is entirely independent even of every figure. And then, as we labor in the dark of enigma, our ignorance will be taught incomprehensibly how we are to think of the Most High more correctly and more truly.

34.  Proceeding, therefore, in this way and beginning under the direction of maximum truth, we are asserting what saintly persons and the loftiest intellects who applied themselves to the study of figures have variously stated. The very devout Anselm, for example, compared maximum truth to infinite straightness.[54] Following him, let us turn to the figure of straightness, which I visualize as a straight line. Others who are very skilled have drawn a comparison between the most blessed Trinity and a triangle that has three equal right angles. Since, as will be shown, such a triangle must consist of infinite sides, it can be called an infinite triangle; and we will also follow their view. Others who have attempted to depict infinite unity have spoken of God as an infinite circle,[55] but those who have considered the most actual existence of God have affirmed that God is as if an infinite sphere.[56]

But we shall show that all these have conceived of the maximum in the right way and that they all share one opinion.

35.  *Chapter Thirteen*
*On the Attributes of the Maximum and Infinite Line*

I maintain, therefore, that if there were an infinite line, it would be a straight line, and also a triangle, a circle, and a sphere; and likewise, if there were an infinite sphere, it would be a circle, a triangle, and a line; and the same is to be said of an infinite triangle and an infinite circle.

In the first place, it is evident that the infinite line would be a straight line. The diameter of a circle is a straight line, and the circumference is a curved line longer than the diameter. If the curved line becomes less curved by as much as the circumference of a circle increases, then the circumference of the maximum circle, which cannot be greater, is minimally curved and therefore maximally straight. Consequently, the minimum coincides with the maximum in such a way that the eye perceives that the maximum line must be maximally straight and minimally curved. And not even the least doubt can remain when we see in the accompanying figure that the arc CD of the larger circle is less curved than the arc EF of the smaller circle and that the arc EF is less curved than the arc GH of the even smaller circle. Consequently, the straight line AB will be the arc of the maximum circle, which cannot be greater. And in this way it is apparent that the maximum and infinite line must be the straightest line, and to it curvature is not opposed; indeed, in the maximum line curvature is straightness. This is the first point that was to be proved.

36. We have said, secondly, that the infinite line is the maximum triangle, circle, and sphere. To demonstrate this, we must consider finite lines and discover what lies in the potentiality of a finite line, and then the object of our inquiry will become clearer to us, for the infinite line is actually whatever lies in the potentiality of a finite line.

First, we know that a line that is finite in length can be longer and straighter, and it was just proved that the maximum line is the longest and the straightest. Second, if with A as the fixed point, the line AB is drawn around until B reaches C, a triangle emerges; and if the rotation of the line is continued until B reaches its original position, a circle is formed. If with A still fixed, B is again drawn around until it reaches D directly opposite its starting point, the lines AB and AD form one continuous line, and a semicircle is described. And if with BD as the fixed diameter the semicircle is rotated, a sphere emerges.

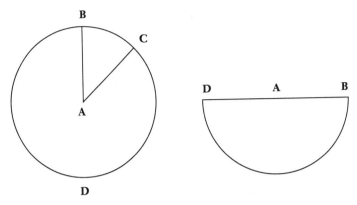

The sphere is the final figure that the line holds in its potentiality; it exists wholly in actuality, for the sphere does not stand in potentiality to any further figure. If, therefore, these figures exist in the potentiality of a finite line and if the infinite line is actually all that a finite line is in potentiality, it follows that the infinite line is a triangle, a circle, and a sphere, and this is what we had to prove.

Since, perhaps, you might wish to see more clearly how the infinite is actually those things that exist in the potentiality of the finite, I will render you most certain of this.

37.

## Chapter Fourteen
### That the Infinite Line Is a Triangle

The imagination, which does not transcend the realm of sensible things, does not grasp that a line can be a triangle, because in quantitative things these are incomparably different; but it will be easy for the intellect to grasp that a line can be a triangle. In fact, it is already evident that there can be only one maximum and infinite thing.[57] Since the sum of two sides of a triangle cannot be smaller than the third, in a triangle that has one side infinite the other two sides obviously cannot be less. And since every part of the infinite is infinite, when a triangle has an infinite side, the others also have to be infinite. And since there cannot be more than one infinite, you understand, in a transcendent way, that an infinite triangle cannot be composed of more than one line, although it is the maximum and truest triangle, which is uncompounded and most simple. And since it is the truest triangle, which it cannot be without having three lines, the one infi-

104

nite line must be three lines and these three must be one most simple line. The same is true of angles, since there will be only one infinite angle; and this angle is three angles, and the three angles are one. This maximum triangle will not be composed of sides and angles, but the infinite line and the infinite angle are one and the same, so that the line is the angle because the triangle is the line.

**38.**     You will also find help in understanding this if you ascend from a quantitative to a nonquantitative triangle. For it is evident that every quantitative triangle has three angles equal to two right angles. Thus, the larger one angle becomes, the smaller the other two are. Although, according to our first principle, any one angle can be increased short of the extent or sum of two right angles, let us suppose, however, that it may be fully increased to the sum of two right angles, without the disappearance of the triangle. In this case it is evident that the triangle has one angle which is three angles and that the three angles are one.

**39.**     In the same way, you can see that a trian-
gle is a line. For any two sides of a quantitative triangle, when joined, are longer than the third side by as much as the angle they make is smaller than two right angles. Thus in the illustration the lines BA and AC, when joined, are much longer than BC because the angle BAC is much smaller than two right angles. Therefore, the greater the angle, for example, BDC, the less the lines BD and DC exceed BC, and the smaller the surface is. If, therefore, we were to suppose that an angle could equal two right angles, the whole triangle would be resolved into a simple line.

Consequently, this supposition, which is impossible with quantitative things, can aid you in ascending to nonquantitative things; what is impossible with quantitative things you see as entirely necessary with nonquantitative things; it is evident, therefore, that the infinite line is a maximum triangle; and this is what we were to show.

**40.**                       *Chapter Fifteen*
       *That the Maximum Triangle Is a Circle and a Sphere*
     You will next see more clearly that a triangle is a circle. Suppose we formed the triangle ABC by drawing the line AB in a rotation

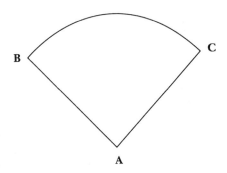

from the fixed point A until B reaches C. If the line AB were infinite and B made a complete revolution until it returned to its starting point, it would, unquestionably, form a maximum circle of which BC would be a part. Because it is a part of an infinite arc, BC is, therefore, a straight line. And because every part of the infinite is infinite, BC is not less than the entire arc of infinite circumference; BC, accordingly, will be both a part of the circumference and also the most complete circumference. Thus, the triangle ABC has to be a maximum circle. Because the circumference BC is a straight line, it is not greater than the infinite line AB, for there is nothing greater than the infinite; nor are they two lines, for there cannot be two infinites. Therefore, the infinite line, which is a triangle, is also a circle, and this is what we set out to prove.

**41.** Moreover, in the following way it becomes very clear that the infinite line is also a sphere. The line AB is the circumference of the maximum circle and, indeed, is also the circle, as we already showed, and in the triangle, AB was moved from B to C, as we said above. But BC is an infinite line, as was just proved. Therefore, AB returned to C by making a complete revolution upon itself, and such a revolution necessarily produces a sphere. And since, as we demonstrated, ABC is a circle, a triangle, and a line, we now have proof that it is also a sphere. These are the things we set out to investigate.

**42.**
*Chapter Sixteen*
*How in a Metaphorical Way*[58] *the Maximum Is Related to All Things as the Maximum Line Is to All Lines*

Now that it is evident that the infinite line is actually and infinitely all that which is contained in the potentiality of the finite line, we can, with regard to the simple maximum, also know, in a metaphorical way, that this maximum is actually and maximally all that lies in the potentiality of absolute simplicity. For the maximum is actually and maximally whatever is possible; not that it is derived from that which is possible, but it maximally is that which is possible. For example, a triangle is produced from a line; but the infinite line is not a triangle as a triangle is produced from a finite line but is actually an infinite triangle, which is identical with the infinite line. Furthermore, just as the infinite line is actually a sphere, so in the maximum, absolute possibility is not other than actually the maximum. It is otherwise in the realm of what is not maximum, for here the potentiality is not the actuality, just as a finite line is not a triangle.

**43.** From these considerations, therefore, we come to an important observation about the maximum: the maximum is such that in it the minimum is maximum, so that the maximum infinitely and completely transcends all opposition. From this principle we can deduce as many negative truths about the maximum as can be written or read; in fact, all the theology that we can grasp comes from this great principle. For this reason, Dionysius the Areopagite, that great seeker of God, writes in his *Mystical Theology* that the very blessed Bartholomew demonstrated a marvelous understanding of theology when he stated that theology is both the greatest and the least.[59] For whoever understands this understands all things and surpasses all created understanding. As the same Dionysius says in his *The Divine Names*, God, who is this maximum, "is neither this nor that, and God is neither here nor there,"[60] for just as God is all things, so God is none of them. For at the end of his *Mystical Theology*, he concludes that "above all affirmation God is the perfect and unique cause of all things, and above the negation of all things is the excellence of the one who is utterly independent of all and beyond all."[61] Hence, in his *Letter to Gaius* he also concludes that God is known above every mind and intelligence.[62]

**44.** Rabbi Solomon[63] concurs, declaring that all the wise have agreed "that the sciences do not apprehend the Creator, but the Creator alone apprehends what the Creator is; our apprehension, by comparison, fails to approach the Creator's apprehension." For this reason he elsewhere concludes: "Praised be the Creator at the comprehension of whose essence the investigation of the sciences falls short, and wisdom is reckoned as ignorance and elegance of diction as foolishness."[64] This is that learned ignorance that we are seeking, and Dionysius attempted in many ways to show that God can be found only by learned ignorance and, in my opinion, by no other principle than this.

**45.** Therefore, let our observation, which we obtain from the fact that infinite curvature is infinite straightness, be applied in a metaphorical way[65] to the maximum's most simple and most infinite essence: We learn that of all essences the maximum's essence is the most simple essence; that in this essence all the essences of things present, past and future are always and eternally actually this essence; that as it is the essence of all essences, so it is all essences; that the essence of all essences is each essence in such a way that it is all essences together and none of them individually; and that as the infinite line is the most adequate measure of all lines, so also the maximum essence is the most adequate measure of all essences.

The maximum, which does not have the minimum for an opposite, is necessarily the most adequate measure of all things; because it is the minimum it is not a greater, and because it is the maximum it is not a lesser. But all that can be measured falls between the maximum and the minimum. Therefore, the infinite essence is the most adequate and most precise measure of all essences.

**46.** To see this more clearly, suppose one infinite line consisted of an infinite number of lengths of one foot and another infinite line consisted of an infinite number of lengths of two feet, yet the two infinite lines would have to be equal, since infinite is not greater than infinite. Therefore, just as in an infinite line one foot is not smaller than two feet, so an infinite line is not longer than the length of one foot more than it is longer than the length of two feet. Indeed, since each part of the infinite is infinite, then one foot of an infinite line is interchangeable with the entire infinite line, just as two feet would be.

Similarly, since in the maximum every essence is the maximum essence, the maximum is not other than the most adequate measure of all essences. No other precise measure of every essence than maximum essence is to be found, for all others are deficient and can be more precise, as we have already most clearly proved.[66]

**47.** *Chapter Seventeen*
*Very Profound Lessons from the Same*

There is still more to be said about this same theme. A finite line is divisible, and an infinite line is indivisible, for the infinite, in which maximum and minimum coincide, has no parts. But a finite line cannot be divided so that it is not a line, for, as we have already seen, with magnitude we do not reach a minimum than which there could not be anything smaller. In its linear essence a finite line is, therefore, indivisible; a line of one foot is no less a line than is a line of one cubit. It follows, therefore, that an infinite line is the essence of a finite line. The simply maximum, therefore, is the essence of all things; the essence, however, is the measure. Hence, in his *Metaphysics,* Aristotle justly states that the First is the rule and measure of all, because it is the essence of all.[67]

48.     Moreover, just as an infinite line, which is the essence of a finite line, is indivisible, and, therefore, immutable and continuous, so the essence of all things, who is the blessed God, is also eternal and immutable. In this we can understand what the great Dionysius meant when he said that the essence of things is incorruptible and what others meant by calling the essence of things eternal.[68] In the same way, Plato, according to Calcidius, stated in the *Phaedo* that, as it exists in itself, there is one exemplar or idea of all, but that, with respect to things, which are plural, there seem to be many exemplars.[69] For when I consider a two-foot line, a three-foot line, and so on, two things are apparent: (1) the essence of the line, which is one and equal in each and every line, and (2) the difference there is between two-foot and three-foot lines. A two-foot line seems to have one essence and a three-foot line another. It is evident, however, that in an infinite line the two lines are not different; an infinite line is the essence of a finite line. Therefore, there is one essence of both lines, and the diversity of things, or of lines, does not result from a diversity of essence, for there is only one essence, but from accident, since the lines do not participate the essence equally. Consequently, there is only one essence of all, which is participated differently.

49.     It is participated differently because, as was proved earlier,[70] two things cannot be perfectly alike and, consequently, participate one essence precisely and equally. For nothing except the maximum, which is the infinite essence, can participate essence with highest equality. Just as there is but one maximum unity, so there can be only one equality of unity, and because it is maximum equality, it is the essence of all things. Also, there is only one infinite line, which is the essence of all finite lines, and since a finite line necessarily falls short of the infinite line, a finite line cannot be its own essence, any more than it can be finite and infinite at the same time. As no two finite lines can be precisely equal, because only precise equality, which is maximum equality, is the maximum, so also no two lines equally participate the one essence of all lines.

50.     Furthermore, as we have already stated,[71] in a line of two feet the

infinite line is neither longer nor shorter than the two-foot line, nor in a line of three feet is it longer or shorter than a three-foot line and so on. Because the infinite line is indivisible and one, it is entire in each finite line. Yet, it is not entire in each finite line according to participation and finiteness; otherwise, it could not be entire in a line of three feet when it was entire in a line of two feet, since a two-foot line is not a three-foot line. The infinite line, therefore, is entire in each line in such a way that it is not in any one of them insofar as one line is distinct from the others through finiteness.

The infinite line, therefore, is entire in each line in such a way that each line is in it. This needs to be considered conjointly; and it is clearly seen how the maximum is in each thing and in no one thing. What is stated here about the infinite line holds for none other than the maximum, since by this same principle the maximum is in each thing, just as each thing is in it, and the principle is that, then, the maximum exists in itself. The fact that the maximum is the rule and measure of all things is not other than the fact that the simply maximum exists in itself, that is, that the maximum is the maximum. Therefore, no thing exists in itself except the maximum, and everything exists in itself as it exists in its essence, because its essence is the maximum.

**51.**     These considerations can assist the intellect, and by the likeness of the infinite line, the intellect can in sacred ignorance move greatly forward, above all understanding, toward the simply maximum. For here we have now seen clearly how we arrive at God by removing the participation of beings. For all beings participate being. Therefore, if participation is removed from all beings, there remains simplest being itself, which is the essence of all things. It is only in learned ignorance that we behold such being, for when I mentally remove all the things that participate being, nothing seems to remain. For this reason the great Dionysius says that an understanding of God approaches nothing rather than something.[72] But sacred ignorance teaches me that what seems nothing to the intellect is the incomprehensible maximum.

**52.**     *Chapter Eighteen*
*How from the Same We Are Led to an Understanding of the*
*Participation of Being*

Furthermore, our insatiable intellect, stirred by this discussion, seeks, with care and great delight, to know how it can more clearly see this participation of the one maximum. And once again with the example of the infinite straight line to assist us, it tells us the following.

A curve, which admits a greater and a lesser, cannot be a maximum or a minimum, nor is a curve as curve anything, for it is a falling away from what is straight. Therefore, the being which is in a curve comes from its participation of straightness, since maximally and minimally a curve is only what is straight. Hence, the less a curve is a curve (as is the circumference of a larger circle), the more it participates straightness: not that it takes a part of it, for infinite straightness cannot be divided into parts. But the longer a finite straight line is, the more it seems to participate the infinity of an infinite maximum line. Now, minimum curvature is reduced to what is straight, and a finite straight line, insofar as it is straight, participates the infinite line according to a more simple participation. A curve's participation, however, is not simple and immediate but mediate and remote, for it participates the infinite line by means of the straightness which it participates. In similar fashion, some beings, such as simple finite substances, more immediately participate maximum being, which exists in itself, while others, such as accidents, participate not in and of themselves but through their substances. Despite the diversity in participation, that which is straight is its own measure and the measure of the oblique, as Aristotle says.[73] And just as an infinite line is the measure of a straight line and of a curve, so the maximum is the measure of all things that, however differently, participate being.

53.     This reveals the meaning of the statement that substance does not receive a greater or a lesser.[74] For this is true just as it is true that a finite straight line, insofar as it is straight, does not receive a greater or a lesser, but because a straight line is finite, then through the diversity of participation of the infinite line, one line is greater or smaller in relation to another, and two lines are never found to be equal. But a curve admits a greater and a lesser in accordance with its participation of straightness, and consequently, as it is something straight through participated straightness, the curve admits a greater and a lesser. For this reason, accidents are the more noble the more they participate substance and even more noble when they participate a more noble substance. From this it is clear that there can be only beings that participate the being of the First either through themselves or by means of others, just as no lines are to be found other than those that are straight or curved. Aristotle, therefore, was right

in dividing all the things that are in the world into substance and accident.[75]

**54.**     Hence, there is one most adequate measure of substance and accident, and this is the most simple maximum. Although it is neither substance nor accident, yet, as should be obvious from what has been stated, it takes the name of those things that immediately participate it, that is, the name of substances rather than of accidents. Accordingly, the great Dionysius calls it "more than substance," or "supersubstantial,"[76] rather than "superaccidental"; and because "supersubstantial" signifies more than "superaccidental," it is more appropriately ascribed to the maximum. Moreover, it is called "supersubstantial," that is, not substantial but above substance, because the substantial is below it. Thus the name "supersubstantial" is negative and therefore more truly appropriate for the maximum, as we will explain below in discussing the names of God.[77]

From these considerations one could investigate many things having to do with the diversity and quality of accidents and substances, but here is not the place for it.

**55.**                                 *Chapter Nineteen*
             *The Infinite Triangle as Metaphor[78] for Maximum Trinity*

Regarding what we have stated and shown above[79] that a maximum line is a maximum triangle, let us now become instructed in ignorance. We have shown that a maximum line is a triangle, and since the line is most simple, it will be a most simple three. Every angle of the triangle will be the line, since the whole triangle is the line. The infinite line, therefore, is three. But there cannot be more than one infinite; this trinity, then, is unity.

Further, since, according to geometry, the angle opposite the larger side is the larger angle and since the maximum triangle has infinite sides only, its angles will be maximum and infinite. Hence, one angle of the maximum triangle is not smaller than the others, nor are two larger than the third, but since quantity could not exist outside infinite quantity, so other angles cannot exist outside the one infinite angle. Consequently, one angle will exist in another, and all three will be the one maximum.

**56.**     In addition, just as a maximum line is not more line or triangle or circle or sphere but is in truth all these without composition, as was shown,[80] thus in similar fashion the simply maximum is like the linear

112

maximum, which we can call essence; it is like the triangular maximum and can be called trinity; it is like the circular maximum and can be called unity; and it is like the spherical maximum and can be called actual existence.

The maximum, therefore, is actually one threefold essence; the essence is not other than the trinity, nor the trinity other than the unity, nor the actuality other than the unity, trinity, or essence, although it is perfectly true that the maximum is these identically and most simply. Just as it is true that the maximum exists and is one, so it is also true that the maximum is three in a way in which the truth of the trinity does not contradict the most simple unity but is the unity.

**57.**     But what we have stated is possible only as the likeness with the maximum triangle makes it understandable. Consequently, from this consideration we come to know the true triangle and the most simple line in the way possible to a human being, and from this knowledge, therefore, we shall, in learned ignorance, attain to the Trinity. For we shall see that we do not find one angle and then another and still a third, as in finite triangles, because there cannot be three different angles in the unity of a triangle that is without composition. Rather we find that the one exists in a threefold way, without numerical multiplication. Therefore, the most learned Augustine justly remarks: "When you begin to count the Trinity you depart from the truth."[81] With God we must, as far as possible, forestall contradictories and embrace them in a simple concept. In God we must not conceive of distinction and indistinction, for example, as two contradictories, but we must conceive of them as antecedently existing in their own most simple beginning, where distinction is not other than indistinction, and then we shall more clearly conceive that trinity and unity are the same. For where distinction is indistinction, trinity is unity, and, conversely, where indistinction is distinction, unity is trinity. And it is the same way with the plurality of persons and the unity of essence; for where plurality is unity, a trinity of persons is the same as a unity of essence; and, conversely, where unity is plurality, a unity of essence is a trinity in the persons.

**58.**     These observations are evident in our example in which the most simple line is a triangle, and, conversely, the simple triangle is linear unity. The example also shows us that the angles of the triangle cannot be numbered "one," "two," and "three," since each angle is in each angle, for as the Son says: "I am in the Father and the Father in me."[82] Again, the truth of a triangle requires three angles; in this example, therefore, there are most truly three angles, and each is a maximum angle and all are the one maximum. Furthermore, the truth of a triangle requires that one angle not be another, and thus in the example the truth of the unity of the most simple essence requires that these three angles not be three distinct things but one thing. And this is true in our example.

Unite, therefore, these apparent opposites antecedently, as I advised, and you will not have one and three or three and one but the "unitrine" or the "triune." And this is absolute truth.

**59.**

*Chapter Twenty*
*Further About the Trinity and That Quaternity or More Is Impossible*
*in God*

Moreover, the truth of the Trinity, which is a triunity, requires that the three be one, since it is called triune. But we may conceive of this only in the manner in which a correlation unites things that are distinct and an order distinguishes them. For example, when we draw a finite triangle, first we make one angle, and then a second, and finally from these two a third, and these angles are so correlated that together they form a single triangle; and in the case of the infinite this is infinitely so. However, it must be understood that priority is conceived to be in eternity in such a way that posteriority does not contradict it; otherwise there could be no priority and no posteriority in the infinite and eternal. Consequently, the Father is not prior to the Son nor the Son subsequent to the Father, but the Father is prior in such a way that the Son is not subsequent. The Father is the first person in such a way that the Son is not afterward the second, but just as the Father is the first person without priority, so the Son is the second person and the Holy Spirit the third person without either being subsequent. But since this was treated more fully above, let this statement suffice.[83]

**60.**

Even so, you may want to note about this ever blessed Trinity that the maximum is three and not four or five or more. This is well worth noting, for anything more than three would be incompatible with the simplicity and perfection of the maximum. For every polygonal figure has as its most simple element a triangular figure, which is the minimum polygonal figure, than which there cannot be a smaller. Now, it was proved that the simply minimum coincides with the maximum.[84] Therefore, what "one" is to numbers so a triangle is to polygonal figures. Therefore, just as every number is resolved to unity, so polygons are resolved to a triangle. Therefore, the maximum triangle, with which the minimum triangle coincides, embraces all polygonal figures, for just as maximum unity is to every number, so the maximum triangle is to every polygon. Moreover, a quadrangular figure is not the minimum figure, as is evident, since a triangular figure is smaller. Therefore, a quadrangular figure, which is not possible without composition, since it is greater than the minimum, can never correspond to the most simple maximum, which can coincide only with the minimum. Indeed, to be maximum and to be quadrangular involves a contradiction. For a quadrangle could not be the adequate measure of triangles since it would always exceed a triangle. How, therefore, could that which would not be the measure of all things be the maximum? Indeed, how would that which would take its existence from another and would be composite, and thus finite, be the maximum?

61.    It is now clear why, as far as polygons are concerned, the first figure to issue from the potentiality of a simple line is a simple triangle, and then a simple circle, and finally a simple sphere. It is also clear why one arrives at only these elemental figures, which are not proportional to one other in finite things and which enfold all figures within themselves. Therefore, suppose we wanted to conceive of the measures of all measurable quantities. First, for length, we would need a maximum infinite line, with which the minimum would coincide; then, also, for rectilinear dimension, a maximum triangle; for circular dimension, a maximum circle; and for depth, a maximum sphere. For it is only with these four that we could attain to all measurable things. Because all these measures would have to be infinite and maximum measures, with which the minimum would coincide, and because there cannot be more than one maximum, we maintain that the one maximum, which should be the measure of all quantities, is all those—that is, line, triangle, circle, and sphere, without which it could not be the maximum measure. Yet, considered in itself, without reference to measurable things, the one maximum is not, nor can it truly be called, any one of these things, but it is infinitely and disproportionally above them. Therefore, because the simply maximum is the measure of all, we give it those names without which we do not understand it to be able to be the measure of all. Thus, although the maximum is infinitely above all trinity, we speak of it as threefold, for otherwise we would not understand it to be the simple cause, rule,

and measure of the things whose unity of being is a trinity, just as, with figures, triangular unity consists of a trinity of angles. Apart from this observation, however, in truth both the name and our concept of "trinity" never properly apply to the maximum but fall infinitely short of this maximum and incomprehensible truth.

62.  Therefore, we consider the maximum triangle to be the most simple measure of all things that exist in a threefold way, just as operations are actions having a threefold existence in potency, object, and act, and it is a similar situation with perceptions, thoughts, acts of will, likenesses, differences, beauty, proportions, correlations, natural appetites, and all other things whose unity of being consists of plurality, especially a nature's being and operation, which consists in a correlation of agent, passive object, and their common effect.

63.
*Chapter Twenty-One*
*The Infinite Circle as Metaphor[85] for Unity*

Now that we have made a few remarks about the maximum triangle, we shall also add some things about the infinite circle. The circle is a perfect figure of unity and simplicity. As we already showed, the triangle is a circle, and so trinity is unity.[86] However, this unity is infinite, just as the circle is infinite; it is, therefore, infinitely more one, or more identical, than every unity that we are able to express and to grasp. In fact, identity in the infinite circle is so great that it precedes even all relative oppositions, because in it "other" and "different" are not opposed to identity. Therefore, because the maximum is of infinite unity, all the things that belong to the maximum are the maximum without diversity or otherness, so that its goodness is not one thing and its wisdom another, but they are the same. For in the maximum all diversity is identity, and the maximum's power, because it is most one, is both most powerful and most infinite. The maximum's most one duration is so great that in its duration the past is not other than the future nor the future other than the present, but they are the most one duration, or eternity, without beginning and without end. For in the maximum the beginning is so great that in the maximum the end is also the beginning.

64.  All this we learn from the infinite circle, which, without beginning or end, is eternal, indivisibly the most one and the most capacious. Because this circle is maximum, its diameter is also maximum, and because there cannot be more than one maximum, this circle is

so greatly one that its diameter is its circumference. But an infinite diameter has an infinite middle, and as the middle is the center, it is clear, therefore, that the center, the diameter and the circumference are the same. Thus, our ignorance is taught that the maximum, to which the minimum is not opposed, is incomprehensible, but in the maximum the center is the circumference.

You see that the whole maximum is most perfectly within all things as simple and indivisible, because it is the infinite center; that while it is outside every being, it encompasses all things, because it is the infinite circumference; and that it penetrates all things, because it is the infinite diameter. It is the beginning of all because it is the center; the end of all because it is the circumference; and the middle of all because it is the diameter. It is the efficient cause because it is the center; it is the formal cause because it is the diameter; and it is the final cause because it is the circumference. It gives being because it is the center; it governs being because it is the diameter; and it preserves being because it is the circumference. Many other similar observations could be added.

**65.** Your intellect, therefore, grasps that the maximum is neither the same as nor different from anything and that all things are in it, from it, and by it,[87] because it is the circumference, the diameter, and the center. Not that it is, in fact, a circle, a circumference, a diameter, or a center, but it is only the most simple maximum and this is what is being investigated by means of these paradigms. We discover that it encompasses all that exists and all that does not; thus in it not-being is maximum being, just as in it the minimum is the maximum. It is the measure of all circular motion from potentiality to actuality and back again from actuality to potentiality; it is the measure of the composition from principles to individuals and of the resolution of individuals to principles; it is the measure of perfect circular forms, of circular operations and motions turning on themselves and returning to their beginning; and it is the measure of all similar motions whose unity consists in a circular perpetuity.

**66.** Many conclusions about the perfection of unity could be drawn from this circular figure, but for the sake of brevity I shall pass over them, since they could easily be reached by anyone who follows our premises. I would urge you to note only that all theology is circular and is established in a circle[88] even to such an extent that the names of the attributes are verified of one another in a circular manner. For example, highest justice is highest truth and highest truth is highest justice, and so it is with all the other attributes. Therefore, if you wanted to extend this inquiry, you could uncover an infinite number of theological truths now hidden to you.

**67.**

*Chapter Twenty-Two*
*How the Providence of God Unites Contradiction*

That we may also learn how through our prior discussion we are brought to a profound understanding, let us now consider the providence of God.[89] Since, as the preceding has shown, God is the enfolding of all things, even of contradictories, nothing is able to escape God's providence. Whether we have done one thing or its opposite or nothing at all, everything has been enveloped in the providence of God. Nothing, therefore, will happen except according to God's providence.

**68.**
Although God could have foreseen many things that God has not foreseen nor will foresee and although God has also foreseen many things that God was able not to foresee, nevertheless, nothing can be added to or taken away from divine providence. Human nature, by comparison, is simple and one; if a person were born who was never even expected to be born, nothing would be added to human nature, just as nothing would be taken from it if a person were not born and nothing is taken from it when those who have been born die. This is so because human nature enfolds those who are and also those who neither are nor will be, although they could have been. Thus, even if what never will be should happen, nothing would be added to divine providence, because it enfolds both those things that do happen and also those that can but do not. Therefore, just as in matter many things exist possibly[90] that will never happen, so, by contrast, whatever things will not happen but can happen, if they are in the providence of God, are not there possibly but actually. Nor thereupon does it follow that these things actually exist. Therefore, we say that human nature enfolds and embraces an infinite number of things, because it includes not only the human beings who have been, who are, and who will be but also those who can be, although they never will be. Thus, human nature embraces mutable things immutably just as infinite unity embraces all number. In this way the infinite providence of God enfolds both the things that will happen and also those that will not but can happen, and it enfolds contraries, as a genus enfolds contrary differentiae. And God's providence does not know the things that it

knows according to a difference of times, because it does not know the future as future nor the past as past, but it knows mutable things in eternal and unchanging ways.

**69.**     God's providence is inevitable and immutable, and nothing is able to exceed it; therefore, all things related to providence are said to have necessity, and justly, because in God all things are God, who is absolute necessity.[91] Thus, it is clear that the things that will never happen exist in the providence of God in the way we have explained, even if they are not foreseen to happen. It is necessary that God foresaw what God foresaw, because God's providence is necessary and immutable, although God was able to foresee even the opposite of what God foresaw. For to posit enfolding is not to posit the thing that was enfolded, but to posit unfolding is also to posit enfolding. Although tomorrow I am able to read or not to read, whichever I shall do, I shall not escape providence, which enfolds contraries. Therefore, whatever I shall do will happen according to the providence of God.

Hence, it is clear how through what we have already discussed, which teaches us that the maximum precedes all opposition because it somehow embraces and enfolds all things, we grasp the truth about God's providence and other similar subjects.

**70.**     *Chapter Twenty-Three*
*The Infinite Sphere as Metaphor[92] for the Actual Existence of God*

It is appropriate to make a few additional observations about the infinite sphere. We find that in the infinite sphere three maximum lines of length, width, and depth converge in the center. However, the center of the maximum sphere is equal to the diameter and to the circumference. Therefore, in the infinite sphere the center is equal to these three lines; indeed, the center is all of them—the length, width, and depth. Thus, the maximum will be, most simply and infinitely, all length, width, and depth, which in the maximum are the one perfectly simple and indivisible maximum. As the center, the maximum precedes all width, length, and depth and is their end as well as their middle, for in the infinite sphere the center, the diameter, and the circumference are the same. Just as the infinite sphere wholly exists in actuality and is most simple, so the maximum wholly and most simply exists in actuality. And just as the sphere is the actuality of the line, the triangle, and the circle, so the maximum is the actuality of all things. Consequently, all actual existence holds from the maximum whatever it has of actuality, and all existence actually exists only insofar as it actually exists in the infinite. The maximum, therefore, is the form of forms and the form of being, or maximum actual being.

71.     In a very subtle reflection, Parmenides said that God is the one for whom to be anything that is, is to be everything that is.[93] Therefore, just as a sphere is the ultimate perfection of figures, beyond which there is none more perfect, so the maximum is the most perfect perfection of all things, so much so that in the maximum every imperfect thing is most perfect, just as the infinite line is a sphere, and curvature is straightness, composition is simplicity, diversity is identity, otherness is unity, and so on. For how could there be any imperfection where imperfection is infinite perfection, possibility is infinite actuality, and so on?

72.     Because the maximum is like the maximum sphere, we now see clearly that the maximum is the one, most simple, and most adequate measure of the whole universe and of everything existing in the universe. For in the maximum the whole is not greater than the part, just as the infinite sphere is not greater than the infinite line. God, therefore, is the one most simple essence of the entire universe, and just as the infinite sphere emerges after infinite revolutions, so God, like the maximum sphere, is the most simple measure of all circular movements. For all animation, motion, and intelligence are from, in, and through God;[94] with God one revolution of the eighth sphere is not less than one of the infinite sphere, because one in whom all motion takes rest as in an end is the end of all motions. God is the maximum rest in which all motion is rest, and as maximum straightness is the measure of all circumferences and as the maximum present, or eternity, is the measure of all times, so maximum rest is the measure of all motions.

73.     In God, therefore, all natural motions come to rest as in their end, and in God all potentiality is completed as in infinite actuality. And since God is the being of all being and since all motion is toward being, one who is the end of motion, who is the form and actuality of being, is motion's rest.

All beings tend toward God. Since they are finite and in comparison to one another cannot participate equally this end, some participate it through intermediaries, just as a line is made into a sphere by means of a triangle and a circle, a triangle is made into a sphere through a circle, and a circle is made into a sphere through itself.

74.

*Chapter Twenty-Four*
*On the Name of God and Affirmative Theology*

Since with God's help and by means of a mathematical example we have now endeavored in our ignorance to become more knowledgeable about the first maximum, let us then investigate the name of the maximum and make our learning even more complete. And if we keep rightly in mind the lessons already stated often enough, the process of discovery will be easy.

Clearly, no name can properly apply to the maximum, for it is the simply maximum itself and has no opposite. When we impose names we do so out of a certain singleness of conception by which we distinguish one thing from another. But where all things are one, there can be no proper name.

75.

Hermes Trismegistus, therefore, is correct in saying: "Because God is the whole of things, no name is proper to God; for since in God's simplicity God enfolds the whole of all things, it would be necessary either to assign every name to God or to call all things by God's name."[95] God's proper name, which we say is ineffable and which is a tetragrammaton, that is, consisting of four letters, is proper to God, because it applies to God according to God's own essence and not through any relation to creatures. Accordingly, God's name should be understood as "One and All," or better, "All in One." Earlier, therefore, we learned of "maximum unity," which is the same as "All in One"; indeed "Unity" seems an even closer and more appropriate name than "All in One." For this reason the prophet says: "On that day there will be one God and God's name will be one."[96] And elsewhere: "Hear, O Israel" (i.e. whoever sees God through the intellect) "for your God is one."[97]

76.

"Unity," however, is not the name of God as we assign the name or understand unity, because just as God transcends all understanding, so God is, a fortiori, above every name. In order to distinguish between things, names are imposed by a movement of reason, which is much inferior to the intellect. But since reason cannot leap over contradictories, there is, in accord with reason's movement, no name to which another is not opposed. So then, according to the movement of reason, plurality or multitude is opposed to unity. Hence, it is not a unity of this sort that properly applies to God, but the unity to which neither otherness nor plurality nor multiplicity is opposed. This unity is the maximum name enfolding all things in its simplicity of unity, and this is the name that is ineffable and above all understanding.

77.     For who could understand infinite unity, which infinitely precedes all opposition, where all things are enfolded, without composition, in simplicity of unity; where there is neither other nor different; where a human does not differ from a lion and sky does not differ from earth? And yet there they are most truly that,[98] not in accord with their finiteness, but in an enfolded way they are maximum unity itself. Therefore, if anyone could understand or name such unity that because it is unity is all things and that because it is the minimum it is the maximum, one would attain the name of God. But since the name of God is God, God's name is known only by that understanding that is itself the maximum and is the maximum name. Consequently, in learned ignorance we reach this conclusion: Although "unity" seems to be a closer name for the maximum, yet it is still infinitely removed from the maximum's true name, a name that is the maximum.

78.     For this reason, it is clear that the affirmative names we attribute to God apply to God in an infinitely diminished way. For such names are attributed to God on the basis of something found in creatures. Since, therefore, no such particular, no such discrete thing, which has an opposite, could apply to God other than in the most diminutive way, affirmations, as Dionysius says, are unsuitable.[99] For if you call God "truth," falsity stands in opposition; if you call God "virtue," vice is the opposite; and if you call God "substance," accident opposes, and so on. But because God is not a substance which is not all things and to which something is opposed and because God is also not a truth which is not all things without opposition, these particular names can apply to God only in an infinitely diminished sense. For no affirmations, as if positing in God something of what is signified, can apply to God, who is not any one thing more than God is all things.

79.     For this reason, if affirmative names apply, they apply to God only in relation to creatures; not that creatures are the reason why such names may apply, for the maximum can hold nothing from creatures, but affirmative names apply according to God's infinite power in relation to creatures. For God was able to create from all eternity, since otherwise God would not have been the highest power. Therefore, although the name "Creator" applies to God with reference to creatures, yet it was also applicable even before a creature was made, for God was able to create from eternity. It is similar with "justice" and all other affirmative names, which we take from creatures and

metaphorically attribute to God because of a perfection signified by the names; even before we attributed them to God, all these names were eternally and truly enfolded in God's highest perfection and in God's infinite name, as were all the things which such names signify and from which we transfer names to God.

**80.** This point is so true of all affirmatives that even the names of the Trinity and of the persons, namely, of the "Father," the "Son," and the "Holy Spirit," are bestowed on God in relation to creatures. For because God is unity, God is begetter and Father; because God is equality of unity, God is begotten or Son; and because God is their connection, God is Holy Spirit. Therefore, it is evident that the Son is called Son because he is the equality of unity, or of entity or being. So too it is evident that because God from eternity was able to create things, even if God had not created them, God is called Son in relation to these things. For God is Son because God is the equality of being these things, an equality than which things could not be more or less. Thus, God is Son because God is the equality of the being of the things that God was able to make, even if God had not been going to make them; and if God were not able to make them, God would not be Father or Son or Holy Spirit—indeed, God would not be God. If, therefore, you consider this more closely, you will see that for the Father to beget the Son was to create all things in the Word.[100] For this reason Augustine asserts that in relation to creatures the Word is both the art and the idea.[101]

**81.** God, therefore, is Father because God begets equality of unity, but God is Holy Spirit because God is the love of both.[102] And God is all—the unity, the equality of unity, and the love—in relation to creatures. For a creature first comes into being because God is Father; it is perfected because God is Son; and it is in harmony with the universal order of things because God is Holy Spirit. And in each thing these are vestiges of the Trinity. This is also the opinion of Aurelius Augustine, who in his exposition of the opening words of Genesis, "In the beginning God created heaven and earth" says that it is because God is Father that God created the foundations of things.[103]

**82.** Whatever, therefore, affirmative theology may say about God is based on a relation to creatures, even those most holy names in which lie hidden the greatest mysteries of divine knowledge, names which were cherished by the Hebrews and Chaldeans. Each name signifies God only according to some particular property, except for the name of four letters, *ioth-he-vau-he*, which we explained above as God's proper and ineffable name. Jerome[104] and Rabbi Solomon, in his book *Dux Neutrorum*,[105] treat these names at great length and may be consulted.

**83.**

*Chapter Twenty-Five*
*Pagans Have Given Various Names to God with Regard to Creatures*

Pagans also gave names to God according to God's various relations to creatures. They called God Jupiter because of the marvelous goodness; Jupiter, says Julius Firmicus, is so favorable a star that if Jupiter alone had reigned in heaven, "human beings would be immortal."[106] They also named God Saturn because of the depth of thoughts and inventions regarding the necessities of life; Mars because of victories in war; Mercury because of prudent counsel; Venus because of the love that preserves nature; the Sun because of the force of natural motions; the Moon because of the preservation of the fluids in which life consists; and Cupid because of the unity of the two sexes. For this last reason they also called God Nature because God preserves the species of things through the duality of sexes. Hermes maintained that two sexes are to be found in all things, animals and nonanimals alike; therefore, he declared that the cause of all things, God, enfolds in Godself both the masculine and feminine sex, of which Hermes believed Cupid and Venus were the unfolding.[107] Valerius the Roman concurred and sang of a Jupiter omnipotent, God the Father and Mother.[108] Hence, the daughter of Venus, that is, of natural beauty itself, they called Cupid, because one thing desires another,[109] but they said that Venus is the daughter of an omnipotent Jupiter, from whom Nature and all her company descend.

**84.**

Also the temples of Peace, Eternity, and Concord, the Pantheon, in the middle of which, in the open air, an altar was dedicated to the Infinite Limit, which is without limit, and similar monuments instruct us that pagans assigned various names to God according to God's relation to creatures. All the names are unfoldings of the enfolding of the one, ineffable name, and as this proper name is infinite, so it enfolds an infinite number of such names of particular perfections. Although there could be many such unfoldings, they are never so many or so great that there could not be more; each of them is to the proper and ineffable name what the finite is to the infinite.

The ancient pagans used to ridicule the Jews, who worshiped

the one, infinite God whom they did not know, while the pagans themselves were worshiping God in God's unfoldings, that is, they were worshiping God wherever they beheld God's divine works. At that time all believed God to be the one maximum, than which there cannot be a greater, but there was this difference between all human beings: Some, like the Jews and the Sissennii,[110] worshiped God in God's most simple unity, as the enfolding of all things is, but others worshiped God in the things where they found the unfolding of God's divinity by taking what they sensibly perceived as a guide to the Cause and Principle. In this last way the simple folk were led astray, for they did not take what was unfolded as an image but as the truth. As a consequence, idolatry was introduced among the common folk, while the wise, for the most part, correctly believed in the unity of God, as can be ascertained by anyone who will carefully examine Cicero's *On the Nature of the Gods*[111] and the ancient philosophers.

**85.**   However, we do not deny that some pagans did not understand that since God is the being of things God exists outside things in another way than by abstraction, unlike prime matter, which exists apart from things only by the abstracting intellect. These worshiped God in creatures and also supported their idolatry with rational arguments. Some even thought that God could be summoned: the Sissennii, for example, summoned God in angels, but the pagans summoned God in trees, as one reads regarding the Sun tree and the Moon tree, and others summoned God in air, water, or temples with specified forms of incantations. Our previous statements show how misled they all were and how far they were from the truth.

**86.**
*Chapter Twenty-Six*
*On Negative Theology*

Since, however, the worship of God, who is to be worshiped "in spirit and in truth,"[112] has to rest on positive affirmations about God, all religion, in its worship, has to ascend by means of an affirmative theology in which it worships God as one and three, as most wise and most good, as "inaccessible light,"[113] as life, as truth,[114] and so on, and thus religion always conducts its worship by faith, which it more truly attains through learned ignorance. It believes that this whom it worships as one is all in one; that this whom it worships as inaccessible light is not light as is corporeal light, whose opposite is darkness, but is most simple and infinite light, in which darkness is infinite light;

and that this infinite light always shines in the darkness of our ignorance but the darkness cannot comprehend it.[115] Therefore, the theology of negation is so necessary to the theology of affirmation that
without it God would not be worshiped as the infinite God but as
creature; and such worship is idolatry, for it gives to an image that
which belongs only to truth itself. It will be useful, therefore, to provide a few more words about negative theology.

87.      Sacred ignorance has taught us that God is ineffable; and this is
the case because God is infinitely greater than all that can be named;
and this is so greatly true that we speak of God more truly through
remotion[116] and negation. For the same reason, the great Dionysius
did not think of God as truth or intellect or light or anything that can
be spoken,[117] and in this Rabbi Solomon[118] and all the wise agree.
According to this negative theology, in which God is infinite only,
there is then neither Father nor Son nor Holy Spirit. Infinity as infinity is neither begetter, nor begotten, nor that which proceeds. Hilary of Poitiers expressed it most subtly when he distinguished the
persons: "Infinity in the eternal; beauty in the image; and use in the
gift."[119] He means that although in eternity we can see only infinity,
nevertheless the infinity, which is eternity, cannot, since it is negative, be understood as begetter but instead can be properly conceived
as eternity, for eternity is affirmative of unity, or maximum presence.
Therefore, "infinity in the eternal" is the beginning without beginning. "Beauty in the image" signifies the beginning from the beginning, and "use in the gift" the procession from both.

88.      All these things are very clear from what we have discussed previously. For although eternity is infinity in such a way that eternity is
not a greater cause of the Father than is infinity, yet, considered in
one way, eternity is attributed of the Father but not of the Son or of
the Holy Spirit, but infinity is not attributed of one of the persons
more than another. Considered from the standpoint of unity, infinity
is the Father; from the standpoint of equality of unity, it is the Son;
from the standpoint of connection it is the Holy Spirit; but when
considered simply as infinity, infinity is neither Father nor Son nor
Holy Spirit. Although infinity, as also eternity, is each of the three
persons, and, conversely, each person is infinity and eternity, yet this
is not so when infinity is considered simply as infinity, as was stated,
because from the standpoint of infinity, God is neither one nor more
than one. According to the theology of negation, nothing other than
infinity is found in God. Consequently, negative theology holds that

God is unknowable either in this world or in the world to come, for in this respect every creature is darkness, which cannot comprehend infinite light, but God is known to God alone.

**89.**     From these considerations it is clear that in theology negations are true and affirmations are inadequate and that, notwithstanding, the negations that remove the more imperfect things from the most perfect are truer than other negations. It is truer, for example, to say that God is not stone than to say that God is not life or intelligence, and truer to say that God is not drunkenness than to say God is not virtue.[120] It is the contrary with affirmations: Here it is truer to assert that God is intelligence and life than to assert that God is earth, stone, or body.

All these points, which should now be very clear, lead us to conclude that the precise truth shines forth incomprehensibly in the darkness of our ignorance. This is the learned ignorance for which we have been searching, and, as we explained, by means of it alone we can draw near the maximum and triune God of infinite goodness, according to the degree of our learning of ignorance, so that with all our strength we may always praise God for showing Godself to us as incomprehensible, who is over all things, blessed forever.[121]

# BOOK TWO

**90.**                    *Prologue*

We have thus used certain symbolic figures to set forth the teaching of ignorance about the nature of the absolute maximum. And now with the help of this nature, which in shadow shines forth a little to us, let us use the same method to examine the things that are all that they are from the absolute maximum.

Moreover, that which is caused originates entirely from its cause and is nothing from itself, and it conforms, as closely as it can, to its source and concept, through which it is that which it is; consequently, it is clear that if the absolute exemplar remains unknown, it is difficult to attain the nature of contraction. It is fitting, therefore, that we be learned in an ignorance beyond our comprehending, so that while not grasping the precise truth as it is, we may at least be led to see that there does exist a precise truth that we are not now able to comprehend. This is the goal I have chosen in this Second Book,[1] which I leave to your clemency to judge and to accept.[2]

91.

*Chapter One*
*Introductory Corollaries for Inferring One Infinite Universe*

It will be very beneficial if, from our principle,[3] we present the introductory corollaries of the teaching of ignorance. For they will provide a facility by which an infinite number of similar points can equally be inferred, and they will make clearer the discussion to follow.

We have held as a basic assumption that with things greater and lesser we do not arrive at a maximum in being and in possibility. Hence, we showed earlier that precise equality applies only to God.[4] It follows, therefore, that, except for God alone, all else that can be given differs. Therefore, no motion can be equal to another; nor can one motion be the measure of another, for the measure necessarily differs from the measured.

Even though these observations should prove useful to you in an infinite number of cases, yet if you transfer to astronomy, you see that the art of calculation lacks precision because it presupposes that the motion of all other planets can be measured by the sun's motion. It is also impossible to have precise knowledge even of the ordering of the heavens with reference to any kind of place or to the risings and settings of the constellations or to the elevation of a pole, or to things attending these. And since no two places precisely agree in time and position, obviously, judgments about the stars are, in the particulars, far from being precise.[5]

92.

If you next apply this rule[6] to mathematics, you see that equality is actually impossible in geometrical figures and that no two things can precisely agree either in shape or in size. Although the rules are true for describing an equal to a given figure as it exists in its definition, yet in actuality equality between different things is impossible. From this ascend to the knowledge that truth, abstracted from the material, sees as in a definition the equality that it is totally unable to experience in things, since equality is found in things only defectively.

93.

Proceed to music where also there is no precision according to our rule. Therefore, no two things agree in weight, length, or thickness; nor between the different sounds of flutes, bells, human voices, and other instruments is it possible to find harmonic proportions so precisely in harmony that a still more precise harmonic proportion could not be given. Nor does the same degree of true proportion exist in different instruments, just as it also does not exist in different human beings, but rather in all things difference according to place, time, combination, and so on is necessary. Consequently, precise proportion is seen only in its definition, and we cannot experience sweetest, faultless harmony in sensible things because it does not exist there. Now ascend to the knowledge that the maximum, most precise harmony is an equality of proportion that no living person can hear in the flesh. For such harmony would draw to itself our soul's reason, because it is all reason, just as infinite light would attract all light; thus freed from the sensible, the soul would not without rapture hear this supremely concordant harmony with the ear of the intellect. Here we could derive great pleasure from contemplating not only the immortality of our intellectual and rational spirit, which in its nature bears incorruptible reason, by which this spirit, of itself, attains to the concordant and the discordant likeness in music, but also the eternal joy into which the blessed are taken, when they are freed from the things of this world. But we will speak of this elsewhere.[7]

**94.**     Furthermore, if we apply our rule to arithmetic, we see that no two things can agree in number. And because numerical difference involves a difference of composition, combination, proportion, harmony, motion, and so on ad infinitum, we, therefore, understand that we are ignorant.

Since no one person is like another in anything, not in sense, or imagination, or intellect, or in an activity, whether writing, painting, or a craft, even if for a thousand years someone zealously attempted to imitate another in anything, one would never arrive at precision, although at times a perceptible difference may go unnoticed. Indeed, art imitates nature[8] as much as it can, but it will never be able to reproduce it precisely. Therefore, medicine and also alchemy, magic, and the other arts of transmutation lack true precision, although, in comparison, one art is truer than another, as for example, medicine is self-evidently truer than the arts of transmutation.

**95.**     As we continue to draw from this same basis,[9] let us go on to state: Since we find degrees of greater and lesser in opposites, such as the simple and the composite, the abstract and the concrete, the formal and the material, and the corruptible and the incorruptible, we never arrive at the pure other of the opposites or at that in which they agree precisely and equally. All things, therefore, issue from opposites with a degree of difference; having more from one opposite and less from another, they receive the nature of one of the opposites through the victory of one over the other. Hence, we investigate the knowledge of things rationally in order to discover that in one thing composition exists in a certain simplicity and in another simplicity exists in composition, that in one thing corruptibility exists in incorruptibility and in another the contrary, and so on, as we will explain in the book *On Conjectures,* where this will be more thoroughly treated.[10] Let these few words suffice to demonstrate the marvelous efficacy of learned ignorance.

**96.**  Descending more to the theme, I say further: Since it is impossible to ascend to the simply maximum or to descend to the simply minimum, so that, as is evident with number and with the division of a continuum, there is no transition to the infinite, it is clear that for any given finite thing, a greater and a lesser, whether in quantity, power, or perfection, and so forth, necessarily can always be given. For neither the simply maximum nor the simply minimum can be posited in things. Nor is this progression to infinity, as we just showed. Because each part of the infinite is infinite, the assertion that where we reach the infinite we find more and less implies a contradiction. For just as more and less cannot apply to the infinite, so they cannot apply to anything that bears some proportional relation to the infinite, because this thing also would have to be infinite. If by ascending one could actually arrive at an infinite number, two in such a number would not be less than a hundred, just as an infinite line consisting of an infinite number of lines of two feet would not be less than an infinite line consisting of an infinite number of lines of four feet. Thus, nothing can be given that would limit the divine power; for to every given thing a greater and a lesser can be given by the divine power, unless the given is also the absolute maximum, as will be brought out in the Third Book.[11]

**97.**  Therefore, only the absolutely maximum is negatively infinite, and for this reason it alone is what there can be in all potentiality. But since the universe embraces all the things that are not God, the universe cannot be negatively infinite, although it is boundless and thus privatively infinite, and in this respect it is neither finite nor infinite. It cannot be greater than it is, and this is the result of a defect; for possibility, that is, matter, does not extend itself further. To say that "the universe can always be actually greater" is no different than saying that "possible being passes over into actually infinite being." But this is impossible, since infinite actuality, which is absolute eternity and actually all possibility of being, could not originate from possibility. Therefore, although with reference to the infinite power of God, which is illimitable, the universe could have been greater, yet, since the possibility of being, or matter, which cannot actually be extended to infinity, opposes, the universe cannot be greater. And so the universe is limitless, for nothing actually greater than it, in relation to which it would be limited, can be given. And so the universe is privatively infinite. But it exists actually only in a contracted way, so that it exists in the best way that its natural condition permits. Indeed, the universe is the creation, which necessarily derives from absolute and simply divine being, as, subsequently, in learned ignorance we will briefly demonstrate as clearly and simply as possible.

**98.**

*Chapter Two*
*That the Being of a Creature Comes from the Being of the First in a*
*Way That Cannot Be Understood*[12]

Sacred ignorance has, in the preceding, taught us that nothing is from itself except the simply maximum, in which "from itself," "in itself," "through itself," and "toward itself" are the same, that it is, in other words, absolute being. We have also learned that everything that exists must be that which it is, insofar as it is, from absolute being.[13] For how could that which is not from itself exist otherwise than from eternal being? But since the maximum is far removed from all envy,[14] it cannot communicate diminished being as such. Therefore, the creature, which is a derived being, does not hold everything that it is—its corruptibility, divisibility, imperfection, diversity, plurality, and other things of this kind—from the eternal, indivisible, most perfect, indistinct, and one maximum, nor from any positive cause.

**99.**

For example, an infinite line is infinite straightness, which is the cause of all linear being, and a curved line as line is from the infinite line; but as curved it is not from the infinite line. Curvature is a consequence of finiteness, for a line is curved because it is not the maximum line. If a curved line were the maximum line, it would not be curved, as was shown above.[15] And it is the same with things: Because

131

they cannot be the maximum, they are diminished, other, distinct, and so on, and these properties are without a cause. Therefore, it is from God that a creature is one, distinct, and joined to the universe, and the more a creature is one, the more it is like God. But the fact that its unity exists in plurality, its distinctness in confusion, and its harmony in discord it does not hold from God or from any positive cause but from a contingent.

**100.**     Who, therefore, can understand the being of the creation by uniting in it both the absolute necessity from which it exists and the contingency without which it does not exist? It seems that the creation, which is neither God nor nothing,[16] is, as it were, subsequent to God and prior to nothing and between God and nothing; in the words of one of the sages, "God is the opposition to nothing by the mediation of being."[17] And yet the creation cannot be composed of being and not-being. It seems, therefore, neither to be, since it descends from being, nor not to be, since it is before nothing, nor a composite of both. Indeed, our intellect, which cannot leap beyond contradictories, does not reach the being of creation either by division or by composition, although the intellect knows that this being originates only from the being of the maximum. Derived being, therefore, is not understandable, since the being from which it exists is not understandable, just as the incidental being of an accident is not understandable if the substance to which it is incidental is not understood. The creation as creation, therefore, cannot be called "one," since it descends from unity, nor "many," since it takes its being from the One, nor both "one and many" conjointly. But its unity exists contingently and in a certain plurality. And this, it seems, ought equally to be said of simplicity and composition, and other opposites.

**101.**     Because the creation was created through the being of the maximum and because, in the maximum, being, making, and creating are the same, creating seems to be no different than God's being all things. If, therefore, God is all things and if this means creating, how can one understand the creation not to be eternal, since the being of God is eternal, indeed, is eternity itself? Insofar as the creation is the being of God, no one doubts that it is eternity; therefore, insofar as it is subject to time, it is not from God, who is eternal. Who, therefore, understands the creation to exist from eternity and also temporally? For in Being itself the creation was unable not to exist in eternity, nor could it exist before time, since before time there was no prior; consequently, it has always existed since the time it could exist.

**102.**     Who, therefore, can understand that God is the form of being[18] but not intermixed with creation? For a composite, which cannot exist without proportion, cannot be formed from an infinite line and a finite curve. However, no one doubts that there can be no proportion between the infinite and the finite.[19] How, therefore, can the intellect grasp that the being of a curved line is from an infinite straight line, which, nevertheless, does not inform the curved line as a form but as a cause and essence? The curve cannot participate the essence of the infinite line by taking a part of it, since the essence is infinite and indivisible; nor can the curve participate it as matter participates form, as, for example, Socrates and Plato participate humanity, or as parts participate the whole, as, for example, the universe is participated by its parts, or as several mirrors participate the same face in different ways. For unlike a mirror, which is a mirror before it receives the image of a face, the being of creation does not exist before derived being; for the being of creation is derived being.

**103.**     Who, accordingly, can understand how the one, infinite form is participated differently by different creatures? For the being of creation cannot be other than a resplendence,[20] but not a resplendence positively received in something other but one which is contingently different. It is, perhaps, as if a work of art were to have no other being than that of dependency, for it would be totally dependent on the idea of the artist. From the artist it would take its being and under the artist's influence it would be preserved, like the image of a face in a mirror if we assume that before and after the image's reflection the mirror would be nothing in and of itself.

Nor can one understand how God can be made manifest to us through visible creatures.[21] God is not like our intellect, which is known only to God and to us and which, when it begins to think, receives from certain images in the memory the form of a color, a sound, or something else; previously the intellect was without form, and after receiving these forms, it assumes another form—of signs, words, or letters, and then manifests itself to others. Whether to make known God's goodness, as the religious believe,[22] or because God is maximum, absolute necessity,[23] or for another reason, God created the world, which obeys God, so that there are those who are compelled and who fear God and whom God judges. Nevertheless, it is obvious that God does not put on another form, since God is the Form of all forms, nor does God appear in positive signs, since these signs themselves, in what they are, would also require other things in which to appear, and so on ad infinitum.

104.     Who could understand how all things, though different contingently, are the image of that single, infinite Form, as if the creature were an occasioned god, just as an accident is an occasioned substance and a woman an occasioned man?[24] The infinite form is received only in a finite way; consequently, every creature is, as it were, a finite infinity or a created god, so that it exists in the way in which this could best be. It is as if the Creator had spoken: "Let it be made," and because God, who is eternity itself, could not be made, that was made which could be made, which would be as much like God as possible. The inference, therefore, is that every created thing as such is perfect, even if by comparison to others it seems less perfect. For the most merciful God communicates being to all in the manner in which it can be received. Therefore, God communicates without difference and envy, and what God communicates is received in such a way that contingency does not permit it to be received otherwise or to a higher degree. Therefore, every created being finds its rest in its own perfection, which it freely holds from the divine being. It desires to be no other created being, as if something else were more perfect, but rather it prefers that which it itself holds, as if a divine gift, from the maximum, and it wishes its own possession to be perfected and preserved incorruptibly.

105.     *Chapter Three*
*How the Maximum Enfolds and Unfolds All Things in a Way*
*Not Understandable*

Nothing can be said or thought about investigable truth that is not enfolded in the first part of this work. Everything in agreement with what is stated there about the first truth is necessarily true, and everything disagreeing is false. There we showed that there can be only one maximum of all maximums.[25] But the maximum is that to which nothing can be opposed and that in which the minimum is the maximum.[26] Infinite unity, therefore, is the enfolding of all things; indeed, "unity," which unites all, designates this. Unity is maximum not merely because it is the enfolding of number but also because it is the enfolding of all things. And just as only unity is found in number, which is the unfolding of unity, so only the maximum is found in all existing things.

In relation to quantity, which is an unfolding of unity, unity is called a point, for nothing but a point is found in quantity. Just as a point is present everywhere in a line no matter where you may divide it, so it is also everywhere in a surface and in a body. There is not more than one point, and this is nothing else than infinite unity, for infinite unity is the point that is the limit, perfection, and totality of line and quantity, which it enfolds. The point's first unfolding is the line, in which only the point is found.

**106.** In such a way rest is unity enfolding motion, and motion, on careful examination, is rest ordered in a series. Therefore, motion is the unfolding of rest. In the same way, the now, or the present, enfolds time. The past was the present, the future will be the present; nothing, therefore, is found in time except the ordered present. Consequently, the past and the future are the unfolding of the present; the present is the enfolding of all present times, and present times are the unfolding of the present in a series, and only the present is found in present times. Therefore, there is one enfolding of all times — which is the present, and the present, indeed, is unity. In the same way, identity is the enfolding of difference, equality the enfolding of inequality, and simplicity the enfolding of divisions or distinctions.

**107.** There is, consequently, one enfolding of all things; there is not one enfolding of substance, another of quality or of quantity, and so on, for there is only one maximum, with which the minimum coincides and in which enfolded difference is not opposed to enfolding identity. For just as unity precedes otherness, so also a point, which is a perfection, precedes magnitude. And that which is perfect is prior to everything that is imperfect; so rest is prior to motion, identity to difference, equality to inequality, and so on, and these are convertible with unity, which is eternity itself. For there cannot be more than one eternal.[27] God, therefore, is the enfolding of all in the sense that all are in God, and God is the unfolding of all in the sense that God is in all.

**108.** In order for us to explain our concept in relation to numbers, we say that number is the unfolding of unity. Number indicates reason, and reason is from a mind; as a result, the beasts, which have no mind, cannot number. Therefore, just as number arises from our mind because we understand as individually many that which is commonly one, so the plurality of things arises from the divine mind, in which the many exist without plurality because they exist in enfolding unity.[28] As things cannot participate equally the equality of being, so

God, in eternity, understood one thing in one way and another in another way. Consequently, there arose plurality, which in God is unity. Plurality or number has no other being than that which it holds from unity. Therefore, unity, without which number would not be number, exists in the plurality. For unity to unfold means that all exist in plurality.

109.     However, the manner of enfolding and unfolding exceeds our mind. Who, I ask, could understand how the plurality of things is from the divine mind, since God's understanding is God's being and God is infinite unity? If you continue with number as similitude and consider that number is the multiplication, by the mind, of the common one, it seems as if God, who is unity, were multiplied in things, since God's understanding is God's being; and, yet, you understand that this unity, which is infinite and maximum, cannot be multiplied. How, therefore, do you understand a plurality whose being is from the one without a multiplication of the one? Or how do you understand a multiplication of unity without there being a multiplication? Indeed, you cannot understand it as you might the multiplication of one species or of one genus in many species or individuals, for apart from individuals neither genus nor species exist except by the abstracting intellect.

110.     No one, therefore, understands how God, whose unity of being does not exist by the intellect's abstracting from things nor as united to or as immersed in things, is unfolded through the number of things. If you consider things apart from God, they are nothing, as number is nothing apart from unity.[29] If you consider God apart from things, God exists, and they are nothing. If you consider God as God is in things, you are considering things as something in which God exists, and here you are in error, as the preceding chapter clearly demonstrated. For the being of a thing is not another thing, as a different thing is, but its being is derived being. If you consider a thing as it is in God, then it is God and unity.

There remains only to say that the plurality of things arises from the fact that God is in nothing. For if God is removed from creation, nothing remains; if substance is removed from a composite, no accident remains, and thus nothing remains. How can our intellect grasp this? Although the accident perishes when the substance is removed, an accident is not, therefore, nothing. Rather, it perishes because its being is incidental being, and, therefore, just as a quantity exists only through the being of a substance, yet since quantity is present, then it is through quantity that the substance is quantitative. But it is not the case here, for the creation is not incidental to God in this way. Indeed, it confers nothing on God, as an accident confers something on a substance; in fact, it confers something on a substance to such a degree that, in consequence, although the accident takes its being from the substance, nevertheless, the substance cannot exist without any accident, but with God there cannot be a similar relationship.

**111.**     How, therefore, can we understand the creation as creation, as derived from God but, in consequence, unable to impart anything to God, who is the maximum? And if as creation it does not have even as much being as an accident but is completely nothing, how can we understand that the plurality of things is unfolded because of the fact that God is in nothing, since nothing is without any being? If you say: "God's omnipotent will is the cause, and will and omnipotence are God's being; for the whole of theology is circular,"[30] you, therefore, have to admit that you are completely ignorant of how enfolding and unfolding come about and that you know only that you do not know the manner. This is the case even if you do know that God is the enfolding and unfolding of all things, that, as God is the enfolding, in God all things are God, and that, as God is the unfolding, God is in all things that which they are, like the truth in an image. Suppose a face were present in its own image, which, according to the image's multiplication, is either a distant or a close multiple of the face; I do not mean according to spatial distance but according to progressive distance from the true face, since the image cannot be multiplied in any other fashion. Then, the one face, incomprehensibly above every sense and mind, would appear in different and multiple ways in the different images multiplied from it.[31]

**112.**                    *Chapter Four*
*How the Universe, Which Is Only a Contracted Maximum,*
*Is a Likeness of the Absolute Maximum*

If by a keen consideration we extend the things that were previously made manifest to us through learned ignorance, from alone knowing that all things are either the absolute maximum or are from it, many things can become clear to us about the world or universe, which, I maintain, is only a contracted maximum. Because that which is contracted or concrete holds all that it is from the absolute, that which is the contracted maximum imitates the maximally absolute as much as it can. Therefore, we may affirm that those things we learned in the First Book about the absolute maximum, as they apply in an absolute way to the maximally absolute, also apply in a contracted way to that which is contracted.

113.     Some illustrations may help the inquirer proceed. God is absolute maximumness and absolute unity, preceding and uniting things that are absolutely different and distant, for example, contradictories, between which there is no mean. Absolute maximumness is, in an absolute way, that which all things are; and in all things it is the absolute beginning, end, and being of things. In it, all things are most simply, indistinctly, and without plurality the absolute maximum, just as an infinite line is all figures. Likewise, the world or universe is a contracted maximum and a contracted "one"; it precedes contracted opposites, that is, contraries; and it is contractedly that which all things are. In all things it is the contracted beginning and the contracted end of things, a contracted being and a contracted infinity, so that it is contractedly infinite. In it all things are, with contracted simplicity and indistinction and without plurality, the contracted maximum, just as a contracted maximum line is contractedly all figures.

114.     All this becomes clear when contraction is considered in the right way. For contracted infinity, or simplicity, or indistinction, in virtue of its contraction, falls infinitely lower than that which is absolute, with the result that the infinite, eternal world falls disproportionally short of absolute infinity and eternity, and the one falls disproportionally short of unity. Absolute unity is free of all plurality. But although contracted unity, which is the one universe, is one maximum, it is not free of plurality because it is contracted, although it is only one contracted maximum. And although it is maximally one, its unity, however, is contracted through plurality, just as its infinity is contracted through finiteness, its simplicity through composition, its eternity through succession, its necessity through possibility, and so on. It is as if absolute necessity communicated itself without commingling and were delimited in a contracted way in its opposite. It is as if whiteness had in itself an absolute being apart from the abstraction of our intellect and from this whiteness that which is white were contractedly white; thus whiteness would be delimited by non-whiteness in that which is actually white, so that whatever would not be white without whiteness is white through whiteness.

115.     From these considerations the inquirer can elicit many things.

For just as God, because God is boundless, is neither in the sun nor in the moon, although in them God is absolutely that which they are, so the universe is neither in the sun nor in the moon but in them is contractedly that which they are. The absolute quiddity of the sun is not other than the absolute quiddity of the moon, for this is God, who is the absolute being and absolute quiddity of all things. But the contracted quiddity of the sun is other than the contracted quiddity of the moon, for whereas the absolute quiddity of a thing is not the thing, the contracted quiddity is not other than the thing. Therefore, it is clear that since the universe is a contracted quiddity, which is contracted in one way in the sun and in another in the moon, the identity of the universe exists in diversity, as unity exists in plurality. Although the universe is not the sun or the moon, yet in the sun it is the sun, and in the moon it is the moon. But God is not in the sun "sun" and in the moon "moon"; rather God is that which is sun and moon without plurality and difference. Universe indicates universality, that is, a unity of many things; consequently, just as humanity is neither Socrates nor Plato, but in Socrates it is Socrates and in Plato it is Plato, so the universe is related to all things.

**116.**    Since we have said that the universe is only the contracted first, and in this respect a maximum, clearly the whole universe came forth into being by a simple emanation of the contracted maximum from the absolute maximum. But all the beings that are parts of the universe, without which the universe, because it is contracted, could not be one, whole, and perfect, came forth into being together with the universe, and not as Avicenna and other philosophers would have it, with intelligence first, the noble soul next, and then nature.[32] Yet, just as in the design of an artisan the whole exists before the part, for example, a house before a wall, so, because all things have come forth into being from God's design, we say that the universe appeared first and all things subsequently, without which there could be neither a universe nor a perfect universe. Therefore, just as the abstract is in the concrete, so we consider the absolute maximum antecedently in the contracted maximum, so that it is subsequently in all particulars, for it is absolutely in that which is contractedly all things. Indeed, God is the absolute quiddity of the world, or universe, but the universe is contracted quiddity. Contraction signifies contraction to something so as to be this or that. God, therefore, who is one, is in the one universe, but the universe is contractedly in all things.

In this way we will be able to understand how God, who is most

139

simple unity and exists in the one universe, is in all things as if subsequently and by mediation of the universe and how also through mediation of the one universe the plurality of things is in God.

117.

*Chapter Five*
*Each Thing Is in Each Thing*

If you carefully attend to what has already been stated, you will not find it difficult to see, perhaps more clearly than Anaxagoras himself, the basis of that truth of the Anaxagorean statement that "each thing is in each thing."[33] In the First Book it was shown that God is in all things in such a way that all things are in God, and now it is evident that God is in all things,[34] as if, by mediation of the universe. It follows, then, that all are in all and each is in each. The universe, as most perfect, has preceded all things in the order of nature, as it were, so that it could be each thing in each thing. In each creature, the universe is the creature, and each receives all things in such a way that in each thing all are contractedly this thing. Since each thing cannot be actually all things, for it is contracted, it contracts all things, so that they are it. If, therefore, all things are in all things, all things are seen to precede each thing. All things, therefore, are not many things, since plurality does not precede each thing. For this reason, in the order of nature all things have, without plurality, preceded each thing. Therefore, many things are not actually in each thing, but rather all things are, without plurality, each thing.

118. The universe is in things only in a contracted way, and every actually existing thing contracts all things so that they are actually that which it is. But everything that actually exists is in God, for God is the actuality of all things. Actuality is the perfection and the end of potentiality. Since the universe is contracted in each actually existing thing, it is obvious that God, who is in the universe, is in each thing and each actually existing thing is immediately in God, as is the universe. Therefore, to say that "each thing is in each thing" is not other than to say that "through all things God is in all things" and that "through all things all are in God."

It takes a keen intellect to grasp these profound truths clearly: that God is, without diversity, in all things, for each thing is in each thing, and that all things are in God, for all things are in all things. But since the universe is in each in such a way that each is in it, in each thing the universe is in a contracted way that which this thing is con-

140

tractedly, and in the universe each thing is the universe, although the universe is in each thing in one way, and each thing is in the universe in a different way.

119.     Consider the following example: An infinite line is obviously a line, a triangle, a circle, and a sphere.[35] But every finite line has its being from the infinite line, which is all that which the finite line is. Hence, in the finite line all that the infinite line is—line, triangle, and so on—is that which the finite line is. In the finite line, therefore, every figure is the line itself, and no triangle, circle, or sphere is actually present in it, because that which is actually one does not become from that which is actually many. Each thing is not actually in each thing, but rather in the line the triangle is the line, and in the line the circle is the line, and so on. To make this clearer: A line can actually exist only in a body, as will be shown elsewhere,[36] and no one doubts that all figures are enfolded in a body with length, breadth, and depth; in an actual line, therefore, all figures are actually the line, in an actual triangle all are the triangle, and so on. Indeed, in a stone all things are stone; in a vegetative soul all are vegetative soul; in life all are life; in the senses all are the senses; in sight all are sight; in hearing all are hearing; in imagination all are imagination; in reason all are reason; in intellect all are intellect; and in God all are God. And now you see how the unity of things, or the universe, exists in plurality and, conversely, how plurality exists in unity.

120.     Consider more keenly and you will see that each actually existing thing is at rest, because in it all things are it and in God it is God. You see that there is a marvelous unity of things, an admirable equality and a most wonderful connection, so that all things are in all things. You also understand that for this reason there is a diversity and a connection of things. Indeed, each thing could not be actually all things, for each thing would have been God, and, therefore, all things would exist in each thing in the way in which they would be able to exist according to that which each thing is; nor could one thing be like another in all respects, as was made clear above;[37] for this reason, all things are made to exist in different degrees, just as that being which could not exist incorruptibly at once is also made to exist incorruptibly in temporal succession. So then all things are what they are because they could not exist in another or a better way.

121.     All things, therefore, are at rest in each thing, because one degree could not exist without another, just as in a body each member contributes to each, and all are content in all. Since the eye cannot actually

be the hand and the foot and all the other members, it is content to be the eye, and the foot is content to be the foot, and all the members contribute to one another, so that each is that which it is in the best way it can be. Neither the hand nor the foot is in the eye, but in the eye they are the eye, insofar as the eye itself is immediately in the person. Thus, also, in the foot all the members are the foot, insofar as the foot is immediately in the person. Consequently, each member through each member is immediately in the person, and the person, or the whole, through each member, is in each member, just as in its parts the whole is in each part through each part.

122.    If, therefore, you were to consider humanity as something absolute, unmixable, and unable to be contracted and to consider a human being in whom absolute humanity exists absolutely and from whom there exists the contracted humanity that the human is, then the absolute humanity would be as if God and the contracted humanity would be as if the universe. The absolute humanity is in the human principally, or antecedently, and is subsequently in each member or each part; the contracted humanity is in the eye "eye," in the heart "heart," and so on, so that in each member is each member contractedly. This hypothesis, therefore, provides us with a likeness of God and of the world and also a guidance for all that we have treated in the last two chapters along with many other notions that follow from this likeness.

123.    *Chapter Six*
*On the Enfolding of the Universe and the Degrees of Its Contraction*

In the preceding sections we discovered, above all understanding, that the universe, or world, is one; its unity is contracted by plurality so that it is unity in plurality. Since absolute unity is first, and the unity of the universe derives from it, the unity of the universe will be a second unity, which consists of a plurality. And since, as we will show in *On Conjectures*,[38] the second unity is tenfold and unites the ten categories,[39] the one universe will be the unfolding, by a tenfold contraction, of the first, absolute, and simple unity. Moreover, in the number ten all things are enfolded, since there is no number above it. The tenfold unity of the universe, therefore, enfolds the plurality of all contracted things. Because the universe's unity is in all things as the contracted principle of all, its unity is the root of all things, as ten is the square root of a hundred and the cube root of a thousand. From this root there first arises, as it were, the square number as a third unity and then the cubic number as a fourth and final unity. The third unity, the hundred, is the first unfolding of the unity of the universe, and the fourth unity, the thousand, is the last unfolding.

**124.** In this way we find three universal unities descending by degrees to the particular, in which they are contracted, so that they are actually the particular. The first and absolute unity enfolds all absolutely, and the first contracted unity enfolds all contractedly. But order imposes that absolute unity be seen as enfolding, as it were, the first contracted unity and by means of it all others; that the first contracted unity be seen as enfolding the second contracted unity and by means of it the third contracted unity; and that the second contracted unity be seen as enfolding the third contracted, which is the last universal unity and fourth from the first, so that by means of the third the second arrives at the particular. And in this way we see that the universe is contracted in each particular through three grades.

Therefore, the universe is, so to speak, all the ten most general,[40] then the genera and then the species. And thus these are universal in accordance with their degrees, and they exist in degrees and, by a certain order of nature, prior to the thing which actually contracts them. And since the universe is contracted, it is found only as unfolded in genera, and genera are found only in species; but individuals exist actually, and in them all things exist contractedly.

**125.** By this consideration we see that universals actually exist only contractedly, and thus the Peripatetics declare a truth when they say that universals do not actually exist outside things. For only the particular exists actually, and in the particular universals are contractedly the particular. Yet in the order of nature universals have a certain universal being that is contractible by the particular. This is not to suggest that they actually exist before contraction and in another way than according to the natural order, that is, in some other way than as a contractible universal that exists not in itself but in that which is actual, just as the point, the line, and the surface precede, in progressive order, the body in which alone they actually exist. For since the universe actually exists only in a contracted way, the same is true of all universals. Although they have no actual existence outside particulars, universals are not rational entities only. They are like the line and the surface, which, although they are not found apart from a body, nevertheless are not rational entities only, for they exist in a body, just as universals exist in particulars. However, through abstraction the intellect gives them existence outside things. This abstraction, indeed, is a rational entity, because absolute being cannot apply to universals. For the entirely absolute universal is God.

126.    We will see in the book *On Conjectures*[41] how the universal exists in the intellect by abstraction, although this can be evident enough from what has already been stated, since in the intellect the universal is only the intellect, and so it exists there intellectually and contractedly. Since the intellect's understanding is a clearer and loftier being, it apprehends in itself and in others the contraction of universals. Dogs and the other animals of the same species are united because of the common nature of their species that is in them; this nature would have been contracted in them, even if Plato's intellect had not created for itself a species from a comparison of likenesses. With regard to its own operation, understanding, therefore, follows being and living, for through its own operation, it cannot give being or living or understanding. But with regard to the things that are understood, the intellect's understanding, through similitude, follows being and living and nature's understanding. Universals, which the intellect makes through comparison, therefore, are a similitude of the universals contracted in things. Universals, therefore, already exist contractedly in the intellect even before the intellect unfolds them by these outward signs, through its understanding, which is its operation. For the intellect can understand nothing that is not present already contractedly in the intellect as the intellect. In understanding, therefore, the intellect unfolds by means of similitudinous marks and signs a certain world of similitudes, which is contracted in it.

Enough has been said here about the universe's unity and its contraction in things. Let us go on to speak more about its trinity.

127.
*Chapter Seven*
*On the Trinity of the Universe*[42]

Absolute unity is necessarily threefold, not contractedly but absolutely, for absolute unity is not other than trinity, which is grasped more humanly in a certain correlation, all of which was sufficiently established in the First Book.[43] Thus, as maximum contracted unity is unity, it is also threefold, not, indeed, absolutely, so that the trinity is unity, but contractedly, so that the unity exists only in a trinity, in the same way that a whole exists contractedly in its parts. In God unity does not exist contractedly in a trinity; it is not as a whole exists

144

in its parts or as a universal in the particulars, but the unity itself is a trinity. Therefore, each of the persons is the unity, and because the unity is a trinity, one person is not another. But, of course, in the universe it cannot be this way. Therefore, the three correlations, which in God are called persons, have actual being only together in unity.

**128.**  We must give careful attention to these points.[44] For in God so great is the perfection of unity, which is a trinity, that the Father is actually God, the Son actually God, and the Holy Spirit actually God; the Son and the Holy Spirit are actually in the Father; the Son and the Father actually in the Holy Spirit; and the Father and the Holy Spirit actually in the Son. But this cannot be so with something contracted, for the correlations exist per se only conjointly. Each correlation, therefore, cannot be the universe, but together all these are the universe; nor is one of them actually in the others, but insofar as the condition of contraction permits, they are so most perfectly contracted to one another that from them there is one universe, which without this trinity could not be one. Indeed, contraction is impossible without that which is contractible, that which contracts, and the connection that is accomplished by the common actuality of the other two.

Contractibility denotes a certain possibility, and this possibility descends from the procreating unity in God, as otherness descends from unity. For such possibility means changeableness and difference,[45] since its meaning is in regard to a beginning. It seems that nothing precedes possibility, for how would anything exist if it had not been possible? Possibility, then, descends from eternal unity.

**129.**  However, that which does the contracting descends from equality of unity, for it sets a limit to the possibility of that which is contractible. Equality of unity, to be sure, is equality of being, for being and one are convertible. Consequently, since that which contracts is that which equalizes the possibility for being one thing or another contractedly, it is correct to say that it descends from equality of being, which in God is the Word. And because the Word, which is the essence, idea, and absolute necessity of things, necessitates and restricts possibility through such a contracting agent, some, therefore, called that which contracts "form" or "soul of the world," and they called possibility "matter"; others named it "fate in substance"; and still others, like the Platonists, spoke of it as "the necessity of connection," since it descends from absolute necessity to become, as it were, a contracted necessity and a contracted form, in which all forms truly exist. But this will be discussed later.[46]

130.    Finally, there is the connection of that which contracts and that which is contractible, of matter and form, or of possibility and the necessity of connection, and this is actually brought about as if by a spirit of love uniting them through a certain motion. And certain ones were accustomed to calling this connection "determined possibility," because the possibility of being is determined toward actually being this or that through the union of the determining form and the determinable matter. But it is evident that this connection descends from the Holy Spirit, who is the infinite connection.

The unity of the universe, therefore, is threefold, for it is from the possibility, the necessity of connection, and the connection, which one can designate as potentiality, actuality, and connection and from this, obtain four universal modes of being. First, there is the mode of being that is called absolute necessity, namely, as God is the form of forms, the being of beings, the essence or quiddity of things, and in this mode of being all things, in God, are absolute necessity itself. Second, there is the mode of being as things exist in the necessity of connection, in which the forms of things, true in themselves, exist with a distinction and order of nature, as in the mind. Whether or not this is so we will see later.[47] Third, there is the mode of being as, in determined possibility, things are actually this or that. Fourth, the lowest mode of being is as things can be, and this is absolute possibility.

131.    The last three modes of being exist in one universality, which is a contracted maximum: From these there is one universal mode of being, for without them nothing can exist. I say "modes of being," for the universal mode of being is not composed of these three as parts as a house is composed of roof, foundation, and wall. But it is from modes of being, for a rose that in the rose garden exists in potentiality during winter and in actuality in summer has passed from a mode of being of possibility to that which is actually determined. From this we see that there is one mode of being of possibility, another of necessity, and a third of actual determination. From these three there is one universal mode of being, for nothing exists without them, and no one mode actually exists without the other.

132.    *Chapter Eight*
*On the Possibility or Matter of the Universe*

In order to explain here, at least in summary, what can make our ignorance learned, let us explain a little further the three modes of being already described, and let us begin with possibility. The ancients have had much to say about possibility. It was their unanimous opinion that from nothing, nothing is made.[48] Consequently, they asserted that there is an absolute possibility of being all things and that it is eternal; they also believed that in absolute possibility all things are enfolded as possibles. It was by reasoning in a contrary manner, just as with absolute necessity, that they formed a concept of this absolute matter or possibility. For instance, they conceived a body incorporeally by abstracting from it the form of corporeity. And thus they attained to matter only ignorantly. For how can a body be understood incorporeally and without form? They said that this matter or possibility is by nature prior to all things, so that it is never true to say "God exists" without it also being true to say "absolute possibility exists." Yet they did not maintain that absolute matter or possibility is coequal with God, since it is from God; it is neither something nor nothing, neither one nor many, neither this nor that, neither quid nor quale,[49] but rather it is the possibility for all things, and it is actually nothing of all.

133.     Because it lacks all form, the Platonists spoke of it as "lack." And because it lacks, it desires, and because it obeys necessity, which commands it or brings it to actual being, just as wax obeys the artisan who wishes to make something from it, it is aptitude. But formlessness proceeds from lack and aptitude and connects them, so that absolute possibility is, as it were, three without compounding, since lack, aptitude, and formlessness cannot be its parts; otherwise, something would be prior to absolute possibility, which is impossible. Therefore, these three (lack, aptitude, and formlessness) are modes without which absolute possibility would not be absolute. For lack exists contingently in possibility. Because possibility does not have the form that it can have, it is said to be lacking. Consequently, it is lack. But formlessness is as if "the form of possibility," which, to Platonists, is as if "the matter of forms." For the soul of the world is connected to matter in accordance with formlessness, which they have called "the vital principle" so that when the soul of the world is intermixed with possibility, the formless vitality is actually brought to the enlivening soul from a motion descending from the soul of the world and from the movableness of possibility or of vitality. For this reason, they asserted that formlessness is as if the matter of forms, which to exist actually is informed through sensitive, rational, and intellectual form.

**134.**   Hermes said that *hyle* is the nurse of bodies and formlessness the nurse of souls,[50] and one of us[51] said that chaos naturally preceded the world and was the possibility of things and in chaos there was the formless spirit in which all souls exist as possibles.

For this reason, the ancient Stoics held that all forms exist actually in possibility but are hidden and appear by the removal of the covering, just as a spoon is made from a piece of wood only by the removal of parts.[52]

**135.**   But the Peripatetics said that forms exist in matter only as possibilities and are brought forth by an efficient cause. Therefore, it is truer to say that forms arise not only from possibility but also through an efficient cause. Surely it is evident that whoever cuts pieces from a block of wood in order to make a statue adds with regard to form. That a craftsman is unable to make a chest from stone is a defect of the material, and that someone who is not a craftsman cannot fashion a chest from wood is a defect of the efficient cause. Therefore, both matter and an efficient cause are needed. Therefore, in a certain way forms are in matter as possibles, and they are brought to actuality in conformity with an efficient cause.

Hence, the Peripatetics declared that the whole of things exists as possible in absolute possibility. And because of its lack of form and its aptitude for all forms, absolute possibility is boundless and infinite, as, for example, the possibility of fashioning wax into the figure of a lion or a hare or anything else is unlimited. Yet this infinity is contrary to the infinity of God, for it is through its lack that it is infinite, but God's infinity is from God's abundance, for in God all things are actually God. Thus, matter's infinity is privative, but God's infinity is negative. This is the position of those who have discussed absolute possibility.

**136.**   We, however, discovered through learned ignorance that it would be impossible for absolute possibility to be. For among possibles nothing can be less than absolute possibility, which comes nearest to not-being — even according to the position of these authors. Consequently, in things receiving a greater and lesser we would arrive at a minimum and a maximum, but this is impossible. Therefore, in God absolute possibility is God, but outside God it is not possible; for nothing can be found that would exist with absolute potentiality, since all things other than the First are necessarily contracted. If, indeed, the different things in the world are found to be so related that more is able to be from one than from another, we do not arrive at a simply and absolutely maximum and minimum, and because such things are found, clearly no absolute possibility can be given.

137.     Every possibility, therefore, is contracted, but it is contracted by actuality. Consequently, pure possibility, completely undetermined by any actuality, is not found; nor can the aptitude of possibility be infinite and absolute, devoid of all contraction. For since God is infinite actuality, God is only actuality's cause, but the possibility of being exists contingently. If, therefore, the possibility is absolute, on what is it contingent? But the contingency of possibility results from the fact that being which derives from the First cannot be actuality entirely, simply, and absolutely. The actuality, therefore, is contracted through the possibility, so that it exists absolutely only in potentiality, and potentiality exists absolutely only when it is contracted by actuality.

But differences and degrees occur so that one thing is more actual, another more potential, without one arriving at the simply maximum and minimum, for maximum and minimum actuality coincide with maximum and minimum potentiality, and they are what we have called the absolutely maximum, as we showed in the First Book.[53]

138.     Furthermore, unless the possibility of things were contracted, no reason for things could be had, but all would occur by chance, as Epicurus mistakenly supposed. That this world rationally came forth from possibility resulted necessarily from the fact that the possibility had the aptitude only for being this world. The aptitude of possibility, therefore, was contracted and not absolute. The same is true of the earth, the sun, and so on, for unless they had been latent in matter, in a contracted possibility, there would have been no greater reason for their coming forth into actuality than not.

139.     Although God is infinite and therefore could have created the world as infinite, nevertheless, since the possibility was necessarily contracted and the aptitude in no way absolute or infinite, therefore, in accord with the possibility of being, the world could not be actually infinite, or greater or different than it is. The contraction of possibility is from actuality, and actuality is from maximum actuality. Since, therefore, the contraction of possibility is from God, and the contraction of actuality is from contingency, the world, necessarily contracted, is, from contingency, finite. We see, therefore, from our knowledge of possibility how contracted maximumness comes from a necessarily contracted possibility, and, indeed, there is this contraction not because of contingency but through actuality. And, thus, the

universe has a rational and necessary cause of contraction, so that the world, which is only contracted being, exists contingently from God, who is absolute maximumness.

**140.**     We must consider this in a singular fashion. Since, therefore, absolute possibility is God, if we consider the world as it is in absolute possibility, then it is as in God, and it is eternity itself. If we consider the world as it is in contracted possibility, then possibility by nature precedes only the world, and this contracted possibility is neither eternity nor co-eternal with God, but rather it falls short of eternity, as the contracted falls short of the absolute; they are infinitely distant from each other.

It is necessary to limit in this manner the discussion of potentiality or possibility or matter according to the rules of learned ignorance. We shall leave to the book *On Conjectures* the question of how possibility by grades proceeds to actuality.

**141.**                              *Chapter Nine*
                        *On the Soul or Form of the Universe*

All the wise agree that possible being can become actual being only through actual being, for nothing is able to bring itself into actual being, otherwise it would be its own cause;[54] indeed, it would be before it existed. Therefore, they said that what makes possibility actual does so intentionally, so that possibility becomes actual by rational ordaining and not by chance.

**142.**     This elevated nature, which renders the possible actual, has been assigned different names: "mind," "intelligence," "soul of the world," and "fate in substance." Some, like the Platonists, have called it "necessity of connection,"[55] and through this necessity they thought that possibility is necessarily determined, so that possibility is now in actuality what it was able to be before by nature. The forms of things, they said, exist in this mind actually and intelligibly, just as they exist in matter as possibilities. And possessing in itself the truth of the forms, along with what accompany them, the necessity of connection, they insisted, moves the heavens according to the order of nature. Consequently, using motion as an instrument, this necessity brings possibility into actuality and, in as conforming a way as possible, into equality with the intelligible concept of truth. As the Platonists conceded, form as it exists in matter, through this operation of the mind and by means of the motion, is the image of the true intelligible form and so is not true form but is very similar to it. Hence, the Platonists maintained that the true forms exist in the soul of the world prior to their existing in things, not however in time but in nature. The Peripatetics disagree, for they insist that the only existence forms have is in matter and, by abstraction, in the intellect, but the abstraction, of course, occurs after the thing.

**143.**    However, it was agreeable to the Platonists that such distinct exemplars in the necessity of connection are, in a natural order, from one infinite essence, in which all are one.[56] Yet they did not believe that the exemplars were created by this infinite essence but that they descended from it in such a way that it was never true to say "God exists," unless it were also true to say "the soul of the world exists." They asserted that the soul of the world is an unfolding of the mind of God in such a way that all things, which in God are one exemplar, in the soul of the world are many and distinct exemplars. They also added that God naturally precedes this necessity of connection, that the soul of the world naturally precedes motion, and that motion as instrument naturally precedes the temporal unfolding of things, so that the things that exist in this soul as true and in matter as possibilities are unfolded in time through motion. This temporal unfolding follows the natural order, which is in the soul of the world and is called "substantial fate,"[57] and the temporal unfolding of substantial fate is the "fate," as many call it, that descends in act and in effect from substantial fate.

**144.**    And so there is in the soul of the world the mode of being according to which we say that the world is intelligible. The mode of actual being, which is, as was stated, the effect of the actual determination of possibility by means of unfolding, is, according to the Platonists, the mode of being according to which the world is sensible. Yet they did not want forms as they exist in matter to be other than those that exist in the soul of the world; rather, forms exist according to different modes of being; in the soul of the world they exist as true and in themselves, but in matter they exist as resemblances, not as in their purity but in shadow. The Platonists also added that the truth of forms is attained only by the intellect, and not by reason, imagination, and sense, which attain nothing but images, as the forms are intermingled with possibility. That is why they did not attain to anything truly, but only as opinion.

**145.**    The Platonists thought that all motion descends from this soul of the world, which, they said, is entire in the whole world and entire

151

in each part of the world. Yet it does not exert the same influence in all parts, just as in a human being the rational soul does not operate in the same way in the hair and in the heart, although it is entire in the whole person and in each part. They insisted, therefore, that all souls, whether in bodies or outside, are enfolded in the soul of the world. For, according to the Platonists, the soul of the world is diffused throughout the entire universe, not through parts, since it is simple and indivisible, but as entire in the earth, where it joins the earth together, as entire in a stone, where it holds the parts steadfast, as entire in water, as entire in trees, and so on in each thing. The soul of the world is the first circular unfolding, with the divine mind as the central point, so to speak, and the soul of the world as the circle enfolding the center; it is also the natural enfolding of the whole temporal order of things. Therefore, because of its distinctness and order the Platonists designated the soul of the world as "self-moving number,"[58] and they maintained that it is from identity and diversity. They also thought that it differs from the human soul only in number, so that the soul of the world is to the universe what the human soul is to the human being. They believed that all souls derive from the soul of the world and in the end are resolved into it, if their transgressions do not stand in the way.

**146.**    Many Christians acquiesced in this Platonic approach. Especially since the essence of stone is distinct from that of a human being and in God there is no distinction and no otherness, they believed that these distinct essences, by which things are distinct, must exist after God but prior to things, for the essence precedes the thing. They also held that the same is true of the intelligence that guides the spheres and that such distinct essences as these are the ever indestructible ideas of things in the soul of the world. Indeed, they held that this soul is comprised of all the ideas of all things in such a way that in it all ideas are its substance, although they acknowledge this to be difficult to express and to understand.

They establish their case on the authority of divine scripture: "God said, 'Let there be light,' and there was light."[59] How would God have said "Let there be light" if the truth of light had not naturally existed beforehand? And once the light was temporally unfolded, why would it have been called "light" rather than something else, if the truth of light had not existed beforehand? They also cite many similar proofs in support of this argument.

**147.**    Although the Peripatetics acknowledge that the work of nature is the work of an intelligence, they, however, refuse to admit that there are exemplars. If by intelligence they do not mean God, I certainly think they are wrong. For if in this intelligence there is no idea, how does the intelligence move according to a purpose? If there is an idea of the thing that is to be unfolded temporally, and this idea is the essence of the motion, then such an idea could not have been abstracted from a thing that does not yet exist temporally. If, therefore, there exists an idea not obtained by abstraction, then this, surely, is the idea about which the Platonists speak: the idea that is not from things but rather things exist according to it. The Platonists did not wish these essences of things to be distinct and different from the intelligence, but rather such distinct essences together form a simple intelligence that enfolds in itself all essences. For example, although the essence of the human being is not the essence of stone but both essences are distinct, nevertheless, the humanity, from which the human descends, as white descends from whiteness, has no being other than in intelligence intelligibly, in accord with the nature of intelligence, and in reality really. It is not as if there were one humanity of Plato and another separate humanity, but rather according to different modes of being the same humanity exists naturally in the intelligence prior to its existence in matter, not prior in time but in the way that the essence by nature precedes the thing.

**148.**     The Platonists discussed in a sufficiently pointed and reasonable manner, while Aristotle's reproach of them was perhaps unreasonable, for he attempted to refute them more on the surface with words than at the core with understanding. But by means of learned ignorance we will ascertain what is the truer. For it has been demonstrated that we do not arrive at a simply maximum,[60] that, thus, neither absolute potency nor absolute form, or absolute actuality, that is not God can exist, that every being except God is contracted, that there is only one form of forms and one truth of truths, and that the maximum truth of the circle is not other than the maximum truth of the quadrangle. Hence, it is only in their contracted existence that the forms of things are distinct; as they exist absolutely they are one indistinct form, which is the Word of God. The soul of the world, therefore, has its existence only together with possibility, through which it is contracted, and it does not exist as a mind separated or separable from things. For if we consider mind as separated from possibility, it is the divine mind, which alone is completely actual. Therefore, many distinct exemplars are not possible, for each exemplar would be to its exemplata the maximum and absolutely true exemplar. But it is not possible for there to be plural maximum and most true exemplars. For only one infinite exemplar is sufficient and necessary. In it all things exist, as the ordered exist in the order, and in it all the essences, however distinct, are most adequately enfolded, so that infinite essence is the truest essence of the circle without being more or less, different or other, and it is the essence of the quadrangle without being more or less, or different, and it is thus with other things, as we understand from the example of the infinite line.[61]

149.     When we consider the differences of things, we are amazed that the one most simple essence of all things is also the different essence of individual things. Yet we know that this has to be so, for learned ignorance shows us that in God difference is identity. Since we see that the difference of the essences of all things most truly exists, then, because this is most true, we grasp the one most true essence of all things, which is maximum truth itself. When, therefore, we say that God created the human being by one essence and stone by another, this is true with respect to things but not with respect to the Creator, just as we see in numbers. The number three is a most simple essence, not receiving more or less, and in itself is one essence, but as it is related to different things, it is, accordingly, a different essence. For there is one essence of three for the three angles in a triangle, another essence of three for matter, form, and their compound in a substance, and another essence of three for a father, mother, and child, or for three human beings or three asses. The necessity of connection, therefore, is not, as the Platonists determined, a mind inferior to the begetting mind, but it is the Word and Son equal with the Father in the divinity, and it is called Logos, or Essence, for it is the essence of all things. Therefore, what the Platonists have proposed about the images of forms amounts to nothing, because there is only one infinite form of forms, of which all forms are images, as we already said in another place.[62]

150.     Therefore, one must understand these things keenly, for the soul of the world ought to be regarded as a certain universal form that enfolds in itself all forms yet has actual existence only by contraction in things and that in each thing is the contracted form of the thing, as was already stated about the universe.[63] Therefore, God, who in one Word makes all things, however different from each other they may be, is the efficient, formal, and final cause of all things, and there can be no creature that is not diminished from contraction and does not

fall infinitely short of the divine work. God alone is absolute; all else is contracted.

Between the absolute and the contracted there is no intermediate, as those imagined who believed the soul of the world to be a mind subsequent to God and prior to the contraction of the world. For God alone is the soul and mind of the world, in such a way that this soul is regarded as something absolute in which all the forms of things actually exist. Because the philosophers were not sufficiently instructed about the divine Word and about the absolute maximum, they regarded this mind and soul and necessity as existing without contraction in a certain unfolding of absolute necessity.

Forms, therefore, actually exist only in the Word as Word and in things as contracted. But the forms that are in the created intellectual nature have a more absolute existence in accord with this nature, yet they do not exist without contraction. Consequently, they are the intellect, whose operation, as Aristotle says, is to understand by means of an abstract similitude.[64] We will have certain things to say about this in the book *On Conjectures*.[65] These remarks about the soul of the world should be sufficient here.

**151.**

*Chapter Ten*
*On the Spirit of All*

Some have thought that motion, by which there is a joining together of form and matter, is a certain spirit[66] as if an intermediary between form and matter and diffused throughout the firmament, the planets, and earthly things. The first motion they called Atropos, that is, "without rotation," for they believed that the firmament is moved in a simple motion from east to west. The second they called Clotho, that is, "rotation," for by a rotation from west to east the planets are moved in a contrary direction to the firmament. And the third they called Lachesis, that is, "fate," since chance governs earthly things.[67]

The motion of the planets is as an evolution of the first motion, and the motion of temporal and earthly things is an evolution of the motion of the planets. In earthly things certain causes of events are latent, as the harvest is latent in the seed; for this reason, these same thinkers stated that the things that are enfolded in the soul of the world, as in a ball, are unfolded and extended through such motion. The wise considered the matter by comparison with a sculptor who wishes to fashion a statue in stone; he has the form of the statue in himself as an idea, and by certain instruments that he moves he creates the form of the statue corresponding to the shape and image of his idea; in the same way, so they thought, the mind or soul of the world bears within itself the exemplars of things and through motion unfolds them in matter. They said that this motion is diffused throughout all things, just as the soul of the world is. They maintained that this motion in the firmament, the planets, and earthly things, which, like fate, descends in act and deed from substantial fate, is the unfolding of substantial fate, for by such motion or spirit a thing's actual being is determined.

152.    They said that this spirit of connection proceeds from both possibility and the soul of the world. Matter, because of its aptitude for receiving form, possesses a certain appetite just as what is base has an appetite for good and privation an appetite for possession. Form desires actual existence but cannot exist absolutely, for it is not its own being, nor is it God. Form, therefore, descends in order to have a contracted existence in possibility. In other words, while possibility ascends toward actual being, form descends so that it limits, perfects, and ends possibility. And in this way, from the ascent and descent there arises a motion that connects the two, and this motion is the means by which potency and act are connected, since from moveable possibility and a formal mover, moving arises as the intermediary.

153.    Therefore, this spirit, which is called nature, is diffused throughout and contracted by the entire universe and by each of its parts. Nature, therefore, is, as it were, the enfolding of all the things that owe their origin to motion. The following example illustrates how this motion is contracted from the universal to the particular while order is preserved throughout its gradations. When I say "God exists," this sentence proceeds in a certain movement but by such a definite order that first, I pronounce the letters, next the syllables, then the words, and finally the sentence, although the hearing does not distinguish the order by degrees. In the same way, motion descends by degrees from the universal to the particular, where it is contracted by the temporal or natural order. But this movement or spirit descends from the divine Spirit, who moves all things by this motion. Just as in speech a breath proceeds from one who speaks and is contracted into a sentence, as just noted, so God, who is Spirit, is the one from whom all motion descends. For Truth states: "It is not you who speak but the Spirit of your Father who speaks in you."[68] It is the same for all other motions and operations.

**154.**     This created spirit, therefore, is a spirit without which nothing is one or is able to exist, but through this spirit, which fills the whole world,[69] the entire world and all that are in it are, naturally and connectively, that which they are, so that by means of this spirit, potentiality is in actuality and actuality is in potentiality. And this spirit is the motion of the loving bond of all things and toward unity, so that there is one universe of all things while all things are moved individually so that they are what they are in the best way and so that none is equally the same as another. Yet each thing, in its own way, contracts and participates the motion of each other thing either mediately or immediately, just as the elements and their compounds contract and participate the motion of the heavens and all the members of the body contract and participate the motion of the heart so that there is one universe. By this motion things exist in the best possible way. And the end of their motion is their preservation in themselves or in species through the natural union of different sexes, and the sexes are united in nature, which enfolds motion, and are separately contracted in individuals.

**155.**     There is, therefore, no simply maximum motion, since it coincides with rest. And no motion is absolute, for absolute motion is rest and is God and enfolds all motions. Just as all possibility exists in absolute possibility, which is the eternal God, and all form and act exist in the absolute form, which is the Word of the Father and of the Son in the divine, so all motion that connects and all proportion and harmony that unite exist in the absolute connection of the divine Spirit, so that God is the one principle of all things. In God and through God all things exist in a certain unity of trinity, and in like fashion they are contracted according to a greater and lesser, between the simply maximum and the simply minimum, according to their own degrees. Consequently, in intelligent beings, where to understand is to move, there is one level of potentiality, actuality, and connecting motion, and in corporeal things, where to be is to move, there is still another level of matter, form, and connection, but we will treat these things elsewhere.[70] We have said enough about the trinity of the universe for now.

**156.**

*Chapter Eleven*
*Corollaries Regarding Motion*

Perhaps those who are reading these things that have never been heard of before will be filled with wonder now that learned ignorance has shown them to be true. From them we now know that the universe is threefold; that there is nothing of all things that is not one from potentiality, actuality, and the motion connecting them;[71] and that none of these three can exist without the others absolutely, so that, of necessity, the three are in all things in very different degrees and so differently that no two things in the universe can be completely equal in these three or in any one of them.[72] Yet there is no reaching to the simply maximum and minimum in any genus, not even in that of motion.[73] Consequently, if we consider the different movements of the spheres, we will see that it is impossible for the world machine to have this sensible earth, air, fire, or anything else for a fixed and immovable center. For in motion there is no simply minimum, such as a fixed center, because the minimum has to coincide with the maximum.

The center of the world, therefore, coincides with the circumference.[74] And, therefore, the world has no circumference. For if it had a center, it would also have a circumference,[75] and thus it would possess within itself its own beginning and end, and the world would be limited in relation to some other thing, and outside the world there would be both something other and there would be place. But all these lack truth. Since it is not possible for the world to be enclosed between a corporeal center and circumference, the world, whose center and circumference are God, is not understood. And although the world is not infinite, it cannot be conceived as finite, since it lacks boundaries within which it is enclosed.

157.      The earth, which cannot be the center, cannot lack all motion. In fact, it is even necessary that it be moved in such a way that it could be moved infinitely less. Therefore, just as the earth is not the center of the world, so the sphere of fixed stars is not its circumference, even though, by comparison of earth with the sky, the earth itself seems nearer the center and the sky nearer the circumference. The earth thus is not the center of the eighth sphere or of any other; nor does the appearance of the six constellations above the horizon prove that the earth is at the center of the eighth sphere. For even if at some distance from the center the earth were revolving on an axis through the poles of the sphere in such a way that one part of the earth would face upward toward one pole of the sphere and the other part downward toward the other pole, then, clearly, only half the sphere would be visible to those on the earth, who would stand at as great a distance from the poles as the horizon is extended. Furthermore, the very cen-

ter of the world is not more within the world than outside it; nor does this earth or any sphere even have a center. Because the center is a point equidistant from the circumference and because it is impossible for there to be a sphere or a circle so perfectly true that a truer one could not be given, it is evident that to any given center an even truer and more precise center could always be given. Precise equidistance to different points cannot be found outside God, for God alone is infinite equality. The one, therefore, who is also the center of the world, namely, God, the ever blessed, is the center of the earth, of all spheres and of all things that are in the world, and is, at the same time, the infinite circumference of all.[76]

**158.** Moreover, there are no immobile and fixed poles in the sky, although the motion of the heaven of fixed stars seems to describe circles gradually smaller in size, smaller colures than the equinoctial, and so also for the intermediaries. But it is necessary that every part of the sky be moved, although unequally by comparison with the circles described by the movement of the stars. Consequently, while certain stars seem to describe a maximum circle, others seem to describe a minimum, but there is no star that does not describe a circle. Therefore, because there is no fixed pole in the sphere,[77] it is evident that there is no exact middle situated as if equidistant from the poles. In the eighth sphere there is no star that in its revolution describes a maximum circle. For it would have to be equidistant from the poles, which do not exist. Consequently, there is also no star that describes a minimum circle.

**159.** The poles of the spheres, therefore, coincide with the center, so that the center is not other than the pole, since center and pole are the blessed God. Since we are able to detect motion only in relation to a fixed point, that is, either poles or centers, which we presuppose in measuring motion, so we find that in our conjectures we are in error in all our measurements, and because we believe that the views of the ancients about centers and poles and measurements are correct, we are astonished when we discover that the stars are not in the position indicated by the rules of the ancients.

It is clear from what has been stated that the earth is moved. We have learned from the movement of a comet that the elements of air and fire are moved and that the moon is moved less from east to west than Mercury, Venus, or the sun and so on level by level; and so the earth is moved least of all. But the earth, as one of the stars, does not describe a minimum circle around a center or pole; nor does the eighth sphere describe a maximum circle, as was just proved.

**160.** Carefully consider, therefore, that just as the stars in the eighth sphere are disposed around conjectural poles, the earth, moon, and planets, as stars, are disposed, at a distance and with different movements, around a pole that we conjecture to be where the center is thought to be. Consequently, although the earth, as a star, may be nearer the central pole, yet it is moved and in its movement does not describe a minimum circle, as we showed. Indeed, even if it may seem otherwise to us, neither the sun nor the earth nor any sphere can describe a perfect circle by its motion, since they are not moved on a fixed point; nor can a circle be given that is so true that a still truer could not be given; nor is a sphere's or a star's motion at one moment ever precisely equal to their motion at another; nor does such motion describe two circles that are ever alike and equal, even if it may not appear that way to us.

**161.** If, therefore, in light of what has just been said you wish truly to understand something about the motion of the universe, you must make use of your imagination as much as possible and enfold the center with the poles. Suppose one observer were situated on the earth and underneath the northern pole and another on the pole itself; just as to the one on the earth the pole would seem to be at the zenith so to the other on the pole the center would appear at the zenith. Just as the antipodes have the sky above, as we have, so to those at either of the two poles the earth would appear to be at the zenith, and wherever a person finds oneself, one will believe one is at the center. Therefore, enfold these different images, so that the center is the zenith and vice versa, and then by means of your intellect, which is aided only by learned ignorance, you come to see that the world and its motion and shape cannot be grasped, for it will appear as a wheel in a wheel and a sphere in a sphere, nowhere having a center or a circumference, as we said.[78]

**162.**

### Chapter Twelve
### On the Earth's Conditions

The ancients did not attain the truths that we have just stated, for they lacked learned ignorance. It is already clear to us that the earth, in truth, is moved, yet it may not appear this way to us, since we detect motion only by a comparison to a fixed point. How would a passenger know that one's ship was being moved, if one did not know that the water was flowing past and if the shores were not visible from the ship in the middle of the water? Since it always appears to every observer, whether on the earth, the sun, or another star, that one is, as if, at an immovable center of things and that all else is being moved, one will always select different poles in relation to oneself, whether one is on the sun, the earth, the moon, Mars, and so forth. Therefore, the world machine will have, one might say, its center everywhere and its circumference nowhere, for its circumference and center is God, who is everywhere and nowhere.[79]

163.    The earth is also not spherical, as some have stated, although it tends to sphericity. For the world's shape, like its motion, is contracted in the world's parts. When an infinite line is regarded as contracted in such a way that as contracted it could not have a greater perfection or capacity, then it is circular, for in the circle the beginning coincides with the end. The more perfect motion, therefore, is circular, and as a result the more perfect solid figure is spherical. Hence, for the sake of perfection, each part's total motion is directed toward the whole. Heavy bodies are moved toward the earth and light things upward; earth toward earth, water toward water, air toward air, fire toward fire. The motion of the whole tends toward the circular as much as possible, and all shape tends toward the spherical, as we find in the parts of animals, in trees, and in the heavens. One motion, therefore, is more circular and more perfect than another, and shapes also differ in the same way.

164.    The earth's shape, therefore, is noble and spherical, and its motion circular, but it could be more perfect. And because in the world there is neither a maximum nor a minimum in perfections, movements, and shapes, as is clear from what has just been said, it is untrue that the earth is the least and lowliest; for although it seems more central with respect to the world, yet for this same reason it also seems nearer the pole, as we have stated.[80] Nor is the earth a proportional or an aliquot part of the world. For since the world has neither a maximum nor a minimum, it has neither a middle nor aliquot parts, nor does a human being or an animal.[81] The hand is not an aliquot part of a person, although its weight seems to be in proportion to the body, and it is the same with size and shape. Nor is the earth's darkness proof of its inferiority, for the sun's brightness, which is apparent to us, would not be apparent to anyone who might be on the sun. The sun's body, on examination, is discovered to have, as it were, a more

central earth, a fiery brightness, as it were, along its circumference, and in between, as it were, a watery cloud and brighter air, just as this earth of ours has its own elements.

165. If someone were outside the region of fire, this earth of ours, which is at the circumference of this region, would, by means of the fire, appear to that individual as a bright star, just as the sun seems very bright to us who are on the circumference of the solar region. If the moon does not appear so bright to us, it is perhaps because we are within its circumference toward the more central parts, that is, in its watery region, so to speak; therefore, its light is not apparent, although it has its own proper light, which is visible to those who are on the extremities of its circumference; but to us only the reflected light of the sun is visible. It is also for this reason that the moon's heat, which undoubtedly results from its motion and is greater on the circumference where the motion is greater, is not communicated to us, as in the case of the sun. Consequently, our earth seems to be situated between the region of the sun and that of the moon, and through the sun and the moon it participates the influence of other stars, which we do not see because we are outside their regions, for we see only the regions of those stars that glimmer.

166. The earth, therefore, is a noble star, which has light, heat, and influence that are different and distinct from those of all other stars, just as each star differs from each of the others in its light, nature, and influence. Each star communicates its light and influence to another but not intentionally, since all stars are moved, and glimmer, only in order to exist in the best possible way, and participation arises as a consequence, just as light shines of its own nature, not in order for me to see, but participation occurs, as consequence, when I use light for the purpose of seeing. The blessed God has so created all things that when each thing strives to preserve its own being as a divine office, it does so in communion with other things. The foot, for example, exists only for walking but in fulfilling its purpose serves not only itself but also the eye, the hands, the body, and the whole person, and it is the same with the eye and the other members of the body, and likewise with the parts of the world. Indeed, Plato called the world an animal. If you conceive God as its soul but without God's immersion in it, many of the things we have stated will be clear to you.

167. The fact that the earth is smaller than the sun and is under its influence is no reason to say that the earth is inferior, for the entire region of the earth, which stretches to the circumference of fire, is

great. Although we know from the earth's shadow and from eclipses that the earth is smaller than the sun, yet we do not know to what extent the sun's region is larger or smaller than the earth's. But they cannot be precisely equal, for no star can be equal to another. Nor is the earth the smallest star, for it is larger than the moon, as the experience of eclipses has shown, and the earth is also larger than Mercury, as some say, and perhaps larger than other stars. Size, therefore, is no proof that the earth is inferior.

**168.** In addition, the influence that the earth receives is no evidence of its imperfection. For as a star it perhaps equally influences the sun and its region, as was stated.[82] Because we have only the experience of being in the center where influences merge, we experience nothing of this return influence. Let us suppose the earth were possibility and the sun, in relation to it, were the soul or formal actuality and the moon their connection, so that these stars (the earth, sun, and moon), situated within one region, would unite their mutual influences, but the other stars, such as Mercury, Venus, and so forth, would remain above, as the ancients and also some moderns have held.[83] Then the correlation of influence would clearly be such that one influence could not exist without the other. The influence, therefore, in each (the earth, sun, and moon) would equally be one and three, according to the degrees of the influence. Obviously, therefore, human knowledge cannot determine, according to influences, whether earth's region exists in a more imperfect and more ignoble degree in relation to the regions of the other stars, such as the sun, the moon, and the rest.

**169.** Nor can this be known according to place, namely, that this place of the world is the habitation of humans, animals, and plants that are in degree less noble than in the region of the inhabitants of the sun and of the other stars. God is the center and circumference of all the regions of the stars and from God proceed the natures of different nobility that inhabit each region, lest so many celestial and stellar places be empty and only the earth, perhaps from among the lesser things, be inhabited. Yet it does not seem possible that according to the intellectual nature a more noble and more perfect could be given than the intellectual nature that exists here on earth and in its region, even if inhabitants of another kind should exist on other stars. The human being, in fact, desires no other nature but only to be perfect in the human being's own nature.

**170.** Improportional, therefore, are the inhabitants of other stars, of whatever kind they might be, to those that dwell on earth. This is so even if with regard to the purpose of the universe, that whole region of other stars should stand in a certain proportion, though unknown to us, to this whole region of the earth so that thus through the medium of the universal region the inhabitants of this earth or region may bear a certain mutual relation to those inhabitants of other regions, just as by means of the hand the individual parts of the fingers are proportionately related to the foot and by means of the foot the individual joints of the foot are proportionately related to the hand, so that all are proportionately ordered to the whole animal.

171. For since that whole region is unknown to us, its inhabitants remain completely unknown. On earth, for example, it happens that animals of one species, which comprise, as it were, one region of species, are united and, because of the common species region, mutually participate the things that belong to their region, while not concerning themselves with other regions and truly grasping nothing of them. In fact an animal of one species cannot grasp a thought that an animal of another species expresses through vocal signs, except extrinsically in very few signs and even then as the result of lengthy experience and only as opinion. Indeed, we are able to know incomparably less about the inhabitants of another region. We surmise that in the sun's region the inhabitants are more solar, bright, illuminated, and intellectual, even more spiritual than those on the moon, who are more lunar, and than those on the earth, who are more material and more weighty. We also presume that these solar intellectual natures are mostly actual and only a little potential, while the earthly natures are more potential and a little actual and the lunar natures fluctuate in between.

172. We have this opinion because of the sun's fiery influence, the moon's influence of both air and water, and the earth's heavy material influence. In similar fashion, we surmise that none of the other stellar regions are uninhabited, as if there were as many individual world-parts of the one universe as there are stars, of which there is no number so that the one universal world is contracted, in a threefold way and in its downward fourfold progression, in so many particular parts that they are countless except to the one who created all things in number.[84]

Not even the fact that the things of earth perish, as we know from experience, is an effective argument that the earth is ignoble. For since there is a single universal world and since there are influential proportions mutually between all the individual stars, we cannot establish that anything is utterly corruptible. Rather, it is better to consider the corruption of things according to one or another mode of being, when these influences, previously contracted, as it were, in an individual, are dissolved so that the mode of being this or that perishes, and death has no place, as Virgil says.[85] Death seems to be only the dissolution of a composite into its components. Who can know whether such dissolution occurs only in earthly things?

173.　　Certain ones have said that there are as many species of things on earth as there are stars. If, therefore, the earth contracts the influence of all the stars to the particular species, why is it not the same in the regions of other stars also receiving stellar influences? And who can know whether all the influences, at first contracted in a composition, return, at the dissolution of that composition, so that an animal that is now a contracted individual of a certain terrestrial species is released from all influence of the stars so that it returns to its beginnings? Or who can know whether only the form returns to the exemplar or soul of the world, as the Platonists maintain,[86] or whether only the form returns to its own star from which the species received actual being on mother earth and matter returns to possibility, while the spirit that unites them remains in the motion of the stars? For, in that case, when this spirit ceases to unite and withdraws itself, because of an indisposition of the organs or for other reasons, so that separation occurs by the spirit's diversity of motion, then the spirit returns, as it were, to the stars, while its form rises above the influence of the stars and its matter descends below it. Or who can know whether the forms of each region come to rest in a higher form, such as the intellectual, and through this higher form reach the end that is the world's end?

174.　　And how do the lower forms attain this end in God by means of a higher form, and how does the higher form ascend to the circumference, which is God, while the body descends to the center, where God also is, so that the motion of all is toward God? For just as the center and circumference are one in God, the body and the soul will one day be united again in God, even though the body seemed to descend as if to the center and the soul to rise as if to the circumference, when not all motion will cease but only that toward generation: It is as though at that time that successive generation will cease and the spirit of union return and connect possibility to its own form, the essential parts of the world, without which the world could not exist, will necessarily return.

No one can know these things from oneself but only as one holds knowledge in a singular way from God. There is no doubt that the excellent God created all things for Godself and wants none of the things God has made to perish, and all know that God is a most generous rewarder of those who honor God. Nevertheless, the manner of the divine activity's present and future reward God alone knows, who is God's own activity. However, later I will have a few more things to say about this,[87] according to divinely inspired truth, but for now it is enough for me, in ignorance, to have touched on these things in such a way.

**175.**

### Chapter Thirteen
### On the Wonderful Divine Art in the Creation of the World and Its Elements

Since it is the unanimous opinion of the wise that through these visible things and their magnitude, beauty, and order we are led to marvel at the divine art and excellence and since we touched upon several of the handiworks of God's marvelous knowledge, let us briefly and in wonder add, regarding the creation of the universe, a few more words about the placement and order of its elements.

In the creation of the world God made use of arithmetic, geometry, music, and astronomy, which we also use when we investigate the proportions of things, including elements and motions. For through arithmetic God joined things together; through geometry God fashioned them in such a way that they receive steadfastness, stability, and mobility, according to their conditions; with music God gave them such proportion that there is not more earth in earth than water in water, air in air, and fire in fire, so that no element is wholly resoluble into another. Therefore, the machine of the world cannot perish. Although part of one element may be resolved into another, yet all air that is mingled with water can never be converted to water, for the surrounding air would prevent this; consequently, there is always an intermingling of elements. God, therefore, arranged it so that parts of the elements would be resolved into one another. Since this occurs with delay, something is generated out of the concord of elements in relation to what is itself generable, and this endures as long as the concord of the elements endures, for if their concord is annulled, that which was generated is annulled and dissolved.

**176.** The elements, therefore, have been established in a wonderful order by God, who created all things in number, weight, and measure.[88] Number pertains to arithmetic, weight to music, and measure to geometry. Heaviness is sustained by lightness, which restricts it, as, for example, by fire the heavy earth is suspended as if in its center, and lightness relies on heaviness, as fire relies on earth. When ordaining these things, Eternal Wisdom employed an inexpressible proportion, so that it foreknew to what extent each element ought to precede another and weighed the elements in such a way that by as much as water is lighter than earth, air would be lighter than water and fire would be lighter than air, and so that, likewise, weight would agree with size and a container would occupy a larger space than that which it contains. And Eternal Wisdom has linked the elements to each other in such a relationship that one element necessarily exists in another. Accordingly, the earth, as Plato says, is as if an animal with stones in place of bones, rivers instead of veins, and trees for hair, and there are animals that are nourished within the earth's hairs like the vermin in the hair of beasts.[89]

**177.**	And, as it were, the earth is to fire as the world is to God. For in relation to the earth, fire has many likenesses to God. There is no limit to its power; it works, penetrates, and illumines all the things on earth and distinguishes and forms all by means of air and water. Hence, it is as if in all things that are brought forth from earth there is nothing except one or another activity of fire, so that the forms of things are different because of the diversity in fire's brightness. Fire, however, is immersed in things, and without them it does not exist, nor do earthly things exist without it. But God alone is absolute. Hence, God, who is light and in whom there is no darkness,[90] is called by the ancients "Absolute Consuming Fire"[91] and "Absolute Brightness." It is God's fiery splendor and brightness, as it were, that all things strive, as far as they can, to participate, as we observe in all the stars, where such brightness is found materially contracted. And this discerning and penetrating brightness is, as it were, immaterially contracted in the life of those who are living by an intellective life.

**178.**	Who would not marvel at this Artisan, who in the spheres and stars and the astral regions also employed such skill that, although without complete precision, there is a harmony of all things as well as a diversity? This Artisan weighed in advance the vastness of the stars and their position and movement in the one world and so ordained the distances between them that unless each region were just as it is, it could neither exist nor exist in such position and order, nor could the universe itself exist. This Artisan gave to all the stars a differing brightness, influence, shape, and color, as well as heat, which causally accompanies the brightness. And this Artisan so proportionately established the proportion of parts to one another that in each thing the movement of the parts is in relation to the whole, with heavy things having downward motion toward the center and with light things having upward motion from the center and around the center, as, for example, we perceive the movement of the stars to be circular.

179.      In these things that are so marvelous and so varied and diverse we discover through learned ignorance, in keeping with what we have already stated, that we are unable to know the reason of all the works of God,[92] but we can only marvel, for the Lord is great and of the Lord's greatness there is no end.[93] Because God is absolute maximumness, as God is the author and knower of all God's works, so God is also their end, so that in God are all things and outside God is nothing. God is the beginning, the middle, and the end of all things, the center and circumference of all, so that God alone is to be sought in all things, for apart from God all are nothing. If God alone is possessed, all things are possessed, for God is all things. If God is known, all things are known, for God is the truth of all things. It is also God's will that we should come to admire so marvelous a machine of the world, but the more we admire it the more God hides it from our view, for God alone wants to be sought with our whole heart and purpose. And because God dwells in inaccessible light,[94] which is sought by all things, only God can open to those who knock and give to those who seek.[95] Of all creatures none has the power to open itself to one who knocks and to show what it is, because without God, who is in all things, they are nothing.

180.      But to one who in learned ignorance inquires what they are or how they exist or to what purpose they exist, all things reply: "Of ourselves we are nothing, nor of ourselves are we able to give any other reply than nothing, since we do not even have knowledge of ourselves, but the One alone has knowledge by whose understanding we are that which that One wills, commands, and knows in us. Indeed, we are all mute; it is that One who speaks in all things. The One who made us alone knows what we are and how and to what purpose we exist. If you wish to know anything about us, seek it in our reason and cause, not in us. There, while seeking one thing, you will find all things. Nor can you find yourself except in that One."

"Therefore, make certain," says our learned ignorance, "that you find yourself in God. And since in God all things are God, nothing can be wanting to you. Yet it is not ours to approach the inaccessible, but it belongs to God, who has given us a face turned toward God and also an exceeding desire to seek God. And when we seek God, God is most compassionate and will not abandon us, but rather after showing Godself to us God will eternally satisfy us, when God's glory will appear.[96]

May God be blessed forever."[97]

# BOOK THREE

**181.**                                        *Prologue*

Now that we have set forth these few things about the universe, how it subsists in contraction, we will, to your admirable diligence,[1] also very briefly explain the concept of Jesus. And so, in a learned way in ignorance, we will, for the increase of our faith and perfection, investigate some things regarding the maximum that is both absolute and contracted, Jesus Christ, the ever blessed. We call on him to be the way to himself who is the truth,[2] that by this truth, now through faith and later through obtaining, we may be made alive in him and by him who is eternal life.

**182.**                                      *Chapter One*
*The Maximum, Contracted to This or That, Beyond Which There Can*
*Be No Greater, Cannot Exist Without the Absolute*

The First Book shows that the one absolutely maximum, which is incommunicable, immersible and incontractible to this or that, persists in itself as eternally, equally, and unchangeably the same. The Second Book explains the contraction of the universe, for the universe exists in no other way than as contractedly this and that. The unity of the maximum exists absolutely in itself; the unity of the universe exists contractedly in plurality. But the many things in which the universe is actually contracted can in no way agree in the highest equality; for then they would no longer be many. Therefore, all things necessarily differ from one another either by genus, species, and number or by species and number, or by number, so that each exists in its own number, weight, and measure.[3] All things, as a result, are distinguished from each other by degrees, so that no one thing coincides with another.

**183.** Therefore, no contracted thing can participate precisely the degree of contraction of another so that each thing necessarily exceeds or is exceeded by any other thing. All contracted things, therefore, stand between a maximum and a minimum, so that there could be given a still greater and lesser degree of contraction than the contraction of any given thing. But not that this process actually continues to infinity, since an infinity of degrees is impossible, for saying that infinite degrees actually exist is no different than saying that none exists, as was explained with regard to numbers in the First Book.[4] With contracted things, there can be no ascent or descent to an absolutely maximum or an absolutely minimum. Just as the divine nature, which is absolutely maximum, cannot be diminished and thus turned into a finite and contracted nature, so neither can the contracted nature be so lessened in contraction that it becomes entirely absolute.

**184.** No contracted thing, therefore, ever reaches the limit either of the universe or of a genus or species, for something can exist that is more or less greatly contracted than it. The first general contraction of the universe is through a plurality of genera, which necessarily differ by degrees. But genera exist only as contracted in species and species only in individuals, which alone exist actually. Therefore, just as, in accordance with the nature of contracted things, the individual is admissible only within the limit of its species, so also no individual can reach the limit of its genus or of the universe; indeed, among the many individuals of the same species different degrees of perfection necessarily occur. For this reason, no individual of a given species will be so maximally perfect that a more perfect could not be given, nor so imperfect that a more imperfect would not be possible. None, therefore, reaches the limit of its species.

**185.** There is only one limit of species and genera, and of the universe, and this is the center, circumference, and bond of all things.[5] The universe does not exhaust the infinite and absolutely maximum power of God so that the universe is simply maximum, setting a limit to God's power. The universe does not reach the limit of absolute maximumness nor do genera reach the limit of the universe, or species the limit of genera, or individual things the limit of species.

170

Therefore, between a maximum and a minimum all things are what they are in the best possible way, and God is the beginning, middle, and end of the universe and of each thing, so that whether they ascend or descend or tend toward the middle, all things approach God. But the bond of all things is through God, so that although all things are different, they are also bound together. Therefore, among genera, which contract the one universe, there is such a bond of the lower and the higher that they coincide in the middle, and among the different species there is such an order of combination that the highest species of one genus coincides with the lowest species of the genus immediately above, so that there is one continuous and perfect universe.

**186.** However, every bond is by degrees, and the maximum is not reached, because this is God. Therefore, the different species of a lower and a higher genus are not bound together in something invisible that does not receive greater and lesser degrees but in a third species, whose individuals differ by degrees, so that no one of them participates both species equally, as if it were a composite of both. On the contrary, the individual contracts the one nature of its own species in its own degree. In relation to the other species, the third seems to be composed of the lower and higher species, though not equally of both, for nothing can be composed of precisely equal components. As this third species falls between the other two species as a middle, it necessarily favors one of them, either the higher or the lower.[6] Examples of this are found in the books of philosophers on oysters, sea mussels, and other things.[7]

**187.** No species, therefore, descends so that it is the minimum species of any genus, for before it reaches the minimum, it is changed into another. And it is equally the case with the maximum species, which is changed into another species before it becomes the maximum. When in the genus animal the human species strives to reach a higher gradation among sensible things, it is caught up into commixture with the intellectual nature; but the lower part, after which the human is called animal, prevails. There are perhaps other spirits, which I will treat in *On Conjectures*,[8] and these are, in a wider sense, grouped with the genus animal because of a certain sensible nature, but since in them the intellectual nature prevails over the other nature, they are called spirits rather than animals, although the Platonists believe that these are intellectual animals.[9] Therefore, we may conclude that species are like a series of sequentially progressive numbers, necessarily finite, so that there is order, harmony, and proportion in diversity, as we demonstrated in the First Book.[10]

188.    It is necessary that, without proceeding to infinity, we reach the lowest species of the lowest genus, than which there is actually no lesser, and the highest species of the highest genus, than which there is actually no greater and higher, although a lesser and a greater than both could be given. Therefore, whether counting upward or downward, we take our beginning from absolute unity, which is God, that is, from the beginning of all things. Consequently, species are as if converging numbers, proceeding from a minimum that is maximum and from a maximum without an opposing minimum. There is nothing in the universe that does not enjoy a certain singularity that cannot be found in any other thing. Therefore, nothing prevails over all others in every respect or over different things equally, just as there can never be anything in every way equal to another. Even if at one time one thing is less than something else and at another time greater, it makes this transition with a certain singularity so that it never attains to an exact equality with the other. For example, a square inscribed in a circle grows in size from a square that is smaller than the circle to a square that is larger than the circle without ever reaching its equal, and an angle of incidence increases from one smaller than a right angle to one larger but without equality mediating. More things of this kind will be elicited in the book *On Conjectures*.[11]

189.    Individuating principles cannot come together in one individual with the same harmonious proportion as in another, so that each thing per se is one and perfect in the way possible to it. In each species, for example, in the human, at a given time some members are found to be more perfect and more excellent than others in certain features: Solomon surpassed others in wisdom, Absalom in beauty, and Samson in strength, and those who exceeded others in the intellective part deserved to be honored before the rest. Yet a diversity of opinions, according to the diversity of religions, sects, and regions, makes for different judgments of comparison[12] so that what is praiseworthy to one is reprehensible to another, and scattered throughout the world are those who are unknown to us. Therefore, we do not know who is more excellent than others in the world, for not even one of all these are we capable of knowing perfectly.

This, indeed, is God's doing so that each, although admiring others, would be content with oneself, with one's native land, so that one's birthplace would alone seem dearest to one, with the customs of one's own country, with one's own language, and so on, so that as far as possible there would be unity and peace without envy. For peace of every sort is present only among those who reign with the one who is our peace that surpasses all understanding.[13]

**190.**

*Chapter Two*
*The Contracted Maximum Is Also Equally the Absolute Maximum, as*
*Both Creator and Creature*

It has been sufficiently demonstrated that the universe is only contractedly a multitude of things, whose actual existence is such that no one thing attains to the simply maximum.[14] I will add further that if an actually existing maximum contracted to a species could be given, then, in accord with the given species of contraction, this maximum would actually be all the things that in the power of that genus or species are able to be. The absolutely maximum is absolutely actually all possible things and thus is absolutely most infinite. Likewise, a maximum contracted to a genus or species is, in accord with the given contraction, actually all possible perfection. In this contraction, the maximum, because a greater cannot be given, is infinite and embraces the whole nature of the given contraction. Just as the minimum coincides with the absolute maximum, so also the contractedly minimum coincides with the contracted maximum.

**191.**

A very clear example of this has to do with the maximum line, which allows no opposition, is every figure, and is the equal measure of all figures and with which the point coincides, as was shown in the First Book.[15] It follows, therefore, that if anything that could be posited were as the maximum contracted individual of some species, such a thing would have to be the fullness of that genus and species so that in the fullness of perfection it would be the way, the form, the essence, and the truth of all the things that would be possible in the species. Such a contracted maximum, existing above the whole nature of that contraction as its final term and enfolding in itself the whole perfection of that contraction, would hold, above all proportion, the highest equality with every given thing in that species, so that it would be neither too great nor too small for anything but would enfold in its fullness the perfections of all the things in the species.

**192.**

Thus, it is clear that the contracted maximum cannot exist as purely contracted, since no such contracted thing could attain the fullness of perfection in the genus of its contraction. Nor would such a contracted thing be God, who is most absolute, but the contracted maximum, that is, God and creature, would have to be both absolute and also contracted by a contraction that could exist in itself only by existing in absolute maximumness. For, as was shown in the First Book,[16] there is only one maximumness through which that which is contracted could be called maximum. If a maximum power so united this contracted maximum to itself that it could not be more united and both their natures be preserved and if, in consequence, with its contracted nature preserved (according to which nature it is the contracted and created fullness of the species), this contracted maximum were both God and also all things because of a hypostatic union, this wonderful union would surpass all our understanding.

193.     It is erroneous to conceive of this as a union in which different things are united. Absolute maximumness is not other or different, for it is all things. It is also incorrect to conceive of this as if two things were once separate but are now united. Divinity does not have a different existence with respect to earlier and later, nor is it this rather than that; nor could this contracted maximum, before the union, be this or that as an individual person existing in oneself. Nor is the union of divinity and the contracted maximum one of parts united in a whole, for God cannot be a part.

194.     Therefore, since the absolute God is unable to be mingled with matter and does not inform it, who could conceive of so wonderful a union, which is unlike the union of form and matter? This union would be greater than all intelligible unions, for that which is contracted, because it is maximum, would exist in such a union only in absolute maximumness and would add nothing to maximumness, for maximumness is absolute, nor would it pass over into the nature of maximumness, for it itself is contracted.[17] That which is contracted, therefore, would so exist in the absolute that if we were to conceive of it as God, we would be mistaken, for the contracted does not change its nature; if we were to imagine it as creature, we would be misled, for absolute maximumness, which is God, does not abandon its nature; and even if we were to think of it as a composite of both, we would be wrong, for of God and creature, of the maximally contracted and the maximally absolute, composition is impossible. We would have to conceive of this as God in such a way that it is also creature and as creature in such a way that it is also God, as both creator and creature without confusion and without composition.

Who, thus, could be raised to such a height that in unity one would conceive difference and in difference unity? Therefore, this union would exceed all understanding.

**195.**

*Chapter Three*<br>*How Such a Maximum Is Possible Only in Human Nature*

Consequently, it is easy next to ask what the nature of this contracted maximum should be. Because this maximum is necessarily one, just as absolute maximumness is absolute unity, and because it is contracted to this or that, it is indeed clear, first of all, that the order of things must require that by comparison with others some things are of a lower nature, as are those lacking life and intelligence; that some are of a higher nature, as are intelligences; and that some lie in between. If, therefore, absolute maximumness is the being of all things in the most universal way and as a result is not more of one thing than of another, obviously that being that is more common to the whole company of beings is more capable of union with the maximum.

**196.**

If the nature of lower things is considered and if one of these lower beings were elevated to maximumness, such a being would be both God and itself. A maximum line would be an example.[18] Since it would be infinite through absolute infinity and maximum through maximumness, to which it is necessarily united if it is maximum, therefore, through maximumness it would be God, and through contraction it would remain a line. It would thus be actually all that a line can become. But a line includes neither life nor intellect. How, therefore, could the line be taken to the maximum gradation, if it would not attain to the fullness of all natures? For it would be a maximum that could be greater and would lack perfections.

**197.**

A similar sort of thing must be said of the highest nature, which does not embrace the lower in such a way that the union of lower and higher natures is greater than their separation. Moreover, it befits the maximum, with which the minimum coincides, to embrace one thing in such a way that it does not forgo another but rather includes all things together. Accordingly, the middle nature, which is the means by which the lower and the higher are united, is alone that nature that can suitably be elevated to the maximum by the power of the maximum and infinite God. This middle nature enfolds all natures within itself, as the highest of the lower nature and the lowest of the higher. Consequently, if, in accord with all comprising it, it ascends to union with maximumness, it is evident that in this nature all natures and the whole universe have in every possible way attained to the highest gradation.

**198.** Indeed, it is human nature that is raised above all the works of God and made a little lower than the angels.[19] It enfolds both intellectual and sensible nature and embraces all things within itself, so that the ancients, with reason, called it a microcosm or miniature world.[20] Hence, it is this nature that, if elevated to a union with maximumness, would be the fullness of all the perfections of both the universe and of individual things, so that in humanity all things would reach the highest gradation.

**199.** Humanity, however, exists in this or that thing only in a contracted way. For this reason, it would not be possible for more than one true human being to be able to ascend to union with maximumness, and, certainly, this being would be a human in such a way as to be God and God in such a way as to be a human. This human being would be the perfection of the universe, holding primacy in everything.[21] And in this individual the least, the greatest, and the middle things of the nature united to absolute maximumness would so coincide that this human would be the perfection of all things, and all things, as contracted, would come to rest in this individual as in their own perfection. The measure of this human would also be that of an angel, as John states in the Apocalypse,[22] and of each thing. For this human being would be the universal contracted being of each creature through this human's union with the absolute, which is the absolute being of all things. Through this human being all things would receive the beginning and the end of their contraction, so that through this human, who is the contracted maximum, all things would come forth from the absolute maximum into contracted being and would return to the absolute through the same intermediary, so to speak, through the one who is the beginning of their emanation and the end of their return.[23]

**200.** But as the equality of being all things, God is the creator of the universe, since the universe has been created according to God. It is to this highest and maximum equality of being all things absolutely that the nature of humanity would be united. As a result, through the assumed humanity, God would, in the humanity, be all things contractedly, just as God is the equality of being all things absolutely. Because this human being would, by the union, exist in the maximum equality of being, this human would be the Son of God, just as this human would be the Word, in whom all things have been made,[24] and the equality of being, which, as we have already shown,[25] is called Son of God. Yet this individual would not cease being the Son of Man, just as this one would not cease being a human being, as will be discussed below.[26]

201.    And these things that can be done by God without variation, diminution, or lessening of God are not contrary to the most excellent and most perfect God, but, instead, they are in keeping with God's immense goodness, so that all things have been created by God and according to God in a most excellently and most perfectly congruent order. Since, then, not anything could be more perfect were this way withdrawn, therefore, no one, unless denying God or God's excellence, could reasonably object to these things. All envy is far removed from God, who is the highest good and whose work can have no defect, but rather as God is maximum, so also God's work, as far as possible, approaches the maximum. However, maximum power is limited only in itself, because there is nothing beyond it, and it is infinite. It reaches its limit in no creature, but, instead, this infinite power can create a better or a more perfect creature than any given one.

202.    But if a human is elevated to unity with this power, so that this human is a creature existing not in itself but in unity with the infinite power, then this power is not limited in the creature but in itself. Furthermore, this is the most perfect work of the maximum, infinite, and illimitable power of God, in which no deficiency is possible. Otherwise, this work would be neither creator nor creature. For how would this be a creature existing contractedly from the absolute divine being if contraction were unable to be united with it? Through it all things would exist as coming from one who exists absolutely, and as contracted they would be from one to whom contraction is united in the highest way. First, therefore, there is God as creator. Second there is God as both God and human, whose created humanity has in the highest way been assumed into unity with God, as if the universal contraction of all things were hypostatically and personally united with the equality of being all things. And therefore, in the third place, through most absolute God and by the mediating of the universal contraction, which is the humanity, all things come forth into contracted being so that they could thus be what they are in the best possible order and manner.

But this order should not be regarded in a temporal way as if God had temporally preceded the first-born of creation or as if the first-born, God and human, had preceded the world temporally. Rather, the first-born preceded it in nature and in the order of perfection above all time, so that, existing with God above time and before all things,[27] the first-born appeared in the world in the fullness of time after many ages had come and gone.

203.
*Chapter Four*
*How This Maximum Is Blessed Jesus, Who Is God and Human*

Our deliberations have now led us, in unwavering faith, to the point that, without hesitation, we firmly hold that the claims we have set forth are most true. Furthermore, we maintain that the fullness of time has passed and that Jesus, the ever blessed, is the first-born of all creation.[28]

Because of what Jesus, existing as a human, divinely worked beyond the power of a human being and because of other things that he found to be true in all things,[29] affirmed about himself, and to these affirmations his companions bore witness in their own blood, we are justified in asserting with an invariable constancy, long upheld by countless infallible proofs, that he is the one whose coming at some future time all creation awaited from the beginning and whose appearance in the world he had himself foretold by the prophets. For he came in order to fill all things, since by will he restored all to health, and as holding power over all things, he made known all the hidden and secret things of wisdom; as God he forgave sins, raised the dead, transformed nature, commanded the spirits, the sea, and the winds, walked on water, and established a law in fulfillment of all laws. According to the testimony of that most singular preacher of truth, Paul, who was enlightened in a rapture from above,[30] we have in Jesus every perfection and the redemption and the remission of sins. He is the image of the invisible God, the first-born of all creation, for in him all things were created in heaven and on earth, visible and invisible, whether thrones or dominions, principalities or powers; all have been created through him and in him. And he is before all things, and in him all abide. He is also head of the body, the church; the one who is the beginning is the first-born from the dead, so that he holds primacy in everything. For it was pleasing that all fullness dwell in him and that through him all things be reconciled to himself.[31]

204.
The saints provide such testimonies, and more elsewhere, about

his being both God and human. In him the humanity was united to the Word in the divinity, so that the humanity did not exist in itself but in the Word, for the humanity could not have existed in the highest degree and in all fullness except in the divine person of the Son.

In order that, above all our intellectual comprehension, as it were, in learned ignorance, we may conceive of this person who united human nature to oneself, let us by an ascent of our intellect consider: Since through all things God is in all and through all things all are in God, as we showed in a certain passage earlier on,[32] and since both these statements must be considered together, in union, as God is in all things in such a way that all things are in God, and since the divine being is of the highest equality and simplicity, hence God, while in all things, is not in them according to degrees, as if communicating Godself by degrees and in parts. But none can exist without a difference of degree; for this reason, all things are present in God according to themselves with a difference of degree. Since, therefore, God is in all things in such a way that all are in God, it is clear that, without any change to God and in the equality of being all things, God exists in unity with the maximum humanity of Jesus, for the maximum human can exist only maximally in God. And thus the eternal Father and the eternal Holy Spirit exist in Jesus, who is the equality of being all things, as they exist in the Son in the Divine, who is the middle person. And all things exist in Jesus as in the Word, and every creature exists in this highest and most perfect humanity, which universally enfolds all creatable things, so that all fullness dwells in him.

205.    Let the following example in some measure lead us to these things. Sense knowledge is a contracted kind of knowledge because the senses attain only to particulars. Intellectual knowledge is universal because in comparison with sense knowledge it is independent of and separate from contraction to the particular. Sensation, however, is contracted to various degrees in various ways. By these contractions various species of animals arise in degrees of nobility and perfection. And although none ascends to the simply maximum degree, as we explained above,[33] nevertheless, in that species that is actually the highest in the animal genus, that is, the human species, the senses produce an animal that is animal in such a way that it is also intellect. For a human being is one's intellect, and in the intellect sense contraction is somehow supposited in the intellectual nature, which exists as a certain divine being, separate and abstract, while the sensory remains temporal and corruptible according to its own nature.

206.    Therefore, by a certain similitude, even if a remote one, we ought similarly to ponder regarding Jesus, in whom the humanity is supposited in the divinity; for, otherwise, his humanity could not be maximum in its own fullness. Because Jesus' intellect is most perfect in existing in actuality completely, it can be personally supposited only in the divine intellect, which alone is actually all things. For the intellect in all human beings is potentially all things; it grows by degrees from potentiality to actuality, so that the greater it exists in act, the less it exists in potentiality. However, because the maximum intellect is the limit of the potentiality of every intellectual nature and exists completely in act, maximum intellect cannot exist at all unless it were intellect in such a way that it were also God, who is all in all.[34] It is as if a polygon inscribed in a circle were the human nature and the circle were the divine nature. If the polygon were to become a maximum polygon, than which there can be no greater polygon, it would in nowise exist per se with finite angles but only in a circular figure. In this way it would not have its own figure of existing, not even intellectually separable from the circular and eternal figure itself.

207.    But the maximumness of the perfection of human nature is seen in what, in human nature, are substantial and essential, namely, with regard to the intellect, which the rest, the corporeal, serve. Therefore, the maximally perfect human being need not be preeminent in accidentals but rather with respect to intellect. For it is not required that such a human being be a giant or a dwarf or of this or that size, color, shape, or other accidental. But it is necessary only that this human's body so avoid extremes as to be a most suitable instrument of the intellectual nature, which it should heed and obey without resistance, complaint, or weariness. Our Jesus, in whom, even while he appeared in the world, all the treasures of knowledge and wisdom were hidden,[35] as if a light in the darkness,[36] is believed to have had, for the purpose of his most eminent intellectual nature, a most suitable and most perfect body, as the most holy witnesses of his life also testified.

208.

*Chapter Five*
*How Christ, Conceived by the Holy Spirit, Was Born*
*of the Virgin Mary*

We should further consider that since this most perfect human nature, which is supposited above,[37] is the terminal contracted precision, it does not completely exceed the limits of its species. Like is begotten from like, and the begotten proceeds from the begetter according to a natural proportion. But this terminus not itself having a terminus is without limitation and proportion. The maximum human, therefore, cannot be begotten in the natural way; nor can such a human entirely lack a beginning from that species whose terminal perfection this maximum human being is. Because this maximum is a human, the maximum human being proceeds in part according to human nature. And because the maximum human is the highest begotten being and is most immediately united to the beginning, this beginning, from which this maximum most immediately exists, is as one who creates and begets, as a father, and the human beginning is as a passive beginning, providing receptive matter. Hence, this maximum human is from a mother without male seed.[38]

**209.** Every operation, however, proceeds from a spirit and a love uniting the active with the passive, as we showed previously in a certain place.[39] And, therefore, beyond all natural proportion, the maximum operation, by which the Creator is united with the creature and which proceeds from a maximum uniting love, must undoubtedly arise from the Holy Spirit, who is absolutely love. By the Holy Spirit alone, with no help from a contracted agent, could the mother conceive, within the extent of her species, the Son of God the Father. Just as by his own Spirit God the Father formed all the things that through God have come forth from not existing into being, so by the same most Holy Spirit God achieved this in a more excellent way when God worked most perfectly.

**210.** An illustration may instruct our ignorance. When some very excellent teacher[40] wishes to reveal his intellectual and mental word to his students so that they may feed spiritually on the conceived truth when shown to them, the teacher proceeds to clothe his mental word in sound, for unless it takes on a sensible form, it is otherwise not capable of being shown to his students. But this can be done only by means of the natural spirit of the teacher, who from the inhaled air adapts a vocal form suited to the mental word. The teacher unites the word with the form in such a way that the sound subsists in the word so that those hearing attain the word by means of the sound.

**211.** Through this likeness, although a very remote one, we are, for the moment, lifted up in our meditation above that which we can understand. By the Holy Spirit, who is consubstantial with the Father, the eternal Father, who of his immense goodness willed to show us the riches of his glory and all the fullness of his knowledge and wisdom,[41] clothed in human nature the eternal Word, his Son, who is this fullness and the fullness of all things. For God took pity on our weaknesses,[42] and because we could not grasp the Word except in a sensible form and in a form similar to ourselves, God revealed the Word according to our capacity. As speech is formed from our breath, so it is as if this Spirit, by breathing into, fashioned the animal body from pure and fruitful virginal blood. And the Spirit added reason so that this would be a human being. The Spirit united the Word of God the Father with this human so inwardly that the Word was the center of existence of the human nature. And all these things were not done seriatim, as a concept is expressed temporally by us, but by an instantaneous operation above all time and in accordance with a will befitting infinite power.

212.    No one, however, should doubt that this mother, who was so full of virtue and provided the material, surpassed all virgins in the complete perfection of virtue and received a more excellent blessing than all other fertile women.[43] In every way preordained to such a unique and most excellent virginal birth, she should properly have been free from what could have opposed the purity or the vigor as well as the singleness of so most excellent a birth. Had the virgin not been chosen beforehand, how would she have been suited for a virginal birth without male seed? Had she not been most holy and blessed most highly by the Lord, how would she have been made the sacristy of the Holy Spirit, in which the Spirit would form a body for the Son of God? Had she not remained a virgin after this birth, she would, beforehand, have furnished to this most excellent birth a center of maternal fertility not in her supreme perfection of brightness but in a divided and diminished way, not proper to so unique and supreme a son. Therefore, if this most holy virgin offered her whole self to God, for whom she fully participated the complete nature of her fertility through the work of the Holy Spirit, then before, during, and after the birth virginity remained in her, immaculate and uncorrupted, beyond all natural ordinary procreation.

213.    Therefore, from the eternal Father and from a temporal mother, the most glorious Virgin Mary, Jesus Christ was born God and human. He was born from the maximum and absolutely most abundant Father and from a mother most full of virginal fertility, filled in the fullness of time with a blessing from on high. For he could not be a human being born of a virgin mother except in time or of God the Father except in eternity. But his temporal birth required a fullness of

perfection in time, just as it demanded a fullness of fertility in his mother.

**214.** When, therefore, the fullness of time came,[44] since he could be born a human being only in time, he was born at a time and place best suited to this, but entirely hidden from all creatures. For the highest fullnesses cannot be compared with our ordinary human experiences. Hence, there was no sign by which reason could apprehend such fullnesses, although by a certain very hidden prophetic inspiration certain obscure signs, darkened by human likenesses, transmitted them, and from these signs the wise could reasonably have foreseen the incarnation of the Word in the fullness of time. But only the eternal Begetter foresaw the exact time, place, or manner and ordained that when all things kept a moderate silence, then during the night the Son would come down from the heavenly citadel[45] into the virginal womb and at the appointed and appropriate time would reveal himself to the world in the form of a servant.

**215.**
### Chapter Six
#### The Mystery of the Death of Jesus Christ

In order to attain to the mystery of the cross more clearly it seems appropriate, in keeping with my expression of intent, first to make a short digression. It is not doubted that a human being is made up of senses and intellect and also reason, which stands between and binds them together. Order subjects the senses to reason and reason to the intellect. The intellect is not of time and the world but free from them. The senses are temporally subject to the motions of the world. Reason is as though on the horizon with respect to the intellect but at the apogee with respect to the senses; so those things that are within time and those that are beyond coincide in reason.

**216.** The senses are of the animal nature and are incapable of the things that are outside time and spiritual. That which is animal, therefore, does not perceive the things that are of God,[46] for God is spirit[47] and more than spirit.[48] For this reason, sense knowledge resides in the darkness of ignorance of eternal things, and in conformity with the flesh it is moved by the power of concupiscence toward the desires of the flesh and by the power of anger toward repelling whatever may hinder it. But supraeminent, reason, because it is able to participate the intellectual nature, contains in its nature certain laws by which, as ruler, it moderates desire's passions and restores them to equanimity, lest a human being make sensible things the goal and thus be deprived of the intellect's spiritual desire. The most important of the laws are that one not do to another what one would not want done to oneself[49] and that eternal things be preferred to temporal things and pure and holy things to impure and profane things. And cooperating to this end are the laws that have been drawn from reason by the most holy lawgivers and decreed, appropriate to different times and places, as remedies for those who sin against reason.

217.     The intellect, rising to greater heights, sees that, even if the senses were in every way subjected to reason and refused to follow their natural passions, the human being would not of oneself be able to attain to the end of one's intellectual and eternal desires. For since the human is begotten of the seed of Adam in carnal pleasure, and in accordance with propagation the animality overcomes the spirituality in the human being, then, one's nature, originally rooted in carnal pleasure, by which one comes into being from a parent, remains completely powerless to transcend the temporal in order to embrace the spiritual. Accordingly, if the weight of carnal delights draws reason and intelligence downward, so that by not resisting, reason and intelligence consent to these motions, it is clear that a person so drawn downward and turned away from God is completely deprived of the enjoyment of the highest good, which is, intellectually, upward and eternal. But if reason rules the senses, it is still necessary that the intellect rule reason, so that above reason and by formed faith[50] the intellect may adhere to the mediator and thus through God the Father be drawn to glory.

218.     No one but Christ Jesus, who descended from heaven, ever had such power over oneself and one's own nature, from its origin so subject to the sins of carnal desire, that one could, of oneself, ascend beyond one's origin to eternal and celestial things, and it is Jesus who ascended by his own power, for in him human nature, born not of the will of the flesh but of God,[51] had nothing to obstruct it from returning, also powerfully, to God the Father.

In Christ, therefore, human nature by its union with the divine nature was exalted to the highest power and was delivered from the burden of temporal and oppressive desires. Christ the Lord willed to mortify completely and, in mortifying, to purge, by his own human body, all the iniquities of human nature that draw us to earthly things, not for his own sake, for he had committed no sin, but for ours so that all persons, of the same humanity with himself, might find in him complete purgation of their sins.[52] That willing and most innocent, that most shameful and most cruel death on the cross of the human Christ was the extinction, satisfaction, and purgation of all the carnal desires of human nature. Whatever humanly can be done that is contrary to the love of one's neighbor is abundantly filled in by the fullness of Christ's love, by which he gave himself up to death even for his enemies' sake.

219.   The humanity in Christ Jesus, therefore, filled in for all the deficiencies of all human beings. Because this humanity is maximum, it embraces the whole potentiality of the species and thus is such equality of being with each human being that it is united to each one much more closely than a sibling or very special friend. For the maximumness of Christ's human nature so works that in each person who adheres to him by formed faith Christ is this same person by a most perfect union with each one's individuality preserved. Through this union the saying of his is true: "Whatever you have done for one of the least of mine you have done for me."[53] And, conversely, whatever Christ Jesus merited in his passion those who are one with him also merited, but different degrees of merit are preserved, according to the different degree of each one's union with Christ through faith formed by love. Hence, in him the faithful are circumcised; in him they are baptized; in him they die; in him they are made alive again through the Resurrection;[54] and in him they are united to God and glorified.[55]

220.   Therefore, our justification does not come from ourselves but from Christ.[56] Because he is all fullness,[57] in him we obtain all things if we possess him. Because we attain to him in this life by formed faith, we can be justified only by faith,[58] which we will discuss more extensively below in another location.[59]

This is that ineffable mystery of the cross of our redemption, in which, beyond what has already been treated, Christ demonstrated that truth, justice, and the divine virtues must be preferred to temporal life, just as eternal things must be preferred to transitory things. And he also showed that in the most perfect human being the highest steadfastness, courage, love, and humility must reside, just as Christ's death on the cross made plain that these and all the other virtues were most greatly present in Jesus, the maximum. The higher, therefore, a person rises in these immortal virtues, the more like Christ one becomes. For minimum things coincide with maximum, as for example, maximum humiliation with exaltation;[60] the most shameful death of a virtuous human being with the most glorious life;[61] and so on. And all these are revealed to us in the life, passion, and crucifixion of Christ.

221.

*Chapter Seven*
*On the Mystery of the Resurrection*

Only if the mortal put on immortality[62] could Christ the human being, passible and mortal, attain to the glory of the Father, who, because he is absolute life, is immortality itself. And this could be done only through death. For how could the mortal put on immortality except by being divested of mortality? How could it be set free of mortality except by satisfying death's debt? Therefore, Truth itself declares that they are foolish and slow of heart who do not understand that Christ had to die and so enter into glory.[63]

But since we previously showed that Christ died a most cruel death for us,[64] we should now add that because it was not fitting for human nature to be led to immortality's triumph by any other way than through victory over death, Christ underwent death in order that human nature might rise again with him to everlasting life and that the animal and mortal body might become spiritual and incorruptible. He could not be a true human being unless he were mortal, and he could not bring mortal nature to immortality unless it were divested of mortality through death.

222.

Hear how eloquently Truth itself, speaking of this, instructs us when saying: "Unless a grain of wheat falls to the ground and dies, it remains alone, but if it dies, it bears much fruit."[65] If Christ, therefore, had always remained mortal, even if he had never died, how as a mortal human being would he have conferred immortality on human nature? And had he not died, he would have remained only a mortal without death. It was necessary, therefore, that through death he had to be freed from the possibility of dying, if he was to bear much fruit, so that lifted up he would draw all things to himself,[66] for his power would extend not only to a corruptible world and to a corruptible earth but also to an incorruptible heaven. But we in our ignorance will be able somewhat to attain this, if we recall the things we have often stated.

223.

We have already shown[67] that the maximum human being, Jesus, could not have in himself a person existing separately from the divinity for he is the maximum. And, for this reason, a communication of properties[68] is allowed, so that the human things coincide with the divine, for Jesus' humanity cannot have separate personal existence; rather, because of their supreme union, his humanity is inseparable from his divinity, as if his humanity were put on and assumed by his divinity. But a human being is a unity of body and soul, and their separation is death. Since, therefore, the maximum humanity is supposited in the divine person, it was not possible for either the soul or the body to have been separated from the divine person at the time of his death, even after the spatial separation of body and soul; for without the divine person the human being Jesus did not exist.

**224.** Christ, therefore, did not die as if his person had defected, but he remained hypostatically united with the divinity, without even a spatial separation with respect to the center in which his humanity was supposited. And in accord with the lower nature, which could suffer a separation of the soul from the body in conformity with the truth of its own nature, a separation occurred temporally and spatially so that at the hour of death soul and body were not present together at the same place and time. Corruptibility, therefore, was not possible in his body and soul, for they were united with eternity. But the temporal birth was subject to death and temporal separation, and thus when the circle of return from temporal composition to dissolution was completed and when, in addition, the body was freed from these temporal motions, the truth of the humanity that is above time and that, as united with the divinity, remained uncorrupted united, as its truth required, the truth of the body with the truth of the soul. When, therefore, the shadowy image of the truth of the human who appeared in time had departed, the true human arose, freed from all temporal suffering. By means of a union of soul with body, which union is above all temporal motion, the same Jesus most truly arose above all temporal motions, never to die again. Without this union the truth of the incorruptible humanity would not have been hypostatically united, most truly and without confusion, with the nature of the divine person.

**225.** Let Christ's example of the grain of wheat[69] assist the meagerness of your intellectual capability and your ignorance. The single grain is destroyed while the specific essence remains whole; by this means nature raises up many grains. If the grain were maximum and most perfect, after having died in a most excellent and most fertile soil, it could bring forth fruit not only a hundredfold or even a thousandfold but as much as the nature of that species embraced in its possibility. This is what Truth declares when stating that the single grain would bring forth much fruit; for a multitude is a limitation but without number.

Therefore, understand this keenly: As Jesus' humanity is considered to be contracted to the human being Christ, so also it is likewise understood to be united with his divinity. As united with the divinity, his humanity is most absolute; but as it is considered to be that true human Christ, his humanity is contracted, so that through the humanity he is a human being. And thus Jesus' humanity is like a middle point between the purely absolute and the purely contracted. It was corruptible, therefore, only in a certain respect, but absolutely it was incorruptible. It was corruptible, therefore, according to temporality, to which it was contracted, and incorruptible according to the fact that it was free from time and above time and united with the divinity.

226.     But truth as contracted temporally is as if a sign and image of supratemporal truth. Thus, the body's temporally contracted truth is as if a shadow of the body's supratemporal truth, and the soul's contracted truth is like a shadow of the soul that is freed from time. For while the soul is in time, where it does not apprehend without mental pictures, it appears to be like the senses or reason rather than the intellect, and when it is elevated above time it is the intellect, which is free and independent of pictures. And because the humanity was, from on high, inseparably rooted in the divine incorruptibility, then, upon the completion of the temporal and corruptible motion, the dissolution could occur only in the direction of the root of its incorruptibility. Therefore, after the end of temporal motion, which end was death, when all these things were removed that temporally fell to the truth of human nature, the same Jesus arose, not with a body that was oppressive, corruptible, shadowy, passible, and of such other qualities that follow from temporal composition, but with a true, glorious, impassible, agile, and immortal body, as the truth that was free from temporal conditions required.

The truth of the hypostatic union of the human and divine nature necessarily demanded this union. For this reason, blessed Jesus had to rise from the dead, as he himself said: "Christ must so suffer and on the third day rise from the dead."[70]

227.

*Chapter Eight*
*Christ, as the First Fruits of Those Who Are Asleep,*
*Ascended into Heaven*

From what has been shown it is easy to see that Christ is the first-born from the dead.[71] For prior to him no one was able to rise from the dead, because human nature had not yet in time attained the maximum and was not yet united, as it was in Christ, with incorruptibility and immortality. All were powerless until he should come who said: "I have the power to lay down my life and to take it up again."[72] Therefore, in Christ, who is also the firstfruits of those who are asleep,[73] human nature put on immortality.

There is, however, only one indivisible humanity and essence of species of all humans, and through it all individuals are numerically distinct beings. Consequently, there is the same humanity in Christ and all human beings, yet the numerical distinction of individuals remains unconfused. Hence, it is clear that the humanity of all human beings, who temporally, either before or after Christ, existed or will exist, has in Christ put on immortality.[74] The conclusion is evident: Because Christ the human arose, all human beings will rise through him after all motion of temporal corruptibility will have ceased, so that they will be forever incorruptible.

**228.** Although there is one humanity of all human beings, there are, however, various and diverse individuating principles that contract it to this or that person.[75] Therefore, in Jesus Christ these principles were only the most perfect and most powerful and the nearest to the essence of the humanity that was united with the divinity. And through this divinity's power, Christ was able to rise by his own power, which came to him from the divinity, and, for this reason, God is said to have raised him from the dead. Because he was God and human he arose by his own power, and apart from him no one can arise as Christ, except in the power of Christ, who is also God.

It is Christ, therefore, through whom, in accordance with the nature of his humanity, our human nature has contracted immortality. And it is through him also, when motion will have ceased, that we, born completely subservient to motion, will rise above time into his likeness;[76] this will be at the end of time. Christ was born temporally, but only as he came forth from a mother, yet with respect to his Resurrection he did not wait for the complete expiration of time. For time did not fully apprehend his birth. Keep in mind that human nature has put on immortality in Christ. Consequently, we will all rise, the good as well as the bad, but we will not all be changed by the glory that transforms us into adopted children through Christ the Son of God. All, therefore, will rise through Christ, but not all will rise as Christ and in him through union, but only those who are Christ's by faith, hope, and love.

229.     Unless I am not mistaken, you see that there is no perfect religion, leading to the final and most desired end of peace, that does not embrace Christ as mediator and savior, God and human, the way, the truth, and the life.[77] Indeed, how incongruous is the belief of the Saracens, who maintain that Christ is the maximum and most perfect human, born of a virgin and conveyed alive into heaven, but deny that he is God.[78] Surely they have been blinded, for they assert the impossible. But even from what was previously discussed it ought to be clearer than light to anyone having understanding that no human being can be in all respects most perfect and maximum, supernaturally born of a virgin, unless that human were also God. The Saracens, who are ignorant of the mysteries of Christ, are, without reason, persecutors of the cross of Christ. They will not taste the divine fruit of his redemption, nor do they expect it on the basis of their law of Mohammed, which promises only to satisfy their desires for pleasure.[79] Hoping that by Christ's death these desires become extinguished in us, we long to possess an incorruptible glory.

230.     The Jews along with the Saracens also confess that the Messiah is the maximum, most perfect, and immortal human, but impeded by the same diabolical blindness, they deny that the Messiah is God.[80] They also do not hope, as we servants of Christ do, for the supreme happiness of the enjoyment of God, nor will they obtain it. And what to me is even more astonishing, both the Jews and the Saracens believe that there will be a general resurrection but do not acknowledge its possibility through the human being who is also God.[81] Indeed, one might say that if the motion of generation and corruption ceases, there can be no perfection of the universe apart from resurrection, for human nature, which is intermediate, is one essential part of the universe; and without human nature the universe would be neither perfect nor even a universe. One might also say that, consequently, it is necessary that if motion ever ceases, either the whole universe will perish or human beings will rise to incorruptibility. In human beings the nature of all intermediate things is complete, so that a resurrection of the other animals would not be necessary, since the human is their perfection. Or one might say that there will be resurrection in order that the whole human being will receive retribution from a just God according to one's merits. Nevertheless, even though all these might be said, it is still necessary, above all, to believe that Christ is God and human; through Christ alone human nature can attain to incorruptibility.

190

**231.**         Therefore, all who believe in resurrection and deny that Christ is the means of its possibility have been blinded, for faith in resurrection is the affirmation of the divinity and humanity of Christ and of the death and resurrection of the one who is the first-born from the dead,[82] as was previously stated. He arose in order that by ascension into heaven he might enter into glory.[83] This ascension, in my judgment, must be understood as having occurred above all motion of corruptibility and above all influence of the heavens.[84] Although in keeping with his divinity Christ is everywhere, nevertheless, his place is more properly said to be where there is never any change, suffering, sadness, or the other things that fall to temporality. And we must speak of this place of eternal joy and peace as above the heavens, although with reference to place it is not apprehensible, describable, or definable.

**232.**         Christ is the center and circumference of intellectual nature,[85] and because the intellect embraces all things, he is above all things. Yet in holy, rational souls and in intellectual spirits, which are the heavens declaring his glory,[86] he resides as if in his own temple. Therefore, we understand Christ to have ascended, above all place and all time, to an incorruptible mansion,[87] beyond everything that can be spoken, for he ascended far above all the heavens so that he might fill all things. Because he is God, he is all in all;[88] because he is truth itself, he reigns in the intellectual heavens; and because as the life of all rational spirits he is their center, he is not, according to place, situated along the circumference but is seated at the center. And, consequently, this one who is to souls both the fountain of life[89] and their end affirms that this kingdom of heaven is also within human beings.[90]

**233.**

### Chapter Nine
*Christ Is the Judge of the Living and the Dead*

Who is a more just judge than the one who is also justice itself? For Christ, the head and genesis of every rational creature, is maximum reason itself, from which all reason originates. Moreover, it is reason that exercises a discriminating judgment. Therefore, Christ is rightly the judge of the living and the dead; he assumed rational human nature with all rational creatures, although he remained God, who is the rewarder of all. He judges all things, above all time, through himself and in himself, for he embraces all creatures, because he is the maximum human being in whom, since he is God, are all things. As God, he is infinite light in which there is no darkness.[91] This light illumines all things, so that in the light all things are most visible to the light. For this infinite, intellectual light enfolds, above all time, the past as well as the present, and the living as well as the dead, just as corporeal light is the hypostasis of all colors. But Christ is like the purest fire, which is inseparable from light and exists not in itself but in light. Christ is that spiritual fire of life and understanding that consumes[92] all things and takes all things into itself and so proves and judges all things, as the judgment of material fire, which tests all things.

234.     All rational spirits are judged in Christ, just as everything inflammable is judged in fire.[93] And of these, one such thing, if held continuously in the fire, is transformed into the likeness of fire, like the best and most perfect gold that is to such an extent gold and so intensely heated that it appears to be as much fire as gold. But others, such as refined silver, bronze, or iron, do not participate the intensity of the fire to so great a degree. Yet they all seem to be transformed into fire, although each in its own degree. And this is the judgment of the fire alone, and not that of the things that are inflamed, for each inflamed thing apprehends in each other thing only that very intense fire and not the differences between them. For example, if we were to observe gold, silver, and copper fused in a maximum fire, we would not apprehend the differences between the metals after their transformation into the form of fire. But if fire itself were intellectual, it would know the degrees of each metal's perfection and to what extent, in accord with these degrees, the fire's capacity of intensity would exist differently in each thing.

235.     Some inflammable materials that persevere incorruptibly in fire are capable of light and heat and because of their purity are transformable into the likeness of fire, but differently, in greater and lesser degrees. However, certain other materials, because of their impurity, are not transformable into light even though they can be heated. So according to one most simple and undivided judgment Christ, the judge, in a most just and unenvying way, communicates created reason's heat to all in a single moment, as if in the order of nature, but not of time. And he does so in order to impart by the heat that is received a divine, intellectual light from above. God, therefore, is all things in all things,[94] and all are in God through this Mediator. And all are equal to God insofar as this is possible according to each's

capability. But some things, because they are more unified and pure, can receive both heat and light, others can scarcely receive heat, but no light, according to the recipient's indisposition.

**236.** Because the infinite light is eternity itself and truth itself, a rational creature who desires to be illumined by that light must turn toward true and eternal things, above these worldly and corruptible things. Corporeal things and spiritual things behave in contrary ways. Vegetative power is corporeal and converts the nourishment that is received from without into the nature of that which is nourished; an animal is not changed into bread, but bread into an animal. However, when an intellectual spirit, whose operation is above time and, as if on eternity's horizon, turns toward eternal things, it cannot convert them into itself, because they are eternal and incorruptible. But because it itself is incorruptible, it is not converted into them so that it ceases to be an intellectual substance; rather, it is converted into them in such a way that it is absorbed into a likeness of eternal things. However, this occurs in degrees, so that the more fervently an intellectual spirit is turned toward eternal things the more thoroughly it is perfected by them and the more profoundly its being is hidden in the eternal being itself. Moreover, since Christ is immortal,[95] and, further, both lives and is the truth and the life,[96] whoever turns to Christ turns to truth and life. The more ardently one does this, the higher one is raised from worldly and corruptible things to eternal things, so that one's life is hidden in Christ.[97] The virtues are eternal; righteousness endures forever,[98] and so also does truth.

**237.** Whoever turns to the virtues walks in the ways of Christ, which are the ways of purity and immortality. Virtues are divine illuminations. Therefore, whoever in this life turns by faith to Christ, who is virtue, will then be found in purity of spirit when this person is set free from this temporal life, so that one is able to enter into the joy of eternal possession.

When according to all its intellectual powers our spirit turns by faith to the purest and eternal truth, to which it subordinates all else, and when it chooses and loves this truth as alone worthy of being loved, then, indeed, there is a turning of our spirit. For to turn by most sure faith to the truth that is Christ is to renounce the world and to tread on it victoriously. But to love Christ most ardently is to hasten toward him by spiritual movement, for he is not only lovable but is love itself. When by the steps of love the spirit hastens to love itself, it is engulfed in love itself not temporally but above all time and all worldly movement.

238.     Therefore, as everyone who loves is in love, so all who love the truth are in Christ. And as every lover loves through love, so all who love the truth love it through Christ. Therefore, they do not know the truth unless the Spirit of Christ is in them. And as it is impossible to be a lover without love, so it is impossible for anyone to have God without the Spirit of Christ, for only in Christ's Spirit are we able to worship God.[99] Consequently, unbelievers, who are not turned toward Christ and are incapable of the light of transforming glory, have already been condemned to darkness and to the shadow of death, because they have turned away from the life that is Christ. Through union with Christ all in glory are filled with his fullness alone. Proceeding from this same foundation I will, for our encouragement, have more to say below about this union when discussing the church.[100]

239.

*Chapter Ten*
*On the Judge's Sentence*

It is clear that no mortal comprehends the judgment and the sentence of this judge. For since it is above all time and motion, it is not set forth in the course of a comparative or presumptive inquiry, or by vocal adducing or within such conditions as involve delay or protraction. But just as in the Word all things were created — for "[the Lord] spoke and they were made"[101] — so in the same Word, which is also called Reason, all are judged. Nor is there any interval separating the sentence and its execution. But this happens in an instant, namely, not even an indivisible moment of time divides the resurrection and the assigning to different ends, whether glorification with the translation of the children of God or damnation with the exclusion of the unconverted.

240.     The intellectual nature is above time and not subject to temporal corruption. From its nature it enfolds within itself incorruptible forms, such as mathematical forms, which in their own way are abstract, and also natural forms, which lie hidden in the intellectual nature and are readily transformed into abstractions. These forms are directive signs to us of intellectual nature's incorruptibility. For the intellectual nature is the incorruptible place of incorruptible forms. By its natural movement this nature is moved toward the most abstract

truth, as if toward the end of its own desires and toward its final and most enjoyable object. And since such an object is all things, because it is God, the intellect, which is insatiable until which time it attains God, is immortal and incorruptible, for it is satisfied only with an eternal object.

241.    But if the intellect, when it is freed from the body, in which it is subject to temporal thoughts, does not reach the desired end but instead falls into ignorance when it should be seeking the truth and when it should be desiring with its deepest yearning only to apprehend the truth, not in an enigma or in signs but with certitude and face to face,[102] then, since at the hour of its separation it is turned away from the truth and toward the corruptible, it falls away toward a corruptible object of desire, toward uncertainty and confusion, and into the dark chaos of pure possibility,[103] where nothing is actually certain. And when this is so, the intellect is justly said to have descended to intellectual death. For the intellectual soul, to understand is to be and to understand the object of its desire is to live. Accordingly, just as for the intellectual soul eternal life, at the end, is to grasp the steadfast eternal object of its desire, so for it, eternal death is to be separated from this steadfast object of desire and to be flung headlong into the chaos of confusion, where the intellectual soul in its own manner is forever tormented by fire.[104] The manner of its torment is not understandable to us otherwise than as that of one who has been deprived not only of vital nourishment and health but also of any hope of ever attaining them, so that, without extinction and without end, this one is forever dying in agony.

242.    Such a life is miserable beyond anything that can be thought. It is such a life that it is death; it is such an existence that it is a nonexistence; and it is such an understanding that is the absence of knowledge. We already proved[105] that the resurrection of humankind takes place above all motion, time, quantity, and all else that is subject to time, so that the corruptible is resolved into the incorruptible and the animal into the spiritual.[106] Thus, in resurrection the whole human being is one's intellect, which is spirit, and the true body is absorbed in one's spirit. The body, therefore, does not exist in itself, as if in its corporeal, quantitative, and temporal proportions, but exists as translated into the spirit. This is in direct contrast to the manner in which our body exists here in this life, where only the body and not the intellect is seen and where the intellect seems imprisoned in the body. But there, in resurrection, the body exists in the spirit, just as

here the spirit exists in the body; and just as here the soul is weighed down by the body, so there the body is lightened by the spirit. Therefore, just as the spiritual joys of the intellectual life are greatest, and they are participated by the body, which is glorified in the spirit, so the hellish sorrows of spiritual death are greatest, and they are experienced also by the body, which is in the spirit. And because our God, who is apprehended as eternal life, is comprehensible above all understanding, these eternal joys, exceeding all our understanding, are greater than any sign can convey.

**243.** In the same way, the punishments of the damned are also beyond every thinkable and describable punishment. All the musical and harmonic signs of joy, happiness, and glory, as signs calling to mind what is known to us, which are found to be indicators of eternal life that have been handed down to us by the Fathers, are only very distant sensible signs, infinitely removed from intellectual things which no imagining can capture. So, too, the punishments of hell, which are likened to sulfurous fire and pitch and to other sensible torments,[107] bear no comparison to those fiery intellectual sufferings from which Jesus Christ, our life and salvation, who is blessed forever,[108] deigns to save us. Amen.

**244.**

### Chapter Eleven
### Mysteries of Faith

Our predecessors all agree that faith is the beginning of understanding. Indeed, all disciplines presuppose certain things as first principles, which are grasped by faith alone and from which is obtained an understanding of the things to be treated. For everyone willing to rise to learning must believe those things without which no ascent is possible. As Isaiah says: "Unless you believe, you will not understand."[109] Faith, therefore, enfolds in itself everything understandable, but understanding is the unfolding of faith. Understanding, therefore, is directed by faith, and faith is extended by understanding. Where there is no sound faith, there is no true understanding. It is obvious to what kind of conclusion erroneous principles and a weak foundation lead. But there is no faith more perfect than truth itself, which is Jesus.

Who does not understand that the most excellent gift of God is a right faith? The apostle John says that faith in the incarnation of the Word of God leads us to truth in order that we may become children of God.[110] In the prologue he presents this simply; next, in accordance with this faith, he narrates the many works of Christ in order to enlighten the intellect in faith; and finally he concludes with the statement: "These things have been written that you may believe that Jesus is the Son of God."[111]

**245.** But the soundest faith in Christ, made firm and constant in simplicity, can, in stages of ascent, be extended and unfolded in accordance with the given teaching of ignorance. The greatest and profoundest mysteries of God, although hidden to the wise, are revealed by faith in Jesus to the little ones and the humble walking in the world.[112] For Jesus is the one in whom all the treasures of wisdom and knowledge are hidden,[113] and apart from him no one can do anything. For, indeed, he is the Word and the Power by which God, alone most high, having power over all things in heaven and on earth, also created the ages. Since God is not knowable in this world, where reason, opinion, and teaching lead us, by means of symbols, from the better known to the unknown, God is grasped only where persuadings leave off and faith enters in. Through faith we are rapt in simplicity so that, while in a body incorporeally, because in spirit, and in the world not in a worldly manner but celestially, we may incomprehensibly contemplate Christ above all reason and intelligence, in the third heaven[114] of the simplest intellectuality. Therefore, we also see that because of the immensity of his excellence he cannot be comprehended. And this is that learned ignorance by which the very blessed Paul, as he ascended, saw that, when he was being lifted higher up to Christ, he was then ignorant of Christ, whom at one time he had known only.[115]

**246.** We who have faith in Christ, therefore, are led in learned ignorance to the mountain that is Christ and that we are forbidden to touch with the nature of our animality.[116] And when we endeavor to look on this mountain with the intellectual eye, we fall into a darkness, and we know that within that very darkness is the mountain on which only all the living who have intellect may dwell. If we approach it with a greater constancy of faith, we will be snatched away from the eyes of those who live by the senses, so that with inward hearing we will perceive the sounds and thunderings and terrible signs of his majesty. And so we will readily perceive that the one alone is Lord whom all things obey, and so step by step we will come upon certain of the Lord's imperishable footprints, as if certain most divine markings. And, there, hearing in the sacred instruments and in the signs of the prophets and of the saints the voice not of mortal creatures but of God, we behold God more clearly, as if through a more transparent cloud.

**247.** Next, the believers, continuously ascending in more ardent desire, are taken up into simple intellectuality,[117] and leaping beyond all sensible things, they pass as if from sleep to wakefulness, from hearing to sight. And, there, those things that are seen cannot be revealed because they are beyond all hearing and beyond all instruction by voice. For if what are revealed there should be told, then the unsayable would be said and the unhearable would be heard, just as there the invisible is seen. For there, incomprehensibly heard, as the end of all speech, is Jesus, blessed forever, the end of all understanding, because he is truth, and the end of all sense, because he is life, and the end, finally, of all being, because he is being itself, and the perfection of every creature, because he is God and human. All speech has come forth from him and ends in him, for all that is true in speech is from him. For all speech is for instruction, and therefore its end is the one who is wisdom itself. "All that was written was written for our instruction."[118] Spoken words are fashioned into written characters. "By the Word of the Lord the heavens were formed."[119] All created things, therefore, are signs of the Word of God. All corporeal speech is a sign of a mental word; the cause of every corruptible mental word is an incorruptible word, which is its underlying principle. Christ himself is the incarnate principle of all principles, for "the Word was made flesh."[120] Jesus therefore is the end of all things.

**248.** Such things are shown in stages to one who ascends to Christ by faith. The divine efficacy of this faith is inexplicable. For if the faith is great, it unites the believer with Jesus so that the believer rises above all that is not in union with Jesus himself. If one's faith is whole, in the power of Jesus with whom the believer is united, one possesses a power over nature and motion and commands even the evil spirits. And it is not the believer but Jesus who, in and through the believer, works marvelous things, as the deeds of the saints testify.

Perfect faith in Christ must be, as far as can be realized, most pure, maximum, and formed by love. For it does not allow anything whatever to be mixed with it because it is faith in the power of purest truth toward all things. In what we have already discussed one very often finds repeated that the minimum coincides with the maximum. This is also true for the faith that is simply maximum in being and in power. This cannot exist in a wayfarer who at the same time is not also possessor of the journey's end, as Jesus was. But the wayfarer must be willing actually to have, for oneself, maximum faith in Christ to an extent that one's faith is elevated to such a level of undoubtable certainty that it is also faith in the least way but the highest certainty free from all doubt in every point.

**249.** This is a powerful faith that is so greatly maximum that it is also minimum so that it embraces everything that can be believed in relation to the one who is truth. Although one person's faith does not attain the degree of another's, because equality is impossible, just as a visible object cannot be seen equally the same by many, yet each one, so far as possible, must actually believe maximally. And, then, even if by comparison with others one would obtain faith scarcely the size of a mustard seed, still one's faith would be of such immense power that even the mountains would be found to obey.[121] For one would command by the power of the Word of God, with whom, as far as possible, one would be maximally united by faith and whom nothing could resist.

**250.** See how great the power of your intellectual spirit is in the power of Christ, if it adheres to him above all else so that it is enlivened through him and, as it were, through union supposited in him as in its own life, although the individuality of your intellectual spirit is preserved. But because this takes place only through the conversion of the intellect, which the senses obey, to Christ by maximum faith, this faith must be formed by uniting love. Without love faith cannot be maximum. If every one who lives loves to live and every one who understands loves to understand, how can we believe Jesus to be immortal life and infinite truth if he is not loved in the highest measure? For life in and of itself is lovable, and if Jesus is most greatly believed to be eternal life, it is impossible not to love him. Without love faith is not living but dead and not faith at all. But love is the form of faith giving it true being; indeed, love is the sign of the most steadfast faith. If, therefore, all things are put aside for the sake of Christ and if in comparison with him body and soul are regarded as nothing, this is the sign of maximum faith.

**251.** Nor can faith be great without the sacred hope of enjoying Jesus. For how would anyone have a certain faith unless one hoped for the things promised one by Christ? If one does not believe that one will possess the eternal life that Christ promised to the faithful, in what way does one believe in Christ? Or rather, how does one believe that Christ is the truth if one does not have undoubting hope in his promises? How would one elect death for Christ's sake if one did not hope for immortality? And since one believes that Christ does not abandon those who hope in him but instead grants them eternal happiness, the believer, therefore, considers it a little thing to suffer all for Christ's sake, because of so great a reward of recompense.[122]

252.     Great, indeed, is the power of faith that makes a person Christ-like so that one forsakes sensible things, strips oneself of the contaminations of the flesh, walks reverently in the ways of God, follows joyously in the footsteps of Christ, and willingly takes up a cross in exaltation.[123] One, therefore, is in the flesh as a spirit for whom, because of Christ, this world is death, and for whom removal from the world in order to be with Christ is life. Who do you suppose is this spirit in whom Christ dwells by faith? Of what kind is this wonderful gift of God that we, who on this pilgrimage are constituted of frail flesh, can by the power of faith be elevated through union to such power over all things that are not Christ? Note well that as one's flesh is successively and gradually mortified by faith one ascends by steps to union with Christ, so that one is absorbed into him by a profound union, so far as it is possible on this path. Leaping beyond all the things that are visible and worldly, one reaches the complete perfection of one's nature.

253.     This is the perfect nature that, after flesh and sin have been mortified, we who have been transformed into Christ's image will be able to obtain in him.[124] But this is not that illusory nature of the magicians who claim that through certain practices one may ascend by faith to a nature of influential spirits that are similar in nature to oneself, so that by the power of such spirits, with which the magicians are united by faith, they work many singular wonders in fire or in water or by the knowledge of harmonies, visible transformations, the unveiling of hidden things, and so on. It is clear that in all these there is a deception and a departure from life and from truth. Such persons are so bound to alliances and pacts of unity with evil spirits that what they believe by faith they exhibit by deed in incense offerings and in acts of worship owed only to God. But they devote them to these spirits with great deference and veneration as if these were capable of granting their requests and were able to be summoned forth by such means. United thus with a spirit to whom they will also adhere in eternal separation from Christ in torment, sometimes by faith they obtain these transitory requests.

Blessed be God who through God's own Son has redeemed us

from the darkness of such ignorance, so that we may know that all things are false and deceptive that are somehow brought about by any other mediator than Christ, who is the truth, and by any other faith than that in Jesus. For there is only one Lord, Jesus,[125] who has power over all things, who fills us with every blessing, and who alone fills all our deficiencies to overflowing.

254.

*Chapter Twelve*
*On the Church*

Even if an understanding of Christ's church can be had from what has already been stated, nevertheless, I will add a brief word so that this work may not omit anything.

Since faith, by necessity, exists in different individuals in unequal degree and thus receives a greater and lesser, no one can attain maximum faith,[126] than which there cannot be a greater power, nor likewise can anyone attain maximum love.[127] For if maximum faith, which could not be a greater power, were to exist in a wayfarer, this would also have to be one who is possessor of the journey's end.[128] For as the maximum in any one genus is the highest limit of that genus, so it is the beginning of a higher genus. Therefore, simply maximum faith can exist in no one who is not also in possession of one's goal. So too simply maximum love cannot exist in a lover who is not at the same time the beloved. Consequently, neither simply maximum faith nor simply maximum love belongs to anyone other than Jesus Christ, who is both wayfarer and possessor, loving human and beloved God. But within the maximum all things are included, since it embraces all things. Hence, in the faith of Jesus Christ all true faith is included and in Christ's love all true love is included, although there are always distinctions of degrees.[129]

255.

Because these distinct degrees lie below the maximum and above the minimum, no one, even if, as far as possible, one actually has maximum faith in Christ, can attain that maximum faith in Christ by which one would comprehend Christ as God and human being. Nor can anyone love Christ so much that he cannot be loved even more, for Christ is love and charity[130] and therefore infinitely lovable. Consequently, no one in this life or the next can so love Christ that one would therefore be Christ and human. All who are united with Christ, with differences of degree remaining, either by faith and love in this life or by attainment and enjoyment in the next, are united in such a way that they could not be more greatly united and their differences of degree remain. Therefore, no one exists in oneself apart from that union nor because of the union loses one's own degree.

256.     This union, therefore, is a church or congregation of the many in the one, just as many members are in one body, and each in one's own rank. Here one member is not another, but each is in the one body, and by the body's mediation each member is united with each other. And here no member can have life and existence apart from the body, although in the body one member is all members only by the body's mediation.[131] Therefore, while we journey here on earth, the truth of our faith can exist only in Christ's spirit, with the order of believers remaining, so that in the one Jesus there is diversity in concordance. And when we are set free from this church militant at the resurrection, we will be able to arise only in Christ, so that thus there will also be one church of the triumphant, with each member existing in one's own order. And at that moment the truth of our flesh will exist not in itself but in the truth of the flesh of Christ, and the truth of our body in the truth of the body of Christ and the truth of our spirit in the truth of the spirit of Christ Jesus, just as branches exist in the vine.[132] Therefore, Christ's one humanity will exist in all human beings, and Christ's one spirit will be in all spirits, so that each member will be present in Christ in such a way that there is but one Christ from all the members. Thus, in this life whoever receives one from all those who are Christ's receives Christ, and what is done to one of the least is done to Christ.[133] For example, whoever injures Plato's hand injures Plato and whoever wounds the smallest toe wounds the whole human being. And in heaven whoever rejoices over the least rejoices over Christ and sees Jesus in each one and through him the blessed God. Thus, by God's Son our God will be all things in all things[134] and in and through the Son each member will be with God and with all things, so that joy may be full with no envy and deficiency.

257.     And since, while we journey here, because faith can be continually increased in us, so also can love. Although each can actually be in such a degree of faith and love that of oneself, as one then is, one cannot actually be in a greater degree; yet when one is in one degree, one has the potentiality for another, although such a progression, through a common basis, cannot be made ad infinitum.[135] Hence, we ought so to work that our possibility may be made actual by the grace of our Lord Jesus Christ, so that we may thus move from virtue to

virtue and from degree to degree by means of the one who is faith and love. In and of ourselves we can do nothing without Christ,[136] but all that we can do we can do in the one who alone fills our deficiencies,[137] so that on the day of resurrection we may be found to be an integral and noble member of Christ. And, without doubt, in believing and loving with all our strength we can by diligent prayer obtain this grace of increased faith and love and draw near Christ's throne with confidence,[138] for Christ is most merciful and allows no one to be defrauded by one's holy desire.

**258.** If in your mind you will meditate on these profound things, and indeed they are profound, a wonderful sweetness of spirit will engulf you. For by an inner savor you will detect, as with the most fragrant incense, the inexpressible goodness of God, which God, handing on, will serve to you[139] and with which you will be filled when God's glory will appear. You will be filled, I say, without surfeit, for this immortal food is life itself. And just as the desire to live ever increases, so the food of life is ever consumed without being changed into the nature of the one who consumes it. For otherwise it would be a disgusting food, which would burden and would be unable to bestow immortal life, for it would be deficient in itself and would be changed into the one who is nourished. But our intellectual desire is to live intellectually, which is to enter more and more into life and joy. And because that life is infinite, the blessed, in their desire, are brought more and more into it. Therefore, they are filled, as if ones filled with thirst who drink from the fountain of life.[140] And because this drinking never passes away into the past, for it is eternal, the blessed are forever drinking and are forever filled, but never have they drunk or been filled.

**259.** Blessed be God who has given us an intellect that cannot be filled within time. Because the intellect's desire does not attain its end, the intellect perceives itself, from its temporally insatiable desire, as above incorruptible time and immortal, and it knows that it can be satisfied by the desired intellectual life only in the enjoyment of the best and maximum and unfailing good. The enjoyment never passes over into the past, for the appetite does not decrease in the enjoyment. To use an illustration from the body, it is as if someone who was hungry were seated at the table of a great king where one was served the food that one longed for, so that one did not desire any other nourishment. The nature of this food would be of such kind that while filling it would also sharpen one's appetite. If such food never gave out, clearly, the individual always consuming it would always be filled, would always desire this same food, and would always eagerly be brought to it. Therefore, one would always be able to eat this food that possesses such power that after having eaten one would continue to be led to the same food with ardent desiring.[141] This, therefore, is the capability of the intellectual nature, that in receiving life into itself it is turned into life according to its turnable nature, just as the air, in receiving into itself the sun's ray, is turned into light. Therefore, since the intellect has a nature that is turnable toward the intelligible, it understands only universal, incorruptible, and enduring things,[142] for incorruptible truth is the intellect's object, and to this the intellect is intellectually brought. Indeed, it apprehends this truth, with quiet peace, in eternity in Christ Jesus.

**260.** This is the church of the triumphant in which is our God, who is forever blessed.[143] And here, in highest union, the true human Christ Jesus is united with the Son of God in so great a union that the humanity exists only in the divinity,[144] and it exists in the divinity through an ineffable hypostatic union in such a way that it cannot be more highly and more simply united, while the truth of the nature of the humanity remains intact.[145] Further, if in this life every rational nature turns to Christ in highest faith, hope, and love,[146] it is united, while the personal truth of each nature remains, with Christ the Lord in such a way that all angels as well as human beings exist only in Christ, and through Christ they exist in God, with the truth of the body of each having been absorbed and attracted through the spirit.[147] Consequently, each of the blessed, while the truth of each's being is preserved, exists in Christ Jesus as Christ and through him in God as God, and God, remaining the absolute maximum, exists in Christ Jesus as Jesus and through him in all things as all things.

**261.** In no other way can the church be more one. For "church" designates a unity of many, with the personal truth of each member preserved without confusion of natures or degrees. The more the church is one, the greater it is. Therefore, this church, the church of the eternally triumphant, is maximum because no greater union of the church is possible. Therefore, contemplate how great this union is where there is found the divine, absolute maximum union; the union of the divinity and the humanity in Jesus; and the union of the church of the triumphant, the union of Jesus' divinity with the blessed. The absolute union is not greater or lesser than the union of the natures in Jesus or of the blessed in heaven. For this is the maximum union that is both the union of all unions and also that which is total union, not taking a greater or lesser but proceeding from unity and equality, as was shown in Book One.[148] Nor is the union of natures in Christ greater or lesser than the unity of the church of the triumphant. For as it is the maximum union of natures, it, therefore, does not receive a greater or lesser.

262.　　　　Hence, all the different things that are united obtain their unity from this maximum union of the natures of Christ, and through this union the church's union is what it is. Indeed, the union of the church is the maximum ecclesiastical union. Therefore, because it is maximum, it coincides on high with the hypostatic union of the natures in Christ. And this union of the natures in Jesus, because it is maximum, coincides with the absolute union, which is God. And the union of the church, which is a union of individual subjects, is also coincident with that absolute union, although the ecclesiastical union does not seem to be one to such an extent as is the hypostatic union, which is a union of natures only, or as the first and most simple divine union, in which there can be no otherness or diversity; nevertheless, through Jesus the union of the church is resolved into the divine union, from which it also has its beginning. And, indeed, this is clearly seen if we give attention to what was often stated above.[149] For the absolute union is the Holy Spirit. The maximum hypostatic union coincides with the absolute union. So, necessarily, the union of natures in Christ exists by and in the absolute union, which is the Holy Spirit. But the ecclesiastical union coincides with the hypostatic, as was shown. Therefore, the union of the triumphant is in Jesus' spirit, which is in the Holy Spirit. So Truth itself declares in John: "The glory that you gave me I have given them that they may be one, as we are one, I in them, and you in me, that they may be made perfect in one,"[150] so that the church may be so perfect in eternal rest that it could not be more perfect and may dwell in such an inexpressible transformation of the light of glory that in all only God appears.[151] To this glory we triumphantly aspire with great affection and beseech God the Father, with suppliant hearts, that by God's Son, our Lord Jesus Christ, and in him by the Holy Spirit, God would, out of God's immense mercifulness, grant us this glory in order that we may eternally enjoy God who is blessed forever.[152]

263.

*Letter of the Author
to Lord Cardinal Julian*[153]

Accept now, Reverend Father, what for so long I desired to attain by different paths of learning but previously could not until returning by sea from Greece[154] when by what I believe was a celestial gift from the Father of Lights,[155] from whom comes every perfect gift, I was led to embrace incomprehensibles incomprehensibly[156] in learned ignorance, by transcending those incorruptible truths that can be humanly known.[157] This learned ignorance I have, in the one who is the truth, now set loose in these books, which on the basis of this same principle can be compressed or expanded.

**264.**     These profound matters should be the subject of all the effort of our human intelligence, so that it may raise itself to that simplicity where contradictories coincide. The concept of the First Book concentrates on this topic, and from this the Second Book makes a few inferences about the universe, which many will find unusual for they go beyond the common pathway of philosophers. And proceeding always from the same foundation, I have now, at last, completed the Third Book on the supremely blessed Jesus. And by an increase of faith the Lord Jesus has become continually magnified in my understanding and love. For no one who has faith in Christ can deny that on this life's journey one would wish to be more highly inflamed with desire, so that after long meditations and ascensions one would see most sweet Jesus as alone to be loved and, forsaking all else, would joyously embrace him as one's own true life and everlasting joy. All things work well for one who so enters into Jesus, and neither any writings nor this world can present one with difficulty, for such a one is transformed into Jesus because of the Spirit of Christ that dwells in one,[158] and Christ is the end of intellectual desires. May you, most devout Father, pray to Christ earnestly and continually for me, a most wretched sinner, that we both may deserve to enjoy him forever.

COMPLETED AT KUES ON FEBRUARY 12, 1440.

# Dialogue on the Hidden God (Dialogus de Deo abscondito 1444/1445)[1]

*A* dialogue between two men, one of whom is a pagan, the other a Christian:

And the *PAGAN* says: I see you prostrated most devoutly and weeping tears of love, not false tears but from the heart. Tell me who you are.

*CHRISTIAN:* I am a Christian.

*PAGAN:* What are you worshiping?

*CHRISTIAN:* God.

*PAGAN:* Who is the God you worship?

*CHRISTIAN:* I do not know.

*PAGAN:* How can you so earnestly worship that which you do not know?[2]

*CHRISTIAN:* It is because I do not know that I worship.[3]

2.     *PAGAN:* It is amazing to see a person devoted to that which he does not know.

*CHRISTIAN:* It is even more amazing to see a person devoted to that which he thinks he knows.

*PAGAN:* Why is this?

*CHRISTIAN:* Because one knows that which one thinks one knows less than that which one knows one does not know.[4]

*PAGAN:* Please explain.

*CHRISTIAN:* Whoever thinks one knows something, although nothing can be known, seems out of one's mind to me.

*PAGAN:* But you seem irrational to me when you say that nothing can be known.

3.     *CHRISTIAN:* By knowledge I understand the apprehension of truth. Whoever says that one knows is saying that one has apprehended truth.

*PAGAN:* And I also believe the same.

*CHRISTIAN:* How, therefore, can truth be apprehended other than through itself? Truth is not then apprehended when the "apprehending" comes first and the "apprehended" afterward.[5]

*PAGAN:* I do not understand your statement that truth can be apprehended only through itself.

*CHRISTIAN:* Do you think that it can be apprehended in another way and in something else?[6]

*PAGAN:* I think so.

*CHRISTIAN:* You are clearly mistaken. For outside truth there is no truth; outside circularity there is no circle; and outside humanity there is no human being. Therefore, truth is not found outside truth neither in some other way nor in something else.[7]

4.    *PAGAN:* But how, therefore, do I come to know what a human being is, or a stone or anything else I know?

*CHRISTIAN:* You know nothing of these; you only think you know. For if I ask you about the quiddity[8] of what you think you know, you will affirm that you cannot express the truth of a human being or of a stone. That you know that a human is not a stone does not result from a knowledge by which you know a human and a stone and their difference, but it results from accident,[9] from a difference of their ways of operating and their shapes, to which when you discern them, you impose different names. For it is a movement in differentiating reason that imposes names.[10]

5.    *PAGAN:* Is there one truth or is there more than one?

*CHRISTIAN:* There is only one truth. For there is only one unity,[11] and truth coincides with unity, because it is true that unity is one. Therefore, just as there is only one unity in a number, so there is only one truth in the many. Hence, whoever does not attain unity will always be ignorant of number, and whoever does not attain truth in unity cannot truly know anything. Although someone may think that one truly knows, one will easily discover that what one thinks one knows can be known even more truly. For what is visible can be seen more truly than it is seen by you. For it would be seen more truly by keener eyes. Therefore, it is not seen by you as it is visible in truth. And it is the same with hearing and the other senses. But all that is known, not however with that knowledge with which it can be known, is known not in truth but otherwise and in another manner, but truth is not known otherwise and in some other manner than the manner truth itself is. Hence, one is out of one's mind who thinks one knows anything in truth but who is ignorant of truth. Would not a blind man be judged out of his mind who thought he knew the differences between colors, when he was ignorant of color?

6.    *PAGAN:* But if nothing can be known, who among human beings, therefore, is knowing?

*CHRISTIAN:* One is deemed to be knowing who knows oneself to be ignorant. One reveres truth who knows that without it one can attain nothing, whether being or living or understanding.[12]

*PAGAN:* Perhaps it is the desire to be in truth that has led you to worship.

*CHRISTIAN:* It is what you say. For I worship God, not whom your paganism falsely thinks it knows and whom it names, but the God who is ineffable truth.

7.

*PAGAN:* I ask you, Brother, since you worship the God who is truth and since we do not intend to worship a god who is not in truth God, what is the difference between you and us?

*CHRISTIAN:* There are many differences. But one and the greatest of them is that we worship the absolute, unmixed, eternal, and ineffable truth itself, but you do not worship truth as it is absolute in itself but as it is present in its works, not absolute unity but unity in number and plurality.[13] And in this you err, for the truth, which is God, is incommunicable to another.

8.

*PAGAN:* I ask you, Brother, to lead me so that I can understand you about your God. Tell me what you know about the God you worship.

*CHRISTIAN:* I know that everything I know is not God and that everything I conceive is not like God,[14] but rather God surpasses all these.[15]

9.

*PAGAN:* Therefore, God is nothing.

*CHRISTIAN:* God is not nothing, for this nothing has the name "nothing."

*PAGAN:* If God is not nothing, then God is something.

*CHRISTIAN:* God is not something, for something is not everything. But God is not something rather than everything.

*PAGAN:* You affirm marvels—the God you worship is neither nothing nor something; no reason grasps this.

*CHRISTIAN:* God is beyond nothing and beyond something, for nothing obeys God in order that something may come into being. And this is God's omnipotence, by which God surpasses everything that is or is not, so that thus that which is not obeys God just as that which is obeys God. For God causes not-being to enter into being and being to enter into not-being.[16] Therefore, God is nothing of those things that are under God and which God's omnipotence precedes. And, consequently, God cannot be called "this" rather than "that," since all things are from God.[17]

10.

*PAGAN:* Can God be named?

*CHRISTIAN:* That which is named is small. That whose magnitude cannot be conceived remains ineffable.[18]

PAGAN: But is God ineffable?

CHRISTIAN: God is not ineffable but beyond everything that is effable, for God is the cause of all nameable things. How is it, therefore, that the one who gives a name to others is oneself without a name?[19]

PAGAN: Therefore, God is both effable and ineffable.

CHRISTIAN: Not this either. For God is not the root of contradiction, but God is the simplicity itself prior to every root. So it should not be said that God is both effable and ineffable.

PAGAN: What, therefore, will you say about God?

CHRISTIAN: That God is neither named nor not named, nor is God both named and not named, but because of the excellence of God's infinity all that can be said disjunctively and unitively, whether by means of agreement or contradiction, does not correspond to God, for God is the one beginning prior to every idea that can be formed of God.[20]

11.  PAGAN: In this way, therefore, being does not correspond to God.

CHRISTIAN: You speak correctly.[21]

PAGAN: Therefore, God is nothing.

CHRISTIAN: God is neither nothing nor not nothing, nor is God both nothing and not nothing, but God is the source and origin of all beginnings of being and not-being.[22]

PAGAN: Is God the source of the beginnings of being and not-being?

CHRISTIAN: God is not.

PAGAN: But you have just said that.

CHRISTIAN: I was speaking the truth when I said it, and I am speaking the truth now, when I deny it. For if there are any beginnings of being and not-being, God comes before them. But not-being does not have a beginning of not-being, but of being. For not-being needs a beginning in order to be. Therefore, in this way there is a beginning of not-being, for without it there is no not-being.

12.  PAGAN: Is God truth?

CHRISTIAN: No, but God precedes all truth.

PAGAN: Is God other than truth?

CHRISTIAN: No. For otherness cannot correspond to God. But God is infinitely excellently prior to everything we conceive and name as "truth."[23]

13.  PAGAN: Do you not name God "God"?

*CHRISTIAN:* We do.

*PAGAN:* Are you saying something true or something false?

*CHRISTIAN:* Neither the one nor the other, nor both. For we are not saying that it is true that this is God's name, nor are we saying that it is false, for it is not false that this is God's name. Nor are we saying that it is true and false, for God's simplicity precedes both all that can be named and all that cannot.[24]

*PAGAN:* Why do you call that "God" whose name you do not know?

*CHRISTIAN:* Because of a likeness of perfection.

*PAGAN:* Please explain.

14.    *CHRISTIAN:* The name "God" comes from *theoro,* which means "I see."[25] For God is in our realm as sight is in the realm of color. For color is attained in no other way than by sight, and in order that sight can freely attain every color, the center of sight is without color. Therefore, because sight is without color, sight is not found in the realm of color.[26] And so to the realm of color sight is nothing rather than something. For the realm of color does not attain any being outside its realm, but it maintains that everything that exists is in its realm. But sight is not found there. Therefore, sight, because it exists without color, is unnameable within the realm of color, for no color's name corresponds to it. But sight has given a name to every color through its differentiating judgment. Hence, in the realm of color all naming depends on sight, but sight's name, the derivation of every color's name, is discovered to be nothing rather than something.[27] God, therefore, is to all things as sight is to visible things.

15.    *PAGAN:* Your explanation pleases me. I clearly understand that neither God nor God's name is to be found in the realm of all creatures and that God flees from every concept rather than being asserted as something. For that which does not have the condition of a creature is not to be found in the realm of creatures. In the realm of composite things the non-composite is not found. And all names that are named are of composite things. That which is composite is not from itself but from that which precedes every composite. And even though both the realm of composite things and all the composite things are what they are only through the non-composite, yet because it is not composite, it is unknown in the realm of composite things.[28] Therefore, may God, who is hidden from the eyes of all the wise of the world, be blessed forever.[29]

## 16. *On Seeking God* (De quaerendo Deum *1445*)[1]

*I* shall now, worthily reverend Brother in Christ, satisfy your desire, as far as I can, and attempt to repeat clearly and briefly in writing what I tried to explain to the people at the Feast of Epiphany[2] about the concept of the name of God. It is my intent that the meditation of us both may thereby be stirred, and that by an intellectual ascent the inner person[3] may be more and more transformed from light to light until in clear recognition and through the light of glory one enters into the joy of one's Lord.[4]

## *I*

17.　　　First of all, excellent Brother, you know well that when Paul, who confesses that he was caught up to the third heaven all the way to a vision of mysteries,[5] proclaimed the Gospel at the Areopagus to persons who at Athens were devoting themselves to the most renowned study of philosophy, he wanted to preach to them on a theme that had as its premise the unknown God,[6] to whom those pagans had consecrated an altar. And when he proceeded to explicate this theme, he set forth as his premise that in one human God had created all human beings and had appointed them a fixed time for being in the world in order to seek God if, perchance, they could grope for God and find God. Nevertheless, Paul says, God is not far from anyone, for in God we exist, live, and move. Then refuting idolatry, he added that there can be nothing in human thought similar to God.[7]

18.　　　Each time I read the Acts of the Apostles I marvel at this process of thought. For Paul wanted to reveal to the philosophers the unknown God whom, he afterward asserts, no human understanding can conceive. Herein, therefore, God discloses—since it is known that every understanding is too small for a figuration or conception of God. But Paul uses the name "God" or, in Greek, *Theos*. If, therefore, the human being has come into this world to seek God and having found God to cling to God, and by clinging to find rest, and since in this sensible and corporeal world one can neither seek nor grope for God, because God is spirit[8] rather than body and cannot be attained through intellectual abstraction, for, as Paul said, nothing can be conceived similar to God, how, therefore, can God be sought in order to be found? Indeed, unless this world aided the seeker, humankind

217

would have been sent into the world to seek God in vain. Therefore, this world must assist whoever seeks God, and the seeker must know that neither in the world nor in all that a human conceives is there anything similar to God.[9]

19.     Let us now see whether the name *Theos,* or "God," provides assistance for these issues. For the name *Theos* is not itself the name of God, who surpasses every concept. Indeed, that which cannot be conceived remains ineffable.[10] For speech is the inward concept expressed externally in sounds or in other figurative signs. Therefore, whoever's likeness is not conceived, the name is unknown. Therefore, *Theos* is the name of God but only as God is sought by humans in this world. Consequently, whoever seeks God should consider carefully that in the name *Theos* there is enfolded a certain path of seeking God on which God may be found so that God can be groped for. *Theos* is taken from *theoro,* which means "I see" and "I run."[11] The seeker, therefore, has to run by means of seeing in order to be able to reach *Theos,* who sees all things. Therefore, seeing bears a likeness to the path on which the seeker has to proceed. It is necessary, therefore, that we enlarge the nature of sensible vision in the presence of the eye of intellectual vision and from this nature construct a ladder of ascent.

20.     Our sight is produced both from a certain lucid and clear spirit that descends from the summit of the brain into the organ of the eye and also, along with the concurrence of external light, from a colored object that reproduces in the eye an appearance like itself.[12] Therefore, in the region of visible things, one finds only color. Sight, however, does not belong to this region but is situated above all visible things. Therefore, sight does not possess color,[13] since it does not belong to the region of things of color; in order for sight to be able to see every color, sight is not contracted to any color; in order for sight to discriminate truly and freely, it does not have more of one color than of another; and in order for its power to extend to all colors, it is not restricted by any color. And in order that its seeing may be true, it is not intermixed with colors.

21.     By experiment we prove that sight is deceived by a colored medium, such as glass or a transparent stone or some other thing. Sight, therefore, is so pure, without every blemish of visible things, that by comparison with it all visible things are only a certain shadow, and, in contrast to the spirit of vision, are a certain corporeal density.

22.     But when we regard the world of visible things with our intellect

218

and ask whether a knowledge of sight is found in it, all this world of color will be ignorant of sight, since it perceives nothing that is not colored. And if we said that sight exists and that it is not colored, yet if this visible world would want to make of it a figure of likeness, it would not find in all its conception anything similar to sight, since its concept is not possible apart from color. And because within the ambit of its region the visible world finds neither sight nor something similar or conformable to it, the world cannot attain sight. Indeed, it cannot attain that sight is anything at all, since apart from color the visible world does not attain anything but judges that everything not colored is not something. Therefore, among all the names that can be named within this region none befits sight, indeed, neither the name "white" nor "black," nor that of the whole mixture of colors, since neither the name of "white" and "non-white" together nor that of "black" and "non-black" together befit sight. Whether this world of visible things denotes all the names from its region individually and separately, or the names of opposing colors together, or whether it regards the union of all the names that can be named, it attains nothing of the name or the essence of sight.[14]

**23.**     If someone declared the preceding to be the case, since color is discerned and known not from itself but from a higher cause, that is, sight, and then if that person asked all visible things if this were true and how they would conceive of this cause, they would answer that that prefect, that is, sight, which gave them their names, is best and most beautiful according to all that can be conceived. But when they start to form a concept of this best and most beautiful, they return to the region of color, without which they cannot form a concept. For this reason, they say that it is more beautiful than any white color, for in the region of color there is no white color so beautiful that it cannot be more beautiful, nor so clear and brilliant that it cannot be more resplendent. Therefore, none of the visible things would claim their king to be any color that actually exists among the visible things of the region, but rather they would maintain that their king is the ultimate of potential beauty of the clearest and most perfect color.

**24.**     Such things, my Brother, and more besides that are similar, you see as most true. Therefore, by a similar relation ascend from sight to hearing and also to taste, smell, and touch, and finally to the common sense, which is set over all the senses, just as hearing is over that which can be heard, taste over that which can be tasted, scent over that which can be smelled, and feeling over that which can be touched.

25.    And thence proceed still higher to the intellect, which is above all intelligible things that are rational. Indeed, the intellect apprehends the rational but is not found in the region of the rational, for the intellect is like the eye and the rational like colors. If you will, consider the matter even more broadly in order to understand better how the intellect is like free sight, namely, a true and simple judge of all reasons; in the intellect there is no mixture of different kinds of reasons, in order that it may possess a clear and intuitive judgment over the reasons in the variety of the rational region. For the intellect judges one reason as necessary, another as possible, and still others as contingent or impossible or demonstrative or sophistical and apparent or topical, and so forth, just as sight deems this color white, another as not-white but black, and still another as more white than black, and so on. Nowhere in the whole region of reason is the intellect attained. But should the world or the universe of reasons wish to describe its king, which is its prefect and judge, it would say that the king is the terminus and the ultimate of perfection.

26.    However, the intellectual natures, likewise, cannot deny that a king is set over them. Just as the visible natures acknowledge that the king set over them is the ultimate of every visible perfection, so the intellectual natures, which are the natures that are intuitive of the truth, affirm that their king is the ultimate of every perfection that is intuitive of all things. And this they name *Theos* or "God," as if their monarch were contemplation or intuition itself because he is the completeness of perfection of seeing all things. Yet in the whole region of intellectual powers, nothing is found to which the king himself is similar; nor in all the intellectual region is there anywhere hidden a concept of his likeness. But above all that is conceived and understood is the one whose name is not intelligible, although it is the name that names and discerns all intelligible things. And that one's nature infinitely precedes all intellectual wisdom in loftiness, simplicity, strength, power, beauty, and goodness, since compared with that one's nature everything inhabiting the intellectual nature is a shadow, an empty space without power, a grossness and paucity of wisdom, and thus regarding an infinite number of similar modes.

27.    Therefore, you can run along this path on which God is found above all sight, hearing, taste, touch, smell, speech, sensation, reason, and intellect. Indeed, one discovers God to be none of these but to be above all things as God of gods and King of all kings.[15] The king of the intellectual world is the King of kings and the Lord of lords[16] in

the universe. For this is the king of the intellectual nature, which rules over the rational; and the rational in turn rules over the sensory; and the sensory rules over the world of the senses, over which sight, hearing, taste, touch, and smell preside as monarchs. And all these kings are discerning, observing, or seeing as far as to the King of kings and Lord of lords, who is Contemplation Itself and *Theos* or God, and has in this King's power all the kings, who hold from the King all that they hold: power, beauty, being, delight, joy, life, and every good thing.

**28.**     For this reason, in the kingdom of the highest and maximum King all beauty of visible forms, variety of colors, agreeable symmetry, splendor of precious stones, greenness of the meadows, luster of gold, and whatever pleases the sight and is that in which sight, when it rests, is delighted, as in the midst of its own kingdom's treasure— all such things at the court of the great King are deemed as nothing, for they are the common straw of the court. And so too in the kingdom of hearing the concordant resonance of all voices and that sweet harmony, the indescribable variety of all instruments, the melodies from golden organs, the songs of the sirens and the nightingales, and all other exquisite riches of the king of the kingdom of hearing are the rubble adhering to the floor at the court of the greatest and most excellent King of kings. So too everything sweet and tart and pleasing to the taste—of the many paradise apples and very delicious fruits and grapes of Engedi,[17] of the wine of Cyprus, of the honey of Attica, of the grain and oil[18] and everything that India and this entire world, its woods and its waters, present to refreshment and offer to the taste are of little importance in the hall of this most powerful Ruler of the world. Nor does the aroma of ointments,[19] of frankincense and myrrh[20] and musk, and of every fragrance belonging to the kingdom of scent have any value in this great palace of the highest King. And of even less worth is everything that pleases the touch by its softness. Indeed, the kingdom of the king of the sense of touch appears vast and extended throughout the whole world, yet it is hardly a dot, almost imperceptible, with respect to the kingdom of the one who originates the universe. The king seems great who commands these kings of the senses, which we have just mentioned, and rules them as his vassals, and this king is the common sense, enfolding all their powers within its power. But this king is only a purchased slave[21] and the least servant in the kingdom of the King who sees and contains all things.

**29.**     Through its incomparable height the intellectual nature has obtained a kingdom above all these others. All the kingdoms that we have previously listed and described depend on the power of the intellectual nature, and it presides over them as lord. But the kings of the intellectual nature themselves belong to the household of the greatest commander and rejoice to be numbered among this commander's army.[22] They wish nothing else than to be able to gain the rank of any position at their sovereign's court so that there through intellectual intuition they can be renewed by the one who is called *Theos*. And all the things that are present in all the kingdoms mentioned above have no cares about anything, just as also they are nothing in comparison with the good that they recognize in their ruler. All things exist in their ruler divinely and most excellently, in completeness and in themselves, but they exist in the other kings not only imperfectly and outside themselves and in shadow or image but also at a contracted distance that is incomparable and improportional.[23]

30.     Color, therefore, which in the visible kingdom is perceived by sight, does not see but is only visible. It does not have life and the motion belonging to life. Nor does it have the perfection of a vegetative principle[24] or of a subsistent form. But the senses that exist in the kingdom of common sense, as they are particular senses, have a nature which, in the vitality and knowledge of the sensible spirit, enfolds within itself the form of the sensible world. Therefore, there is not less in the kingdom of the senses than there is in the kingdom of sensible things. However, everything that exists in an unfolded way in the kingdom of sensible things exists in the kingdom of the senses in an enfolded and vital way more vigorously and more perfectly. For the kingdom of sensible things finds its rest in the senses. So also those things that belong to the kingdom of the senses exist in a much clearer and more perfect way in the kingdom where they exist intellectually. For color that has an incorruptible nature in the intellectual being of the intellectual kingdom differs in perfection from color of the sensible world, as the everlasting differs from the corruptible, as intellectual life from death, and as light from darkness.

31.     But in the kingdom of the Almighty, where the kingdom is the King;[25] where all things that exist in all the kingdoms are the King himself; where color is neither sensible nor intellectual color but is divine, indeed, is God; where everything lacking motion and life in the sensible world and everything possessing vegetative, sensitive, rational, or intellectual life is the divine life itself, which is immortality itself, which God alone inhabits,[26] and in God all things are God,[27]

there the joy of all the pleasures that we derive from the eyes, ears, taste, touch, smell, sense, life, motion, reason, and intelligence is the infinite, divine, and inexpressible joy and final rest of all pleasure and delight, for God is *Theos*, Vision, and Discursus, who sees all things, is in all things, and runs through all things.[28] All look to God as to the King. At this king's command all things are moved and run forth,[29] and every running to the goal of rest is toward the king. Therefore, *Theos*, who is the beginning from which everything flows forth, the middle in which we move, and the end to which everything flows back again,[30] is everything.

Therefore, on this path, my Brother, strive to seek God with the most diligent vision, for God who is everywhere is impossible not to find if God is sought in the right way. And then in keeping with God's name, God is rightly sought to the end that, in keeping with God's name, praise of God may reach to the limits of the power of our earthly nature.[31]

32.

## II

Now let us turn more fully to the second part of the question and see by what way we will be led on a ladder of ascent of the vision we have spoken of,[32] for we are not moved toward something completely unknown. And in order to investigate this, let us consider sight.

33.

In the first place, two lights concur in order for sight to perceive visible things discriminately. For it is not the spirit of sight that assigns a name to colors but the spirit of its parent,[33] which is in it. For the spirit that descends from the brain through the optic channels into the eye is confronted by the image of an object opposite it, and a confused sensation arises. The sensitive power[34] wonders at this sensation and strives to discern. Therefore, it is not the spirit in the eye that discerns, but a higher spirit that produces discernment in it. Indeed, we discover this to be true in our daily experience. For often we do not recognize passersby, even though their images are reproduced in the eye, if we are concerned with other things and do not really pay attention to them, and if several people are talking to us, we understand only the one to whom we direct our attention.[35] This demonstrates to us that it is true that the spirit that is present in sense accomplishes its work by means of a higher light, namely, that of reason. When, therefore, the eye says that this is "red" and that is "blue," it is not the eye speaking but rather the spirit of its parent speaking in it, namely, that sensitive spirit[36] whose eye this is.

34.     But even though the attention of someone who wishes to see is present, color is still not for that reason visible, for it is necessary that color be made visible by a second light, from what illuminates the visible. For in darkness and shadow the visible has no aptitude to be seen. Its adaptation occurs through the light that illuminates it. Therefore, just as that which is visible is apt to be seen only in light, for in and through itself the visible cannot transmit itself into the eye, the visible must be illuminated, since light is of the nature of that which in and through itself is transmitted into the eye. The visible, therefore, can be transmitted into the eye when the visible stands in the light, which itself has the power to be transmitted. But color exists in light not as in some other thing, but rather as in its own principle, because color is nothing other than a terminus of light in what is diaphanous, as we observe in a rainbow. For as the ray of the sun is terminated in a rain cloud first in one way and then in another, it generates different colors. It is evident that color is visible in its own principle, that is, in light,[37] because exterior light and the visual spirit communicate in a clarity.[38] Hence, that light which illuminates the visible transmits itself to a corresponding light and conveys the image of color, which is imparted to sight.

35.     From these things, my Brother, set out a course for yourself to inquire how the unknown God surpasses everything by which we are moved toward God. For even though it is already clear to you that the sensitive spirit[39] within the spirit of the eye discerns and that the light makes the visible apt to be seen, nevertheless, sight grasps neither the spirit itself nor the light. For light does not belong to the region of colors, because it is not colored. Therefore, it is found in no region ruled by the eye. Light, therefore, is unknown to the eye and yet remains pleasing to the sight. Just as it is the discriminating reason that in the eye discerns between visible objects, so it is the intellectual spirit that in reason understands, and it is the divine spirit that illuminates the intellect. But the discriminating animate light in the eye, ear, tongue, nose, and sensory nerve in which touch thrives is one light, which is received in different ways in different organs in order that according to the diversity of these organs it discerns variously between the things that belong to the sensible world. And this light is the beginning, the middle, and the end of the senses, because the senses have no other end than discernment between sensible things;

and the senses are derived from this spirit alone and are moved in no other. In it too all the senses live. For it is the life of sight to see and the life of hearing to hear, and the more perfect such a life is, the more discriminating it is. For sight that discerns the visible more perfectly is the more perfect, and the same is true of hearing. Therefore, life and perfection, joy and rest, and whatever all the senses may desire are present in the discriminating spirit, and from it they have everything they have. And when the sense organs become infected and the life in them diminishes in activity, life, however, does not diminish in the discriminating spirit, from which they receive the same life back again when the blemish or infirmity is removed.

36.      In equal fashion, conceive the same regarding the intellect, which is the light of discriminating reason, and from the intellect lift yourself up to God, who is the light of the intellect. For while you thus run by means of what you have learned about sight, you will discover that our God, who is blessed forever,[40] is all that is in every existing thing,[41] just as the discriminating light is in the senses and the intellectual light is in reasons; that it is God through whom the creature has what it is and has life and movement; and that in God's light is all our knowledge, so that it is not we ourselves who know, but rather it is God who knows in us.[42] When we ascend to the knowledge of God, although God is unknown to us, yet we are moved only in God's light, which transmits itself into our spirit, so that we proceed toward God in God's light. Therefore, just as being depends on God, so does being known. In the same way, just as the being of color depends on corporeal light, so does the knowledge of color, as we previously stated.[43]

37.      It ought to be observed, therefore, that God, who is wondrous, has among God's works created light.[44] In its simplicity, light surpasses the other corporeal things, so that it is an intermediary between the spiritual and the corporeal natures; and through light this corporeal world, as if through its own simplicity, ascends to the spiritual world.[45] For light conveys figures to sight so that in this way the form of the sensible world ascends to reason and to the intellect and through the intellect attains its end in God. And the world itself has thus come into being so that this corporeal world is what it is by participation of the light and the more corporeal things participate light, the more perfect in their own corporeal genus they are judged to be, as we experience in gradations with the elements. And in the same way, the creature possessing the spirit of life[46] is more perfect,

the more it participates the light of life.[47] So too the creature having intellectual life is more perfect, the more it participates the light of intellectual life.[48] But God is imparticipable and is the infinite light shining forth in all things, as the discriminating light in the senses. But the variable termination of this imparticipable and unmixable light displays a variable creature, just as the variable termination of the corporeal light displays a variety of color in that which is diaphanous, although the light itself remains unmixable.

38.

*III*

I have no doubt, my Brother, that from these considerations you are able to proceed in clarity to grasp that just as color is visible only by means of light, that is, as color can ascend to its rest and to its end only in the light of its principle, so our intellectual nature can attain to the happiness of its rest only in the light of its intellectual principle. And just as sight does not discern, but rather a discriminating spirit discerns in it, so it is with our intellect, which is illuminated by the divine light of its principle in accord with its aptitude for the light to be able to enter. We will not understand or live the intellectual life in and of ourselves, but rather God, who is infinite life, will live in us.[49] This is that eternal happiness where the eternal intellectual life, surpassing in inexpressible joy every concept of living creatures, thus lives in us in strictest unity, just as discriminating reason lives in our most perfect senses and as intellect lives in our most clear reason.

39.

It is now obvious to us that we are drawn to the unknown God by the movement of the light of the grace of one who can be known only by self-disclosure.[50] And God wills to be sought[51] and wills to give to seekers the light without which they are unable to seek God. God wills to be sought, and God also wills to be apprehended, for it is God's will to uncover and to disclose Godself to those who seek. Therefore, God is sought with the desire of apprehending, and then whenever God is sought with greatest desire, God is sought contemplatively[52] and with a running that leads the runner to motion's rest. Hence, we proceed rightly toward attaining wisdom only if it is sought with the deepest desire. And when wisdom is pursued in this way, it is sought along the right path on which it is certain to be found, for it reveals itself there. No other path has been given to us than this,[53] and no other has been passed on to us in all the teaching of the saints, who have attained wisdom.

**40.**     For this reason those who were proud, who were presumptuous, who according to themselves were wise, who trusted in their own intelligence, who, in ascending pride, reckoned themselves to be like the Most High, who assumed for themselves a knowledge of gods— all these have erred. For they closed off to themselves the path to wisdom, because they did not suppose there was any other than that which they measured with their own intellect. In their vanities they fell short and embraced the tree of knowledge but did not apprehend the tree of life.[54] Therefore, the end of the philosophers who did not honor God was nothing other than to perish in their vanities.

**41.**     But those who saw that they could not attain wisdom and eternal intellectual life unless they were given by a gift of grace and that the goodness of almighty God would be so great that God would hear those who call on God's name, "and they were saved,"[55] have become humble, acknowledging themselves to be ignorant, and have ordered their life as those desiring eternal wisdom. This is the life of the virtuous, who press on in the desire for the other life, which is commended to us by the saints. The tradition of the holy prophets and of those who have received the grace of the divine light in this life is not other than this: that whoever is willing to approach the intellectual life and immortal divine wisdom must first believe that God is[56] and is the giver of all best gifts;[57] that one must live in the fear of God and proceed in love of God; and that one must in utter humility beseech immortal life itself from God and that, in order to have ability to attain it, one must embrace all things that are ordered to immortal life, in highest devotion and in most sincere worship.

**42.**     You see now, Brother, that no virtue of any kind justifies us so that we deserve to receive this most excellent gift, nor does any worship or law or instruction. But a virtuous life, observance of the commandments, outward devotion, mortification of the flesh, contempt for the world, and the other things of this kind accompany those who rightly seek the divine life and eternal wisdom. If these things are not present in the seeker, it is clear that one is not on the path but outside it. Moreover we can detect the signs that one has not strayed but remains on the path from the works that accompany one who journeys in the right manner. For whoever most ardently desires to apprehend eternal wisdom prefers nothing to it in one's love, is afraid to offend it, affirms all else to be nothing in comparison with it, and considers all others to be nothing and holds them in contempt. And one applies one's whole effort to please the beloved wisdom, but one knows that one cannot please it, if one adheres to another, to the world's corruptible prudence, or to sensible pleasure. For this reason, forsaking all these things, one quickly hurries forward in the fervor of love. As the deer longs after the fountain of water, so one's soul desires God.[58] Indeed, we do not then merit the incomparable treasure of glory[59] from the works we have done,[60] but rather God loves those who love God,[61] for God is charity and love[62] and gives Godself to the soul so that it may forever enjoy this greatest good.

43.     You see now, my Brother, that the end toward which you have come into this world is to seek God, as we stated earlier in the introduction. You see that God is called *Theos* to those who seek and that you are able to seek God along a certain path. And if you tread upon it, it will be your own path and will be more known to you; on it you will take delight because of its beauty and the abundance of fruit found all around it. Apply yourself, therefore, by increased acts and contemplative ascents, and you will find pastures[63] that augment and strengthen you on your journey and daily inflame you more in desire. For our intellectual spirit has the power of fire within it. It has been sent by God to earth for no other end than to glow and to spring up in flame. It increases when it is excited by wonder, as if wind blowing on fire excites its potency to actuality.[64] Therefore, through the knowledge of the works of God we marvel at eternal wisdom and are stirred by an external wind of works and of creatures of such various powers and operations that our desire may burst into love of the Creator and into a contemplation of that wisdom that has wonderfully ordered all things.

44.     For when we observe the smallest mustard seed and with the eye of our intellect contemplate its strength and its potency, we discover a vestige that stirs us in wonder at our God.[65] For although it is so small in body, yet its power is without limitation. In this seed there is a large tree with leaves and small branches and many other seeds in which there also exists this same power beyond all reckoning. And so in the intellect I see the power of the mustard seed: If its potential should be unfolded in actuality, this sensible world would not suffice, nor indeed would ten or a thousand or all the worlds that one could count.

45.     Who reflecting on these things will not marvel when one adds that the human intellect embraces all this power of the seed, that it apprehends this as true, that in its apprehension it thus surpasses all capacity of the whole sensible world, and not only of this one world

but also of an infinite number of worlds? And in this way our intellectual power embraces every corporeal and measurable nature. How great a magnitude there is in our intellect! If, therefore, the magnitude of our intellectual spirit, though as small as a point, embraces all possible sensible and corporeal magnitude with an infinitely greater capacity, then how great and how praiseworthy is the Lord,[66] whose magnitude infinitely surpasses that of the intellect. Consequently, since the Lord is so great, everything in comparison to the Lord is nothing and in the Lord can be nothing other than God, who is blessed forever.[67] Then, through similar ascents, you will be able to ascend from the power of the millet seed and likewise from the power of all vegetable and animal seeds.[68] The power of no seed is less than that of the mustard seed, and there are an infinite number of such seeds.

**46.** Oh, how great is our God, who is the actuality of all potency![69] For God is the goal of all potency[70] and not the goal of a potency contracted to a mustard or millet seed or the goal of a grain of wheat or the goal of our father Adam or of others and so on ad infinitum. But since in all these there is immeasurable power and potency that is contracted according to their genus, then in God, there is, without contraction, absolute potency, which is also infinite actuality.[71] Who seeking the power of God in this manner would not be stunned in amazement? Who would not be inflamed to the greatest ardor to fear and to love the Almighty? And if one considers the potency of the least spark of fire, who would not marvel at God, who is beyond all that can be expressed? If the potency of a spark is so great that, when it exists in actuality—for the potential spark has become actual by the motion of iron against flint—, it is in its power to resolve everything into its own nature and to turn potential fire into actual, wherever it is in this world, even if there were an infinite number of worlds, Oh, how great is the power of our God, who is a fire that consumes fire.[72] And when you, Brother, turn to the nature and conditions of fire, which number twenty-four, as Dionysius, that highest contemplator of the divine, set forth in his *Angelic Hierarchy*,[73] you will have a wonderful path for seeking and finding God. Look there, and you will marvel.

**47.**
*IV*

If, therefore, you are seeking still another path to the wisdom of our Master, consider the following. For with the eye of the intellect you perceive that in a small piece of wood, in this very tiny stone, in a portion of ore or gold, in a mustard or millet seed, all artificial corporeal forms exist in potentiality. Indeed, you do not doubt that in each of them there is found the circle, the triangle, the rectangle, the sphere, the cube, and whatever else geometry names and also the forms of all animals, fruit, flowers, foliage, and trees and the likeness of all the forms that exist in this world and that could exist in an infinite number of worlds.

48.    If, therefore, that artisan is great who knows how to educe from a small piece of wood the face of a king or of a queen, an ant, or a camel, then of what great mastery is one who can bring forth into actuality everything that lies in all potency?[74] Of marvelous subtlety, therefore, is God, who from the smallest particle can make all things in the likeness of all forms that are possible in this world and in an infinite number of worlds. But of still more wonderful power and knowledge is the one who created the millet seed and placed such strength within it. Of what astonishing mastery belongs to that wisdom which knows how to rouse all the possible forms within the seed, not in accidental likeness but in essential truth! And beyond all understanding is the indescribable astonishment that this wisdom knows how to rouse living human beings not only from stones[75] but also from nothing and how to call into being those things that are not, as those that are.[76] And since it is certain that all created arts attain something only in something else, that is, they attain some likeness, not without defect, in something created as, for example, from bronze they fashion a statue that is in some way like a human being, who is this Master who without any material form brings forth into being not a likeness with a defect but a true essence?

Indeed, it is on such journeys that we hasten to God with fervent wonder, and then the spirit will glow with the desire of finding God unfailingly and will languish in love until it is shown final salvation.

49.                      *V*

Finally, there is still a path of seeking God within yourself: the path of the removal of limits.[77] For when an artist seeks the face of a king in a block of wood, the artist rejects everything else that is limited except the face itself. For the artist sees in the wood, through the concept of faith, the face that the artist is seeking to observe as visibly present to the eye. For the face is future to the eye but present by faith to the mind in an intellectual concept.

When, therefore, you conceive that God is better than can be conceived, you reject everything that is limited and contracted. You reject the body—saying that God is not body, that is, God is not limited by quantity, place, form, or position. You reject the senses, which are limited; for you do not see through a mountain or into the hidden depths of the earth or at the brightness of the sun, and the same is true of hearing and of the other senses. Indeed, they are all limited in potency and strength. Therefore, they are not God. You reject the common sense, fantasy, and imagination, for they do not exceed corporeal nature; indeed, the imagination does not attain anything incorporeal. You reject reason, for it often fails and does not attain to all things. You might want to know why this is a human being and that a stone, and you do not attain to the reason of all the works of God. The power of reason, therefore, is small; so God is not reason. You reject the intellect, for the intellect itself is also limited in its power, although it embraces everything. Yet it cannot attain perfectly anything's quiddity in its purity, and it sees that whatever it does attain can be attained in a more perfect way.[78] Therefore, God is not intellect. But if you seek further, you find nothing in yourself like God, but rather you affirm that God is above all these as the cause, beginning, and light of life of your intellective soul.[79]

**50.** You will rejoice to have found God beyond all your interiority as the source of the good, from which everything that you have flows out to you. You turn yourself to God by entering each day more deeply within yourself[80] and forsaking everything that lies outside in order that you be found on that path on which God is met so that after this you can apprehend God in truth. May God grant this to you and me, for God, who is blessed forever,[81] gives Godself abundantly to those who love God.

# On the Vision of God
## (De visione Dei 1453)[1]

## To the Abbot and Brothers of Tegernsee[2]

**1.**    *I* will now explain, dearest brothers,[3] what I had earlier promised you about the facility of mystical theology.[4] For I know that you are led by a zeal for God, and I count you worthy for the uncovering of this most precious and bountiful treasure. But I pray first the Word from on high and the all-powerful Discourse, which alone can disclose itself, may be given to me in order to set forth, according to your grasp, the wonders which are revealed beyond all sensible, rational, and intellectual sight.[5] But by means of a very simple and commonplace method I will attempt to lead you experientially[6] into the most sacred darkness. While you abide there, feeling the presence of the inaccessible light, each of you, in the measure granted him by God, will of himself endeavor to draw continuously nearer and in this place to foretaste, by a most delicious sampling, that feast of eternal happiness to which we have been called in the Word of Life[7] through the Gospel of the ever blessed Christ.

### Preface

**2.**    In the effort to transport you to divine things by human means, I must use some kind of similitude.[8] But among human works I have found no image more suitable for our purpose than that of an all-seeing figure. Through the painter's subtle art its face is made to appear as if looking on all around it.[9] Many excellent pictures of this kind may be found, such as that of the archeress in the forum of Nuremberg; that of the great artist Roger in the very valuable painting which hangs in the court at Brussels;[10] that of a veronica[11] in my chapel at Koblenz;[12] that of the angel holding the arms of the church in the castle at Brixen; and many others elsewhere. However, so that you not be deficient in the exercise, which requires a sensible image of this kind, I am sending, to your charity, a painting that I was able to acquire containing an all-seeing image, which I call an icon of God.[13]

**3.**    Hang this up some place, perhaps on a north wall. And you

235

brothers stand around it, equally distant from it, and gaze at it. And each of you will experience that from whatever place one observes it the face will seem to regard him alone. To a brother standing in the east, the face will look eastward; to one in the south, it will look southward; and to one in the west, westward. First, therefore, you will marvel at how it is possible that the face looks on all and each one of you at the same time. For the imagination of the one who is standing in the east cannot conceive that the icon's gaze is turned in any other direction, such as the west or the south. Next, let the brother who was in the east place himself in the west, and he will experience the gaze as fastened on him there just as it was before in the east. Since he knows that the icon is fixed and unchanged, he will marvel at the changing of its unchangeable gaze.

Even if while fixing his gaze on the icon, a brother walks from west to east, he will discover that the icon's gaze continuously follows him. And if he returns from east to west, it will likewise not leave him. He will marvel at how its gaze was moved, although it remains motionless, and his imagination will not be able to grasp how it is moved in the same manner with someone coming forth to meet him from the opposite direction. If he wishes to experience this, let him have one of his brothers pass across from east to west while looking at the icon, as he himself moves from west to east. When they meet let him ask the other whether the icon's gaze continuously turns with him, and he will hear that it moves just the same in the opposite direction. He will believe him, but unless he believed him, he would not imagine this to be possible. And when he is shown this by his brother, he will discover that the face looks unfailingly on all who walk before it even from opposite directions.

Therefore, he will experience that the immobile face is moved toward the east in such a way that it is also moved simultaneously toward the west, that it is moved toward the north in such a way that it is also moved toward the south, that it is moved toward a single place in such a way that it is also moved simultaneously toward all places, and that it beholds a single movement in such a way that it beholds all movements simultaneously.

4.     And while the brother observes how this gaze deserts no one, he will see that it takes diligent care of each, just as if it cared only for the one on whom its gaze seems to rest and for no other, and to such an extent that the one whom it regards cannot conceive that it should care for another. He will also see that it has the same very diligent

concern for the least creature as for the greatest, and for the whole universe.

It is by this sensible appearance that I propose to uplift you, very beloved Brothers, through a certain devotional exercise, to mystical theology,[14] and to this end I will first discuss three important premises.[15]

### Chapter One
*That the Perfection of the Appearance Is Verified of God,*
*the Most Perfect*

5.  As a first premise, I believe it should be presupposed that nothing concerning the gaze of the icon of God can be apparent that is not truer in the true gaze of God. For God, who is the very summit of every perfection and greater than can be thought, is called *Theos* because of the fact that God looks on all things.[16] If, therefore, the painted gaze in the icon can appear to be observing all and each at the same time, and since this faculty is of the perfection of sight, it cannot truly pertain to the truth less than it apparently pertains to the icon or appearance. For if one person's sight is sharper than another's, if one's sight hardly distinguishes things nearby while another's sees things at a distance, and if one's sight perceives an object slowly and another's sight perceives more quickly, then without question absolute sight, the source of all the sight of those who see, excels all sharpness, all quickness, and all power of all who actually see and all who can become seeing.

6.  Suppose I examine abstract sight, which in my mind I have made absolute from all association with eyes and organs. And suppose I consider how this abstract sight in its own contracted being, just as seeing persons see through sight, is contracted to time and regions of the world, to individual objects and to other such contracted conditions, and that abstract sight is similarly abstracted and made absolute from these conditions. Then I correctly grasp that it is not of the essence of sight to regard one object more than another, although it does belong to sight in its contracted being that while it regards one thing it cannot also look on another or on all things absolutely.

God, however, as God is true uncontracted sight, is not less than what the intellect can conceive of abstract sight, but God is incomparably more perfect. The appearance of the icon's sight, therefore, is less able to approach the summit of excellence of absolute sight than conception is. There is no doubt, therefore, that what appears to exist in the image exists more excellently in absolute sight.

## Chapter Two
### *Absolute Sight Embraces All Modes of Seeing*

7.     As a second premise, observe that sight varies in those who see because of the variety of its contraction. For our sight follows the dispositions of the organ and of the spirit. Consequently, a person may now see lovingly and joyfully, but later sadly and irascibly, now childishly, but later maturely, and finally gravely and agedly. However, sight that is absolute from every contraction, as if the most adequate measure and the truest exemplar of all visions, embraces, at one and the same time, each and every mode of seeing. For without absolute sight there can be no contracted sight. Sight that is absolute embraces in itself all modes of seeing, and it embraces all modes in such a way as to embrace each, and it remains entirely absolute of every variety. For all contracted modes of seeing exist in absolute sight without contraction. Every contraction of sight exists in the absolute, because absolute sight is the contraction of contractions. Moreover, it is a contraction that is not contractible. The most simple contraction, therefore, coincides with the absolute. Indeed, without contraction nothing is contracted. Thus, absolute vision exists in all sight because every contracted vision exists through absolute vision and is utterly unable to exist without it.

## Chapter Three
### *What Things Are Said[17] of God Do Not Differ in Reality*

8.     As a final premise, notice that all things that are said of God cannot differ in reality because of God's highest simplicity. Even so, we attribute different names to God according to different reasons. Since God is the absolute reason of all formable reasons, God enfolds in Godself the reasons of all things.[18] Although we attribute to God sight, hearing, taste, smell, touch, sense, reason, intellect, and so on, according to the different significations of each word, yet in God seeing is not other than hearing, tasting, smelling, touching, sensing, and understanding. Therefore, all theology is said to be established in a circle,[19] because any one of the attributes is affirmed of another and because God's having is God's being, God's moving is God's standing

still, God's running is God's resting, and so on with the remaining attributes. Although we thus attribute to God "moving" for one reason and "resting" for another, yet because God is the absolute reason in which all otherness is unity and all diversity identity, then a diversity of reasons, which, as we conceive it, is not identity itself, cannot exist in God.

### Chapter Four
*That God's Vision Is Called Providence, Grace, and Eternal Life*

**9.**     Now, brother contemplative, approach the icon of God. First stand to the east, then to the south, and finally to the west. And because the icon's gaze regards you equally everywhere and does not leave you wherever you may go, a contemplation will arise in you, and you will be stirred saying:[20]

"Lord, in this image of you I now behold your providence by a certain sensible experience. For if you do not abandon me, the vilest of all, you will never abandon anyone. Indeed, you are present to all and to each, just as being, without which they cannot exist, is present to all and to each. For thus you, who are the absolute being of all,[21] are present to all as if you had concern for no other.[22] And for this reason there is nothing which does not prefer its own being to all others and its own way of being to all other ways of being, and it so upholds its own being that it would rather allow the being of all others to perish rather than its own.[23] For you, Lord, so look on anything that exists that no existing thing can conceive that you have any other care but that it alone exist in the best manner possible for it and that all other existing things exist only for the purpose of serving the best state of the one which you are beholding.

**10.**     By no imagining, Lord, do you allow me to conceive that you love anything other than me more than me, for it is I alone that your gaze does not abandon. And since the eye is there wherever love is,[24] I experience that you love me because your eyes rest most attentively on me, your humble servant. Your seeing, Lord, is your loving. And just as your gaze looks upon me so attentively that it never turns away from me, so it is with your love. Since your love is always with me and since your love, Lord, is nothing other than you yourself, who love me, you are always with me. You do not forsake me, Lord; you guard me on every side, for you take most diligent care of me. Your being, Lord, does not desert my being, for I exist only insomuch as you are with me. And since your seeing is your being, therefore, because you regard me, I am, and if you remove your face from me, I will cease to be.

**11.** But I know that your gaze is that maximum goodness which is unable not to communicate itself to all capable of receiving it. You, therefore, can never forsake me so long as I am able to receive you. For my part, then, insofar as I can, I ought to make myself ever more able to receive you. And I know that the capacity which warrants union is nothing other than likeness. But incapacity stems from the want of likeness. If, therefore, I render myself similar to your goodness in every way possible, then according to the degree of the likeness, I will be capable of truth.

O Lord, you have given me being of such kind that it can make itself ever more capable to receive your grace and goodness. And this power, which I hold from you and in which I possess a living image of your almighty power, is free will.[25] By it I can increase or restrict my capacity for your grace. I am able to increase it through conformity, when I strive to be good because you are good, to be just because you are just, and to be merciful because you are merciful, when all my striving is turned only toward you because all yours is turned toward me, when I give all my attention only to you and never remove my mind's eyes because you hold me in your constant vision, and when I direct my love to you alone because you, who are love, are turned toward me alone.

And what, Lord, is my life, except that embrace in which the sweetness of your love so lovingly holds me! I love my life supremely because you are my life's sweetness.

**12.** Now I contemplate eternal life in a mirror, in an icon, in an enigma,[26] for that is nothing other than the blessed vision by which you never forsake regarding me most lovingly even to the innermost places of my soul. Your seeing is nothing other than your bringing to life, nothing other than your continuously imparting your sweetest love. And through this imparting of love, your seeing inflames me to the love of you and through inflaming feeds me and through feeding kindles my desires and through kindling gives me to drink of the dew of gladness and through drinking infuses a fountain of life within me and by infusing causes to increase and to endure. Your seeing communicates your immortality and confers the imperishable glory of your heavenly and highest and greatest kingdom. Moreover, it makes me partaker of that inheritance which is of the Son alone and renders me possessor of eternal happiness. Here is the source of all the delights that can be desired. Nothing better can be thought by any human being or angel, and nothing better can exist by any mode of being, for this source is the absolute maximumness,[27] unable to be greater, of every rational desire.

*Chapter Five*
*That Seeing Is Tasting, Seeking, Having Mercy, and Working*

**13.** How great is the multitude of your sweetness, which you have hidden away for those who fear you![28] It is an inexhaustible treasure of the most joyous of gladness. For to taste your sweetness is to know through the touch[29] of experience the sweetness of every delight at its source. It is to attain in your wisdom to the reason of every desirable thing. Therefore, to see Absolute Reason, the Reason of all things, is nothing other than mentally to taste you, O God, because you are the sweetness itself of being, of life, and of intellect.[30]

What other, O Lord, is your seeing, when you look upon me with the eye of mercy, than your being seen by me? In seeing me you, who are the hidden God,[31] give yourself to be seen by me. No one can see you except in the measure you grant to be seen. Nor is your being seen other than your seeing one who sees you.[32]

**14.** In the icon, this image of you, I perceive, O Lord, how inclined you are to show your face to all those seeking you.[33] For you never close your eyes, never turn them elsewhere; and although I turn myself away from you when I direct my attention entirely to something other, yet notwithstanding this, you change neither your eyes nor your gaze. If you do not look upon me with the eye of grace, I am at fault because I have separated myself from you by turning away toward some other, which I prefer to you. Yet, even so, you do not turn completely from me, but on the contrary, your mercy follows me so that should I ever wish to turn back to you, I would be capable of grace. If you do not regard me, it is because I do not regard you but reject and despise you.

O infinite Mercy, how unhappy is every sinner who forsakes you, who are the source of life, and seeks you, not in yourself, but in that which in itself is nothing and would have remained nothing had you not called it forth out of nothing! How foolish is one who seeks you, who are goodness, and while seeking you withdraws from you and turns one's eyes away! Everyone, therefore, who is seeking seeks only the good and everyone who seeks the good and withdraws from you withdraws from that which one is seeking. Every sinner, therefore, strays from you and wanders afar off. Yet as soon as the sinner returns to you, without delay you hurry to meet the sinner, and before the sinner sees you, you cast your eyes of mercy on the sinner in parental affection.[34]

15.      For with you having mercy is no different than seeing. Your mercy follows after every person as long as one lives and wherever one may go, just as your gaze never abandons anyone. So long as one lives, you do not cease to follow each person and, with a sweet and inward warning, to incite one to depart from error and to turn toward you in order to live happily.

You, O Lord, are my journey's companion; wherever I go your eyes always rest on me. Moreover, your seeing is your moving. Therefore, you are moved with me and never cease from moving so long as I am moved. If I am at rest, you are with me. If I ascend, you ascend, and if I descend, you descend. Wherever I turn, you are there.[35] Nor do you forsake me in a time of tribulation.[36] However often I call upon you, you are near,[37] for to call upon you is to turn to you. You cannot fail one who turns to you; nor can anyone be turned toward you unless you were already there. You are present before I turn to you. For unless you were present and did incite me, I would be utterly ignorant of you. And how would I turn toward you of whom I would be ignorant?

16.      You, therefore, are my God, who sees everything, and your seeing is your working. And thus you work all things. Therefore, not to us, O Lord, not to us, but to your great name, which is *Theos*, do I sing eternal glory.[38] For I possess nothing that you do not give. Nor would I keep what you have given were you not preserving it. You minister all things to me. You are the Lord, powerful and good, who gives all things; you are the minister who ministers all things; you are the provider, the guardian, and the preserver. And all these things you work with your one simplest glance, you, who are blessed forever.[39]

*Chapter Six*
*On Facial Vision*

17.      The longer I behold your face, O Lord, my God, the more keenly you seem to fix your glance on me. And your gaze prompts me to

consider how this image of your face is thus portrayed in a sensible fashion since a face could not have been painted without color and color does not exist without quantity. But I see the invisible truth of your face, represented in this contracted shadow here, not with the eyes of flesh, which examine this icon of you, but with the eyes of the mind and the intellect. Your true face is absolute from every contraction. It has neither quality nor quantity, nor is it of time or place, for it is the absolute form, which is the face of faces.[40]

**18.** When, therefore, I consider how this face is the truth and the most adequate measure of all faces, I am numbed with astonishment. For this face, which is the truth of all faces, is not a face of quantity. It is, therefore, neither greater nor smaller nor equal to any, since it is not of quantity but is absolute and superexalted. Therefore, it is the truth, which is equality, absolute from all quantity. Thus, O Lord, I comprehend that your face precedes every formable face, that it is the exemplar and truth of all faces and that all are images of your face, which is not subject to contraction and participation. Every face, therefore, which can behold your face sees nothing that is other or different from itself, because it sees there its own truth. Moreover, the truth of the exemplar cannot be other or different, but otherness and diversity happen to the image because the image is not itself the exemplar.

**19.** Therefore, while I look at this painted face from the east, it likewise appears that it looks at me in the east, and when I look at it from the west or from the south it also appears to look at me in the west or south. In whatever direction I turn my face, its face seems turned toward me. Thus, too, your face is turned to all faces which look on you. Your vision, Lord, is your face. Consequently, whoever looks on you with a loving face will find only your face looking on oneself with love. And the more one strives to look on you with greater love, the more loving will one find your face. Whoever looks on you with anger will likewise find your face angry. Whoever looks on you with joy will also find your face joyous, just as is the face of the one who looks on you. So indeed the eye of flesh, while peering through a red glass, judges that everything it sees is red or if through a green glass, that everything is green. In the same way, the eye of the mind, wrapped up in contraction and passivity,[41] judges you, who are the object of the mind, according to the nature of the contraction and passivity.

A human being cannot judge except in a human way. When a

person attributes a face to you, one does not seek it outside the human species since one's judgment is contracted within human nature and in judging does not depart the passivity of this contraction. In the same manner, if a lion were to attribute a face to you, it would judge it only as a lion's face; if an ox, as an ox's; if an eagle, as an eagle's.

O Lord, how wonderful is your face, which a young man, if he wished to conceive it, would fashion as youthful; a grown man as manly; and an older man as elderly!

20.     Who could conceive of this sole, truest, and most adequate exemplar of all faces, in such a way that it is the exemplar of all and of each individually and is so most perfectly the exemplar of each as if it were the exemplar of no other? One must leap beyond the forms of all formable faces and beyond all figures. And how would one conceive a face when one would transcend all faces, and all likenesses and figures of all faces, and all concepts that can be formed of a face, and all color, decoration, and beauty of all faces? Whoever, therefore, undertakes to see your face, so long as one conceives anything, is far removed from your face. For every concept of a face is less than your face, O Lord. And every beauty that can be conceived is less than the beauty of your face. Every face has beauty, but none is beauty itself. Your face, Lord, has beauty, and this having is being. It is thus absolute beauty itself, which is the form that gives being to every form of beauty. O immeasurably lovely Face, your beauty is such that all things to which are granted to behold it are not sufficient to admire it.[42]

21.     In all faces the face of faces is seen veiled and in enigma.[43] It is not seen unveiled so long as one does not enter into a certain secret and hidden silence beyond all faces where there is no knowledge or concept of a face. This cloud, mist, darkness, or ignorance into which whoever seeks your face enters when one leaps beyond every knowledge and concept is such that below it your face cannot be found except veiled. But this very cloud reveals your face to be there beyond all veils, just as when our eye seeks to view the light of the sun, which is the sun's face, it first sees it veiled in the stars and in the colors and in all the things which participate its light. But when the eye strives to gaze at the light unveiled, it looks beyond all visible light, because all such light is less than what it seeks. But since the eye seeks to see the light which it cannot see, it knows that so long as it sees anything, what it sees is not what it is seeking. Therefore, it must leap beyond every visible light. Whoever, therefore, has to leap beyond every light

must enter into that which lacks visible light and thus is darkness to the eye. And while one is in that darkness, which is a cloud, if one then knows one is in a cloud, one knows one has come near the face of the sun. For that cloud in one's eye originates from the exceeding brightness of the light of the sun. The denser, therefore, one knows the cloud to be the more one truly attains the invisible light in the cloud. I see, O Lord, that it is only in this way that the inaccessible light,[44] the beauty, and the splendor of your face can be approached without veil.[45]

*Chapter Seven*
*What the Fruit of Facial Seeing Is and How This Will Be Obtained*

22.  So great is that sweetness by which you, O Lord, now feed my soul that it helps itself, howsoever it may, with those things that it experiences in this world and through those most acceptable likenesses that you inspire. For since you, O Lord, are that power or principle from which all things come and since your face is that power and principle from which all faces are what they are, I then turn myself toward this great and lofty nut-tree and seek to perceive its principle.[46] With my sensible eye I see it as tall and wide, colored, and heavy with branches, leaves, and nuts. And then with the eyes of the mind I perceive that this tree existed in the seed, not as I look at it now, but virtually. I study with care the wonderful power of this seed, in which existed this entire tree and all its nuts and all their seminal power, and all trees existed in the seminal power of the nuts. I also see how this power can never at any time be fully unfolded by the movement of the heavens. But this power of the seed, although not able to be completely unfolded, is nevertheless contracted, because it has power only in this one species of nuts. Consequently, although I see the tree in the seed, I still see it only in a contracted power. Then, O Lord, I consider the power of the seeds of all the different species of trees, a power that is contracted to the species of each, and in these seeds I see the trees in their potential.

23.  If, therefore, I wish to see the absolute power of all such seminal powers, which is the power and also the principle giving power to all seeds, I must leap beyond every seminal power that can be known and conceived and enter into that ignorance in which nothing at all remains of seminal power or energy. And then in the cloud I find a most astonishing power, approachable by no power that can be thought.

This is the principle that gives being to every power both seminal and not seminal. This absolute and supereminent power gives to each seminal power that power in which it virtually enfolds a tree, together with all the things that are required for a sensible tree and all that accompany the being of a tree. Therefore, this principle and cause, in an enfolded and absolute way, holds within itself as cause, whatever it gives to its effect. And thus I perceive that this power is the face or exemplar of every arboreal face and of each tree. In this power I see this nut-tree not as in its contracted seminal power but as in the cause and creator of that seminal power.

24.     Hence, I see this tree as a certain unfolding of the power of the seed and the seed as a certain unfolding of omnipotent power. And I perceive that just as in the seed the tree is not a tree but is the power of the seed and that the seed's power is that from which the tree is unfolded, so that nothing can be found in the tree that does not proceed from the power of the seed, so in its cause, which is the power of powers, the seminal power is not seminal power but absolute power. And thus in you my God the tree is you yourself, and in you it is the truth and exemplar of itself. Similarly, also in you the seed of the tree is the truth and exemplar of itself. And of both the tree and the seed, you, O God, are the truth and the exemplar. And that power of seed, which is contracted, is that of the natural power of a species, which is contracted to its species and dwells therein as a contracted principle. But you, my God, are absolute power and, consequently, the nature of all natures.

O God, you have led me to that place in which I see your absolute face to be the natural face of all nature, the face which is the absolute entity of all being, the art and the knowledge of all that can be known.

25.     Whoever, therefore, merits to see your face sees all things openly and nothing remains hidden to this person. Whoever has you, O Lord, knows all things and has all things, and whoever sees you has all things. For no one sees you unless one has you. No one can approach you because you are unapproachable. No one, therefore, will grasp you unless you give yourself to this person. How do I have you, O Lord, I who am not worthy to appear in your presence? How will my prayer reach you, who are unapproachable by every means?[47] How will I beseech you, for what would be more absurd than to ask that you give yourself to me, you who are all in all?[48] And how will you give yourself to me if you do not at the same time give me heaven

and earth and all that are in them?[49] And, even more, how will you give me yourself if you do not also give me myself?

And when I thus rest in the silence of contemplation, you, Lord, answer me within my heart, saying: "Be yours and I too will be yours!"[50]

O Lord, the Sweetness of every delight, you have placed within my freedom that I be my own if I am willing. Hence, unless I am my own, you are not mine, for you would constrain my freedom since you cannot be mine unless I also am mine. And since you have placed this in my freedom, you do not constrain me, but you wait for me to choose to be my own. This depends on me and not on you, O Lord, for you do not limit your maximum goodness but lavish it on all who are able to receive it. But you, O Lord, are your goodness.

26.    But how will I be my own unless you instruct me? You teach me that sense should obey reason and that reason should be lord and master. When, therefore, sense serves reason, I am my own. But reason has no guide except you, O Lord, who are the Word and the Reason of reasons. I see now that if I listen to your Word, which does not cease to speak in me and which continually shines forth in my reason, I will be my own, free and not the slave of sin. And you will be mine and will grant me to see your face, and then I will be saved.[51] May you be blessed, therefore, in your gifts, O God, who alone are able to comfort my soul and to lift it up so that it might hope to attain to you and to enjoy you as its very own gift and as the infinite treasury of all that is desirable.

### Chapter Eight
*How God's Vision Is the Loving, Causing, Reading, and Holding in Itself of All Things*

27.    My heart is restless, O Lord, because your love has inflamed it with such desire that it can find rest only in you.[52] I began to pray the Lord's Prayer, and you inspired me to consider in what manner you are our Father. Your loving is your seeing. Your fatherhood is your vision, which embraces us all in the manner of a father, for we say: "Our *Father*." You are equally universal and individual father, for each says of you: "*Our* Father." Your fatherly love clasps all and each of your children. For a father loves all his children as he does each one because he is the father of all just as he is of each one. He so loves

each child that each believes that one is preferred to all the others. If, therefore, you are a father and our father, we are your children.

**28.** But paternal love precedes filial. As long as we, your children, look on you as children, you do not cease to regard us as father. Therefore, you will be our fatherly provider, having a father's care for us. Your vision is your providence. But if we, your children, renounce you as our father, we cease to be your children. Nor are we, then, free children in our own power, but separating ourselves from you, we set off into a far country[53] and endure an oppressive bondage under a prince who is your adversary, O God. But because of the liberty granted us, since we are the children of you who are liberty itself,[54] you, Father, allow us to depart and to squander our liberty and our best substance in accord with the corrupt desires of our senses. Yet you do not wholly forsake us, but you are present continually urging us. And you speak within us and call us back to return to you, always ready to look on us as before with a father's eye, if we turn away and if we turn again toward you. O merciful God, look on me: Filled with remorse, I now turn back from my wretched servitude in the slimy filth of the swine, where I was perishing with hunger, and seek to be fed whatever there may be in your house.[55]

**29.** Feed me with your gaze, O Lord, and teach me how your gaze sees every sight that sees, everything that can be seen and every act of seeing and also every power of seeing, every power of being seen and every actual seeing that results from them both. Since your seeing is causing, you who cause everything see everything.

Teach me, Lord, how with one glance, you discern [all things] and each individual thing at one and the same time. When I open a book to read, I see the whole page as a jumble and if I want to discern the individual letters, syllables, and words, I must consider each single item individually and in succession. And I cannot read except successively one letter after another, one word after another, and passage by passage. But you, Lord, see the whole page at once and read it instantly. When two of us read the same book, one more quickly and the other more slowly, you read with us both, and you seem to read within time since you read with those reading. And beyond time you see and read all things at once. For your seeing is your reading. From eternity and beyond the limits of time, you have seen and read, together and once for all, every book written and all that can be written. And, too, you read them one after the other with all those who read them. But you do not read one thing in eternity and another with those who read in time, but the same; you do both, in the same way, because you are not changeable but are fixed eternity. However, because eternity does not forsake time, it seems to be moved with time, although in eternity motion is rest.[56]

**30.** You, Lord, see and have eyes. You are, therefore, an eye, because your having is being. You thus observe all things in yourself. For if in me my sight were an eye as in you, my God, then in myself I would see all things. For the eye is like a mirror, and a mirror, however small, figuratively takes into itself a vast mountain and all that exists on the mountain's surface. And in this way the species of all things are observed in the eye. Nevertheless, our sight, through the mirror of the eye, sees only, and in a particular manner, the object toward which it turns its attention, because its power can be determined only in a particular manner by the object. Therefore, it does not see all the things that are captured in the mirror of the eye. But since your sight is an eye or living mirror, it sees all things in itself. Even more, since it is the cause of all that can be seen, it embraces and sees all things in the cause and reason of all, that is, in itself. Your eye, O Lord, reaches toward all things without turning. Our eye must turn itself toward an object because of the quantum angle of our vision. But the angle of your vision, O God, is not quantum but infinite. It is also a circle, or rather, an infinite sphere because your sight is an eye of sphericity and of infinite perfection.[57] For your sight sees all things simultaneously around and above and below.

**31.** Oh, how wonderful to all those who examine it, O God, is your sight, which is *Theos!*[58] How fair and lovely it is to all who love you! How terrible it is to all who have forsaken you, O Lord my God! For by your sight, Lord, you give life to every spirit and make the blessed glad, and drive off every sorrow. Look on me, then, with mercy and my soul is saved!

*Chapter Nine*
*How God's Seeing Is Both Universal and Particular,*
*and the Way to Seeing God*

**32.** You look on all and each together, even as does this painted image that I contemplate, and so I marvel, O Lord, at how in your visual faculty the universal coincides with the particular. But I am mindful that my imagination does not grasp how this may be so, for I seek your vision within my own faculty of sight. And since your vision is not contracted to the sensible organ as is mine, I am deceived in judgment.

Your sight, Lord, is your essence. If, therefore, I consider humanity, which is simple and one in all humans, I find it in all and in each. Although in itself it is neither eastern, nor western, nor southern, nor northern, yet in human beings who are in the east, it is in the east and in those who are in the west, it is in the west. Thus, although neither motion nor rest are of the essence of humanity, nevertheless, it is moved with human beings who move, rests with those who rest, and stands with those who stand, and all this it does at one and the same moment, because humanity does not desert humans whether they are moved or not moved and whether they sleep or rest.

33.　　If this human nature, which is contracted and is not found outside humans, is such that it is not more present in one individual than in another and is so perfectly present in one as if it were in no other, in a far higher way will it be so with uncontracted humanity, which is the exemplar and idea of the contracted human nature and which is as the form and truth of the contracted humanity. For the uncontracted humanity can never abandon the humanity contracted in individuals. For it is the form which gives being to this formal nature. Therefore, no specific form can exist without it, since none in and of itself has being. The specific form stems from the form which exists in and of itself and before which there is no other. That form, therefore, which gives the being of species is absolute form. And this you are, O God, who forms heaven and earth and all things.[59]

34.　　When, therefore, I consider contracted humanity and through it absolute humanity—namely, by seeing the absolute in the contracted as the cause in an effect and the truth and the exemplar in an image—you appear to me, O my God, as the exemplar of all humans and as human per se, that is, as absolute. When in the same way I consider the form of forms in all species you appear to me as the idea and exemplar in them all. Since you are the absolute and most simple exemplar, you are not the composite of many exemplars, but you are the one exemplar, most simple and infinite, so that you are the truest and most adequate exemplar of each and of all that can be formed. You are, therefore, the essence of essences granting to contracted essences to be what they are.[60] Apart from you, therefore, O Lord, nothing can exist.

35.　　If, therefore, your essence penetrates all things, so too does your sight, which is your essence. Just as nothing that exists is able to flee from its own proper being, so neither can it flee from your essence, which gives essential being to all things, nor, therefore, can it flee from your sight. You, Lord, see all things and each single thing at the same time. You are moved with all that are moved and stand with all that stand. Because some are moved while others remain standing, you, Lord, stand and are moved and also proceed and rest at one and the same time. For if both being moved and resting are found at the same time contractedly[61] in different beings, and if nothing can exist apart from you, neither motion nor rest exist apart from you. O Lord, you are wholly present at the same time to all these things and to each. Yet you neither are moved nor rest, since you are superexalted and absolute from all these things that can be conceived or named. Therefore, you stand and you proceed, and at the same time you neither stand nor proceed. The painted face demonstrates this for me. For if I am moved, its gaze seems to be moved with me, because it does not leave me. If while I am moving, another who looks at the face remains standing, the gaze likewise does not abandon this person but stands still with the one standing and looking. However, neither standing nor being moved can properly befit a face absolute from these conditions, because it exists above all standing and motion, in simplest and most absolute infinity. Subsequent to this infinity are motion and rest and opposition and whatever can be expressed or conceived.

**36.** Hence, I experience how necessary it is for me to enter into the cloud and to admit the coincidence of opposites, above all capacity of reason, and to seek there the truth where impossibility confronts me. And above reason, above even every highest intellectual ascent when I will have attained to that which is unknown to every intellect and which every intellect judges to be the most removed from truth, there are you, my God, who are absolute necessity. And the more that cloud of impossibility is recognized as obscure and impossible, the more truly the necessity shines forth and the less veiled it appears and draws near.

**37.** Therefore, I thank you, my God, because you make clear to me that there is no other way of approaching you except that which to all humans, even to the most learned philosophers, seems wholly inaccessible and impossible.[62] For you have shown me that you cannot be seen elsewhere than where impossibility confronts and obstructs me. O Lord, you, who are the food of the mature,[63] have given me courage to do violence to myself,[64] for impossibility coincides with necessity, and I have discovered that the place where you are found unveiled is girded about with the coincidence of contradictories. This is the wall of paradise, and it is there in paradise that you reside. The wall's gate is guarded by the highest spirit of reason, and unless it is overpowered, the way in will not lie open. Thus, it is on the other side of the coincidence of contradictories that you will be able to be seen and nowhere on this side. If, therefore, impossibility is necessity in your sight, O Lord, there is nothing which your sight does not see.

*Chapter Ten*
*How God Is Seen Beyond the Coincidence of Contradictories,*
*and How Seeing Is Being*

38.  I stand before this image of your face, my God, which I observe with the eyes of sense, and I attempt with inward eyes to behold the truth that is designated in the picture. The thought occurs to me, O Lord, that your gaze speaks, for your speaking is not other than your seeing, because they are not in reality different in you, who are absolute simplicity itself. Therefore, I experience clearly that you see all things and each thing together. For when I preach, I speak at one and the same time both to the church congregated and to each individual present in the church. I preach only one word, and with this one word, I speak to each person individually. What is for me the church is for you, O Lord, the entire world and every single creature which exists or can exist. Thus, you speak to individuals, and you see those to which you speak.

39.  O Lord, you are the supreme comfort of those who hope in you. You inspire me to praise you from myself. For, as you willed, you have given me one face, and those to whom I preach see it individually and at the same time. Each one sees my individual face, and each hears in whole this simple sermon of mine. However, I cannot at the same moment hear separately all who speak, but only one at a time, nor can I at the same moment see them separately, but only one by one. But if such great power existed in me that being heard would coincide with hearing and being seen with seeing and also speaking with hearing, as in you, O Lord, who are the highest power, then I would hear and see all and each one at the same time. Just as I would speak to individuals simultaneously, so also in the very same moment in which I were speaking I would see and hear the responses of all and each.[65]

40.  Consequently, when I am at the door of the coincidence of opposites, guarded by the angel stationed at the entrance of paradise,[66] I

begin to see you, O Lord. For you are there where speaking, seeing, hearing, tasting, touching, reasoning, knowing, and understanding are the same and where seeing coincides with being seen, hearing with being heard, tasting with being tasted, touching with being touched, speaking with hearing, and creating with speaking. If I were to see just as I am visible, I would not be a creature, and if you, O God, did not see just as you are visible, you would not be God, the Almighty. You are visible by all creatures and you see all. In that you see all you are seen by all. For otherwise creatures cannot exist since they exist by your vision. If they did not see you who see, they would not receive being from you. The being of a creature is equally your seeing and your being seen.[67]

By your word, you speak to all that are and call into existence all that are not.[68] You call them to hear you, and when they hear you, then they are. When, therefore, you speak, you speak to all and all to which you speak hear you. You speak to the earth, and you call it into human nature. The earth hears you, and its hearing this is its becoming human being. You speak to nothing as if it were something, and you call nothing into something, and nothing hears you since what was nothing becomes something.[69]

**41.** O infinite Power, your conceiving is your speaking. You conceive sky, and it exists as you conceive it. You conceive earth, and it exists as you conceive it. While conceiving, you see and you speak and you work and you do all else that one is able to name.

You inspire wonder, my God. You speak once; you conceive once. How is it, therefore, that all things do not exist simultaneously, but many come into being successively? How do so many diverse things exist out of a single concept? You enlighten me, stationed at the threshold of the door, for your concept is simplest eternity itself. Nothing, however, can be made subsequent to simplest eternity. Infinite duration, which is eternity itself, embraces all succession. Everything, therefore, that appears to us in succession in no way exists subsequent to your concept, which is eternity. For your unique concept, which is also your Word, enfolds all things and each single thing. Your eternal Word cannot be manifold, diverse, variable, or subject to change, because it is simple eternity. Thus, O Lord, I see that nothing exists subsequent to your concept, but all things exist because you conceive them. Moreover, you conceive in eternity. But in eternity succession is, without succession, eternity itself, your Word itself, O Lord my God. You have not conceived before it existed anything that appears to us in time. For in eternity, in which you conceive, all temporal succession coincides in the same now of eternity. Therefore, nothing is past or future where future and past coincide with the present.

42.     But that things in this world exist according to earlier and later stems from the fact that you did not conceive such things earlier so that they would exist. Had you conceived them earlier, they would have existed earlier. But one is not almighty in whose thought earlier and later occur, so that one first conceives one thing and afterward another. Thus, since you are God the Almighty, you are in Paradise inside its wall. The wall, moreover, is that coincidence where later coincides with earlier, where the end coincides with the beginning, and where the alpha and the omega are the same.[70]

Therefore, things exist always because you tell them to exist, and they do not exist earlier because you do not earlier speak. When I read that Adam existed so many years ago and that one such as he was born today, it seems impossible that Adam existed then because you then willed it and likewise that someone else was born today because now you have willed it, and that nevertheless you did not earlier will Adam to exist than you willed the one born today to exist. But that which seems impossible is necessity itself. For *now* and *then* exist after your word. And, therefore, to one approaching you, *now* and *then* meet in coincidence within the wall that surrounds the place where you dwell. For *now* and *then* coincide in the circle of the wall of paradise. But it is beyond *now* and *then* that you, my God, who are absolute eternity, exist and speak.

### Chapter Eleven
#### *How in God Succession Is Seen Without Succession*

43.     I experience your goodness, my God, which not only does not reject me, a wretched sinner, but sweetly nourishes me with a certain longing. You have inspired a likeness pleasing to me about the unity of your mental word or concept and its variety, successively, in appearances. The simple concept of a most perfect clock directs me so that I might be more delightfully caught up to the vision of your concept and your word. For the simple concept of a clock enfolds all temporal succession. If, let us assume, the clock were a concept, then although we hear the sixth hour strike before the seventh, nevertheless, the seventh is heard only when the concept orders it. The sixth

hour is not earlier in the concept than the seventh or the eighth, but in the single concept of the clock, no hour is earlier or later than another, although the clock never strikes the hour except when the concept orders it. It is true to say upon hearing the sound of the sixth hour that the sixth strikes then because the concept of the master wills it so.

**44.**     Since in the concept of God the clock is the concept, we perceive to some small extent how succession is in the clock without succession being in the word or concept; that in this most simple concept are enfolded all motions and sounds and whatever we experience in succession; that everything that occurs successively does not in any way evade the concept, but is the unfolding of the concept, so that the concept gives being to each; and that nothing existed before it occurred, since it was not conceived before it existed.

**45.**     If, therefore, the concept of a clock were as though eternity itself, in the clock the movement is succession. Eternity, therefore, enfolds and unfolds succession. For the concept of a clock, when the concept is eternity, equally enfolds and unfolds all things.

Blessed be you, O Lord my God, who feed and nourish me with the milk of likenesses until you grant me more solid food.[71] Lead me, Lord God, by these paths to you. For unless you lead me, I cannot remain on the path because of the frailty of my corrupt nature and of the futile vessel that I bear.[72]

**46.**     Trusting in your help, O Lord, I return again in order to find you beyond the wall of the coincidence of enfolding and unfolding.[73] When at the same time I go in and go out through this door of your word and concept, I discover the sweetest nourishment. I enter when I find you as power that enfolds all things. I go out when I find you as power that unfolds. I both go in and go out when I find you as power that both enfolds and unfolds.[74] I go in proceeding from creatures to you, the Creator, from the effects to the cause; I go out from you, the Creator, from the cause to the effects. I go in and go out simultaneously when I see how to go out is to go in and to go in is simultaneously to go out. In the same way one who is counting unfolds and enfolds alike; as one counts one unfolds the power of unity and enfolds number in unity.[75] For the creature's going forth from you is its entering into you, and to unfold is to enfold. When I see you, O God, in paradise, which this wall of the coincidence of opposites surrounds, I see that you neither enfold nor unfold, whether disjunctively or together. For disjunction and conjunction alike are the wall

255

of coincidence beyond which are you, absolute from all that can be spoken or thought.

### Chapter Twelve
### *That Where the Invisible Is Seen, the Uncreated Is Created*

47.    Formerly you appeared to me, O Lord, as invisible by every creature because you are a hidden, infinite God.[76] Infinity, however, is incomprehensible by every means of comprehending. Later you appeared to me as visible by all, for a thing exists only as you see it, and it would not actually exist unless it saw you. For your vision confers being, since your vision is your essence. Thus, my God, you are equally invisible and visible. As you are, you are invisible; as the creature is, which exists only insofar as the creature sees you, you are visible. You, therefore, my invisible God, are seen by all, and in all sight you are seen by everyone who sees. You who are invisible, who are both absolute from everything visible and infinitely superexalted, are seen in every visible thing and in every act of vision.

Therefore, I must leap across this wall of invisible vision to where you are to be found. But this wall is both everything and nothing. For you, who confront as if you were both all things and nothing at all, dwell inside that high wall which no natural ability can scale by its own power.

48.    At times you confront me so that I think you see all things in yourself as a living mirror in which all things are reflected. But because your seeing is knowing, then it occurs to me that you do not see all things in yourself as a living mirror would, for in this case your knowledge would arise from things. Then you seem to me to see all things in yourself as a power looking on itself. If, for example, the power of the seed of a tree looked on itself, it would see in itself the virtual tree, since the power of the seed is virtually the tree. But, afterward, it occurs to me that you do not see yourself and all things in yourself as a power. For to see a tree in the potency of its power is different from the sight by which a tree is seen in actuality. And then I discover how your infinite power surpasses the power of a mirror or a seed and exceeds the coincidence of radiating and reflecting and of both cause and effect. I learn how your absolute power is absolute vision, which is perfection itself and above all the modes of seeing; for your vision, which is your essence, my God, is, without mode, all the modes, which make manifest the perfection of vision.

**49.**     Yet, most merciful Lord, permit a paltry creature to address you. If your seeing is your creating and if you see nothing other than yourself, but you yourself are your own object, for you are the seer, the seeable, and the seeing, how, therefore, do you create things that are other than yourself? For you seem to create yourself even as you see yourself. But you strengthen me, Life of my spirit. For I am confronted by the wall of absurdity, which is the wall of the coincidence of creating with being created, as if it were impossible for creating to coincide with being created. For it seems that to admit this would affirm that a thing exists before it exists; for when a thing creates, it is, and yet it is not since it is created. Nevertheless, this wall is not an obstacle, for your creating is your being. Creating and being created alike are not other than communicating your being to all things so that you are all things in all things[77] and yet remain absolute from them all. To call into being things which are not[78] is to communicate being to nothing. Thus, to call is to create, and to communicate is to be created.[79] Beyond this coincidence of creating with being created are you, O God, absolute and infinite, neither creating nor creatable, although all things are what they are because you are.

**50.**     O Depth of riches, how incomprehensible you are![80] So long as I conceive a creator creating, I am still on this side of the wall of paradise. And so long as I imagine a creatable creator, I have not yet entered, but I am at the wall. But when I see you as absolute infinity to whom is suited neither the name of creating creator nor that of creatable creator, then I begin to behold you in an unveiled way and to enter the garden of delights. For you are not anything that can be named or conceived but are absolutely and infinitely superexalted above all such things. You are not, therefore, creator but infinitely more than creator, although without you nothing is made or can be made. To you be the praise and the glory through all eternity.[81]

### Chapter Thirteen
#### That God Is Seen to Be Absolute Infinity

**51.**     O Lord God, helper of those who seek you, I see you in the garden of paradise, and I do not know what I see, because I see nothing visible. I know this alone that I know that I do not know what I see and that I can never know. I do not know how to name you, because I do not know what you are. Should anyone tell me that you are named by this or that name, by the fact that one gives a name I know that it is not your name. For the wall beyond which I see you is the limit of every mode of signification by names. Should anyone express any concept by which you could be conceived, I know that this concept is not a concept of you, for every concept finds its boundary at the wall of paradise. Should anyone express any likeness and say that you ought to be conceived according to it, I know in the same way that this is not a likeness of you. So too if anyone, wishing to furnish the means by which you might be understood, should set forth an understanding of you, one is still far removed from you. For the highest wall separates you from all these and secludes you from everything that can be said or thought, because you are absolute from all the things that can fall within any concept.[82]

52.    Accordingly, when I am lifted up to the highest, I see you as infinity. For this reason you cannot be approached, comprehended, named, multiplied, or seen. Whoever, therefore, approaches you must ascend above every end, every limit, and every finite thing. But how will one reach you, who are the end to which one strives, if one must ascend above the end? Does not whoever ascends above the end enter into what is indeterminate and confused and thus, with respect to the intellect, into ignorance and obscurity, which belong to intellectual confusion? The intellect, therefore, must become ignorant and established in darkness if it wishes to see you. But what, my God, is intellect in ignorance if not learned ignorance?[83] O God, you are infinity, and no one can approach you except one whose intellect abides in ignorance, that is, one whose intellect knows that it is ignorant of you.

How can the intellect grasp you, who are infinity? The intellect knows that it is ignorant and that you cannot be grasped because you are infinity. For to understand infinity is to comprehend the incomprehensible. The intellect knows that it is ignorant of you because it knows that you can be known only if the unknowable could be known, and the invisible seen, and the inaccessible reached.

53.    My God, you are absolute infinity itself, which I perceive to be the infinite end,[84] but I am unable to grasp how an end without an end is an end. You, O God, are your own end, since you are whatever you have; if you have an end, you are an end. You are, therefore, an infinite end, because you are your own end, for your end is your essence. The essence of end is not bounded or ended in anything other than end but in itself. The end, therefore, which is its own end is infinite, and every end that is not its own end is a finite end. You, Lord, since you

are the end limiting all things, are the end that has no end, and thus you are an end without end, or infinite end, which eludes all reason, for it involves a contradiction. When, therefore, I assert the existence of the infinite, I admit that darkness is light, ignorance knowledge, and the impossible necessary. Since we admit the existence of an end of the finite, we necessarily admit the infinite, the final end, or the end without an end. We cannot but admit that finite beings exist; thus, we cannot refuse to admit the infinite. We are admitting, therefore, the coincidence of contradictories, above which is the infinite. But this coincidence is a contradiction without contradiction, and it is an end without end.

**54.**      You, Lord, tell me that just as in unity otherness is without otherness because it is unity, so in infinity contradiction is without contradiction because it is infinity. Infinity is simplicity itself of all that are spoken; contradiction does not exist without otherness. Yet in simplicity otherness exists without otherness because it is simplicity itself. For all that can be said of absolute simplicity coincides with it, because in absolute simplicity having is being. The opposition of opposites is an opposition without opposition, just as the end of finite things is an end without an end. You are, therefore, O God, the opposition of opposites, because you are infinite, and because you are infinite, you are infinity itself. In infinity the opposition of opposites is without opposition.[85]

**55.**      Lord, my God, strength of the weak,[86] I see that you are infinity itself. Therefore, there is nothing that is other than, or different from, or opposite you. For infinity is incompatible with otherness; for since it is infinity, nothing exists outside it. Absolute infinity includes and embraces all things. If there were infinity and another outside it, then there would be neither infinity nor something other, for infinity is unable to be greater or less. Nothing, therefore, exists outside it. Unless infinity included in itself all being, it would not be infinity, and if there were no infinity, there would be no end, nor anything other or different, since these cannot exist without otherness of limits and ends. If, therefore, the infinite is removed, nothing remains. Infinity, therefore, exists and enfolds all things and nothing is able to exist outside it. Consequently, nothing exists that is infinity's other or that is different from it. Infinity, therefore, is all things in such a way that it is no one of them.[87] No name can fit infinity, for every name can have its contrary. But to infinity, which is unnameable, there can be no contrary. Neither is infinity a whole to which a part is opposite, nor can it be a part. It is neither great nor small, nor any of all the things that can be named in heaven or on earth. Infinity is above them all.

56.     Infinity is neither greater nor less than nor equal to anything. But when I consider that infinity is not greater or less than any given thing, I affirm that it is the measure of all things, since it is neither greater nor less. And thus I conceive it as the equality of being.[88] But such equality is infinity, and in this way it is not the equality whose opposite is inequality, but in this equality inequality is equality. For in infinity inequality is without inequality, because it is infinity. In this way, too, in infinity equality is infinity. Infinite equality is an end without end. Granted it is neither greater nor less, yet it is not for this reason the equality that is understood as contracted; rather it is the infinite equality that does not admit of greater or less. And so it is not more equal to one than to another but is equal to one in such a way that it is equal to all and to all in such a way as to none. For the infinite is not contractible but remains absolute. If the infinite were able to be contracted away from infinity, it would not be the infinite. Therefore, the infinite cannot be contracted to equality with the finite, although it is not unequal to anything. For how could inequality suit the infinite to which neither more nor less belong? The infinite, therefore, in relation to any given thing, is neither greater nor less, nor unequal; nor, consequently, is it equal to the finite, for it is infinitely above everything finite. It exists per se; the infinite, therefore, is wholly absolute and uncontractible.

57.     O Lord, how exalted you are above all things[89] and also how lowly,[90] for you are in all![91] If infinity were contractible to any nameable thing, such as a line, or a surface, or a species, it would attract to itself that to which it would be contracted, and, thus, that the infinite is contractible implies a contradiction,[92] for the infinite is not contracted but attracts. For if I say that the infinite is contracted to a line, as, for example, when I speak of an infinite line, then the line is attracted into the infinite, for the line ceases to be a line when it does not have quantity and an end. An infinite line is not a line, but in infinity a line is infinity. Just as nothing can be added to the infinite, so the infinite cannot be contracted to anything so as to be other than the infinite. Infinite goodness is not goodness but infinity; infinite quantity is not quantity but infinity; and so with all else.

You are great, O God, and your greatness has no end,[93] and thereby I see that you are the immeasurable measure of all things, just as you are their infinite end. Therefore, O Lord, because you are infinite, you are without beginning and end. You are the beginning without beginning and the end without end. You are the beginning without end and the end without beginning, the beginning in such a way as to be the end and the end in such a way as to be the beginning. You are neither beginning nor end, but above beginning and end you are absolute infinity itself, forever blessed.

### Chapter Fourteen
### *How Without Otherness God Enfolds All Things*

**58.**  From the infinity of your mercy, I see, O Lord, that you are infinity embracing all things. There is nothing that exists outside you, but all things in you are not other than you. You teach me, Lord, how otherness, which is not in you, does not exist in itself, nor can it exist. Nor does otherness, which does not exist in you, make one creature other than another, although one creature is not another. The sky is not the earth, although it is true that the sky is sky and the earth is earth. If, therefore, I seek otherness, which exists neither in you nor outside you, where will I find it? And if it does not exist, how is it that the earth is another creature than the sky? This is inconceivable without otherness.

But you speak in me, O Lord, and tell me that otherness has no positive principle, and thus it does not exist.[94] For how could otherness exist without a principle unless it were itself principle and infinity? Otherness, however, is not the principle of being, because its name is derived from not-being. Because one thing is not another, it is therefore called "other." Otherness, therefore, cannot be the principle of being, since it receives its name from not-being, and it does not have a principle of being, since it stems from not-being. Otherness, therefore, is not anything.[95] That the sky is not the earth is because the sky is not infinity itself, which embraces all being.

**59.**  Accordingly, because infinity is absolute infinity, thence it follows that one thing cannot be another. For example, the essence of Socrates[96] embraces all Socratic being, and in the simple Socratic being there is no otherness or diversity. For the being of Socrates is the individual unity of all that is in Socrates. And so in this single being is enfolded the being of all that exists in Socrates, namely, in the individual simplicity where nothing other or diverse is found. But in this single being, all things that have Socratic being exist and are enfolded, and outside it they neither exist nor can exist. However, in this most simple being, the eye is not the ear, and the head is not the heart, sight is not hearing, and sense is not reason. But this does not result from any principle of otherness, but given the most simple Socratic being, it follows that the head is not the feet because the head is not the most simple Socratic being itself. The head, therefore, does not embrace the whole Socratic being. And thus I see, because you illumine me, O Lord, that the being of one member is not the being of another since the simple Socratic being is utterly incommunicable and cannot in any way be contracted to the being of any one member. Rather, this simple Socratic being is the being of all Socrates' members, and in it all the variety and otherness of being that befalls the members is a simple unity, just as the plurality of the forms of the parts is a unity in the form of a whole.[97]

60.     Thus, somehow, O God, does your being, which is absolutely the being of infinity, stand in relation to all the things that exist; but by "absolutely" I am saying: as the absolute form of being of all contracted forms. Hence, when the hand of Socrates is separated from Socrates, although after the amputation it would no longer be Socrates' hand, yet it endures in some sort of way as the being of a cadaver. This is so because the form of Socrates, which gives being, does not give being simply but gives a contracted being, namely, Socratic being. From this the being of the hand can be separated, and it endures but under another form. But if at any time the hand were separated from the completely uncontracted being, which is infinite and absolute, it would totally cease to exist, because it would be separated from all being.

I give thanks to you, O Lord my God, who generously disclose yourself to me, insofar as I can comprehend, that you are infinity itself, enfolding the being of all things by a most simple power, which would not be infinite unless it were infinitely united. For power united is stronger. A power that is so united that it cannot be more united is therefore infinite and omnipotent. You are omnipotent, O God, because you are absolute simplicity, which is absolute infinity.

*Chapter Fifteen*
*How Actual Infinity Is Unity in Which the Image Is Truth*

61.     Sustain further your little servant, who is surely without wisdom except so much as you grant that he may speak to you, his God. I see

in this painted face[98] an image of infinity, for its gaze is not limited to an object or a place and thus is infinite. For those who look on it, it is not turned more to one than to another. Although its gaze is infinite in itself, yet it seems limited by anyone looking on it, because it so fixes its gaze on anyone beholding it as if it saw this person alone and nothing else. You appear to me, therefore, O Lord, as if you were absolute and infinite power to be,[99] formable and determinable by every form. For we say that the formable potency of matter is infinite, since it will never be entirely brought to a determinate end.

But, you, O Infinite Light, answer in me that absolute potency is infinity itself, which is beyond the wall of coincidence, where the power to be made coincides with the power to make, where potency coincides with act.[100] Although prime matter is in potency to an infinite amount of forms, however it cannot possess them in act; instead the potency is determined by one form, and when this is taken away, the potency is determined by another.[101] If, therefore, the power to be of matter should coincide with act, it would be potency in such a way as to be act; and just as it would be in potency to an infinite amount of forms, so in act it would be formed an infinite number of times.[102] However, infinity in act is without otherness, and there cannot be infinity if it is not unity. Therefore, there cannot be infinite forms in actuality, but actual infinity is unity.

**62.** You, therefore, O God, who are infinity itself, are the one God, in whom I see that all power to be exists actually. For power absolute from all potency that is contracted to prime matter or to any passive potency is absolute being. For whatever exists in infinite being is simplest infinite being itself. Thus, in infinite being, the power to be all things is infinite being itself. Similarly, in infinite being, actually being all things is infinite being itself. Therefore, in you, my God, absolute power to be and absolute actual being are only you, my infinite God. You, my God, are all power to be.[103]

Prime matter's power to be is material and thus contracted and not absolute; so too sensible or rational power to be is contracted, but completely uncontracted power coincides with the simply absolute, that is, with the infinite.[104]

**63.** Therefore, my God, when you confront me as if formable prime matter, because you receive the form of whoever beholds you, then you lift me up that I may see how one looking on you does not give you form, but rather one sees oneself in you, for one receives from you that which one is. Thus, what you seem to receive from one who looks on you is your gift, as if you were the living mirror of eternity, which is the form of forms. While anyone looks into this mirror, one sees one's own form in the form of forms, which is the mirror. And one judges the form which one sees in the mirror to be the image of one's own form since this is the case with a polished material mirror. Yet the contrary is true. For that which one sees in this mirror of eternity is not an image but what one sees is the truth of which one who sees is an image. Therefore, in you my God the image is the truth and the exemplar of all things and of each one of them that exists or can exist.

64.     O God, you are wondrous to every mind. You, who are light, at times are seen as if you were shadow. For as long as I see how, according to my changing, the gaze of your icon seems to be changed and your face seems to be changed because I am changed, you confront me as if you were a shadow which follows the changing of the one walking about. But since I am a living shadow and you are the truth, I conclude from the changing of the shadow that the truth is changed. Therefore, my God, you are shadow in such a way that you are truth. You are the image of me and everyone else in such a way that you are the exemplar.

O Lord God, who illumines hearts, my face is a true face because you, who are truth, have given it to me. My face is also an image because it is not the truth itself but an image of absolute truth. In my thought I enfold the truth and the image of my face, and I see that in my face the image coincides with facial truth so that insomuch as my face is image it is true.

65.     Then you show me, O Lord, how according to the changing of my face your face is equally changed and unchanged. It is changed because it does not forsake the truth of my face; it is unchanged because it does not follow the changing of the image. For this reason, just as your face does not abandon the truth of my face, so also it does not follow the changing of an image that can be changed, for absolute truth is unchangeability. The truth of my face is changeable, for it is truth in such a way as to be image. But yours is unchangeable, for it is image in such a way as to be truth. Absolute truth cannot abandon the truth of my face, for if it should, my face, which is a changeable truth, could not exist. Thus, O God, because of your infinite goodness, you seem changeable since you do not forsake changeable creatures. But because you are absolute goodness, you are not changeable, since you do not follow after changeability.

O profoundest Depth, my God, you who do not abandon your creatures and at the same time do not follow after them! O inexplicable Loving-kindness, you offer yourself to any of us looking on you, as though you receive being from us, and you conform yourself to us so that we will love you more the more you seem like us. For we cannot hate ourselves. Therefore, we love that which participates and accompanies our being. We embrace our likeness because we are shown ourselves in an image and we love ourselves in it.

**66.**     Out of the humility of your infinite goodness, O God, you present yourself as though you were our creature that thus you may draw us to you. For you draw us to yourself by every possible means by which a free and rational creature can be drawn. In you, O God, being created coincides with creating. For the likeness that seems to be created by me is the Truth that creates me, so that in this way at least I may grasp how greatly I should be bound to you, since in you being loved coincides with loving. For if I ought to love myself in you, my likeness, then I am greatly constrained to do this when I see that you love me as your creature and your image. How can a father not love a son who is a son in such a way as to be a father? And if one who is in esteem a son and in knowledge a father is much loved, are you not most greatly lovable who in esteem exceed a son and in knowledge exceed a father? You have willed, O God, that filial love be established in esteem, and you will to be esteemed as one who is more similar than a son and to be known as one who is more intimate than a father, because you are love enfolding both filial and paternal love. May you, therefore, my God, who are my sweetest love, be blessed forever.[105]

### Chapter Sixteen
### That If God Were Not Infinite, God Would Not Be the End of Desire

**67.**     Fire does not cease to burn and neither does the desiring love that is directed to you, O God, who are the form of every desirable thing and the truth which is desired in every desiring. Through your gift, as sweet as honey, I have begun to taste your incomprehensible sweetness, which is more pleasing to me the more infinite that it appears. Therefore, I perceive that the reason you, O God, are unknown to all creatures[106] is that they may have in this most sacred ignorance a greater rest, as if in an incalculable and inexhaustible treasure.[107] For a much greater joy fills anyone who finds such a treasure which one knows to be utterly innumerable and infinite than any who finds a treasure that can be counted and is finite. This most sacred ignorance of your greatness is, therefore, the most desirable nourishment for my intellect, especially when I find such a treasure in my own field[108] so that the treasure is mine.

**68.**  O Fountain of riches, you will to be grasped and possessed by me and yet to remain incomprehensible and infinite. For you are the treasure of delights of which no one can desire an end. For how could the appetite desire not to exist? For whether the will desires to be or not to be, the appetite itself cannot find rest but is borne to eternity. You come down, Lord, that you may be comprehended, and you remain innumerable and infinite, and unless you remained infinite, you would not be the end of desire.

You are, therefore, infinite that you may be the end of all desire. For intellectual desire is not borne toward that which can be greater or more desirable. But everything this side of infinite can be greater. Therefore, the end of desire is infinite.

You, therefore, O God, are infinity itself, which alone I desire in every desiring. But I cannot approach the knowledge of this infinity more closely than to know that it is infinity.

**69.**  The more I comprehend you, my God, to be incomprehensible, the more I attain you because the more I attain the end of my desire. I reject as misleading whatever I come across that attempts to show that you are comprehensible. My desire in which you shine forth leads me to you because it rejects all that is finite and comprehensible, for in these it can find no rest, because by you it is led to you. Moreover, you are the beginning without beginning and the end without end. Therefore, desire is led by the eternal beginning, from which it comes to be desire, to the end without end, and this end is infinite. If, therefore I, a paltry human being, would not be content with you, my God, if I knew you to be comprehensible, it is because I am led by you to you, who are incomprehensible and infinite.

**70.**  I see you, O Lord my God, in a certain mental rapture, because if sight is not satisfied by seeing, nor the ear by hearing, then even less is the intellect satisfied by understanding. Therefore, that which satisfies the intellect, or that which is its end, is not that which the intellect understands. Nor can that which the intellect utterly does not understand satisfy it, but only that which it understands by not understanding. For the intelligible which the intellect knows does not satisfy it, nor does the intelligible of which it is totally ignorant, but only the intelligible which the intellect knows to be so intelligible that this intelligible can never be fully known can satisfy the intellect, just as someone who has an insatiable hunger is not satisfied by a small portion which one can eat or by a meal not set down for one, but only by that meal brought to one, and which, though continually eaten, can never be fully consumed, because, since it is infinite, it is not diminished by being eaten.[109]

### Chapter Seventeen
### *That God Can Be Seen Perfectly Only as Triune*

**71.**     You have disclosed yourself to me, O Lord, as so lovable that you cannot be more lovable. For you are infinitely lovable, my God. Never, therefore, can you be loved by anyone as you are lovable except by one who is infinitely loving. For unless there were one who is infinitely loving, you would not be infinitely lovable; for your lovableness, which is the power to be loved infinitely, exists because there is a power to love infinitely. From the power to love infinitely and the power to be loved infinitely arises an infinite bond of love between the infinite lover and the infinite lovable. But the infinite cannot be multiple. You, therefore, my God, who are love, are the loving love, the lovable love, and the love which is the bond of loving love and lovable love.[110]

I see in you, my God, loving love and from the fact that I see in you loving love and lovable love, I see the bond of love of each. This is not other than what I see in your absolute unity,[111] in which I perceive the unity which unites, the unity which is unitable, and the bond of each.

**72.**     But whatever I see in you, this you are, my God. You are, therefore, that infinite love which cannot be seen by me as natural and perfect love without one who is loving, one who is lovable, and the bond between them. For how can I conceive of a most perfect and most natural love without one who loves, one who is lovable, and their bond? For in contracted love I experience that it is of the essence of perfect love that love be loving, lovable, and the bond of the two. Now, that which is of the essence of perfect contracted love cannot be lacking to absolute love from which contracted love possesses whatever perfection it has.

Moreover, the simpler love is, the more perfect it is. But you, my God, are the most perfect and the most simple love. You, therefore, are the most perfect, the most simple, and the most natural essence of love. Consequently, in you, as love, the lover is not one thing, the lovable another, and the bond between them still other, but they are the same; they are you yourself, my God. Since, therefore, in you the lovable coincides with the lover and being loved coincides with loving, the bond of this coincidence is an essential bond. For there is nothing in you which is not your essence itself.

73.     Therefore, these which present themselves to me as three, namely, the lover, the lovable, and the bond, are the absolute and most simple essence itself. Thus, they are not three but one. Your essence, my God, which appears to me to be most simple and most one, is not most natural and most perfect without these three. Your essence, therefore, is triune, and yet there are not three in it, since it is most simple. Thus, the plurality of these three names is plurality in such a way as to be unity and their unity is unity in such a way as to be plurality. And their plurality is a plurality without plural number, for a plural number cannot be simple unity because it is a plural number.[112] Therefore, there is no numerical distinction between these three because such a distinction would be essential, for number is essentially distinguished from number. Since their unity is triune, it is not the unity of a singular number, for the unity of a singular number is not triune.[113]

74.     O most wondrous God, who are neither of singular number nor of plural, but above all plurality and singularity, you are one in three and three in one. Therefore, I perceive that at the wall of paradise, wherein you reside, my God, plurality coincides with singularity and that you dwell beyond, exceedingly far off.

Teach me, Lord, how I can conceive as possible that which I see as necessary. For I am confronted by the impossibility that the plurality of the three, without which I cannot conceive you as perfect and natural love, is a plurality without number, as if a man said *one, one, one*; he says *one* three times, and he does not say *three* but *one*, and this *one* three times. Yet he cannot say *one* three times without the number three, although he does not say *three*. For when he says *one* three times, he repeats it without counting. For to count is to alter the one, but to repeat one and the same thing three times is to make plural without number.[114]

75.     The plurality, therefore, which I see in you, my God, is an otherness without otherness, since it is an otherness which is identity. For when I perceive that the one who loves is not the lovable and that the bond is neither the lover nor the lovable, I do not thus see the

lover not to be the lovable as if the lover were one thing and the lovable another. But I perceive that the distinction between the one who loves and the lovable exists inside of the wall of the coincidence of unity and otherness.[115] Therefore, this distinction, which is inside of the wall of coincidence, where the distinct and the indistinct coincide, precedes all otherness and diversity that can be understood. For the wall shuts out the power of every intellect, although the eye looks beyond into paradise. Yet that which the eye sees it can neither name nor understand; for what is seen is the eye's secret love and a hidden treasure, which remains hidden after having been found, because it is discovered inside of the wall of the coincidence of the hidden and the revealed.

76.     But I cannot be drawn away from the sweetness of this vision before in some way I draw to myself the revelation of the distinction between the lover, the lovable, and the bond between them. For it seems that in some way one can enjoy by a figure a slight foretaste of its sweetest savor. You, O Lord, thus grant that I see love in myself because I see myself as one who loves. And since I see me loving myself, I see myself as lovable and as the most natural bond between them. I am lover, I am the lovable, I am their bond. The love, therefore, without which none of these three could exist, is one. I the lover am one; I the lovable am this same one; and I the bond arising from the love by which I love myself am the same one. I am one and not three.

77.     Suppose, therefore, that my love were my essence, as with you, my God, then the unity of these three would exist in the unity of my essence, and the unity of my essence would exist in their trinity. In my essence, all would exist in a contracted way even in the manner in which I see them existing truly and absolutely in you.

Furthermore, the love that loves would not be the love that is lovable or their bond, and this I experience in the following application. For through the love that loves that I extend outside myself to another object, as if to something lovable which is the external of my essence, there follows the bond by which I am united to that object as much as I am capable of being. The object is not joined to me by this bond since my love's object does not love me. Therefore, although I love it in such a way that my love that loves extends itself upon it, yet my love that loves does not draw out with itself my love that is lovable. For I do not become lovable to the object. For it does not care for me, although I love it greatly, as sometimes a son does not care about his mother who loves him most tenderly. And thus I experience that the love that loves is neither the love that is lovable nor their bond, but I perceive that the lover is distinguished from the lovable and from their bond. This distinction, to be sure, is not in the essence of love, since I cannot love either myself or another than myself without love. Thus, love is of the essence of the three. And in this way I perceive a most simple essence of the three, although they are distinguished among themselves.

78.    I have set forth, Lord, by a likeness a kind of foretaste of your nature. But you who are merciful, be sparing, for I am attempting to depict the undepictable taste of your sweetness. For if the sweetness of an unknown fruit remains unable to be depicted by every picture and symbol or unable to be expressed by every word, who am I, wretched sinner, to strive to show you who cannot be shown and to depict as visible you who are invisible and to presume to make savory your infinite and utterly inexpressible sweetness? I have never yet merited to taste it. And through that which I describe here I diminish rather than magnify it. But so great is your goodness, my God, that you even permit the blind to speak of the light and to herald the praises of one of whom they neither know anything nor can know unless it is revealed to them.

79.    Revelation, however, does not attain to this taste; the ear of faith does not attain this tasteable sweetness.[116] Yet, O God, you have revealed to me that ear has not heard nor has there descended into the human heart the infinity of your sweetness, which has been prepared for those who love you.[117] This was revealed to us by Paul, your great apostle, who was caught up, beyond the wall of coincidence, into paradise,[118] where alone you, who are the Fountain of delights, can be seen without veil. Trusting in your infinite goodness, I have ventured to surrender myself to rapture in order to see you, who are invisible, and the unrevealable vision revealed. You know how far I have reached, but I do not; yet your grace is sufficient for me;[119] by it you both assure me that you are incomprehensible and also lift me up into the firm hope that through your guidance I may come to enjoy you forever.

*Chapter Eighteen*
*That If God Were Not Three, There Would Not Be Happiness*

80.    Would, Lord, that all who by your gift have received eyes of the mind would open them and would see with me how you, who are a

jealous God,[120] can hate nothing because you are the love that loves. For in you, who are a lovable God, enfolding all that is lovable, you love all that which is lovable, so that thus they would see with me by what alliance or bond you are united to all things.

You love, O loving God, all things in such a way that you love each single thing. You stretch forth your love to all. Yet many do not love you but prefer another to you. However, if lovable love were not distinct from love that loves, you would be so lovable to all that they could not love anything besides you, and all rational spirits would be compelled to love you. But you are so magnanimous, my God, that you will for rational souls to be free to love you or not to love you. For this reason it does not follow that because you love, you are loved. You, therefore, my God, are united to all by a bond of love, for you stretch forth your love upon all your creatures. But not every rational spirit is united to you, because it extends its love not to your lovableness but to another to which it is united and bound.

By your love that loves, you have betrothed every rational soul, but not every bride loves you, her Bridegroom, but very often clings to another. But how, my God, could your bride, the human soul, attain her end if you were not lovable so that thus by loving you, the lovable, she could attain to the happiest bond and union?

81.      Who, therefore, can deny that you, O God, are triune, when one sees that if you were not three and one, you would not be a noble or a natural and perfect God, nor would there be the spirit of free choice nor could one arrive at the joy of you and at one's own happiness? Because you are intellect that understands and intellect that can be understood and the bond between them, the created intellect can reach in you, its intelligible God, union with you and happiness. Thus, because you are[121] lovable love, the created will which loves can obtain in you, its lovable God, union and happiness. For whoever receives you, O God, who are rational receivable Light, will be able to come to such a union with you that one will be united to you as a child to a parent.

I see, Lord, as you illumine me, that unless you are lovable and intelligible the rational nature cannot obtain union with you. Human nature, therefore, cannot be united to you as loving God, for as such you are not its object, but it can be united to you as its lovable God, since the lovable is the object of the one who loves. In the same way the intelligible is the object of the intellect; and this object we call truth. Since you, my God, are intelligible Truth, the created intellect, therefore, can be united to you.

**82.**     And in this way I see that rational human nature can be united only to your intelligible and lovable divine nature and that a person, in receiving you, the God who can be received, crosses over into a bond with you so close that it can be named "filiation." For we know no closer bond than that of filiation.[122]

If this bond of union is maximum, than which there can be no greater bond—and this will necessarily follow since you, the lovable God, cannot be more loved by a human—then this bond will attain to the most perfect filiation so that this filiation will be the perfection enfolding every possible filiation, by which all children will attain to final happiness and perfection. In this highest Son filiation is as art in a master or as light in the sun, but in the other children, it is as art in disciples or as light in the stars.

*Chapter Nineteen*
*How Jesus Is the Union of God and Human Being*

**83.**     I give inexpressible thanks to you, O God, Life and Light of my soul. For I now perceive the faith which the Catholic Church holds by the revelation of the apostles: that you who are loving God beget of yourself lovable God and that you who are begotten lovable God are absolute Mediator. For it is through you that everything which exists or can exist does exist. For you who are loving and willing God enfold all things in yourself, who are lovable God. For all that you, O God, will or conceive is enfolded in you who are lovable God. Nothing whatsoever can exist unless you will it to be. Therefore, all things have their cause or reason for being in your lovable concept. Nor is there another cause of all things except that it so pleases you. Nothing pleases a lover, as lover, but the lovable. You, therefore, lovable God, are the Son of God, the loving Father. For in you is all the Father's pleasure.[123] Thus, all createable being is enfolded in you who are lovable God.[124]

Therefore, O loving God, since God who is lovable is from you, as a son is from a father, in that you are God the loving Father of God your lovable Son, you are the Father of all things that exist. For your concept is the Son and all things are in him.[125] Your union and your concept is act and an arising work, in which are the act and unfolding of all things.

**84.**  Therefore, just as from you, the loving God, is begotten the lovable God—the generation is a conception—so from you, the loving God, and from your lovable concept, begotten from you, proceeds your act and that of your concept. This act is the connecting bond and is the God uniting you and your concept, as loving unites the lover and the lovable in love. And this bond is named Spirit; for spirit is like motion, which proceeds from that which moves and that which can be moved.[126] Consequently, motion is the unfolding of the concept of the mover. All things, therefore, are enfolded in you, God the Holy Spirit, as they are conceived in you, God the Son.

I see, therefore, because you, O God, show me, how all things are in you, God the Son of God the Father, as in their reason, concept, cause, or exemplar, and how the Son is the intermediary of all things, because he is the reason. For by means of reason and wisdom, you, God the Father, work all things, and the Spirit or Motion puts the concept of reason into effect, just as in our experience, the artisan by means of the motive power in the artisan's hands puts into effect the chest that exists in the artisan's mind.

**85.**  I see, therefore, my God, that your Son is the intermediary of the union of all things, so that all may find rest in you by mediation of your Son. And I see that blessed Jesus, as human son, was most profoundly united to your Son and that the human son could not be united to you, God the Father, except by mediation of your Son, the absolute mediator.

Who while earnestly considering these things would not be enraptured in the highest way? For such a secret you, my God, uncover for me, wretch that I am, that I may perceive that a person can understand you, the Father, only in your Son,[127] who is intelligible and is the mediator, and that to understand you is to be united to you. The human being, therefore, can be united to you through your Son, who is the means of union.[128] And the human nature most profoundly united to you, in whatever human being this may be, cannot be more united to the intermediary than it is. For without an intermediary, it cannot be united to you. Therefore it is maximally united to the intermediary, yet it does not become the intermediary. Consequently, although it cannot become the intermediary, since it cannot be united to you without an intermediary, nevertheless, it is so joined to the absolute intermediary that nothing can mediate between human nature and your Son, who is the absolute intermediary. For if anything could mediate between human nature and the absolute intermediary, then human nature would not be united to you in the profoundest way.

**86.**     O good Jesus, I see that in you human nature is joined most profoundly to God the Father by the profoundest union through which it is joined to God the Son, the absolute Mediator. Therefore, in you, O Jesus, since you are human son, human filiation is most profoundly united to divine filiation so that you are deservedly called Son of God and human son, because in you nothing mediates between human son and Son of God.[129] In absolute filiation, which is the Son of God, every filiation is enfolded, and to absolute filiation your human filiation, O Jesus, is supremely united. Your human filiation, therefore, subsists in divine filiation not only as enfolded but as that which is attracted subsists in that which attracts, that which is united in that which unites, and that which becomes substance in that which substantiates. Therefore, no separation of human son from Son of God is possible in you, Jesus.[130] For possibility of separation occurs where a union could be greater, but where union cannot be greater nothing can mediate. No separation, therefore, will occur where nothing can mediate between the things united. But where that which is united does not subsist is that which unites, the union is not the highest. For the union is greater where what is united subsists in that which unites than where it subsists separately. For separation is removal from maximum union.

Thus, in you, my Jesus, I see how the human filiation by which you are human son subsists in the divine filiation, by which you are Son of God just as in a maximum union that which is united subsists in that which unites. Glory be to you, O God, for evermore!

*Chapter Twenty*
*How Jesus Is Understood as the Joining of the Divine Nature*
*and the Human Nature*

**87.**     You show me, O never-failing Light, that the maximum union by which in my Jesus human nature is united to your divine nature is in no way similar to infinite union. For the union by which you God the Father are united to God the Son is God the Holy Spirit, and therefore it is an infinite union, for it attains absolute and essential identity. It is not so where human nature is united to the divine. For human nature cannot cross over into essential union with the divine, just as the finite cannot be infinitely united to the infinite, because the finite would cross over into an identity with the infinite, and thus, when infinite would be proved true of it, the finite would cease to be finite.[131] Consequently, the union by which human nature is united to the divine is nothing other than the attraction of the human nature to the divine in the highest degree in such a way that human nature as such is unable to be more highly attracted. The union, therefore, of the human nature of Jesus, as human, to the divine is maximum, because it is unable to be greater, but it is not simply maximum and infinite as is the divine union.[132]

**88.** Therefore, through the goodness of your grace, in you, Jesus, the human son, I see the Son of God, and in you, the Son of God, I see the Father. But in you, the human son, I see the Son of God because you are human son in such a way as to be Son of God. In the finite nature that is attracted I see the infinite nature that attracts. In the absolute Son I see the absolute Father, for the son cannot be seen as son unless the father is seen. I see in you, Jesus, the divine filiation, which is the truth of every filiation, and at the same time I see the highest human filiation, which most approaches the image of absolute filiation. Therefore, just as an image between its exemplar and which a more perfect image cannot mediate subsists most closely in the truth of which it is the image, so I see your human nature subsisting in the divine nature.

I see, therefore, in your human nature all that I also see in the divine nature, but what in your divine nature is the divine truth itself I see existing in your human nature in a human way. Whatever I see existing in a human way in you, O Jesus, is a likeness to divine nature, but the likeness is joined to the exemplar without an intermediary in such a way that no greater likeness can exist or can be thought.

**89.** In the human or rational nature, I see that the rational human spirit is most closely united to the divine Spirit, which is absolute Reason,[133] and that likewise your human intellect and all things in your intellect, O Jesus, are united to the divine intellect. For you, Jesus, as God, understand all things, and this understanding is to be all things. As human being, you understand all things, and this understanding is to be the likeness of all things. For nothing is understood by a human except in a likeness.[134] A stone is not in the human intellect as it is in its cause or its proper reason but as it is in its representation and likeness. Therefore, in you, Jesus, human understanding is united to the divine understanding itself, just as the most perfect image is united to its exemplar truth. If I should consider in the mind of an artisan the ideal form of a chest and the representation of a most perfect chest, fashioned by that master according to the master's idea, then, as the ideal form is the truth of the representation and is united to it in the one master as truth is united to image, so in you, Jesus, the Master of masters, I see that the absolute idea of all things and the resembling representation of these are equally united in the highest way.

I see you, good Jesus, within the wall of paradise, because your intellect is equally truth and image, and you are equally God and creature, equally infinite and finite.[135] And it is not possible that you should be seen on this side of the wall,[136] for you are the joining of the divine creating nature and the human created nature.

90.     However, between your human intellect and that of any other human being I perceive this difference: None else among human beings knows all that can be known by a human being, because no human's intellect is so joined to the exemplar of all things, as the likeness to the truth, but that it could not be even more closely joined and could not be brought to still more actuality; and thus it does not understand so much that it could not understand more through access to the exemplar of things, from which everything actually existing has its actuality. But your intellect actually understands all that a human can understand, since in you human nature is most perfect and is most fully joined to its exemplar. Because of this union, your human intellect exceeds every created intellect in perfection of understanding. All rational spirits, therefore, are far beneath you; you, Jesus, are the Master and Light of them all, and you are the perfection and fullness of all, and through you they draw near to the absolute truth, as through their mediator. For you are the way to the truth and equally the Truth itself;[137] you are the Way to the life of the intellect and equally Life itself; you are the aroma of the food of joy and equally the taste which gives joy. Therefore, most sweet Jesus, may you be blessed forever!

*Chapter Twenty-One*
*That Without Jesus Happiness Is Not Possible*

91.     O Jesus, End of the universe, in whom every creature rests as in the ultimacy of perfection, you are utterly unknown to all the wise of this world, for of you we affirm contradictories as most true, since you are equally creator and creature, equally attracting and attracted, equally finite and infinite.[138] They declare it folly to believe this is

possible; therefore, they flee your name and do not receive your light, by which you have illumined us. But even though they suppose themselves wise, they remain forever foolish and ignorant and blind.[139] Yet if they would believe that you are Christ, God and human, and if they would receive and treat the words of the Gospel as being those of so great a Master, they would at long last see most clearly that in comparison with that light hidden there in the simplicity of your words, all things are thickest shadows and ignorance. Therefore, only the believing little ones attain to this most gracious and life-giving revelation.[140] For in your most holy Gospel, the food of heaven, there is hidden, as in manna,[141] all desire's sweetness, which can be tasted only by one who believes and eats. But if anyone believes and accepts it, one will most truly know by experience that you descended from heaven and that you alone are the Master of truth.

**92.**     O good Jesus, you are the Tree of Life in the paradise of delights.[142] For none can be fed by that desirable life except from your fruit. You are, O Jesus, the fruit prohibited to all the children of Adam, who, expelled from paradise, seek their means of living in the earth in which they toil.[143] Therefore, everyone who hopes to taste the food of life within the paradise of delights must put off the old human of presumption and put on the new human of humility, who is in accord with you.[144] The nature of the new human and of the old is one, but in the old Adam it is animal; in you, the new Adam, it is spiritual,[145] because in you, O Jesus, it is united to God, who is Spirit.[146] Just as everyone is bound to you, O Jesus, by a human nature common to oneself and to you, so one must also be united to you in one spirit in order that thus in one's nature, which is common with you, Jesus, one can draw near to God, the Father, who is in paradise. Therefore, to see God the Father and you, Jesus, his Son, is to be in paradise and everlasting glory. For outside paradise one cannot have such a vision since neither God, the Father, nor you, Jesus, are able to be found outside paradise. Therefore, every human being who has attained happiness is united to you, O Jesus, as a member is united to its head.

**93.**     No one can come to the Father unless one is drawn by the Father.[147] The Father drew your humanity, Jesus, by his Son, and through you, Jesus, he draws all human beings. Just as your humanity, Jesus, is united to the Son of God the Father, as to the means by which the Father drew it, so the humanity of each human is united to you, Jesus, as to the one means by which the Father draws all human beings. Therefore, without you, Jesus, it is impossible for anyone to attain happiness. O Jesus, you are the revelation of the Father. For the Father is invisible to all humans and visible only to you, his Son, and after you to one who, through you and your revelation, will merit to see the Father.[148] You, therefore, are the one uniting everyone who is happy, and everyone who is happy subsists in you, as that which is united subsists in that which unites.

None of the wise of this world can grasp true happiness since they do not know you. None can see anyone happy except with you, Jesus, inside paradise. Of someone happy, as of you, Jesus, contradictories are verified, since one is united to you in a rational nature and in one spirit. For everyone of happy spirit subsists in your Spirit, as the vivified in the vivifier.[149] Every happy spirit sees the invisible God and is united in you, O Jesus, to the unapproachable and immortal God.[150] And thus in you the finite is united to the infinite and to that which cannot be united, and the incomprehensible is seized by an eternal fruition, which is a most joyous and inexhaustible happiness. Have mercy, O Jesus, have mercy, and grant me to see you without veil, and my soul is saved!

## Chapter Twenty-Two
### How Jesus Sees and Has Worked

94.    The eye of the mind cannot be satiated in seeing you, O Jesus, because you are the completion of all mental beauty, and at this icon I conjecture about your exceedingly wonderful and astonishing gaze, O Jesus, who are blessed above all. For while you walked in this world of sense, you, Jesus, used eyes of flesh similar to ours. With them you saw objects one after another, no differently than we human beings, for there was in your eyes a certain spirit that was the form of the organ, like the sensible soul in an animal's body.[151] In this spirit was a noble and discriminative power by which you, Lord, saw distinctly and discretely this object as colored in one way and that object as colored in another. And even more, according to the forms of the face and of the eyes of the people whom you saw, you were the true judge of the soul's passions, of its anger, joy, and sorrow. And more subtly still, from a few signs you comprehended what lay hidden in the mind of a human being. For nothing is conceived in the mind that is not in some way signaled in the face, most greatly in the eyes, because the face is the heart's messenger.

**95.**     For in all these judgments you reached the inward places of the soul much more truly than any created spirit. For from any one sign, however slight, you saw a person's whole concept, as from a few words those who have understanding foresee the entire, lengthy preconceived discourse that is to be unfolded and as those who are well learned, after having glanced at a book for a short time, recite the author's purpose as if they had read it through.

In this kind of sight you, Jesus, excelled all the perfection, quickness, and acuity of all human beings past, present, and future, and this sight, not perfected without the eye of flesh, was human. Yet it was astonishing and wonderful. For if there are those who, by long and precise examination, read the mind of a writer under, then, newly devised characters and signs not seen before, you, O Jesus, saw all things under every sign and figure.

**96.**     If sometimes one reads that there was a man who through certain signs of the eye perceived the thought of someone questioning him, even if his questioner were mentally singing some verse,[152] you, Jesus, better than all grasped every concept from every gesture of the eyes. I myself have seen a deaf woman who from the movement of her daughter's lips understood as if she had heard it. If by long usage this is possible among the deaf and the mute and the religious who converse by signs, you, O Jesus, who actually knew all that can be known, as if the Master of masters, more perfectly formed a true judgment about the heart and its thought from the slightest and to us invisible changes and signs.

**97.**     But to this your most perfect, although finite, human sight, contracted to an organ, there was united an absolute and infinite sight, and through it you, as God, equally saw all things and each, absent as well as present, past as well as future. Therefore, with your human eye, O Jesus, you saw the visible accidents,[153] but with your divine and absolute sight you saw the substance of things. No one constituted in flesh, except you, O Jesus, ever perceived the substance or quiddity of things. You alone most truly saw the soul and spirit and whatever else there is in the human being.[154] For just as in the human the intellective power is united to the animal faculty of sight, so that a human being not only sees as an animal but also discerns and judges as a human, so in you, Jesus, absolute sight is united to the human intellectual power, which is discernment in the animal sight. In the human, the faculty of animal sight subsists not in itself but in the rational soul as in the form of the whole. Thus, in you, O Jesus, the intellectual faculty of sight subsists not in itself but in the absolute power of sight.

Oh, how wonderful is your sight, most sweet Jesus!

**98.**     Sometimes it is our experience to catch a glimpse of a passerby, but since it was not our intent to discern who that was, although we know that someone passed by, if asked, we cannot give the name of the one we know to have passed by.[155] Therefore, we have seen the passerby as an animal sees, but not as a human, since we have not applied the faculty of discernment. From this we discover that the natures of our powers, even if they are united in the one form of the human being, nevertheless remain distinct and have distinct workings. Thus, in you who are one, O Jesus, I see that the human intellectual nature was united in a similar way to the divine nature and that as human being you did many works and at the same time as God many wonderful and superhuman works. I see, most merciful Jesus, that the intellectual nature is absolute in regard to the sensible and not at all, as is the sensible, limited and bound to an organ, as, for example, the visual faculty of the senses is bound to the eye; but the divine power is incomparably more absolute and above the intellectual. For the human intellect, to be brought into act, needs phantasms, and phantasms cannot be acquired without the senses, and the senses do not subsist without the body. Consequently, dependent on these, the power of the human intellect is contracted and slight. But the divine intellect is necessity itself, independent and requiring nothing; yet all things require it, and without it they cannot exist.

**99.**     I consider more closely how the discursive faculty, which in reasoning discursively runs hither and yon[156] and seeks, is one thing, and another is the faculty which judges and understands. We see a dog run hither and yon and seek its master and recognize him and hear his call.[157] In the nature of animality this discursus exists in the degree of perfection of the canine species. There are still other animals whose discursus is more discerning in accord with their more perfect species, and with the human this discursus most nearly approaches the intellectual faculty, so that it is the highest extreme of perfection of the sensible faculty [having][158] many degrees of perfection, and indeed innumerable ones, below the intellectual faculty, as the species of animals make clear to us. For there is no species that does not receive its proper degree of perfection to itself. Indeed, each species has a latitude of degrees within which we see individuals of the species variously participating the species. Similarly, the intellectual nature has innumerable degrees below the divine nature. Just as in the intellectual nature, all the degrees of sensible perfection are enfolded, so in the divine nature are enfolded all the degrees of intellectual perfection and thus all the degrees of sensible perfection and of the perfection of all things.

**100.**     Therefore, in you, my Jesus, I see all perfection. For since you are the most perfect human, I see that in you the intellect is united to the rational or discursive power, which is the summit of sensible power. And thus I see that the intellect is in reason as in its own place, like a candle placed in a room, which illuminates the room and all the walls and the whole building, according, however, to the greater or less degree of distance they are from it. Then I see that the divine Word is united to the intellect in its highest and the intellect itself is the place where the Word is received, just, as in regard to ourselves, we discover that the intellect is the place where the word of a teacher is received, as if the light of the sun were joined to the candle just mentioned. For the Word of God illumines the intellect just as the light of the sun illumines this world. Therefore, in you, my Jesus, I see the sensible life as illumined by the intellectual light, the intellectual life as a light that illumines and is illumined, and the divine life as a light that illumines only. For in your intellectual light I see the Fountain of light, that is, the Word of God, which is the Truth enlightening every intellect.[159] You alone, therefore, are the highest of all creatures, because you are creature in such a way that you are the blessed Creator.

### Chapter Twenty-Three
#### How Jesus Died but His Union with Life Endured

**101.**     O Jesus, the mind's most delectable food, when I behold you inside the wall of paradise, how wonderful you appear to me! For you are the Word of God humanified, and you are the human deified. However, it is not as if you were composed of God and human.[160] Between component parts there must be a proportion without which there can be no composition. But there is no proportion of the finite to the infinite.[161] Nor are you the coincidence of creature and Creator in which coincidence makes one thing to be another. For human nature is not divine, nor is divine nature human. For the divine nature cannot be altered or changed into another nature, since it is eternity itself; nor does any nature because of its union with the divine pass over into another nature, as when an image is united to its truth. For when there is a passing over, the nature cannot then be said to be altered, but rather it retreats from otherness, since it is united to its own truth, which is inalterability itself.

Nor, most sweet Jesus, can you be said to be an intermediate between the divine nature and the human nature, since between them no middle nature can be posited that participates them both.[162] For the divine nature cannot be participated, since it is completely and absolutely most simple; nor, therefore, blessed Jesus, would you be either God or human being.

**102.** But I see you, Lord Jesus, above all understanding, as one person,[163] because you are one Christ, in the same way that I see your human soul as one; in it, as in each human soul, I see that there was a sensible and corruptible nature subsisting in an intellectual and incorruptible nature.

This soul was not composed of corruptible and incorruptible, nor does the sensible nature coincide with intellectual. But I see the intellectual soul to be united to the body through the sensible power vivifying the body. When the intellective soul should cease to vivify the body without being separated from it, then the human being would be dead, since life would have ceased. Yet one's body would not be separated from life, since the intellect is the body's life.[164] It would be as when a person who attentively sought through sight to discern someone approaching but was captured by other considerations and afterward one's attention ceased its search, although one's eyes were no less directed toward the one approaching, one's eye would not then be separated from one's soul, although it would be separated from the discriminative attention of the soul. But if when captured by other considerations, one ceased not only from a discerning vivification of the eye but also from a sensory vivification, one's eye would be dead because it would not be vivified. All the same, it would not for this reason be separated from the intellective form, which is the form that gives being, just as a withered hand remains united to the form that unites the whole body.

**103.** According to Saint Augustine, there are people who know how to withdraw the vivifying spirit and appear dead and deprived of sensibility.[165] In this case the intellectual nature would remain united to the body, because the body would not be under another form than before; indeed, it would have the same form and remain the same body. The vivifying power would not cease to exist but would remain in union with the intellectual nature, although it would not extend itself into the body in actuality. I see such an individual to be truly dead because that individual would lack vivifying, for death is the absence of that which vivifies, and yet this dead body would not be separated from its life, which is its soul.

**104.**     In this way, most merciful Jesus, I see the absolute life, which is God, to be inseparably united to your human intellect and by this to your body. For this union is such that it cannot be greater. A union that can be separated is far inferior to a union that cannot be greater. It, therefore, was never true, nor will it ever be true, that your divine nature is separated from your human nature, nor even from your soul or from your body, without which things human nature cannot exist. Although it is most true that your soul ceased to vivify the body and that you truly suffered death, yet you never separated from the truth of life.

**105.**     If that priest, whom Augustine mentions,[166] had such a power so as to remove from the body that which vivifies by drawing it into the soul, as if a candle illuminating a room were living and without being separated from the room were to draw to the center of its light the rays by which it illuminated the room,[167] and as if this attraction were only the candle's ceasing to emit rays, is it any wonder, therefore, if you, Jesus, because you are the freest living light, had the power to offer and to withdraw your vivifying soul? And when you willed to withdraw it, you suffered death, and when you willed to offer it, you rose by your own power.[168]

But the intellectual nature, when it vivifies or animates the body, is called the human soul, and the soul is said to be withdrawn when the human intellect ceases to vivify it. For when the intellect ceases its function of vivifying and, in this respect, separates itself from the body, it is not therefore simply separated from it.

**106.**     Although I am most unworthy, you, O Jesus, inspire these thoughts that you may show yourself to me, insofar as I can grasp, and that in you I may contemplate that mortal human nature has put on immortality so that in you all those with the same human nature may be able to obtain resurrection and the life divine.[169] Since we find all that is in our nature in you, O Jesus, who alone can do all things and give most generously without finding fault,[170] what, therefore, is sweeter and what more pleasing than to know this? O inexpressible Tenderness and Mercy! You, O God, who are Goodness itself, could not satisfy your infinite mercy and generosity without giving us yourself! Nor could this be done more fittingly, in a way more possible for our receiving than that you took on our nature, for we could not approach yours. Thus, you have come to us and are called Jesus, the ever blessed Savior.

### Chapter Twenty-Four
### How Jesus Is the Word of Life

107.    By your own best and maximum gift, I contemplate you, my Jesus, preaching the words of life[171] and abundantly sowing the divine seed in the hearts of those hearing you.[172] And I see those depart who have not perceived the things that are of the Spirit. But I see the disciples remaining who already have begun to taste the sweetness of the teaching that vivifies the soul. On behalf of all these, that prince and the chief of the apostles, Peter, confessed that you, O Jesus, had the words of life, and he was amazed that those seeking life should depart from you.[173] Paul in rapture heard the words of life from you, Jesus,[174] and thereafter neither persecution, nor the sword, nor bodily hunger could separate him from you.[175] None of all who have tasted the words of life could ever forsake you.

108.    Who can separate a bear from honey after it has tasted the sweetness? How great is the sweetness of truth that bestows the most delectable life beyond every corporeal sweetness; for it is absolute sweetness, from which flows all that is desired by every taste. What is stronger than the love from which all that is lovable has that it is loved? If the bond of contracted love is sometimes so great that the fear of death cannot sunder it, of what kind, therefore, is the bond of that tasted love, from which comes all love? I do not wonder that cruel punishments were regarded as nothing by other soldiers of yours, O Jesus, to whom you have given yourself as foretasteable life.

109.    O Jesus, my Love, you have sown the seed of life in the field of the believers and have watered it by the witness of your blood. By your bodily death, you have shown that truth is the life of the rational spirit. The seed grew in good soil and bore fruit.[176]

Show me, Lord, how my soul is the breath of life[177] in relation to the body, into which it breathes and infuses life, and it is not life in relation to you, O God, but as if a potency for life. And since you cannot but grant petitions if they are asked in the most attentive faith,[178] you inspire me to see that in a child there is a soul which has a vegetative power in act, for the child grows. The soul also has a sensible power in act, for the child senses; and it has an imaginative power, but not yet in act. It also has a reasoning power, whose actuality is still more distant, and it has an intellective power, but in a more remote potency. Thus, we know by experience that the one soul exists in act first in relation to its lower powers and afterward in relation to its higher, so that the human is an animal before being spiritual.[179]

**110.** In similar fashion, we experience that a certain mineral power, which can also be called a "spirit," exists in the bowels of the earth and that it is present there in a potency from which the mineral of stone or the mineral of salt may arise, and there is another spirit that exists in a potency that the mineral of metal may arise. There are various such spirits according to the variety of stones, salts, and metals. There is, however, one spirit of the mineral of gold, which, continually more and more refined through the influence of the sun or the heavens, is at last fashioned into such gold as cannot be corrupted by any element. And in this gold much of the incorruptible celestial light shines forth, for the gold becomes much like the corporeal light of the sun.

Indeed, we have experience of the vegetative and sensible spirit in a similar way. For in the human the sensible spirit conforms itself closely to the motive and influential celestial power, and under this influence it receives successive increase until it is set in perfect act. But since it is drawn out from the power of the body, its perfection ceases with the failing of the body's perfection on which it depends.

**111.** There is next the intellectual spirit, which in its perfection's actuality does not depend on the body but is united to it by means of the sensitive power; this spirit, since it is independent of the body, is not subject to the influence of the celestial bodies; nor does it depend on the sensible spirit or thus on the motive celestial power. But just as the movers of the celestial spheres are subject to the Prime Mover, so also is this mover which is the intellect. But since the intellect is united to the body by means of the sensitive power, it does not arrive at perfection without the senses. For all intellect that attains to perfection reaches it from the sensible world by means of the senses. Nothing such, therefore, can exist in the intellect that did not first exist in the senses.[180] But the more the senses are pure and perfect, the imagination clear, and the discursive reasoning able, the less impeded and the more prompt the intellect is in its intellectual operations.

112.     But the intellect is nourished by the Word of Life under whose influence it is established, like the moving powers of the spheres, although perfected differently as even the spirits that are subject to the influences of the heavens are perfected in different ways. And the intellect is not perfected by the sensible spirit except accidentally,[181] just as an image does not perfect, although it excites a search for the truth of the exemplar. The image of the Crucified, for example, does not inspire devotion but rouses the memory in order to inspire it. Since the intellectual spirit is not compelled by the influence of the heavens but is wholly free, it is not made perfect unless it submits itself through faith to the Word of God, like a free disciple, independent of jurisdiction, who is not perfected unless one submits oneself by faith to the word of a master. For one must trust in one's master and listen to the master. The intellect is made perfect by the Word of God and increases and becomes continually more receptive to, more fit for, and more like the Word. This perfection, which thus comes from the Word through which it had being, is not a corruptible perfection, but Godlike, just as the perfection of gold is not corruptible, but of heavenly form.

113.     But every intellect must submit itself through faith to the Word of God and hear with utmost attention that inward teaching of the supreme Master, and by hearing what the Lord says in the Word the intellect will be made perfect. For this reason, you, O Jesus, one and only Master,[182] have preached that faith is necessary for all who approach the Fountain of life, and you have shown that the inflowing of the divine power is according to the degree of faith.[183]

O Christ, our Savior, you have taught two things only: faith and love. By faith, the intellect approaches the Word; by love, it is united to it. The nearer the intellect approaches, the more it is given increase in power; the more it loves, the more it is established in the light of the Word. But the Word of God is within the intellect, and the intellect need not seek outside itself, for it will find the Word within and will be able to approach the Word by faith. And that the intellect can draw still nearer it will be able to obtain by prayer. For the Word will increase faith by the communication of its light.

114.     I give thanks to you, O Jesus, that I have come to this by your light. For in your light, O Light of my life, I see how you, the Word, flow life into all who believe and make perfect all who love you. What teaching, good Jesus, was ever briefer and more efficacious than yours? You persuade us only to believe and command us only to love.

What is easier than to believe God? What is sweeter than to love God? How agreeable is your yoke and how light is your burden,[184] O one and only Master![185] To those who keep this teaching, you promise all that they desire, for you teach nothing difficult for a believer and nothing a lover can refuse. Such are the promises you make to your disciples, and they are most true, because you are the Truth who can promise only the true. Yes, and in fact, you promise only yourself, who are the perfection of every perfectible thing. To you be the praise, the glory, and the thanksgiving for all eternity! Amen.

*Chapter Twenty-Five*
*How Jesus Is the Consummation*

**115.**   What is it, Lord, that you send into the spirit of the human whom you make perfect? Is it not your good Spirit, which is fully and actually the power of all powers and the perfection of the perfect, since it is that which works all things? The sun's energy, descending into the vegetable spirit, moves it so that it is perfected and so that by the most pleasing and most natural ripening from the heavenly warmth a good tree yields good fruit. So too your Spirit, O God, comes into the intellectual spirit of a good person and by the warmth of divine love ripens its potential power so that the intellectual spirit is perfected and so that fruit is borne that is most acceptable to the Spirit.

We experience, O Lord, that your simple Spirit, infinite in its power, is received in many ways. For it is received in one way in one in whom it produces a prophetic spirit, in another in one who is given skill to interpret, and in another by one to whom it teaches knowledge, and it is received still otherwise in others.[186] For its gifts are diverse and are perfections of the intellectual spirit, just as the same heat of the sun produces different fruit of different trees.

**116.**   I see, Lord, that your Spirit cannot be lacking to any spirit, because it is the Spirit of spirits and the movement of movements and fills the whole world,[187] but it disposes all that do not have an intellectual spirit by means of the intellectual nature that moves the heavens, and by their movement all things that are subject to it. But your Spirit has reserved for itself alone the disposition and the governance in the intellectual nature. For it has espoused to itself this nature, in which it has chosen to rest as though in a dwelling place and in a heaven of truth, for nowhere can truth be grasped in and of itself except in the intellectual nature.

117.        O Lord, who work all things for yourself,[188] you have created this entire world because of the intellectual nature, as if you were a painter who mixes different colors in order finally to be able to paint oneself and to have an image of oneself wherein one may be delighted and one's art find rest. And although such a painter is one and cannot be multiplied, yet this painter can be multiplied in the way in which it is possible, in a very resembling likeness. But the painter makes many images because the likeness of this painter's infinite power can be unfolded more perfectly only in many figures, and all intellectual spirits are serviceable to each spirit. Moreover if they were not innumerable, you, O infinite God, could not be known in the best possible way. For each intellectual spirit sees in you, my God, something which must be revealed to the others if they would attain to you, their God, in the best possible way. The spirits, full of love, therefore, reveal their secrets to one another, and thereby the knowledge of the beloved is increased as well as the desire for the beloved, and the sweetness of joy grows ardent.

118.        Not yet, O Lord God, would you have brought your work to perfection without Jesus, your Son, the Christ, whom you have anointed above his companions.[189] In his intellect the perfection of createable nature is at rest, for he is the last, the most perfect and immultiplicable likeness of God, and there can be only one such supreme likeness. But by this Spirit, all other intellectual spirits are likenesses, and the more perfect they are the more they are like it. All come to rest in this Spirit as in the final perfection of the image of God, of whose image they have attained likeness and some degree of perfection.

119.        Therefore, by your gift, my God, I possess this whole visible world and all of Scripture and all the ministering spirits[190] in support of my advancing in the knowledge of you. All things rouse me to turn toward you; all Scripture strives to do nothing else but to disclose you; all intellectual spirits have no other work but to seek you and to reveal as much of you as they have found. Above all, you have given me Jesus as Master, as the Way, the Life, and the Truth,[191] so that nothing at all can be lacking to me. You strengthen me by your Holy Spirit, through whom you inspire choices of life and holy desires. You draw me by a foretaste of the sweetness of the life of glory to love you, the infinite Good. You enrapture me in order to be above myself and to foresee the place of glory to which you invite me. You show me many most delectable dishes which draw me by their excel-

lent savor. You permit me to see the treasury of riches, of life, of joy, and of beauty. In nature as well as in art, you uncover the fountain from which flows all that is desirable. You keep nothing secret. You do not hide the channel of love, nor of peace, nor of rest. You offer all things to me, wretched as I am, whom you have created from nothing.

**120.** Why then do I delay? Why do I not hasten to the aroma of the ointments of my Christ?[192] Why do I not enter into the joy of my Lord?[193] What holds me back? If ignorance of you, Lord, has restrained me, and the vain delight of the sensible world, they will hold me back no longer. For because you grant me to will, I will to forsake the things of this world, for the world wills to forsake me. I hasten toward the goal; I have almost finished my course; I look forward to its end, for I strive after the crown.[194] Draw me, Lord, for no one may come to you unless drawn by you,[195] so that drawn to you, I may be made absolute from this world and may be joined to you, the absolute God, in the eternity of the glorious life. Amen."[196]

# On the Summit[1] of Contemplation (De apice theoriae 1464)[2]

1.

Speakers:
The most Reverend Lord Cardinal of St. Peter and Peter of Erkelenz, Canon in Aachen[3]

*PETER:* I see you rapt[4] for several days in such deep meditation that I was afraid it would disturb you if I beset you with questions occurring to me. But now since I find you more relaxed and joyous as if you had discovered some great thing, I hope that you will forgive me if I question you beyond what is usual.

*CARDINAL:* It will please me. For I often wondered about your very long silence, especially since already for fourteen years you have heard me say many things, publicly and privately, about what I discovered in my studies[5] and since you have collected more of the tracts that I have written. Surely now that you have obtained the divine status of the most sacred priesthood through God's gift and my ministry,[6] the time has come that you begin to speak and to ask your questions.

2.

*PETER:* I am embarrassed because of my inexperience; yet I feel encouraged by your kindness to ask what new discovery has come to you in your meditation during these Paschal days.[7] I thought that you had completed all your speculation, which you had explained in your many different books.

*CARDINAL:* If the apostle Paul, caught up to the third heaven,[8] still does not comprehend the incomprehensible,[9] then none will ever be so satisfied but that one will always press on eagerly to comprehend better the One who is greater than all comprehension.[10]

*PETER:* What are you seeking?[11]

*CARDINAL:* You speak correctly.

*PETER:* I am asking a question, and you deride me. When I ask what are you seeking, you reply "you speak correctly," although I said nothing but merely posed a question.

*CARDINAL:* When you say, "*What* are you seeking," you speak correctly, since I am seeking *what*. Whoever seeks is seeking *what*. For unless one were seeking something or *what*, one would not be seeking at all. Therefore, like all the studious,[12] I am seeking *what*, for I very much desire to know what this *what* or *whatness*[13] is that is so greatly sought.

293

*PETER:* Do you believe it can be found?

*CARDINAL:* Certainly. For the motion that is present in all the studious is not in vain.[14]

3.

*PETER:* If no one has yet found the *what*, are you making an attempt beyond all the rest?[15]

*CARDINAL:* I believe that in some way or other many have both seen it and in their writings left behind their vision of what they have seen. For if whatness, which has always been sought, is being sought, and will be sought, were entirely unknown, how would it be sought when it would remain unrecognized even if discovered? Therefore, a wise man once said that it is seen by all, though from afar.[16]

4.

Although for many years I had seen that it had to be sought beyond all power of knowing and prior to every diversity and opposition,[17] I had not perceived that whatness subsisting in itself is the invariable subsistence of all substances, that, therefore, it is unable to be multiplied or made many, and that hence, there is not one whatness for one entity and then another for different entities but rather there is the same hypostasis for all.[18] Afterward I saw that one must admit that this same hypostasis or subsistence of things "can be."[19] And since it can be, assuredly it cannot be without *Posse* Itself.[20] For how could it be without *posse?* Therefore, *Posse* Itself, without which nothing whatever can be, is that than which nothing can be more subsistent. Therefore, this is the *What* that has been sought or Whatness Itself, without which nothing at all can be. And it is this contemplation that has occupied my thoughts with great delight during these holy days.

*PETER:* Since, as you say, without *posse* nothing whatever can be (and I see that what you say is true), and since without whatness nothing at all is, I see well that *Posse* Itself can be called "whatness."[21] But since earlier you already said much about *Possest*[22] and explained it in a trialogue,[23] I wonder why this does not suffice?

5.

*CARDINAL:* You will see further on[24] that "*Posse* Itself," than which nothing can be more powerful or prior or better,[25] names far more appropriately that without which nothing whatsoever can be, or live, or understand than "*Possest*" or any other term. For if it can be named, certainly "*Posse* Itself," than which nothing can be more perfect, will name it better. I do not believe that another name that is clearer, truer, or easier can be given.

*PETER:* How do you say "easier" when to me there is nothing more difficult than something that has always been sought but never entirely found?

*CARDINAL:* The clearer the truth is the easier it is. I once thought that it could be found better in darkness.[26] But of great power is the truth in which *Posse* Itself shines brightly. Indeed, it shouts in the streets,[27] as you have read in my tract *On the Ignorant.*[28] With great certainty it shows itself everywhere easy to find.[29]

6.    What child or youth does not know *Posse* Itself since each says one can eat, one can run, or one can speak? Nor is there anyone with a mind who is so ignorant that one does not know, without a teacher, that nothing is unless it can be and that without *posse* nothing whatever can be or can have, can do or can undergo. What young boy or young girl, when asked if they could carry a stone and having answered that they could, when further asked if they could do this without *posse*, would deny it emphatically? For the youth would consider the question absurd and superfluous, as if no one of sane mind would have doubts about this, that anything could be made or become without *Posse* Itself.

For everyone "who can"[30] presupposes *Posse* Itself as so necessary that if it were not presupposed, nothing whatever could be. For if anything can be known, surely there is nothing more known than *Posse* Itself; if anything can be easy, surely there is nothing easier than *Posse* Itself; if anything can be certain, nothing is more certain than *Posse* Itself. Likewise nothing is either prior, or stronger, or more solid, or more substantial, or more glorious, and so forth. But that which lacks *Posse* Itself can neither be nor be good nor be anything else.

*PETER:* I see nothing more certain than these things, and I believe that the truth of these cannot remain hidden to anyone.

7.    *CARDINAL:* The only difference separating you and me is our attention. For if I asked you what you see in all the descendants of Adam who have been, who are, and who will be, even if there were an infinite number, would you not immediately answer, if you gave your attention, that you saw in them all only the paternal *posse* of the first parent?

*PETER:* Yes, by all means.

*CARDINAL:* If I also asked what you see in lions and eagles and all the animal species, would you not answer in the same way?

*PETER:* Certainly and not otherwise.

*CARDINAL:* What if I asked what you see in all things that are caused and originated?[31]

*PETER:* I would say that I see only the *posse* of the first cause and first principle.

*CARDINAL:* And what if I questioned you further: Since the *posse* of all such "firsts" is completely inexplicable, whence does such a *posse* have this strength? Would you not soon answer that it has its strength from the absolute, completely uncontracted, omnipotent *Posse* Itself, than which nothing more powerful can be sensed or imagined or understood? For this is the *Posse* of all *posse*, than which nothing can be prior or more perfect, and if it did not exist, nothing whatever could endure.

*PETER:* That is indeed what I would say.

8.    *CARDINAL:* Hence, *Posse* Itself is the whatness and the hypostasis of all things. In its power are necessarily contained those things that are as well as those that are not.[32] Would you not say that this entirely ought to be so affirmed?

*PETER:* I would say so entirely.

*CARDINAL:* *Posse* Itself, therefore, is called "light" by certain holy ones,[33] not the sensible, rational, or intelligible light but rather the light of all that can emit light.[34] For nothing can be brighter, clearer, or more beautiful than *Posse* Itself. Consider, therefore, sensible light, without which there cannot be sensible vision. Notice that there is no other hypostasis in every color and in every visible thing than light appearing differently in the different modes of being of the colors. And observe too that if the light were withdrawn, then neither color nor what is visible nor seeing could remain. But the brightness of light, as it is in itself, surpasses the power of sight. Therefore, light is not seen as it is, but it manifests itself in visible things, more brightly in one thing and more dimly in another. The more clearly something visible exhibits the light, the more noble and beautiful it is. But light enfolds the brightness and beauty of all visible things and excels them. Light does not manifest itself in visible things in order to show itself as visible but rather to manifest itself as invisible, for its brightness cannot be grasped in visible things. For whoever sees the brightness of light in visible things as invisible sees it more truly.[35] Do you understand this?

*PETER:* The more I have heard it from you the easier it is for me to understand.

9.    *CARDINAL:* Therefore, transfer these sensibles to intelligibles;

for example, transfer the *posse* of light to *Posse* simply or the absolute *Posse* Itself, and transfer the being of color to simple being. For simple being, which is visible only to the mind, is related to the mind as the being of color is related to the sense of sight.[36] Pay close attention to what the mind sees in the various entities, which are only what they can be and which can have only what they have from *Posse* Itself. You will then see that various beings are only various modes of appearance of *Posse* Itself, but that their whatness cannot be various, because it is *Posse* Itself appearing variously.

**10.**     In things which are or live or understand, nothing other can be seen than *Posse* Itself, whose manifestations are *posse* to be, *posse* to live, and *posse* to understand. For what else can be seen in every power other than the *posse* of every power? Yet in all powers of being or of knowing, *Posse* Itself cannot be most perfectly grasped as it is. But it appears in them and in one more powerfully than in another. It appears more powerfully, for example, in the intellectual *posse* than in the sensible, in the measure that the intellect is more powerful than sense. But in itself *Posse* Itself is seen more truly above all cognitive power, yet by means of the intelligible *posse*, when it is seen to excel every power of the capacity of intelligible *posse*. What the intellect grasps, it understands. When, therefore, the mind in its own *posse* sees that *Posse* Itself cannot be grasped because of its eminence, the mind then sees with a sight beyond its capacity, just as a child sees that a stone's size is greater than the child's strength's capacity could carry. The *posse* of the mind to see, therefore, surpasses the *posse* to comprehend.

**11.**     Hence, the simple vision of the mind is not a comprehensive vision, but it elevates itself from a comprehensive vision to seeing the incomprehensible. When, for example, it sees comprehensively[37] one thing to be greater than another, then it elevates itself in order to see that than which nothing can be greater. And this is infinite, greater than all that is measurable or comprehensible.

This *posse* of the mind to see beyond all comprehensible faculty and power is the mind's supreme *posse*.[38] In it *Posse* Itself manifests itself maximally, and the mind's supreme *posse* is not brought to its limit this side of *Posse* Itself. For the *posse* to see is directed only to *Posse* Itself so that the mind can foresee that toward which it tends, just as a traveler foresees one's journey's end so that one can direct one's steps toward the desired goal. So unless the mind could see from a distance the goal of its rest and desire and of its joy and gladness, how would it run that it might comprehend? The Apostle duly admonishes us so to run that we might comprehend.[39] Therefore, think over these matters that you may see that all things are so ordained that the mind could run toward *Posse* Itself, which it sees from afar, and comprehend the incomprehensible in the best way it can. For *Posse* Itself, when it will appear in the glory of majesty, is alone able to satisfy the mind's longing. For it is that *what* which is sought.

Do you see what I have said?

12.     *PETER:* I see that what you have said is true, even if it surpasses one's capacity. For what could satisfy the longing of the mind other than *Posse* Itself, the *Posse* of every *posse*, without which nothing whatever can? Indeed, if something other than *Posse* Itself could be, how could it without *posse*? And if it could not without *posse*, then, by all means, it would have what it could from *Posse* Itself.[40]

The mind is satisfied only when it comprehends that than which nothing better can be. And that can only be *Posse* Itself, namely, the *Posse* of every *posse*. Therefore, you rightly see that only *Posse* Itself, the *what* that is sought by every mind, is the beginning of the mind's desire, since it is that to which nothing prior can be, and you see that it is also the goal of the same desire of the mind, since nothing can be desired beyond *Posse* Itself.

13.     *CARDINAL:* Excellent. You now see, Peter, how much the conversations we are accustomed to having and your reading of my tracts help you to understand me easily. Whatever I see concerning *Posse* Itself you undoubtedly will also soon see when you apply your mind to it. For since every question regarding "can" presupposes *Posse* Itself, no doubt can be raised about it, for no doubt extends to *Posse* Itself. Indeed, whoever would ask whether *Posse* Itself is, if one pays attention, sees immediately that the question is impertinent, because without *posse* no question could be asked about *Posse* Itself. And even less could it be asked whether *Posse* Itself is this or that, since both the *posse* to be and the *posse* to be this or that presuppose *Posse* Itself. And hence, it is evident that *Posse* Itself precedes every doubt that can arise. Therefore, there is nothing more certain than *Posse* Itself, since doubt cannot do otherwise than presuppose it, nor can anything be conceived more sufficient or more perfect. So nothing at all can be added to it nor be separated or subtracted from it.

14.     *PETER:* Now please tell me only this: whether you wish to reveal anything clearer than before about the First. For you have often spoken extensively of it, though not as much as can be said.

*CARDINAL:* I propose now to present a facility not communicated openly before, which I consider most secret, namely, that all speculative precision is to be placed only in *Posse* Itself and its appearance and that all who saw rightly have tried to express this.[41]

Indeed, those who affirmed "the One" only were looking to *Posse* Itself. Those who spoke of "the One and the many" looked to *Posse* Itself and the many modes of being of its appearance.[42]

Those who said that there could be nothing new[43] looked to the *Posse* Itself of every *posse* to be or to become. But those who affirmed the newness of the world and of things turned their mind to the appearance of *Posse* Itself. It is as if someone turned one's mind's eye to the *posse* of unity, then that individual would certainly see in every number and plurality nothing other than the *posse* itself of unity, than which nothing is more powerful, and that person would see every number as nothing than the appearance of the *posse* itself of innumerable and unlimitable unity. For numbers are nothing but the special modes of appearance of the *posse* itself of unity. And this *posse* appears better in the uneven number "three" than in the number "four" and better in the certain perfect numbers than in others. Similarly genera, species and such are to be referred to the modes of being of appearance of *Posse* Itself.

15. Those who deny that there are many forms that give being looked to *Posse* Itself, than which there is nothing more sufficient. And those who claim that there are many species forms direct their attention to the species modes of being of the appearance of *Posse* Itself.

Those who said that God is the source of ideas and that there are many ideas wished to say what we are saying, that God is *Posse* Itself, which appears in various and specifically different modes of being. And those who reject the ideas and such forms looked to *Posse* Itself, which alone is the *what* itself of all *posse*.[44]

Those who say that nothing can perish look to the eternal and incorruptible *Posse* Itself. Those who say that death is something and believe that things perish turn their sight to modes of being of the appearance of *Posse* Itself. Those who say that God, the almighty Father, is the creator of heaven and earth say what we are saying, that *Posse* Itself, than which there is nothing more omnipotent, created heaven and earth and all things through its appearance. For in all things that either are or can be, nothing else can be seen but *Posse* Itself; just as in all things made and to be made nothing can be seen

299

but the *posse* of the first maker and in all things moved and to be moved nothing but the *posse* of the first mover can be seen. Therefore, by such resolutions you see all things easy and every difference pass over into concordance.

**16.** Consequently, my dear Peter, you should be willing to turn your mind's eye to this secret with keen attention and by means of this resolution enter under our writings and your other reading and thoroughly occupy yourself with our booklets and sermons, especially *On the Gift of Light*,[45] which, when properly understood in accordance with what already has been said here, contains the same as this tract. You should also store away in your memory the booklets *On the Icon or the Vision of God* and *On Seeking God*[46] in order to become more familiar with these theological issues. And to them you should, with great goodwill, add the following Memorial of the *Summit of Contemplation*, which I submit now in as brief as possible form.[47] You shall be, it is my hope, an accepted contemplator of God, and may you constantly pray for me in holy worship.

**17.** *Memorial of* The Summit of Contemplation

The summit of contemplation is *Posse* Itself, the *Posse* of all *posse*, without which nothing at all can be contemplated. Indeed, how could it without *posse?*

I. Nothing can be added to *Posse* Itself, since it is the *Posse* of every *posse*.[48] *Posse* Itself, therefore, is not the *posse* to be or the *posse* to live, or the *posse* to understand, nor is it any *posse* with something added, although *Posse* Itself is the *posse* of the *posse* to be and of the *posse* to live and of the *posse* to understand.

**18.** II. Nothing exists except that which can be.[49] To be, therefore, does not add to the *posse* to be. So a human being does not add anything to the *posse* to be a human.[50] Nor does a young person add anything to the *posse* to be a young person or a grown person. And since a *posse* with an addition adds nothing to *Posse* Itself, whoever contemplates keenly sees nothing other than *Posse* Itself.

**19.** III. Nothing can be prior to *Posse* Itself. For how could it without *posse?* So nothing can be better, more powerful, more perfect, simpler, clearer, more known, truer, more sufficient, stronger, more stable, easier, and so forth, than *Posse* Itself. And since *Posse* Itself precedes every *posse* that has an addition, *Posse* Itself can neither be nor be named, sensed, imagined, or understood. Indeed, that which

*Posse* itself signifies precedes all these, although it is the hypostasis of all, just as light is the hypostasis of colors.

20.      IV. A *posse* with an addition is an image of *Posse* Itself, than which nothing is simpler. Hence, the *posse* to be is an image of *Posse* Itself, the *posse* to live an image of *Posse* Itself, and the *posse* to understand an image of *Posse* Itself. However, the *posse* to live is a truer image of it, and the *posse* to understand is an even truer image. The contemplator, therefore, sees *Posse* Itself in all things, just as truth is seen in an image.[51] And just as an image is an appearance of truth, so all things are nothing but appearances of *Posse* Itself.

21.      V. *Posse* Itself manifests itself in all things just as the *posse* of Aristotle's mind manifests itself in his books,[52] not that they disclose it perfectly, even though one book may do so more perfectly than another, and the books were produced for no other purpose than for his mind to reveal itself,[53] not that his mind was compelled to produce books, for a free and noble mind wished to disclose itself.[54] The mind, to be sure, is like an intellectual book, which sees in itself, and for all, the intention of the author.[55]

22.      VI. Although Aristotle's books contain only the *posse* of his mind, nevertheless, those who are unknowing do not perceive this. And although the universe contains only *Posse* Itself, nevertheless, those who lack mind cannot see this. But the living intellectual light, which is called "mind," contemplates in itself *Posse* Itself. Therefore, all things exist for the sake of the mind, and the mind exists for the sake of seeing *Posse* Itself.

23.      VII. The *posse* to choose enfolds in itself the *posse* to be, the *posse* to live, and the *posse* to understand. And the *posse* of free will[56] in no way depends on the body, as does the *posse* of concupiscent animal desire. Therefore, it does not follow the infirmity of the body. For it never grows old or diminishes as concupiscence and the senses do in the elderly, but it always remains and commands the senses. For it does not always permit the eye to look when it is inclined, but it turns it away in order to keep it from seeing vanity and scandal,[57] and likewise it prevents one who feels hunger from eating, and so forth. The mind, therefore, sees laudable and scandalous things, virtues and vices, which the senses do not see, and the mind can compel the senses to adhere to its judgment and not to their own desire.

And thus we experience that *Posse* Itself appears powerfully and incorruptibly in the *posse* of the mind and has a being separate from the body. This is less astonishing to anyone who experiences that the powers of certain herbs are contained in aqua vitae as extracted from the plant bodies themselves, when one observes in the aqua vitae the same effectual power that the herb had before it was immersed in the aqua vitae.

24.　　　VIII. What the mind sees are intelligibles, and they are prior to sensibles. The mind, therefore, sees itself. And because it sees that its own *posse* is not the *Posse* of every *posse*, since many things are impossible to it, so the mind sees that it is not *Posse* Itself but an image of *Posse* Itself. Therefore, since the mind in its *posse* sees *Posse* Itself but is only its own *posse* of being, it then sees that it is a mode of appearance of *Posse* Itself. And it likewise sees that in all things that exist. All things that the mind sees, therefore, are modes of appearance of the incorruptible *Posse* Itself.

25.　　　IX. The body's being, although less noble and least of all, is seen only by the mind. For what the senses see is accident, which does not exist except as incidental.[58] Indeed, this being of the body, which is nothing other than the body's *posse* to be, is not attained by any of the senses, because it is neither quality nor quantity. Therefore, it is neither divisible nor corruptible.[59] If, for example, I divide an apple, I do not divide body, for a part of the apple is body just as the whole apple is. A body is long, wide, and deep; without these there is neither body nor perfect dimension.[60] The being of the body is the being of perfect dimension. Bodily length is not separated from width and depth, just as width is not separated from length and depth, nor depth from length and width. Nor are they parts of the body, for a part is not the whole. Indeed, the length of the body is body, and the same is true of the width and the depth. And the length of bodily being, which is body, is no other body than the width or the depth of bodily being. But each one of these is the same indivisible and unmultiplicable body. Although the length is not the width or the depth; nevertheless, the length is the principle of width, and the length together with the width is the principle of the depth. So the mind sees *Posse* Itself appearing incorruptibly in the unitrine being of body.

And because the mind sees it thus in the lowest being, in that of body, so it sees it also appearing in a nobler and more powerful way in every nobler being and in the mind itself more clearly than in a living or corporeal being. But how the *Posse* Itself as unitrine clearly appears in the remembering, understanding, and willing mind, St. Augustine's mind has seen and revealed.[61]

26.　　　X. In activity or in making, the mind sees most certainly *Posse*

Itself appear in the *posse* to make of the maker, in the *posse* to become of the makeable, and in the *posse* of the connection of both.[62] But there are not three *posses*, but rather one and the same is the *posse* of the maker and of the makeable and of their connection. And similarly the mind sees in sensation, sight, taste, imagination, understanding, will, choice, contemplation, and in all good and virtuous deeds the unitrine *posse* as the reflection of *Posse* Itself, than which nothing is more efficacious or more perfect. But because *Posse* Itself does not shine forth in evil deeds, the mind experiences them as empty, bad, and dead, as works that darken and infect the light of the mind.

27.        **XI.** There can be no other substantial or quidditive principle, either formal or material, than *Posse* Itself. And those who have spoken of various forms and formalities, of various ideas and species, did not look to *Posse* Itself, how it discloses itself at will[63] in the various modes of being of genera and species. And wherever it does not shine forth, those things lack hypostasis as, for example, in emptiness, deficiency, error, vice, sickness, death, corruption, and so on, these lack hypostasis, and these lack entity, because they lack the appearance of *Posse* Itself.

28.        **XII.** By "*Posse* Itself" is signified the three and one God, whose name is the "Omnipotent" or the "*Posse* of All Power," with whom all things are possible and nothing impossible, who is the strength of the strong and the power of powers. God's most perfect appearance, than which none can be more perfect, is Christ leading us by word and example to the clear contemplation of *Posse* Itself. And this is the happiness which alone satisfies the highest longing of the mind.

What words can suffice are only these few.

# NOTES TO TEXTS

## On Learned Ignorance: Book One

[1] This is a translation of the text of *De docta ignorantia* ed. Ernst T. Hoff-mann and Raymond Klibansky, *Nicolai de Cusa opera omnia iussu et auctoritate Academiae Heidelbergensis*, vol. I (Leipzig, 1932). I have also consulted the revised version ed. Paul Wilpert and Hans Gerhard Senger, *Nicolai de Cusa. De docta ignorantia. Die belehrte Unwissenheit*, 2nd ed., "Schriften des Nikolaus von Kues in deutscher Übersetzung," vols. 15a–c (Hamburg, 1970–1971). Hereafter references to *De docta ignorantia* will be designated by DDI, and all references to Cusa's *opera* will be to the Heidelberg edition unless otherwise noted. The paragraph enumeration follows that of Wilpert and Senger.

[2] The work was completed in February 1440 and dedicated to Giuliano Cesarini (1398–1444), the future cardinal, who was a mentor and friend from Cusa's student days at the University of Padua and a president of the Council of Basel when Cusa was incorporated as a member. He may have influenced Cusa's decision to leave the council in favor of Pope Eugene IV in 1437. See also Gerald Christianson, *Cesarini, the Conciliar Cardinal: The Basel Years, 1431–1438* (St. Ottilien, 1979).

[3] Cusa insisted that he first received this notion as a gift from God and subsequently found confirmation of it in studies undertaken after his revelatory experience en route from Constantinople (Nov. 1437–Feb. 1438). See the dedicatory epistle appended to Book III of DDI below and his *Apologia doctae igno-rantiae* (h II.12–13). For the expression *docta ignorantia* see Augustine, Epistle 130 *Ad Gaium* 15.28. Compare also Augustine, Serm. 117.3.5 and Serm. 301.4.3, and Bonaventure, *Breviloquium* V, 6.260a.

[4] To this statement E. Hoffmann and R. Klibansky DDI I (h I.1, n. 16) cite Avicenna, *Canon* III.fen 13.tract. 1, xvi (ed. Venet. 1562 fo. 287ʳ), and Averroes, *Colliget* III.32 (ed. Venet. 1553 fo. 26ʳ). Cusa owned copies of both: The former is now included in Harleian. Cod. 3757 and the latter in Cus. Cod. 301 and 310.

[5] Cf. Aristotle, *Metaphysica* I.2.982ᵇ, 12f.

[6] This is an important thesis in *De docta ignorantia;* see also DDI I.3.9 and II.2.102 (h I.8 – 9; 67) and *De visione Dei* 23.101.

[7] That is, "according to essence or according to accessory (or nonessential) quality."

[8] Cf. Aristotle, *Metaphysica* I.5.985ᵇ, 25ff.

[9] Plato, *Apology* 23 B.

[10] Eccl 1:8.

[11] Jb 28:20 – 21.

[12] "First Philosophy" means metaphysics, apparently also embracing ontology, natural theology and epistemology. On the analogy of the owl and the sun, see Aristotle, *Metaphysica* II.1.993ᵇ, 9 – 11.

[13] *Maximitas,* i.e., the state, condition, or nature of being maximum.

[14] The first maximum Cusa speaks of is the Absolute that is God. Cf. Anselm's descriptions of God in *Proslogion* 2 and 15 as that "quo maius nihil cogitari potest." Note Jasper Hopkins, *A Concise Introduction to the Philosophy of Nicholas of Cusa,* 2nd ed. (Minneapolis, 1980), pp. 14 – 15, on the distinction between the uses to which Anselm and Cusa put the notion of *maximum.*

[15] 1 Tm 6:16.

[16] This second type of maximum is the contracted or restricted maximum and universe, unlike the first type, which is absolute, uncontracted, one, and God. Unlike the absolute maximum, the contracted exists in a restricted way, contractible to this or that, and thereby subject to differentiation and multiplicity.

[17] The third maximum, unlike the first two types, is both absolute and contracted, which, for Cusa, is Christ. Therefore, God, as the absolute maximum, is the subject of Book One; the universe, as the contracted maximum, is encompassed by Book Two; and Christ, as the maximum of both kinds, is the topic of Book Three.

[18] Cf. Aristotle, *De caelo* I.6.274ᵃ, 7 and I.7.275ᵃ, 13 and Cusa's two early sermons (1431): "Hoc facite" Serm. III.11 and "Fides autem catholica" Serm. IV.34 (h XVI/1.48; 71).

[19] In *De venatione sapientiae* 26.79 (h XII.76, 1 – 3), Cusa recites what he calls "the *ratio* of the rule of learned ignorance": "that in those things that receive a greater and a lesser, one never arrives at the simply maximum or the simply minimum." "Haec est ratio regulae doctae ignorantiae, quod in recipientibus magis et minus numquam devenitur ad maximum simpliciter vel minimum simpliciter, licet bene ad actu maximum et minimum."

[20] See Cusa's argument extended below in DDI II.1.91 – 92 (h I.61 – 62).

[21] Cf. Cusa's remarks about the search for quiddity in *De apice theoriae* ¶3 and ¶14 – 15 (h XII.118 – 119 and 126 – 129).

[22] Cusa's phrase "cum sit omne id quod esse potest" can also be translated "since [the absolutely maximum] is all that *it* can be."

[23] Later in *Trialogus de possest* ¶29 (h IX/2.96, 12ff.), Cusa will speak of *non esse* in God as *posse ipsum.*

[24] See below DDI I.10 and successive chapters.

[25] Dt 6:4.

[26] Mt 23:8–9.

[27] That is, the rule of learned ignorance. See above DDI I.3.9 (h I.8–9).

[28] Phil 2:9.

[29] Cusa may have confused Varro's work with Josephus, *Antiquitates Iudicae* XV.371–379 and XVIII.18, which speaks of the Essenes. Hoffmann and Klibansky (h I.15, n.) list several possible sources for the error.

[30] Hoffmann and Klibansky (h I.15, n. 2ff.) cite Cusa's source as John of Salisbury, *De septem septenis* VII PL CXCIX, 961 C.

[31] Cf. Thierry of Chartres, "Tractatus (De septem diebus)" ¶40, p. 197, in *Commentaries on Boethius by Thierry of Chartres and His School*, ed. Nikolaus M. Häring (Toronto, 1971).

[32] John of Salisbury, *De septem septenis* VII PL CXCIX, 961 B.

[33] For a fuller documentation of Cusa's reliance on Thierry of Chartres in this chapter, see the citations in Wilpert's Latin-German edition of DDI I (*Schriften* 15a.117–118). Cusa's etymology here seems to stem from Thierry of Chartres, "Lectiones" II, ¶48, p. 170, and VII, ¶5, p. 224; "Glosa" V, ¶18, p. 297; and especially "Commentum" II, ¶22, p. 75.

[34] Cf. Pseudo-Bede, *Commentum in Boethii De Trinitate* PL CXCV, 400B C. In *De pace fidei* 8.24 (h VII[2].25), Cusa uses the ternary of *unitas, iditas, et idemptitas* where he also makes reference to the persons of the Trinity as *unitas, aequalitas,* and *nexus.*

[35] See Augustine, *De doctrina Christiana* I.5.

[36] See DDI I.24 below.

[37] See above DDI I.7.18 and 21 (h I.14–16).

[38] Martianus Capella, *De nuptiis philologiae et Mercurii* II 135, p. 59, ed. Adolf Dick (Leipzig, 1925). According to Hoffmann and Klibansky (h I.19, n. 18–20), Cusa is apparently using John of Salisbury, *De septem septenis* VII PL CXCIX, 961 C, which substitutes the term *philosophia* for *philologia.*

[39] See above DDI I.4.11f. (h I.10f.).

[40] See above DDI I.5.13–14 (h I.11–13).

[41] *Transumptive,* that is, figuratively or metaphorically, in the sense of transferring from one thing to another.

[42] Cf. Rom 1:25 and 9:5; 2 Cor 11:31.

[43] Rom 1:20.

[44] 1 Cor 13:12.

[45] Boethius, *De institutione arithmetica* I.9–10.

[46] See I.1.3 above.

[47] Augustine, *Orosium contra Priscillanistas et Origenistas* 8, and Boethius, *De institutione arithmetica* I.2.12, 14–17.

[48] *Metaphysica* VIII.3.1043[b], 33ff.

[49] *De anima* II.3.414[b], 29–31.

[50] *De quantitate animae* 6–12 PL XXXII, 1042–1047.

[51] *De institutione arithmetica* I, 1, p. 9.

[52] "Peripatetics," or those walking round, refers to the followers of Aristotle, who was reputed to have taught while walking about, from the Greek περιπᾳτήσις, hence in Latin, Aristotle was sometimes referred to as the "Peripateticus."

[53] According to Hoffmann and Klibansky in DDI I (h I.24, n. 1–5), Cusa drew this conclusion from Albertus Magnus, *Metaphysica* I.tract. 3.14–4, 2.

[54] Anselm, *De veritate* X.

[55] According to P. Wilpert, *De docta ignorantia. Die belehrte Unwissenheit* I (*Schriften* 15a.120.n.34), Cusa is relying here on Heimericus de Campo [Heimeric van den Velde], *Tractatus de sigillo aeternitatis* Cod. Cus. 106, fo. 77f.

[56] Cusa may be referring to the dictum repeated in Meister Eckhart, *In Ecclesiasticum* 24.20 (LW II), ed. K. Weiß and J. Koch (Stuttgart, 1957), p. 248: "Deus . . . est sphaera intellectualis infinita, cuius centrum est ubique cum circumferentia, et cuius tot sunt circumferentiae, quot puncta."

[57] See above DDI I.5.14 and 6.17 (h I.12–13; 16).

[58] *Translative*, a synonym of *transumptive* and *metaphorice*.

[59] Pseudo-Dionysius, *De mystica theologia* 1.3 (*Dionysiaca* I.572).

[60] *De divinis nominibus* 5.8 (*Dionysiaca* I.355f.).

[61] *De mystica theologia* 1.1 (*Dionysiaca* I.601f.).

[62] *Epistola I ad Gaium* (*Dionysiaca* I. 607).

[63] According to Hoffmann and Klibansky DDI I (h I.31, n. 13–16), Cusa confuses the name of Rabbi Moysen [Moses Maimonides] with Rabbi Salomon Issac (Raschi).

[64] The citations to the *Dux neutrorum* [*Guide to the Perplexed*] I 57 and 58 of Maimonides are apparently taken from Meister Eckhart's *Expositio libri Exodi* (LW II), ¶18, p. 158, and ¶174, p. 151. See P. Wilpert, *De docta ignorantia. Die belehrte Unwissenheit* I (*Schriften* 15a.121–122.n. 44).

[65] *Transumptive*.

[66] See above DDI I.3.9–10 (h I.8–9).

[67] Aristotle, *Metaphysica* X.1.1052$^b$, 18–19.

[68] *De divinis nominibus* 4.23 (*Dionysiaca* I.273–4).

[69] Apparently, Cusa erroneously cites *Phaedo* here in place of *Timaeus*. See Calcidius, *Commentarius in Timaeum* 330, ed. J. H. Waszink (*Plato Latinus* IV) (London, 1962), pp. 324–325. Calcidius is referring to *Timaeus* 31 A.

[70] See above DDI I.3.9 (h I.8–9).

[71] See above DDI I.16.46 (h I.32).

[72] *De caelesti hierarchia* 2.73 (*Dionysiaca* II.757). Cf. also *De divinis nominibus* 1.1 and 1.5 (*Dionysiaca* I.10ff.; 355ff.).

[73] *De anima* I.5.411$^a$, 5–7.

[74] Aristotle, *Categoriae* 5.3$^b$, 33–34 and 5.4$^a$, 8–9.

[75] *Metaphysica* V.7.1017$^a$, 7–8.

[76] Pseudo-Dionysius, *De divinis nominibus* 1.1 and 5.8 (*Dionysiaca* I.10ff.; 355ff.).

[77] See below DDI I.26.86ff. (h I.54ff.).

[78] *Transumptio*, literally, the taking of the one for the other, or the representation of one thing for another.

[79] See above DDI I.13–14.35ff. (h I.25ff.).

[80] See above DDI I.13–15.35ff. (h I.25ff.).

[81] The citation is uncertain. The idea but not the exact wording can be found in Augustine, *De trinitate* VI.7 and V–VIII *passim*. Cf. Cusa's *Apologia doctae ignorantiae* (h II.24, 6–9).

[82] Jn 10:38 and 14:10.

[83] See above DDI I chs. 7–9 and 19.

[84] See above DDI I.4.11–12 (h I.10–11).

[85] *Transumptio.*

[86] See above DDI I.15.40 (h I.29).

[87] Cf. Rom 11:36.

[88] On theology as circular, see DDI I.21.66 and II.3.111 (h I.44; 69); *Apologia doctae ignorantiae* (h II.23); *Complementum theologicum* 14 (p II fo.100$^r$); and *Idiota de sapientia* II.29–30 (hV$^2$.60–61). On Lull's influence here see E. Colomer, *Nikolaus von Kues und Raimund Llull* (Berlin, 1961), pp. 88ff. In the *De divinis nominibus* 4.8–9 and 9.9 (*Dionysiaca* I.189ff.; 177ff.), Dionysius the Pseudo-Areopagite describes God's motion as circular as well as the motions of the divine intelligences and of the soul.

[89] Regarding this topic, as Cusa so often does elsewhere when he appeals to the notion of *complicatio-explicatio*, he draws from Thierry of Chartres. On divine providence see especially "Lectiones" II ¶6, p. 156.

[90] *Possibiliter*, i.e. in a possible way or as possibilities.

[91] See Thierry of Chartres, "Lectiones" II, ¶60, p. 174 and "Glosa" II, ¶23, p. 271.

[92] *Transumptio.*

[93] Cusa's citation apparently stems from what other medieval writers had ascribed to Parmenides; Hoffmann and Klibansky (h I. 46, n. 22ff.) cite Pseudo-Bede, *Commentarius in librum Boetii de trinitate* PL XCV, 397C, and also John of Salisbury, *De septem septenis* VII, PL CXCIX, 961B.

[94] Rom 11:36.

[95] *Asclepius* 20 in *Corpus Hermeticum* II, ed. A. D. Nock and A. J. Festugière (Paris, 1945), p. 321. Cusa may have obtained this citation from Thierry of Chartres, "Lectiones" IV ¶11, pp. 189–190.

[96] Zec 14:9.

[97] Dt 6:4. Jerome, in *Liber interpretationis hebraicorum nominum, De exodo* CCSL LXXII, 75, defines Israel as *videre Deum* and *mens videre Deum*.

[98] *Ipsum*, which probably refers to *maximum*.

[99] *De caelesti hierarchia* II, ¶3 (*Dionysiaca* II.759).

[100] Cf. Col 1:16.

[101] *De trinitate* VI.10.11–12.

[102] That is, the love of both unity and its equality.

[103] *De genesi ad litteram* I.4.

[104] On Jerome see *De decem Dei nominibus* PL XXIII, 1333ff.

[105] On the confusion of Solomon and Maimonides, see above DDI I.16.44 (h I.31).

[106] E. Hoffmann and R. Klibansky (h I.52, n. 4–6) cite Firmicus Maternus, *Matheseos* II.13.6, ed. W. Kroll, F. Skutsch, and K. Ziegler (Leipzig, 2 vols., 1898 and 1913), vol. I, pp. 56–57.

[107] *Asclepius* 21 in *Corpus Hermeticum* II.321, 18ff.

[108] E. Hoffmann and R. Klibansky cite Valerius Soranus as apparently drawn from Marcus Varro in Augustine, *De civitate Dei* VII.9.202.

[109] Note the play on words: "They called [her] *Cupid*, because one thing desires [*cupit*] another."

[110] See above DDI I.7.18 (h I.14–15).

[111] *De natura deorum* II.28.70.

[112] Jn 4:24.

[113] 1 Tm 6:16.

[114] Jn 14:6.

[115] Jn 1:5.

[116] That is, by *removing* or denying that which is not God. See *De quaerendo Deum* 5.49 (h IV/1.33).

[117] *De mystica theologia* 5. (*Dionysiaca* I.597ff.).

[118] P. Wilpert, *De docta ignorantia. Die belehrte Unwissenheit* I (*Schriften* 15a.126.n. 87), cites Maimonides, *Dux neutrorum* I 57. See above DDI I.16.44.

[119] *De trinitate* II.1.51 A.

[120] Pseudo-Dionysius, *De mystica theologia* 3 (*Dionysiaca* I.591–593).

[121] Rom 1:25 and 9:5; 2 Cor 11:31.


## On Learned Ignorance: Book Two

[1] On the relationship of Book I to Book II, see DDI I.2.6 (h I.7, 16–25).

[2] The prologue to each of the three books of DDI and the letter appended to the treatise are addressed to Cardinal Julian Cesarini.

[3] Cf. DDI I.3.9 (h I.8–9).

[4] DDI I.17.49 (h I.34).

[5] Cf. DDI II.11.159–161 (h I.102–103).

[6] This refers to the rule in ¶91 above that precise equality belongs only to God and in consequence all else differs.

[7] Cusa is perhaps referring to his statements on harmony in *De coniecturis* II.2.83 and 6.105 (h III.80–81; 102, 9–15).

# NOTES TO TEXTS

[8] This frequently cited dictum apparently stems from Aristotle, *Physica* II.194ª,21. Cf. *De coniecturis* II.12.131 (h III.127, 10).

[9] See ¶91 above.

[10] Cf. *De coniecturis* I.10.44f. (h III.47f.). On Cusa's concept of *coniectura* and differences between the completed book *De coniecturis* [1440–1445] and Cusa's discussion of his original intentions in DDI II, see Josef Koch, *Die Ars coniecturalis des Nikolaus von Kues*. (*Arbeitsgemeinschaft für Forschung des Landes Nordrhein-Westfalen, Geisteswissenschaften*, Hft. 4) (Cologne, 1956). See also Winfried Happ's introduction to the Latin-German edition of *De coniecturis* (*Schriften* 17.ix-xxi) and Clyde Lee Miller, "Nicholas of Cusa's *On Conjectures* (*De coniecturis*)" in *Nicholas of Cusa in Search of God and Wisdom*, ed. Gerald Christianson and Thomas M. Izbicki (Leiden, 1991), pp. 119–140.

[11] Cf. DDI III.2 (h I.123–125).

[12] *Inintelligibiliter*, that is, in a way not discernible by the active intellect.

[13] Cf. DDI I.6.15 (h I.13).

[14] The reference to divine communication *absque invidia* occurs in several places in DDI and, according to P. Wilpert (*Schriften* 15b.118.n.17), may stem from Calcidius' translation of Plato, *Timaeus* 29 E, ed. J. H. Waszink (*Plato Latinus* IV) (London, 1962), p. 22. Cf. DDI II.2.104; III.3.201; 9.235; 12.256 (h I.68; 128; 147; 158–159).

[15] DDI I.13.35 (h I.25–26).

[16] Cf. *Apologia doctae ignorantiae* (h II.22–23).

[17] Pseudo-Hermes Trismegistus, *Liber XXIV philosophorum, propositio* 14 BGPThM XXV.211.

[18] Cf. DDI I.8.22 (h I.17).

[19] Cf. DDI I.1.3 and 3.9 (h I.5–6; 8–9).

[20] That is, a "shining brightly" or "splendor," perhaps even simply a "shining again" or "reflection."

[21] Cf. DDI I.11.30 (h I.22).

[22] Cf. Pseudo-Dionysius, *De divinis nominibus* 4.2 (*Dionysiaca* I.155ff.).

[23] Cf. DDI I.6.17; 22.69 and II.7.129–131 (h I.14; 45; 82–84).

[24] *Occasionatus* may simply indicate something as caused or qualified from something else. However, in *STh* Ia 92.1.ob.1 and ad 1 and 99.2.ob.1 and ad 1 and 2, Thomas Aquinas seems to use the term more narrowly to designate something misbegotten. In 2 *Sent*. 20.2.1.ob.1 he defines it as: "quod non est per se intentum, and ex aliqua corruptione vel defectu proveniens" and in *STh* Ia.99.2.ob.1 he speaks of woman as "mas occasionatus," where he is citing Aristotle, *De generatione animalium* II.3.737ª.27.

[25] Cf. DDI I.2 and 5 (h I.7–8; 11–13).

[26] Cf. DDI I.4 (h I.10–11).

[27] Cf. DDI I.7.21 (h I.16).

# NOTES TO TEXTS

[28] On the relationship of mind to number and of the human mind to the divine, see Cusa's *De coniecturis* I.2.7 and 1.5 (h III.11–12 and 21–28).

[29] Cf. DDI II.13.179 (h I.113).

[30] Cf. DDI I.21.66 (h I.44).

[31] Cf. Cusa's description of the human vision of God's face in *De visione Dei* 6.

[32] Avicenna, *Metaphysica tractatus* IX.4. Wilpert (*Schriften* 15b.121.n. 49) also cites Macrobius, *Commentarii in somnium Scipionis* I.14; Proclus, *Elementatio theologica* 129, and *Liber de causis* VIII.87.

[33] See *Die Fragmente der Vorsokratiker* II, ed. H. Diels and W. Kranz (Zùrich-Berlin, 1964), 59 B 1.

[34] Cf. DDI I.2.5 (h I.7).

[35] Cf. DDI I.13–15 and II.4.113 (h I.25–30; 73).

[36] Cf. DDI II.6.125 (h I.80) and also *De coniecturis* II.4.92 (h III.89–90).

[37] Cf. DDI II.1.91–95 (h I.61–63).

[38] The four unities, however, appear in *De coniecturis* I.4.12ff. (h III.18ff.) as God, intelligence, soul, and body.

[39] In *De coniecturis* I.6.22 (h III.28–29) the second unity is the intellectual.

[40] That is, all the ten most general categories.

[41] Cf. Cusa's discussion of the intellect in *De coniecturis* II.13.134 and 16.159 (h III.130–132; 158–160), which takes a different tack than that described here in DDI II.

[42] On the trinitarian theme in Cusa, see Rudolf Haubst, *Das Bild des Einen und Dreieinen Gottes in der Welt nach Nikolaus von Kues* (*Trier theologische Studien* Bd. 4) (Trier, 1952).

[43] See especially chs. 7–10, 19–20, and 24.

[44] In developing his notion of the relationship between unity and trinity in the universe below in chs. 7–9, Cusa seems to have given close attention to certain writers from the School of Chartres, especially Thierry. For fuller documentation consult the detailed references in the Heidelberg edition of E. Hoffmann and R. Klibansky and the German-Latin edition of H. G. Senger.

[45] To the received text: "Dicit enim mutabilitatem et alteritatem, cum in consideratione principii," Wilpert, *De docta ignorantia. Die belehrte Unwissenheit* II.128 (*Schriften* 15b.50, 18–19), adds the following: "nihil prius sit unitate. Sed tamen nihil in esse producitur, quod prius esse non possit."

[46] Cf. DDI I.8–9 (h I.17–19).

[47] Cf. DDI II.9.149–150 (h I.95–96).

[48] Cf. Aristotle, *Metaphysica* XI.6.1062$^b$. See also *Physica* I.4.187$^a$.

[49] That is, neither a "what" or essence nor a "what sort" or quality, following Aristotle's ten categories or predicables.

[50] *Asclepius* 14 in *Corpus Hermeticum* II.313, 12ff. Cf. *Compendium* 719–720 (h XI/3.16).

[51] The reference is uncertain. Wilpert (*Schriften* 15b.126.n. 95) refers the reader to Wis 11.18 and Augustine, *De genesi contra Manichaeos* I.5.

[52] Cf. Calcidius, *Commentarius in Timaeum* 311, ed. J. H. Waszink (*Plato Latinus* IV) (London, 1962), p. 338.

[53] Cf. DDI I.16.42 (h I.30).

[54] Cf. Aristotle, *Metaphysica* IX.8.1049$^b$, 24–25.

[55] For a brief history of the *anima mundi* theme from Plato's *Timaeus* 34 B through the twelfth century, see Wilpert (*Schriften* 15b.127. n.105).

[56] Cf. Thierry of Chartres, "Lectiones" II.10.157.

[57] Cf. Calcidius, *Commentarius in Timaeum* 143ff., ed. J. H. Waszink (*Plato Latinus* IV) (London 1962), p. 182.

[58] See Aristotle's reference in *De anima* I.2.404$^b$, 27–30.

[59] Gn 1:3.

[60] Cf. DDI I.3.9; II.1.96 and 8.136 (h I.8; 63; 87–88).

[61] See Cusa's extended treatment of the analogy of the maximum and infinite line in DDI I.13–17 (h I.25–35).

[62] Cf. DDI I.23.70 and II.2.103–104 (h I.46; 66–68).

[63] Cf. DDI II.4–6 (h I.72–78).

[64] Cf. Aristotle, *De anima* III.8.431$^b$f.

[65] Cusa's discussion of the intellectual nature in *De coniecturis* II.13.134 and 16.159 (h III.130–132; 158–160) is more broadly focused than his remarks suggest here.

[66] Cf. Calcidius, *Commentarius in Timaeum* 144, ed. J. H. Waszink (*Platinus Latinus* IV) (London 1962), pp. 182–183.

[67] On the probable Chartrian sources for Cusa's descriptions here, see P. Wilpert (*Schriften* 15b.130.n.133).

[68] Mt 10:20.

[69] Wis 1:7.

[70] Cusa perhaps means *De coniecturis* II.8–10 (h III.108ff.).

[71] Cf. DDI II.7.127 and 130 and 10.154 (h I.81–82; 83–84; 98).

[72] Cf. DDI I.3.9; 17.49; II.1.91 and 95 (h I.8–9; 34; 61; 63).

[73] Cf. DDI II.1.96; 8.136–137; and 9.148 (h I.63; 87–88; 94).

[74] Cf. DDI I.23.70 (h I.46).

[75] As in the paragraph above, Cusa here is speaking of a fixed center and a fixed circumference.

[76] Cf. DDI II.11.159 and 12.162 (h I.102; 103–104).

[77] That is, in the eighth sphere.

[78] Cf. DDI II.11.157 (h I.100–101).

[79] Cf. DDI I.23.70 and II.11.157 and 159 (h I.46; 100–101; 102). Cusa may be relying here on the notion Meister Eckhart takes from Pseudo-Hermes Trismegistus, *Liber XXIV philosophorum, propositio* 2 BGPThM XXV.208, 8. See Dietrich Mahnke, *Unendliche Sphäre und Allmittelpunkt* (Halle, 1937), pp. 76–106 and 144ff. and Herbert Wackerzapp, *Die Einfluss Meister Eckharts aud die*

*ersten philosophischen Schriften des Nikolaus von Kues (1440–1450).* BGPThM XXXIX.141ff.

[80] Cf. DDI II.11.159ff. (h I.102–103).

[81] Plato, *Timaeus* 30 B and 38 E. Cf. Cusa's use of the body analogy elsewhere in DDI: DDI II.5.121 and 13.176 (h I.78; 111).

[82] See above DDI II.12.166 (h I.105–106).

[83] Plato, *Timeaus* 38 CD and, according to Wilpert (*Schriften* 15b 133.n.170), William of Conches, *Philosophia* II 23 and *Glosae super Platonem In Timaeum* XCVIII.

[84] Cf. Wis 11:21.

[85] *Georgics* 4.226.

[86] Cf. Macrobius, *Commentarii in somnium Scipionis* 1.6, 8–9, ed. J. Willis (Leipzig, 1963).

[87] Cf. DDI III.9.233 (h I.146).

[88] Cf. Wis 11:21.

[89] Cf. Plato, *Timaeus* 30 B; 38 E. See also DDI II.12.166 (h I.106).

[90] Cf. 1 Jn 1:5.

[91] Dt 4:24; Heb 12:29.

[92] Cf. Eccl 8:17.

[93] Ps 144:3 (145:3).

[94] Cf. 1 Tm 6:16.

[95] Cf. Mt 7:7–8; Lk 11:9–10.

[96] Ps 16(17):15.

[97] Cf. Rom 1:25 and 9:5; 2 Cor 11:31.

## *On Learned Ignorance: Book Three*

[1] The work is dedicated to Cardinal Julian Cesarini. See the prologue DDI I.1 (h I.1–2).

[2] Cf. Jn 14:6.

[3] Cf. Wis 11:21.

[4] Cf. DDI I.5.13 (h I.12). See also DDI I.6.15 (h I.13).

[5] Cf. DDI II.12.162 and 174; 13.179 (h I.103–104; 109–110; 113).

[6] That is, within the middle species, the nature of the two species of which the middle species is composed, either the higher or the lower will necessarily prevail over the other because the third species is not composed equally of the other two.

[7] Cf. Aristotle, *De partibus animalium* IV.5.679[b], 15–16. See Senger (*Schriften* 15c.103–104. n. 186,13) for additional citations.

[8] Cf. *De coniecturis* II.10.123 and 128; 13.137–138 (h III.118–119; 121–122; 133–136).

[9] See Senger (*Schriften* 15c.104–105. n. 187,12) for a list of Platonist writ-

ings on "daemones," especially Apuleius, *De deo Socratis*, according to Senger, a copy of which (cod. Brux. B.R. 10054–56) Cusa owned and annotated.

[10] Cf. DDI I.5.13 (h I.12).

[11] Cf. *De coniecturis* I.2.82 (h III.79–80).

[12] Cf. *De coniecturis* II.15.146ff. (h III.147ff.).

[13] Phil 4:7.

[14] Cf. DDI II.1.96; 4–6; 8.137 (h I.63–64; 72–81; 88).

[15] DDI I.13–17 (h I.25–35).

[16] Cf. DDI I.2.5–6; 5.14 (h I.7; 12–13).

[17] Cf. *De visione Dei* 23.101.

[18] Note Cusa's first reference to the analogy of the "maximum line": DDI I.13 (h I.25–27).

[19] Cf. Heb 2:7,9 and Ps 8:6–8 (8:5–6).

[20] Cf. *De coniecturis* II.14.143 (h III.143). See the selection from Democritus in *Die Fragmente der Vorsokratiker* II, ed. H. Diels and W. Kranz (Zürich-Berlin, 1964), 68 (55) B 34.

[21] Cf. Col 1:18.

[22] Cf. Rv 21:17.

[23] Cf. John Scotus Eriugena, *Periphyseon (De divisione naturae)* III.4, ed. I. P. Sheldon-Williams, *Scriptores Latini Hiberniae* VII.60, 30–31 (Dublin, 1968).

[24] Cf. Col 1:16.

[25] Cf. DDI I.24.80 (h I.50–51).

[26] Cf. DDI III.4.203 (h I.129–130).

[27] Cf. Col 1:15–20.

[28] Cf. Col 1:15.

[29] Cf. Eph 4:10.

[30] Cf. 2 Cor 12:2–4.

[31] Cf. Col 1:14–20.

[32] Cf. DDI II.5 (h I.76–78).

[33] Cf. DDI III.1.183ff. (h I.119–123).

[34] Cf. Col 3:11.

[35] Cf. Col 2:3.

[36] Cf. Jn 1:5.

[37] *Sursum suppositata*, i.e., supposited in the divinity. Cf. DDI I.4.206 and 7.223 (h I.131; 140).

[38] Cf Mt 1:18; Lk 1:35.

[39] Cf. DDI II.7.130 and 10.154 (h I.83; 98).

[40] A similiar analogy occurs elsewhere in Cusa's treatises: see *De filiatione Dei* IV.74 (h IV/1.54–55) and *De genesi* IV.165 (h IV/1.118–119).

[41] Cf. Eph 3:16; Col 1:27 and 2:2–3.

[42] Cf. Heb 4:15.

[43] Cf. Lk 1:28.

[44] Cf. Gal 4:4.

[45] Cf. Wis 18:14–15.

[46] Cf. 1 Cor 2:14.

[47] Cf. Jn 4:24.

[48] According to the consideration of infinity, Cusa says in DDI I.26.88 (h I.55), God as infinity is neither Father nor Son nor Holy Spirit, for in God nothing is to be found other than infinity. Cf. also DDI I.18.54 (h I.37).

[49] Tb 4:16. Compare with the positively stated "golden rule" in Mt 7:12; Lk 6:31.

[50] For Cusa's explanation of the paucity of faith alone and the need for "faith formed" in love, see DDI III.6.219 and 11.248 and 250 (h I.138; 154; 155) and *De pace fidei* 16.58 (h VII.54–55).

[51] Cf. Jn 1:13.

[52] Cf. Heb 1:3.

[53] Mt 25:40.

[54] Cf. Col 2:11–13.

[55] Cf. Rom 8:29–30.

[56] Cf. Rom 5:18–21.

[57] Cf. Col 2:9.

[58] Cf. Rom 3:28; Gal 2:6.

[59] Cf. DDI III.11.248–252 (h I.154–156).

[60] Cf. Mt 23:12; Lk 14:11; 18:14.

[61] Cf. Phil 2:6–11.

[62] Cf. 1 Cor 15:53–55.

[63] Cf. Lk 24:25–26.

[64] Cf. DDI III.6.218 (h I.137).

[65] Jn 12:24–25.

[66] Cf. Jn 12:32.

[67] Cf. DDI III.2.193–194; 4.204 (h I.124–125; 130–131).

[68] *Communicatio idiomatum*, i.e., an interchange of the properties of the divine and human natures in Christ, while each of the natures remains distinct though hypostatically and inseparably united in the one person. See the discussion in Rudolf Haubst, *Die Christologie des Nikolaus von Kues* (Freiburg 1956), pp. 132–135.

[69] Jn 12:24–25.

[70] Lk 24:46.

[71] Col 1:18; Acts 26:23; Rv 1:5.

[72] Jn 17:18.

[73] Cf. 1 Cor 15:20, 23.

[74] Cf. 1 Cor 15:12–22.

[75] *Suppositum*, that is, also subject or individual substance.

[76] Cf. 1 Jn 3:2.

[77] Cf. Jn 14:6.

[78] What follows is a series of criticisms of the Islamic and Jewish rejection of Christ's divinity and Resurrection. Much of the argumentation is developed later in Cusa's *Cribratio Alkorani* and *De pace fidei*.

[79] Cf. *De pace fidei* 15.50–52 (h VII.47–49) and *Cribratio Alkorani* II.18.149 (h VIII.121).

[80] Cf. *De pace fidei* 12.41 (h VII.39).

[81] Cf. *De pace fidei* 13.42f. (h VII.40–41) and *Cribratio Alkorani* II.15.130 (h VIII.104).

[82] Col 1:18.

[83] Cf. Lk 24:26.

[84] Cf. Eph 4:10.

[85] Cf. DDI II.11.156–157 and III.1.185 (h I.100–101; 120).

[86] Cf. Ps 18:2 (19:1).

[87] Cf. Jn 14:2.

[88] Cf. Eph 4:10 and Col 3:11.

[89] Ps 35:10 (36:9).

[90] Cf. Lk 17:21.

[91] Cf. 1 Jn 1:5.

[92] Cf. Dt 4:24 and Heb 12:29. Cf. DDI II.13.177 (h I.112).

[93] Cf. 1 Cor 3:13.

[94] Cf. 1 Cor 15:28.

[95] Cf. Rom 6:9.

[96] Cf. Jn 14:6.

[97] Col 3:3.

[98] Cf. Ps 111 (112):9 and 2 Cor 9:9.

[99] Cf. Jn 4:24.

[100] Cf. DDI III.12.254 (h I.157–158).

[101] Ps 32 (33):9; 148:5.

[102] Cf. 1 Cor 13:12.

[103] Cf. DDI II.8.134 (h. I.86).

[104] Cf. Mt 25:41.

[105] Cf. DDI III.8 (h I.143–145).

[106] Cf. 1 Cor 15:42ff.

[107] Cf. Rv 14:10; 19:20; 21:8.

[108] Cf. Rom 1:25 and 9:5; 2 Cor 11:31.

[109] Is 7:9b according to the Septuagint.

[110] Jn 1:12.

[111] Jn 20:31.

[112] Cf. Mt 11:25 and Lk 10:21.

[113] Col 2:3.

[114] Cf. 2 Cor 12:2.

[115] Cf. 1 Cor 2:2 and 5:16–17. See also *De apice theoriae* 2 (h XII.118, 5–8).

[116] Cf. Heb 12:18–22.

[117] Cf. DDI I.2.8 (h I.8).

[118] Rom 15:4

[119] Ps 32 (33):6.

[120] Jn 1:14.

[121] Cf. Mt 17:20.

[122] Cf. Rom 8:18.

[123] Cf. Mt 16:24; Mk 8:34; Lk 9:23.

[124] Cf. 2 Cor 3:18.

[125] Cf. 1 Cor 8:16.

[126] DDI III.11.248–249 (h I.154–155).

[127] DDI III.11.250 (h I.155).

[128] DDI III.11.248 (h I.154).

[129] DDI III.6.219 (h I.138).

[130] Cf. 1 Jn 4:8. See below in the notation to *De quaerendo Deo* III.42 (h IV/1.29).

[131] Cf. Rom 12:4; 1 Cor 12:12ff.

[132] Jn 15:4ff.

[133] Mt 25:40.

[134] Col 3:11; Eph 1:33 and 4:6.

[135] DDI I.3.9; 6.15; II.1.96; III.1.183 and 188 (h I.8; 13; 63–64; 119; 121–122).

[136] Jn 15:5.

[137] Phil 4:13.

[138] Heb 4:16.

[139] Lk 12:37.

[140] Rv 21:6.

[141] Cf. *De visione Dei* 16.70. This may have come from an analogy in Eckhart, *Sermones et lectiones super Ecclesiastici* 42–43 (LW II 271–272).

[142] Cf. DDI II.6.125–126 (h I.80–81).

[143] Cf. Rom 1:25 and 9:5; 2 Cor 11:31.

[144] Cf. DDI III.4.204 and 7.223 (h I.130; 140).

[145] Cf. DDI III.2.192 and 7.226 (h I.124; 142).

[146] 1 Cor 13:13.

[147] Cf. DDI III.252 (h I.156).

[148] Cf. DDI I.5.14; 9.24–25; and 10.28 (h I.12–13; 18; 20–21).

[149] Cf. DDI I.24.80–81; II.7.128–130 (h I.50–51; 82–84).

[150] Jn 17:22–23.

[151] Cf. 2 Cor 3:18.

[152] Cf. Rom 1:25 and 9:5; 2 Cor 11:31.

[153] See the dedication to Cardinal Julian Cesarini in the prologue DDI I.1 (h I.1–2).

[154] This refers to Cusa's embassy to Constantinople in 1437 to assist in winning the support of the Greek leadership to Pope Eugene IV's proposal for a

union council in Italy. The return journey began on November 27, 1437, and ended on February 8, 1438. See *Acta Cusana. Quellen zur Lebensgeschichte des Nikolaus von Kues,* ed. Erich Meuthen, I.1. (1401–1437) (Hamburg, 1976), pp. 197–199, nrs. 294–296. See also Erich Meuthen, *Nikolaus von Kues 1401–1464. Skizze einer Biographie* 4th ed. (Münster, 1979), pp. 49–52.

[155] Jas 1:17. Note Cusa's later treatise *De dato patris luminum* Prol.91 and I.92 (h IV/1.67–68).

[156] Cf. DDI I.2.5; 4.11–12; 5.13; 12.33; 26.89 (h I.7; 10–11; 12; 24; 56). See also *De visione Dei* 13.15 and *De apice theoriae* ¶11 (h XII.124–125).

[157] In *Apologia doctae ignorantiae* (h II.12–13; 32; and 34), Cusa explains his experience of the discovery of "learned ignorance" initially as a gift that he later traces in earlier writers.

[158] Rom 8:11.


## Dialogue on the Hidden God

[1] Cf. Is 45:15. The following translation and enumeration of paragraphs is from the text edited by Paul Wilpert in *Nicolai de Cusa opera omnia iussu et auctoritate Academiae Heidelbergensis,* vol. IV. *Opuscula* I. (Hamburg, 1959). Although the precise date of composition of the dialogue is uncertain, it is considered to have been written before Cusa's *Apologia doctae ignorantiae* (1449) and probably before his *De quaerendo Deum* (1445). See Wilpert (h I.ix); E. Vansteenberghe, *Le Cardinal Nicolas de Cues: L'action-la pensée* (Paris, 1920), p. 268; and J. Koch, ed., *Cusanus-Texte I. Predigten 2./5. Vier Predigten im Geiste Eckharts* (HSB, Phil.-his. Kl., Jahrg. 1936/1937, 2. Abh.), p. 33.

[2] Jn 4:22.

[3] Cf. DDI I.25.84 and 26.88 (h I.53; 55–56) and *Apologia doctae ignorantiae* (h II.13).

[4] Cf. DDI I.1.4 (h I.6) and *Apologia doctae ignorantiae* (h II.2, 10–13).

[5] Cf. DDI I.4.11 (h I.10).

[6] Cf. DDI I.3.10 (h I.9).

[7] Cf. DDI I.3.10 (h I.9).

[8] *Quidditas,* quiddity or "whatness," designates a thing's essence.

[9] *Ex accidenti,* that is, by or on the basis of an incidental property of a thing.

[10] Cf. *De quaerendo Deum* II.35 and 36 (h IV/1.25).

[11] Cf. DDI I.17.49 and II.3.105 (h I.17; 69).

[12] Cf. DDI II.6.126 (h I.81).

[13] Cf. DDI I.5.14; II.4.114; and III.1.182 (h I.12–13; 73–74; 119).

[14] Cf. Acts 17:29 and *De quaerendo Deum* I.18 (h IV/1.14).

[15] See Cusa's explanation of *theologia negativa* in DDI I.26.86 (h I.54).

[16] Cf. Rom 4:17.

[17] Cf. Rom 11:36.

[18] Cf. *De coniecturis* V.18 (h III.24) and *De quaerendo Deum* I.19 (h IV/1.14).

[19] Cf. Pseudo-Dionysius, *De divinis nominibus* 1.6 (*Dionysiaca* I.44–45).

[20] Cf. DDI I.19.57 (h I.38–39) and *De coniecturis* I.5.21 and 6.24 (h III.26–27; 30–32). See especially *De filiatione Dei* III.63 (h IV/1.47–48): "Nam deus in se triumphans nec est intelligibilis aut scibilis, nec est veritas nec vita, nec est, sed omne intelligibile antecedit ut unum simplicissimum principium."

[21] Cf. DDI I.6.17 (h I.14).

[22] Cf. Rom 4:17 and DDI I.6.17 (h I.14).

[23] Cf. DDI I.24.78 (h I.50).

[24] Cf. DDI I.24.77 (h I.49).

[25] For the notion that "God," or *Theos*, derives from *theoro* see: *De quaerendo Deum* I.19 (h IV/1.14); *De visione Dei* 1.5 and 8.31; *Complementum theologicum* 14 (p II fo. 100ʳ); and *Directio speculantis seu de Non Aliud* 23 (h XIII.104, 12–14).

[26] Cf. *De quaerendo Deum* I.20 (h IV/1.25).

[27] Cf. *De quaerendo Deum* I.26–27 and 3.38 (h IV/1.18–19).

[28] Cf. DDI I.20.60; 24.77; II.2.102; and III.68.194 (h I.40–41; 49; 67; and 125).

[29] Cf. Rom 1:25 and 9:5; 2 Cor 11:31.

## On Seeking God

[1] The following translation and enumeration of paragraphs is from the text edited by Paul Wilpert in *Nicolai de Cusa opera omnia iussu et auctoritate Academiae Heidelbergensis*, vol. IV. *Opuscula* I. (Hamburg, 1959). The work was completed in the early months of 1445.

[2] Cf. Cusa's sermon "Dies sanctificatus illuxit nobis," delivered at Mainz on January 6, 1445, Sermon XXXIX according to J. Koch and XLVIII according to R. Haubst. See E. Hoffmann and R. Klibansky, eds., *Cusanus-Texte I. Predigten. 1. "Dies Sanctificatus" vom Jahre 1439.* (HSB, Phil.-his. Kl., Jahrg. 1928–1929, 3. Abh.). In his preface to *De quaerendo Deum*, P. Wilpert (h IV/1.ix–x) dates the composition of the treatise as falling within a few months of the sermon, that is, most likely between January 6 and March 20, 1445. The *frater in Christo* to whom the treatise is addressed remains unknown.

[3] Cf. Rom 7:22; 2 Cor 4:16; and Eph 3:16.

[4] Cf. Mt 25:21f.

[5] 2 Cor 12:2.

[6] Cf. *Apologia doctae ignorantiae* (h II.6 and 13).

[7] Cf. Acts 17:16ff.

[8] Jn 4:24.

[9] Cf. *De Deo abscondito* ¶8 (h IV/1.7,4).

[10] Cf. *De Deo abscondito* ¶10 (h IV/1.7,2–7).

# NOTES TO TEXTS

[11] That is, the Greek verb θεωρέω. Cf. *De Deo abscondito* ¶14 (h IV/1.9–10); *De visione Dei* 1.5 and 8.31; *Complementum theologicum* 14 (p II fo. 100ʳ); *Directio speculantis seu de Non Aliud* 23 (h XIII.104,12–14). (Paragraph reference numbers for the last are according to those utilized in Paul Wilpert's German translation *Vom Nichtanderen* [*Schriften* 12].) The etymology apparently stems from Plato's *Cratylus* 397, but here Cusa may be drawing from John Scotus Eriugena, *Periphyseon* (*De divisione naturae*). See I.12 in the edition by I. P. Sheldon-Williams, *Scriptores Latini Hiberniae* VII.60, 16–25 (Dublin, 1968). On Cusa's marginal notes in this regard, see the descriptions of Cod. Addit. 11035 in "Kritisches Verzeichnis der Londoner Handscriften aus dem Besitz des Nikolaus von Kues," in MFCG 3 (1963), p. 88.

[12] Cf. Witelo *Perspectiva* III.4 BGPThM III.2.135, 17.

[13] *De Deo abscondito* ¶14 (h IV/1.9, 2–10).

[14] Cf. *De Deo abscondito* ¶11 (h IV/1.8, 13–16).

[15] Dt 1:17; Ps 135 (136):2–3.

[16] 1 Tm 6:15; Rv 17:14 and 19:16.

[17] Cf. Sg 1:13.

[18] Cf. Ps 4:8 (7).

[19] Cf. Sg 1:3.

[20] Cf. Mt 2:11.

[21] Cf. Ex 12:44.

[22] Cf. Lk 2:13.

[23] That is, at a distance not comparable or proportional to *Theos*.

[24] *Stirpes vegetationis*, literally, a plant stirps or stem. Cf. DDI II.8.133 (h I.86, 12).

[25] Cf. *De beryllo* ¶16 (h XI².19) and the source Cusa cites there: Plato Ep. II 312ᶜ1–3.

[26] Cf. 1 Tm 6:16.

[27] Cf. DDI I.22.69; II.3.11; 5.120; 8.135; 13.180 (h I.45, 16; 72,14–15; 77, 25; 87, 17–18; 114, 2). See also Eckhart, *Sermo* VI.4.75 (LW IV.72, 3).

[28] Cf. John Scotus Eriugena, *Periphyseon* (*De divisione naturae*) I.12, ed. I. P. Sheldon-Williams, *Scriptores Latini Hiberniae* VII.60, 30–31 (Dublin, 1968).

[29] Ibid. VII.62, 15–16.

[30] On the beginning-middle-end motif, cf. DDI I.21.64; II.13.179; III.1.185 (h I.43; 113; 120). Cf. Proclus, *In Platonis Theologiam* VI.5, and Pseudo-Dionysius, *De divinis nominibus* 5.8 (*Dionysiaca* I.354).

[31] Cf. Ps 47:11 (48:10).

[32] See ¶19 above.

[33] Cf. Mt 10:20.

[34] *Virtus animalis*, which could also be translated "the animate [animal] power" or "the power of the sensitive [animate or animal] nature."

[35] Cf. *De visione Dei* 22.98 and Augustine, *De trinitate* XI.8.15.

[36] *Spiritus animalis,* which could also be translated "the animate [animal] spirit" or "the spirit of the sensitive [animate or animal] nature." Cf. n. 34 above.

[37] Cf. *De coniecturis* II.16.161 (h III.162–163) and Aristotle, *De anima* II.7.418ᵃ,29ᵇ–30.

[38] That is, a light from the outside joins the spirit of sight and together they generate clarity.

[39] See n. 37 above.

[40] Rom 1:25 and 9:5; 2 Cor 11:31.

[41] Cf. DDI II.3.111 and 13.180 (h I.72, 15; 113, 28–29).

[42] Cf. Mt 10:20. See also DDI II.13.180 (h I.113, 22–25) and Augustine, *Confessiones* XIII.31.46.

[43] Cf. *Directio speculantis seu de Non Aliud* 3 (h XIII.7, 8–14).

[44] Cf. Gn 1:3.

[45] For Cusa's discussion of the properties of light and especially the mediation of light, cf. Robert Grosseteste, *De luce seu de inchoatione formarum* BGPThM IX.52 and Witelo, *Liber de intelligentiis* BGPThM III.7–8.

[46] Rom 8:2.

[47] Jn 8:12.

[48] On the hierarchical communication of light, cf. *De coniecturis* I.13.67 (h III.65f.).

[49] Cf. Gal 2:20.

[50] Cf. *De visione Dei* Prol.¶1.

[51] Cf. DDI II.13.180 (h I.113, 12–15).

[52] *Theorice.*

[53] Cf. Acts 4:12.

[54] Cf. Gn 2:9; Rom 1:20–22.

[55] Ps 21:6 (22:5); cf. also Jl 2:32; Acts 2:21; and Rom 10:13.

[56] Heb 11:6.

[57] Jas 1:17.

[58] Ps 41:2 (42:1).

[59] Cf. Rom 9:23; Eph 3:16.

[60] Cf. Tit 3:5.

[61] Cf. Prv 8:17.

[62] *Caritas et amor.* Cf. 1 Jn 4:8 DDI III.12.255 (h I.158). On the attribution of both *eros* and *agape* to God, see Pseudo-Dionysius, *De divinis nominibus* 4.12 (*Dionysiaca* I.208) and Thomas Aquinas, *STh* I–II, 26, 3. For the distinction Cusa himself makes in his sermons, consult E. Bohnenstaedt's discussion in *Nikolaus von Kues. Drei Schriften vom verborgenen Gott* (*Schriften* 3.87, n. 50).

[63] Cf. Jn 10:9.

[64] Cf. *De coniecturis* II.16.160–161 (h III.160ff.).

[65] Cf. Mt 13:31–32; Mk 4:30–32; Lk 13:18–19. See also Cusa's use of the seed-tree analogy in *De visione Dei* 7.22–24.

[66] Cf. Ps 47:2 (48:1); 95 (96):4; 144 (145):3.

[67] Rom 1:25 and 9:5; 2 Cor 11:31.

[68] That is, from observing and then contemplating the power of the millet seed and also that of all the seeds of vegetables and animals. See the reference to the mustard seed in ¶44 above.

[69] Cf. DDI I.23.73 (h I.47, 20–21).

[70] Cf. DDI II.5.118 (h I.76–77).

[71] Cf. DDI I.16.42; 23.71, 73; II.1.97; 8.136 (h I. 30, 15–17; 47, 4–5; 64 14ff.; 88, 2); *De visione Dei* 15.61–62.

[72] Cf. Dt 4:24; 9:3; Heb 12:29.

[73] Pseudo-Dionysius, *De caelestis hierarchia* 15.2 (*Dionysiaca* II.995–999). Cf. DDI II.13.177 (h I.112).

[74] Cf. DDI II.8.135 (h I.87, 1–12).

[75] Cf. Lk 3:8.

[76] Cf. Rom 4:17.

[77] *Ablationis terminatorum*, i.e., the taking away of things that receive bounds or limits or of things that are terminated in something. Cf. *De filiatione Dei* III.70 (h IV/1.51, 1). See also the notion of negation and ablation in Pseudo-Dionysius, *De divinis nominibus* 1.5 (*Dionysiaca* I.34–39) and DDI I.26.87 (h I.54).

[78] Cf. DDI I.3.10; *De Deo abscondito* ¶4 (h I.9, 24–26; IV/1.4, 1–9).

[79] Cf. Meister Eckhart, *Sermo* XI.2.119 (LW IV.113.5).

[80] Cf. Augustine, *Confessiones* III.6.11 and *De vera religione* 39.72.

[81] Rom 1:25; 9:5; 2 Cor 11:31.

## *On the Vision of God*

[1] The version of the text in p I fo. 99ʳ–114ʳ is very problematic. This translation is largely from Cus. Cod. 219, fo. 1ʳ–24ʳ of c. 1460. The particular edition in Cod. 219 of Cusa's *opera*, which he commissioned and corrected in his own hand, is the nearest we have to an official and final version of most of Cusa's philosophical and theological writings. It perhaps represents the version that he would have preferred later scholars to have consulted. But, for variations, see Rudolf Haubst's "Zur Filiation der Handschriften von 'De visione Dei,' " in MFCG 19 (1991): 143–153, and Jasper Hopkins's descriptive list of manuscripts in *Nicholas of Cusa's Dialectical Mysticism* (Minneapolis, 1985), pp. 101–105 and 359–368. I considered it useful to number sections of the text according to the planned critical edition of the Latin text to have been prepared by the late Martin Bodewig for vol. VI of the Heidelberg Academy's *Nicolai de Cusa Opera Omnia*. See Rudolf Haubst's foreword to Helmut Pfeiffer's translation, Nikolaus von Kues, *De visione Dei. Das Sehen Gottes* (Trier, 1985), p. 4. Until this volume is published, readers are urged to refer to the reprint, ed. Paul Wilpert, of the Strasbourg edition of 1488, vol. I (Berlin, 1967), pp. 292–338, to Jasper Hopkins's edition above, to the edition of Giovanni Santinello in [Nicolaus Cusanus]

# NOTES TO TEXTS

*Scritti Filosofici* II (Bologna, 1980), and to that of Leo Gabriel [Nikolaus von Kues] *Philosophisch-Theologische Schriften* III (Vienna, 1967). The reader is especially referred to the citation of manuscripts in the Hopkins edition, which this translator carefully and gratefully consulted.

2 Cod. Cus. 219, fo. 1ʳ reads: "De visione dei. Tractatus reverendissimi in Christo patris et domini domini Nicolai tituli sancti Petri ad vincula presbyteri cardinalis episcopi Brixinensis ad abbatem et fratres in Tegernsee de visione dei."

3 For Cusa's correspondence with the Benedictine monastery at Tegernsee, see especially his Letter 4 of September 22, 1452, and Letter 5 of September 14, 1453, in the appendix to E. Vansteenberghe, *Autour de la Docte Ignorance. Une controverse sur la Théologie mystique au XVe siécle* BGPThM 14 (Münster, 1915): 111ff. In addition to Vansteenberghe's summary and characterization of the letters in Chapters I–III, consult also the recent reexamination by Margot Schmidt, "Nikolaus von Kues im Gespräch mit den Tegernseer Mönchen über Wesen und Sinn der Mystik," MFCG 18 (1989): 25–49.

4 See Letter 5, E. Vansteenberghe, *Autour*, pp. 115–116. Cusa indicates that he had already begun his treatise on mystical theology by extending one segment of *De theologicis complimentis* [*Complementum theologicum* (p II fo. 100ʳ⁻ᵛ)]. Note also Cusa's preceding statement in the letter: "Verum quomodo possimus ad misticam theologiam nos ipsos transferre, ut degustemus in impossibilitate necessitatem et in negacione affirmacionem, difficiliter tradi potest, nam degustacio illa, que sine summa dulcedine et caritate non potest esse, in hoc mundo perfecte non potest haberi. Et michi visum fuit quod tota ista mistica theologia sit intrare ipsam infinitatem absolutam, dicit enim infinitas contradictoriorum coincidenciam, scilicet finem sine fine; et nemo potest Deum mistice videre nisi in caligine coincidencie, que est infinitas. Sed de hoc lacius videbitis, Deo duce, que ipse dederit."

5 On the humility and caution required by mystical theology, see Pseudo-Dionysius, *De mystica theologia* 1.2 (*Dionysiaca* I.569–572) and Cusa's *Idiota de sapientia* I. 8–16 (h V².13–16).

6 *Experimentaliter*. Letter 3, composed before September 22, 1452, from Caspar Aindorffer, abbot of the Benedictine monastery in Tegernsee, questioned Cusa about issues of mystical theology, especially the views of Jean Gerson, Hugh of Balma, and others regarding the roles of *affectus* and *synderesis* in the experience of God—Vansteenberghe, *Autour*, p. 110: "Est autem hec quaestio utrum anima devota sine intellectus cognicione, vel etiam sine cogitacione previa vel concomitante, solo affectu seu per mentis apicem quam vocant synderesim Deum attingere possit, et in ipsum immediate moveri aut ferri." Regarding Gerson and the appeal to experience, see Vansteenberghe, *Autour*, pp. 110 and 193.

7 1 Jn 1:1.

8 In *Trialogus de possest* ¶58 (h XI/2.69, 12), Cusa speaks of a "conveniens aenigma," proposed in what he calls his "libello *Iconae*." See also his reference to the work in his *De apice theoriae* ¶16, where he titles it "De icona sive visu Dei" (h XII.130, 6).

# NOTES TO TEXTS

[9] Letter 5, p. 116, speaks of a reference to such an image in his *Complementum theologicum:* ". . . et inserui capitulum quomodo ex imagine simul omnia et singula videntis, quam depictam habeo, quodam sensibili experimento ducamur ad misticam theologiam." See *Complementum theologicum* XIV (p II fo. 100ʳ⁻ᵛ).

[10] The painting of Roger van der Weyden (1400–1464), now lost, may have been a self-portrait, which is apparently now preserved in a Flemish tapestry. See G. Heinz-Mohr and W. Eckert, *Das Werk des Nicolaus Cusanus* (Köln, 1963), pp. 30 and 72, and E. Panofsky, "*Facies illa Rogeri maximi pictoris,*" in *Late Classical and Mediaeval Studies in Honor of A. M. Friend, Jr.* (Princeton, 1955), pp. 392–400. E. Vansteenberghe, tr., *La vision de Dieu par le cardinal Nicolas de Cuse (1401–1464)* (Paris, 1925), also notes that Cusa had been well received in Brussels by Philip the Good at the end of 1452 and asks if perhaps it was then that Cusa had seen this remarkable painting (p. 3, n. 1).

[11] See Rudolf Haubst's comment to E. Meuthen, "Die Pfründen des Cusanus," in MFCG 2 (1962): 25, n. 56a. Also see E. Panofsky's explanation of the "veronica" reference as *vera icona*, a portrait of Christ in Cusa's chapel, *Facies*, p. 395. But see Haubst's note in MFCG 18 (1989): 68 and the accompanying reproduction of the Christ image in the "cloth of Veronica" in the cloister of St. Nicholas's Hospital at Kues.

[12] According to E. Bohnenstaedt, tr., *Von Gottes Sehen. De visione Dei*. 2nd ed. (*Schriften* 4.163.n.4), Cusa was dean at the St. Florin church in Koblenz from 1431 to 1439, and the chapel with the "veronica" was in Cusa's residence there.

[13] The icon that Cusa sent is no longer extant. Bohnenstaedt, *De visione Dei* (*Schriften* 4.163–164.n.4), reports that in the Eisleben ms. 960 I (D19) an icon was attached to fo. 10ᵛ, but now only the caption can be seen. Also the Münich ms. Clm 18711 (Tegernsee 711), which includes letters to the abbot and brothers of Tegernsee, contains an image of the so-called towel of Veronica on the foreleaf.

[14] Cf. *Idiota de mente* 13,146ff. (h V².198ff.) on the art of portraiture and the image of God.

[15] These are treated successively in each of the three chapters that follow.

[16] Cusa assumes the Greek word for God, *theos*, to be derived from *theorein*, to look at or behold. See his description above in *De Deo abscondito* ¶14 (h IV/ 1.9, 1): "Deus dicitur a theoro, id est video." See also his discussions in *De quaerendo Deum* I.19 (h IV/1.14); *Complementum theologicum* 14 (p II fo. 100ʳ); and *Directio speculantis seu de Non Aliud* 23 (h XIII.104, 12–14).

[17] *Dicuntur*, "are said," is scratched through in the manuscript.

[18] In DDI I.23.70 (h I.46) Cusanus speaks of God as the form of forms and of being. See also his *Apologia doctae ignorantiae* (h II.8 and 26).

[19] See DDI I.21.66 (h I.44).

[20] The rest of the treatise is a prayer that the all-seeing image is to arouse in the contemplative.

[21] DDI II.2.98 (h I.65) and *Apologia doctae ignorantiae* (h II.17 and 33).

[22] Cf. Letter 5, p. 116.

[23] DDI II.2.104 and 5.120–21 (h I.68; 77–78) and *De dato patris luminum* I.93 (h IV/1.68–69).

[24] Jb 31:7; Lk 12:34.

[25] See *Idiota de mente* 13.149 (h V².204–205, 12–22).

[26] 1 Cor 13:12.

[27] *Absoluta maximitas.*

[28] Ps 30:20 (Ps 31:19).

[29] *Contractu* in the text is in error and should read *contactu*, "touch."

[30] See *Idiota de sapientia* I.10 (h V².17–19).

[31] Is. 45:15. See also *De abscondito Deo* above.

[32] Cf. Hagar's declaration in Gn 16:13–14.

[33] Dt 4:29 and Jer 29:13.

[34] Lk 15:20.

[35] Ps 138 (139):7ff.

[36] Ps 9:10–11.

[37] Ps 144 (145):18.

[38] Ps 113:B1 (Ps. 115:1).

[39] Cf. Rom 1:25 and 9:5; 2 Cor 11:31.

[40] *Idiota de mente* 9.124 (h V².177).

[41] From *passione* [*passio*], which suggests a state or condition of being acted upon and which can also mean susceptibility, receptivity, affection, emotion from the sensate appetites, and weakness.

[42] See Cusa's sermon "Tota pulchra es . . . ," in *Excitationum* VIII (p II fo. 139ᵛ–141ʳ), Sermon CCXL, on the nativity of Mary, 1456, as numbered and dated by Josef Koch, *Cusanus-Texte I. Predigten. 7. Untersuchung über Datierung, Form, Sprache und Quellen. Kritisches Verzeichnis sämtlicher Predigten.* (HSB, Phil.-his. Kl., Jahrg. 1941–1942, 1. Abh.), p. 169.

[43] 1 Cor 13:12.

[44] 1 Tm 6:16.

[45] On the cloud and sun imagery see DDI I.1.4 and III.11.246 (h I.6; 153); *Apologia doctae ignorantiae* (h II.2, 12, and 20); and Letter 5, p. 114. Cf. also Pseudo-Dionysius, *De mystica theologia* 1.1f. (*Dionysiaca* I.565–569).

[46] On the analogy of the tree and seed, see Augustine, *De genesi ad litteram* V.23. See also *De quaerendo Deum* III.44–45 (h IV/1.30–31).

[47] 1 Tm 6:16.

[48] 1 Cor 15:28.

[49] Rv 14:15.

[50] On the interior search for God see Cusa's *De quaerendo Deum* IV.50 (h IV/1.35) and *De venatione sapientiae* 17.49–50 (h XII.46–48).

[51] Ps 79:20 (80:19).

[52] Augustine, *Confessiones* I.1.

[53] Lk 15:13.

[54] Rom 8:21.

[55] Lk 15:14–16.

[56] See Cusa's *Trialogue de possest* ¶18–19 (h XI/2.23–25).

[57] DDI I.15.40 and II.11.157 (h I.29; 100–101).

[58] See ch. I.5 above.

[59] On God as absolute form see *Apologia doctae ignorantiae* (h 26) and *De dato patris luminimum* II.98 (h IV/1.72–73).

[60] On God as the essence of essences see DDI I.16.45 (h I.32).

[61] *Contractum* in the text should read *contracte.*

[62] Letter 5, pp. 114–115.

[63] Heb 5:14.

[64] Notice the powerful idiom *ut vim mihi ipsi faciam,* i.e., to do violence to the rational nature by entering the cloud of impossibility beyond reason and above the highest intellectual ascent.

[65] On the analogy of the preacher, see Augustine, *Epistolae* CXXXVII.II.7.

[66] Cf. Gn 3:24.

[67] On the soul's relationship to God's seeing and being seen, cf. Meister Eckhart, *Predigten* 10 (DW), p. 173, and *Predigten* 12 (DW), p. 201.

[68] Rom 4:17.

[69] Gn 1:3ff.; Ps 49 (50):1; Jn 1:1–3.

[70] Rv 1:8; 2:8; 21:16; and 22:13. See also Is 41:4; 44:6; and 48:12.

[71] Heb 5:12 and 14.

[72] For "futile vessel" Cod. Cus. 219 has *futili vasi* along with a correction to *futilis.* Other manuscripts read *fictili* or *fictilis,* "earthen," which corresponds with 2 Cor 4:7: "Habemus autem thesaurum istum in vasis fictilibus." See Hopkins, *Nicholas of Cusa's Dialectical Mysticism* (Minneapolis, 1985), pp. 170 and 364.

[73] On the "wall" metaphor, see Rudolf Haubst, "Die erkenntnistheoretische und mystische Bedeutung der 'Mauer der Koinzidenz,'" MFCG 18 (1989): 167–191.

[74] Jn 10:9.

[75] Cf. Cusa's notion of *progressio* and *regressio* in *De coniecturis* I.10.53 (h III.54).

[76] Is 45:15.

[77] 1 Cor 15:8.

[78] Rom 4:17.

[79] On how God may be said to create and to be created, cf. John Scotus Eriugena, *Periphyseon (De divisione naturae)* I.12, ed. I. P. Sheldon-Williams, *Scriptores Latini Hiberniae* VII.62–64 (Dublin, 1968).

[80] Rom 11:33.

[81] Ps 110 (111):10 and 144 (145):21.

[82] Cf. Pseudo-Dionysius, *Epistolae* I (*Dionysiaca* I.605–607).

[83] Letter 4, p. 112.

[84] *Finis* translated here as "end" means "goal" and the opposite of a beginning and not just "limit."

[85] On Cusa's and Eriugena's notion of *oppositio oppositorum sine oppositione*, see Walter Beierwaltes, "*Deus opposito oppositorum*," *Salzburger Jahrbuch für Philosophie* 8 (1964): 175–185, and Dermot Moran, "Pantheism from John Scottus Eriugena to Nicholas of Cusa," *American Catholic Philosophical Quarterly* 64 (1990): 143, n. 25.

[86] Is 25:4.

[87] DDI I.16.43 and *Apologia doctae ignorantiae* (h I.30–31; II.31.) See also Pseudo-Dionysius, *De divinis nominibus* 5.8 (*Dionysiaca* I.356).

[88] DDI I.8.22 (h I.17).

[89] Is 33:5 and 57:15.

[90] Mt 11:29.

[91] 1 Cor 15:28.

[92] Leo Gabriel's edition [Nikolaus von Kues], *Philosophisch-Theologische Schriften* III (Vienna, 1967), p. 152, sensibly adds *contradictionem* to the clause *ita implicat infinitum esse contrahile.*

[93] Ps 144 (145):3.

[94] *Positivum principium.* Otherness or alterity (*alteritas*) has a negative principle or beginning, which is not-being (*non esse*). Cf. Thomas Aquinas on God as "the active principle," *STh* I q. 25 a. 1.

[95] Finite things, not being infinite or absolute, suffer otherness. Only the infinite enjoys absolute equality. See Cusa's discussion on unity and otherness in *De coniecturis* I.9.37ff. (h III.42ff).

[96] The name "Socrates" in medieval philosophy often stands for any given human being.

[97] On the analogy of Socratic being, see also *De dato patris luminum* II.100 (h IV/1.74–75).

[98] That is, the icon of an omnivoyant image, accompanying the treatise, that Cusa had sent to the Benedictine brothers at Tegernsee. See above, preface ¶2.

[99] *Posse esse.*

[100] See Cusa's *Idiota de mente* 11.130–131 (h V².184–185) and *Trialogus de possest* ¶6 (h XI/2.6–8).

[101] Cf. Thomas Aquinas, *STh* I q. 44 a. 2, where Thomas asserts primary matter as created but not without form; rather, it is "contracted" by form to a determinate species.

[102] On matter as *posse fieri*, see DDI I.8.22–23 (h I.17).

[103] See also DDI I.5.14 and *Trialogus de possest* ¶14 (h I.12–13; XI/2.17–18).

[104] See *Trialogus de possest* ¶29 (h XI/2.34–35, 1–10).

[105] Cf. Rom 1:25 and 9:5; 2 Cor 31.

[106] Cf. Is 45:15 and Acts 17:23.

[107] On the image of a numberless treasure see *Idiota de sapientia* I.11 (h V².21–22, 11f.).

[108] Cf. the treasure hidden in a field in Mt 13:44.

[109] See the similar and more extended analogy in DDI III.12.259 (h I.160–161). Compare also Eckhart, *Sermones et lectiones super Ecclesiastici* 42–43 (LW II 271–272).

[110] See Augustine, *De trinitate* VIII.14 and IX.2.

[111] In DDI I.5.14 (h I.12–13) Cusa examines unity as the principle, the maximum, and the minimum of all number and absolute unity, which is neither plural nor any number, as an appropriate description for the unknowable God.

[112] DDI I.8.23 and 19.55 (h I.17; 37).

[113] DDI I.19.57 (h I.38–39).

[114] DDI I.8.23 (h I.17).

[115] *Intra murum*, "inside the wall," here means within and not outside the wall surrounding paradise, where the infinite God is to be found.

[116] Cf. *Idiota de sapientia* I.19 (h V².41–42) where Cusa stresses tasting wisdom experientially in oneself by an interior tasting.

[117] 1 Cor 2:9.

[118] Is 64:4 and 2 Cor 12:4.

[119] 2 Cor 12:9.

[120] Ex 34:14.

[121] *Sit*, "it is," in the text may have been confused with *sis*, "you are."

[122] Cf. Cusa's treatment of filiation as *theosis* or *deificatio* in *De filiatione Dei*, especially I.52 (h IV/1.40–41).

[123] Is 42:1; Mt 3:17 and 12:18; Mk 1:11; Lk 3:22; and 2 Pt 1:17.

[124] Rv 4:11.

[125] See Cusa's description of the Word of God as "concept" in ¶41 above and *Trialogus de possest* ¶38 (h XI/2.46, 10–13).

[126] Cf. Cusa's description of nature as spirit or motion descended from the divine Spirit and as the motion of the loving bond of all things in DDI II.10.153–154 (h I.97–98).

[127] Jn 14:5–6.

[128] DDI III.2.194 (h I.125).

[129] Note Cusa's basic Christological statements in DDI III.2–4.190–207 (h I.123–132).

[130] On the enduring hypostatic union of the two natures in Christ, see DDI III.3.202 and 7.224 (h I.128–129; 140–141).

[131] DDI III.2.194 (h I.125).

[132] The *unio divina* is that of the Trinity, which Cusa describes as an absolutely and infinitely essential union of persons, unlike the hypostatic union of the human and divine natures in Christ, which is a maximal but not an infinite union, for the hypostatic union is a union of the finite and the infinite. See Cusa's distinction of three unions in DDI III.12.261–262 (h I.161–162): (1) the divine

union of the Trinity; (2) the union of Christ's natures; and (3) the union of the church.

[133] This is a correction of the punctuation in the text, which seems misplaced. If, as it stands, in "natura humana seu rationali" does not begin a new sentence, then the ending of the prior sentence would read: "No greater likeness can exist or can be thought in the human or rational nature."

[134] On the distinction between the human mind as assimilative and the divine as creative, see *Idiota de mente* 3.72(h V².109–110) and *De ludo globi* II (p I fo. 164ᵛ).

[135] DDI III.2.192 (h I.124).

[136] Because of the union of Christ's natures, Cusa as the contemplative is beholding Jesus not *citra* but *intra*, not outside but only on the inner side of "the wall of paradise."

[137] Jn 14:6.

[138] On the incomprehensible nature of the hypostatic union, see DDI III.2.194 (h I.125).

[139] Rom 1:21–22; 1 Cor 1:18–21 and 3:18–19.

[140] Mt 11:25.

[141] Jn 6:59.

[142] Gn 2:8ff.

[143] Gn 3:17ff.

[144] Rom 6:4–6; Eph 4:22–24; and Col 3:8–10.

[145] 1 Cor 15:45.

[146] Jn 4:24.

[147] Jn 6:44.

[148] Mt 11:27 and Jn 1:18.

[149] *Unificatus in unificante* in the text should be corrected to *vivificatus in vivificante*. See Leo Gabriel's edition in *Philosophisch-Theologische Schriften* III (Vienna, 1967), p. 192, and Jasper Hopkins, *Nicholas of Cusa's Dialectical Mysticism* (Minneapolis, 1985), p. 236.

[150] 1 Tm 6:16.

[151] On the "spirit" in the operation of human sight, see *De quaerendo Deum* II.33 (h IV/1.23–24).

[152] *Idiota de staticis experimentis* ¶191 (h V².238–239).

[153] *Accidentia* here are the accessory and unessential qualities of things not belonging to their substance or essence.

[154] Jn 2:25.

[155] *De quaerendo Deum* II.33 (h IV/1.35).

[156] *Discurrit.* Notice the play on the word *discursus* as both the activity of running from one place to another such as a dog's hunt for its master and also the activity of reasoning as, for example, when proceeding from a premise to a conclusion.

[157] On discursive reasoning and the hunting dog analogy, see Cusa's letter

to Abbot Caspar Aindorffer (Feb. 12, 1454), Letter 9, p. 122, and *Apologia doctae ignorantiae* (h II.14–15). On the rationally discriminative capacity in animals, see *Idiota de mente* 5.84 (h V².126–127).

[158] From other ms. sources, Jasper Hopkins, *Nicholas of Cusa's Dialectical Mysticism* (Minneapolis, 1985), pp. 243–244, adds here "virtutis et infirmum intellectualis. Habet igitur vis animalis sensibilis."

[159] Jn 1:9.

[160] DDI III.2.194 (h I.125).

[161] This is a favorite theme in *De docta ignorantia*; see DDI I.1.3; I.3.9; and II.2.102 (h I.5–6; 8–9; 67).

[162] DDI III.3.198 (h I.126–127).

[163] *Suppositum* here is perhaps the Latin translation of the Greek *hypostasis*. It means subject or substance, but when it refers to an individual of a rational nature its synonym would be *persona*. See also DDI III.8.228 (h I.143).

[164] DDI III.7.224 (h I.140–141) and *Idiota de mente* 5.80 (h V².121–122, 8–15).

[165] Augustine, *De civitate Dei* XIV.24.2. Augustine cites a specific priest named Restitutus, reported to have had such powers. Cusa makes this same reference in *De ludo globi* II (p I fo. 165ʳ).

[166] See ¶103 above.

[167] See above: *De visione Dei* 22.100.

[168] Cf. Is 53:7 and Jn 10:17–18.

[169] 1 Cor 15:53–54 and 2 Cor 5:2–4.

[170] Jas 1:5.

[171] Jn 6:64 in the Vulgate, 6:63 in modern editions.

[172] Mt 13:18–23; Mk 4:13–20; and Lk 8:11–15.

[173] Jn 6:67–69.

[174] Acts 9:3ff. and 2 Cor 12:2–10.

[175] Rom 8:38ff.

[176] Mt 13:8 and Lk 8:8.

[177] Gn 2:7.

[178] Mt 21:22; Mk 11:24; and 1 Jn 3:22.

[179] 1 Cor 45:44–49.

[180] *Idiota de mente* 2.65 (h V².100, 4–7). See also in c. 4.74ff. (h V².112ff.), where Cusa argues that there are no "concreate" ideas in the soul that have become lost in the body but instead the soul possesses a "concreate" power that requires a body to proceed to act.

[181] *Per accidens*, i.e., incidentally and not through a circumstance or attribute essential to the intellect's nature.

[182] Mt 23:10.

[183] DDI III.11.244–253 (h I.151–157).

[184] Mt 11:29–30.

[185] Mt 23:8, 11.

[186] 1 Cor 12:4–10.

[187] Wis 1:7.

[188] Prv 16:4.

[189] Ps 44 (45):8 and Heb 1:9.

[190] Heb 1:14.

[191] Jn 14:6.

[192] Sg 1:3–4.

[193] Mt 25:21.

[194] 1 Cor 9:24–25 and 2 Tm 2:5; 4:7–8.

[195] Jn 6:44.

[196] The explicit reads: "Reverendissimi domini Nicolai cardinalis sancti Petri ad vincula Brixinensis episcopi liber de visione dei."


## On the Summit of Contemplation

[1] The following translation and enumeration of paragraphs is from the text edited by Raymond Klibansky and Hans Gerhard Senger in volume XII of the Heidelberg Academy edition of Cusa's *opera*. On the title and the concept of *apex*, see the introduction and *adnotationes* to *De apice theoriae* (h XII.xviff.; 161–163) and the appendix "Materialsammlung zur Verwendung des Begriffs *apex* in der theologia mystica" in Senger's annotated Latin-German edition (*Schriften* 19.157–164).

[2] *Theoria*, translated here as "contemplation," can also simply mean sight or observation.

[3] Peter Wymar of Erkelenz of the diocese of Liege and canon at Aachen. He may have become Cusa's secretary as early as 1451 during Cusa's apostolic legation journey in Germany. Peter copied and edited several of Cusa's writings and was present with Cusa when he died at Todi on August 11, 1464. Peter was made rector of the charitable institution and library that Cusa bequeathed at Kues. On Peter's life and his relationship with Cusa, see E. Meuthen, "Peter von Erkelenz (ca. 1430)–1494," in *Zeitschrift des Aachener Geschichtsvereins* (1977/78): 701–744.

[4] Cf. his *Apologia doctae ignorantiae* (h II.12) in which Cusa describes how one is to approach absolute Truth: "through a certain incomprehensible intuition as if by means of a momentary rapture."

[5] Literally, "of my studious discoveries," *de studiosis inventionibus*. Notice below the continuing play on the word *studiosus*, which can sometimes mean eager or scholarly or even philosophical.

[6] Senger believes Peter's ordination to have occurred on Friday of Easter week, March 31, 1464, just prior to the "dialogue" of the treatise. See Senger, *De apice theoriae* (*Schriften* 19.61.n.2,3f.), and E. Meuthen, "Peter von Erkelenz," p. 719.

[7] According to Cusa's reckoning of the fourteen-year duration of their re-

lationship and Peter's reference to Easter, the work must have been composed after Easter in the late spring or early summer before Cusa's death in August 1464.

[8] 2 Cor 12:2.

[9] Rom 11:33 and Phil 3:12–13.

[10] See DDI I.3.10 (h I.9).

[11] "Quid quaeris?" Notice below Cusa's play with *quaerere*, which means both "to ask" and "to seek," and also with *quid*, i.e. *what* a thing is, its essence.

[12] By *studiosi* Cusa means those eagerly seeking or inquiring.

[13] *Quidditas*, "whatness," designates a thing's essence, because the definition of a thing, in answer to the question what (*quid*) a thing is, requires a statement of the essence of the thing. See Thomas Aquinas, *De ente et essentia* c.1.

[14] Cf. DDI I.1.4 (h I.6, 17f.).

[15] In DDI I.3.10 (h I.9) Cusa speaks of the quiddity of things as "the truth of beings," which all philosophers have investigated but none have found as it is. See also *Apologia doctae ignorantiae* (h II.33), which describes God as "absolute quiddity" and as "quiddity of quiddities," and *Directio speculantis seu de Non Aliud* 18.83 (h XIII.44, 9–18). In the *De apice theoriae* the search is not for the quiddity of this or that thing but for quiddity itself.

[16] Cf. Jb 36:25.

[17] Cf. DDI I.3.10 and 22.69 (h I 9; 45).

[18] Senger traces the development of Cusa's conceptualization of quiddity in his Latin-German edition of *De apice theoriae* (*Schriften* 19.70ff., n.4, 1–14).

[19] In Latin *posse esse*. Notice yet another word play: Cusa comes to see that the absolute, unvarying *substantia-subsistentia-hypostasis* both "can be" (*posse esse*) and also is the one, absolute "Can" (*Posse*) Itself.

[20] *Posse ipsum* is difficult to render smoothly into English. *Posse* is the infinitive for the verb *possum*, which is usually translated as "I can" or "I am able." I have retained the Latin because "Can Itself" or "To Be Able Itself" seems very awkward, although the equivalences in German, *können*, and in French, *pouvoir*, work very well. "Potentiality Itself" or even "Possibility Itself" might seem less clumsy but ruin the more direct and fluid power of the verb.

[21] On God as absolute Whatness cf. DDI II.4.15–16 (h I.74–75).

[22] This is a term that apparently Cusa coined from the two verbs *posse* and *est*, and it is difficult to translate into English. Literally it means the "Can-Is" or the "Can-That-Is." Jasper Hopkins in *A Concise History Introduction to the Philosophy of Nicholas of Cusa*, 3rd ed. (Minneapolis, 1986), translates it as "Actualized Possibility." But see Peter J. Casarella's discussion of the term in "Nicholas of Cusa and the Power of the Possible," *American Catholic Philosophical Quarterly* 64, no. 1 (Winter 1990): 7–26.

[23] Cusa wrote the treatise *Trialogus de possest* (h XI/2) in 1460. See also *De venatione sapientiae* 13: "De secundo campo, possest" (h XII.34–38).

[24] *Infra.* See ¶14 below.

[25] Cf. Cusa's earlier descriptions of *possibilitas* and *posse* as anterior to his use of *posse* here: DDI II.7.128 (h I.82,21) and *Compendium* 10.29 and *epilog.* ¶45 and ¶46 (h XI/3.23, 5ff. and 34–35, 10–11).

[26] See especially DDI I.26.89 (h I.56, 13f.) and the preface to *De visione Dei* prol.¶1.

[27] Prv 1:20.

[28] *Idiota de sapientia* I.3 (h V².41–43).

[29] Wis 6:13.

[30] *Omnis potens.* This refers to all who can do or can be anything, i.e., all having *posse* or potency.

[31] *Principiatis.*

[32] Rom 4:17.

[33] Cf. Mi 7:8; Jn 1:4ff.; and Jas 1:17. Cf. Pseudo-Dionysius, *De divinis nominibus* 4.4–6 (*Dionysiaca* I.159–177).

[34] Cf. DDI I.26.86; II.13.177; and III.9.233 (h I.54, 10–12; II.112,9; and III.146, 10ff.).

[35] On the manifestation of the invisible in the visible, cf. *De quaerendo Deum* II.34f. and *De dato patris luminum* IV.108–111 (h IV/1.24f.; 79–82).

[36] Cf. *De quaerendo Deum* I.19 (h IV.15).

[37] That is, from a comprehensive power of sight.

[38] Cf. Cusa's discussion of the mind's sight in relation to *posse* in the epilogue to his *Compendium* ¶45–47 (h XI/3.33–36).

[39] 1 Cor 9:24. Cf. *De quaerendo Deum* I.19 (h IV.15, 10f.). See Cusa's sermon CCLXXXVI: "Sic currite ut comprehendatis" (1459) *Excitationum* X (p II fo. 188ᵛ–189ᵛ) as numbered and dated by Josef Koch, *Cusanus-Texte I. Predigten. 7. Untersuchung über Datierung, Form, Sprache und Quellen. Kritisches Verzeichnis sämtlicher Predigten.* (HSB, Phil.-his. Kl., Jahrg. 1941–1942, 1. Abh.), p. 191.

[40] Cf. *Compendium* 10.29 and *epilog.* ¶46 (h XI/3.23–24,5–11; 35, 12–14).

[41] What follows in the text is a kind of typology of schools of thought that have "seen correctly" by looking either at *Posse* Itself or at its appearances. Cusa provides no list of sources, but the reader is referred to the numerous references proposed in Hans Gerhard Senger's Latin-German edition (*Schriften* 19.106–121) and the *adnotationes* to *De apice theoriae* in the Heidelberg *opera* edition of Raymond Klibansky and H. G. Senger (h XII.166–168).

[42] Cf. the two chapters on unity in *De venatione sapientiae* c. 21–22 (h XII.56–65).

[43] Eccl 1:10.

[44] On Cusa's earlier treatment of Platonic forms and ideas, see DDI II.9 (h I.93–96.)

[45] The text (h XII.130, 4) reads *De dato lumine. De dato patris luminum* [1445/1446] (h IV.65–87).

[46] The text has *De icona sive visu Dei. De visione Dei* [1453] (p I fo. 99^r–114^r ); *De quaerendo Deum* [1445] (h IV.11–35).

[47] By *memoriale* Cusa means an abridgement to aid the memory. A somewhat different version of this addendum exists as a separate work, *Memoriale*, in ms. cod. Magdeburgensis 166, fo. 434^r–v, of the Deutschen Staatsbibliothek Berlin. See the description in Senger's Latin-German edition of *De apice theoriae* (*Schriften* 19.124.n.16,14f.) and in the excerpts cited *passim.* in the "apparatus locorum similium" of the Heidelberg Academy edition of *De apice theoriae* (h XII).

[48] Cf. *De venatione Dei* 39.120 (h XII.110–111, 10–14)

[49] Cf. DDI II.7.128 (h I.82.21–22).

[50] Cf. DDI I.22.68 (h I.44, 22f.).

[51] Cf. DDI II.3.111 (h I.72.16); *Idiota de sapientia* I.25 and *Idiota de mente* 5.85 (h V^2.51; 127–128).

[52] Cf. *Trialogus de possest* ¶29 (h XI/2.35).

[53] Cf. *De beryllo* ¶65–66 (h XI/1^2.76–77.)

[54] On the notion of the liberty of God in willing and creating, cf. *De dato patris luminum* IV.110 (h IV.80–81) and *Idiota de mente* 13.145f. (h V^2.197f.).

[55] On the metaphor of a book and its author for explaining the relationship of the creator to the creation, cf. *Idiota de sapientia* I.4 (h V^2.7,7–11); *Trialogus de possest* ¶29 (h XI/2.36f.); *De filiatione Dei* I.61 (h IV.45–46); and *Compendium* 7.21 (h XI/3.16).

[56] Cf. *De venatione Dei* 19.54 and 20.58 (h XII.51, 18; 55, 1–7).

[57] Ps 118 (119):37.

[58] See Aristotle, *Metaphysica* V.30.1025^a, 14ff. Cf. DDI II.3.110 (h I.71.21).

[59] Cf. *De beryllo* ¶44 (h XI/1^2.50–51).

[60] Cf. *De beryllo* ¶22–23 (h XI/1^2.25–26).

[61] Augustine, *De trinitate* X.11.17ff.; XV.7.12 and 20.39.

[62] Cf. *De venatione sapientiae* 39.115–117 (h XII.107–109).

[63] See above ¶21.

# A BRIEF GLOSSARY
## OF CUSAN TERMS

The following are limited to the texts translated in this volume, include only favorite Cusan terms that have meaning especially shaped to specific theological and philosophical purposes in these texts, and do not include all other possible applications in these or in Cusa's other writings. Set here out of context, they can offer only an interpretative glimpse at a possible range of meaning Cusa seems to attribute to certain crucial terms and metaphors.

(See also Eduard Zellinger, *Cusanus-Konkordanz. Unter Zugrundelegung der philosophischen und der bedeutendsten theologischen Werke* [München, 1960]; and Rudolf Haubst, *Streifzüge in die Cusanische Theologie* [*Buchreihe der Cusanus-Gesellschaft*] [Münster, 1991], especially pp. 65–74, 21–26, 117–163, and 195–215.)

---

**Coincidentia oppositorum (coincidence of opposites)**
 [*coincidere* from *co* (together) + *incidere* (to fall upon or into or to occur), used as a metaphor, perhaps originally from geometry and astronomy, when two geometric figures or astral bodies may be said to fall together or to occur in the same space or time]

**A state or condition in which opposites no longer oppose each other but fall together into a harmony, union, or conjunction.**
 [*oppositus* perfect passive participle from *opponere, ob* (in front of, over against) + *ponere* (to place, set), also used metaphorically, possibly also from geometry and astronomy, to designate things that are

335

placed or are lying over against each other on the contrary side of an intervening line or space]

**Those which stand in a contrary or contradictory relationship to each other in position, nature, character, etc.** Aristotle, *Categoriae* 10.11b.15ff., listed four "senses" in which things are said to oppose each other: (1) as correlatives, e.g. as "double" to "half"; (2) as contraries, e.g. as "bad" to "good"; (3) as privatives, e.g. as "blindness" to "sight"; and (4) as affirmatives to negatives, as "he sits" to "he does not sit."

**The coincidence of opposites is a certain kind of unity perceived as coincidence, a unity of contrarieties overcoming opposition by convergence without destroying or merely blending the constituent elements.** Although in one sense not obliterated, in another the constituent elements shed their multiple, differentiated status. Examples would include the coincidence of rest and motion, past and future, diversity and identity, inequality and equality, and divisibility and simplicity.

God is not the coincidence of opposites, but rather, in some sense, it might be said that opposites coincide in God, but not with God. Moreover, coincidence does not really describe God. Rather it sets forth the way God works, the order of things in relation to God and to each other, and the manner by which humans may approach and abide in God. God is beyond the realm of contradictories. God, the absolute maximum, precedes opposites, is undifferentiated, not other, incomparable, and without opposite, precedes distinctions, opposition, contrariety, and contradiction. In other words, the absolute unites opposites because it is their cause from which they are derived. So in it they coincide antecedent to opposition.

**Complicatio, complicare; explicatio, explicare (enfolding, enfold; unfolding, unfold)**
[*complicare* from *com* + *plicare* (to fold), used metaphorically perhaps from an expression for things enwrapped or folded together, like a large sheet of paper folded into four leaves or vellum enfolded into a manuscript quarto; *explicare* from *ex* (from or out of) + *plicare* meaning to unfold or to unwrap]

**Metaphors describing the manner in which it may be said that a thing (1) exists within its principle [i.e., as enfolded] as that principle, and (2) exists as created and individuated [i.e., as unfolded] from, and outside, its principle and as differentiated from other unfolded things.**

Things *enfolded* exist in something as that thing without differentiation. However, things *unfolded* exist as distinct from their enfolding source and from each other. Things as enfolded in God exist without differentiation and precede plurality or otherness. As enfolded in God, all are God but as unfolded in creation, they are themselves as plural and differentiated. They are unfolded from God but are not God unfolded, whereas enfolded things exist in God as God.

To say that all things are enfolded in God and unfolded from God is to say (1) that all things are present in God as God and not as contracted and finite and that God is present in all things but not as God is in Godself and (2) that God is all things but only as they are enfolded in God, and although God is present in all things, God is not all things as each created thing originated and unfolded from God. To say that things exist enfolded in God is to say that they exist there ontologically before they are created and not as themselves in plurality, etc., but as God. Consequently, every actually existing thing is enfolded in God, but not everything enfolded in God is created or actually exists.

**Contractio, contrahere, contractum (contraction, contract, contracted)**

[*contrahere* from *con* + *trahere* (to draw), used to designate the action of bringing objects together, but also both the action of reducing to smaller compass by narrowing or diminishing in extent and, metaphorically, that of simply bringing about, occasioning or making]

*Constriction (e.g. of a universal or a genus or a species) or reception in a restricted way to or by something so as to be this or that, i.e. delimitation to something so as to be individuated and differentiated, as for example, one may say human nature is contracted to the individual human being* Socrates *or that Socrates contracts the species humanity. So too the universe, itself contracted (Cusa's* maximum contractum*), may be said to be contracted to a determinate genus, and a genus to some determinate species, as well as a species to a determinate individual.*

The universal is contractible to [not *into* or *within*], but is neither this particular thing nor that, but in the one thing it is that and in the other it is the other, e.g., humanity is neither Socrates nor Plato, but in Socrates Socrates and in Plato Plato. That to which the universal is contracted possesses the following characteristics: delimited and derived as opposed to absolute and self-subsistent; individuated and differentiated as opposed to universal and undifferentiated; plural as opposed to one only; finite, perishable, divisible, imperfect, and other as opposed to infinite, eternal, indivisible, perfect, and indistinct; unequal as opposed to equal; and comprehensible as opposed to incomprehensible.

God, however, is uncontracted for God alone is absolute [*absolutus* = utterly free and unrestricted] and therefore uncontracted to one thing or another. God, however, is present in the universe, and through the universe God is present in each part although uncontractedly. The world is the contracted likeness or image or reflection of God. All things may be said to be individualized or contracted within the world's unity, the *universum*, but all ontologically exist antecedently as one in God and proceed by contraction into individual and multiple existence, subject to materiality and otherness. The world, therefore, is a created, finite, and constricted maximum.

**Docta ignorantia (learned ignorance)**
[*docta* (instructed or learn*ed*) and *ignorantia* from *ignorare* (not to know, to be unknowing), used together either to comprise an oxymoron, e.g., "wise fool," or to suggest ignorance become instructed and self-aware]

**In three senses: (1) an instructed ignorance so that one now knows one's ignorance, i.e., the limits of one's knowledge, and is no longer uninstructed or ignorant that one is ignorant (a not knowing one has learned of as opposed to a not knowing that one remains ignorant of); (2) an ignorance that renders one wiser the more one knows or becomes instructed that one is ignorant; and (3) knowledge, given to the ignorant, viz., that God or the Infinite is incomprehensible and cannot be known as God is in Godself. One can conceive only what God is not.**

# A BRIEF GLOSSARY OF CUSAN TERMS

A genuinely learned ignorance recognizes the thoroughgoing transcendence of God-in-God's-self, always infinite, absolute, and hidden to human eyes. It teaches us that what we presume to discover about the divine nature we cannot reconcile rationally. One cannot know God's truth, which is incomprehensible, except by leaping across the image to the incomprehensible truth incomprehensibly. Seeing the truth is seeing beyond or through the image. Learned ignorance, therefore, is the experiential source of theology. Through it one is elevated to the vision of divine things, "lifted up to the simplicity of understanding and to the greater knowing of the unknowable God." Furthermore, learned ignorance entails wonder. "Not a knowledge by which someone believes one knows what is unable to be known, rather [such ignorance] is that in which knowing is knowing that one is not able to know." It furnishes revelatory insight into the reality of things that properly lie beyond human comprehension. Through it we can see truths otherwise inaccessible and solve problems otherwise insoluble. Cusa frequently prompts the reader to see beyond apparent contrariety by reviewing the problem "in the light of learned ignorance."

Learned ignorance operates theologically on at least two levels: (1) as recognition of one's incapacity to know God as God is, which is the subject of the first section of *On Learned Ignorance;* and (2) as the reconciliation of human ignorance through God's self-disclosure in Christ, which is the subject of the third part. But Christ converts oblique knowledge into effective knowledge by disclosing God otherwise hidden. Learned ignorance becomes sacred ignorance when it is ignorance enlightened through Christ. So too learned ignorance, as the knowledge of faith in Christ, is the necessary means by which we come to an appropriate theological method.

**Posse; possest; posse ipsum (can, can-is; can itself)**
    [*posse* (to be able, to have power or efficacy, to avail); *possest* (coined by Nicholas of Cusa, *posse* + *est* = can-is); *posse ipsum* (can itself, having power itself, possibility itself)]

*Possest,* a combining of *posse est,* is a Cusan title for God, significantly used in his trialogue by the same name *De Possest* (1460). It designates God as the "Can-Is" or the "Can-That-Is." Later Cusa's *De apice theoriae* (1464) substitutes as the preferred title:

339

*Posse ipsum,* "Can-Itself," "Can" as substantive rather than modal auxiliary, self-subsistent and prior to anything added, the "Can," beyond, antecedent to, behind, and present in all that "is."

*Possest* signifies the union in God of possibility [as both capacity and potency] and actuality. It names God as the *posse* that is, i.e., actually existing potency, as in *De quaerendo Deum* 3.46, which speaks of God as "the actuality of all potency." *Posse ipsum,* as Cusa's later name for God, designates the one and only Self-Subsistent in all things, the "Essence in itself" present in all. This means that all are nothing else than the differing ways *Posse* Itself appears.

The absolute, one, divine *Posse* is self-evident in every *posse.* Everything that "is" presumes "can"; every "can" be or "can" do requires a simple "can"; and every "can" presupposes, as necessary, a single "Can" with nothing added, a *Posse* behind all *posse,* or *Posse* Itself. Nothing, therefore, "can be" more anything, i.e., more known, easier, more certain, etc., than Can Itself. Christ, moreover, is the most perfect appearance of *Posse* Itself. The triune God appears brightly everywhere, in every mode of being, more powerfully in intelligible being but perfectly only in Christ. But like all *posse* God appears invisibly for God is invisibly seen as the *Posse* Itself of every *posse.* God is not just present in all being, God appears in all, while Christ is the perfect *apparitio* of God

# SELECT BIBLIOGRAPHY

## 1. CUSA'S WRITINGS

### 1.1 Opera

*Opera.* Edited by Faber Stapulensis [Jacques LeFèvre d'Étaples]. Paris, 1514 edition. 3 vols. Reprinted Frankfurt/M.: Minerva, 1962.

*Opera omnia iussu et auctoritate Academiae Litterarum Heidelbergensis.* Leipzig-Hamburg: Meiner, 1932–.

*Opuscula* in Cod. Cus. 218–219 at the library of the Cusanusstift of St. Nikolaus Hospital, Bernkastel-Kues, Germany.

*Philosophisch-Theologische Schriften.* Edited by Leo Gabriel. 3 vols. Vienna: Herder, 1967.

*Schriften des Nikolaus von Kues in deutscher Übersetzung im Auftrag der Heidelberger Akademie der Wissenschaften.* Leipzig-Hamburg: Meiner, 1936–.

*Scritti filosofici.* 2 vols. Edited by Giovanni Santinello. Bologna: Zanichelli, 1965–1980.

*Werke. Neuausgabe des Strassburger Drucks von 1488.* Edited by Paul Wilpert. 2 vols. Berlin: De Gruyter, 1967.

341

# SELECT BIBLIOGRAPHY

## 1.2 Special Editions

*Acta Cusana. Quellen zur Lebensgeschichte des Nikolaus von Kues im Auftrag der Heidelberger Akademie der Wissenschaften.* Edited by Erich Meuthen and Hermann Hallauer. Hamburg: Meiner, 1976–.

"Correspondance de Nicolas de Cuse avec Gaspard Aindorffer et Bernard de Waging." In Edmond Vansteenberghe, *Autour de la docte ignorance. Une controverse sur la théologie mystique au XV<sup>e</sup> siècle.* (BGPThM 14.) Münster: Aschendorff, 1915. Pp. 107–162.

*Cusanus-Texte,* issued in the *Sitzungsberichte der Heidelberger Akademie der Wissenschaften,* Philosophisch-historische Klasse (HSB). Heidelberg: C. Winter, 1928–.

I. *Predigten*

Vol. I. *"Dies Sanctificatus" vom Jahre 1439.* Edited by Ernst Hoffmann and Raymond Klibansky. (HSB Jg. 1928–1929, 3. Abh.).

Vols. IV–V. *Vier Predigten im Geiste Eckharts.* Edited by Josef Koch. (HSB Jg. 1936–1937, 2. Abh.).

Vol. VI. *Die Auslegung des Vaterunsers in vier Predigten.* Edited by Josef Koch and Hans Teske. (HSB Jg. 1938–1939, 4. Abh.).

II. *Traktate*

Vol. I. *De auctoritate presidendi in concilio generali.* Edited by Gerhard Kallen. (HSB Jg. 1935–1936, 3. Abh.).

III. *Marginalien*

Vol. I. *Nicolaus Cusanus und Pseudo-Dionysius im Lichte der Zitate und Randbemerkungen des Cusanus.* Edited by Ludwig Baur. (HSB Jg. 1940–1941, 4. Abh.).

# SELECT BIBLIOGRAPHY

V. *Brixener Dokumente*

Vol. I. *Erste Sammlung. Akten zur Reform des Bistums Brixen.* Edited by Hans Hürten. (HSB Jg. 1960, 2. Abh.).

*De apice theoriae. Die höchste Stufe der Betrachtung.* Edited by Hans Gerhard Senger. Vol. 19 of *Schriften des Nikolaus Cusanus.* Hamburg: Meiner, 1986.

*De docta ignorantia. Die belehrte Unwissenheit. Buch I.* Edited by Paul Wilpert and revised by Hans Gerhard Senger. 2nd rev. ed. Vol. 15a of *Schriften des Nikolaus Cusanus.* Hamburg: Meiner, 1970.

*De docta ignorantia. Die belehrte Unwissenheit. Buch II.* Edited by Paul Wilpert and revised by Hans Gerhard Senger. 2nd rev. ed. Vol. 15b of *Schriften des Nikolaus Cusanus.* Hamburg: Meiner, 1977.

*De docta ignorantia. Die belehrte Unwissenheit. Buch III.* Edited by Hans Gerhard Senger. Vol. 15c of *Schriften des Nikolaus Cusanus.* Hamburg: Meiner, 1977.

*De visione dei.* Edited by Jasper Hopkins, *Nicholas of Cusa's Dialectical Mysticism. Text, Translation and Interpretive Study of "De visione Dei."* Minneapolis: Banning, 1985. Pp. 107–269.

"Der *Dialogus concludens Amedistarum errorem ex gestis et doctrina concilii Basiliensis.*" Edited by Erich Meuthen in MFCG 8 (1970): 11–114.

"*Reformatio generalis.*" In Stephan Ehses, "Der Reformentwurf des Kardinals Nikolaus Cusanus," *Historisches Jahrbuch der Görresgesellschaft* 32 (1911): 281–297.

"Vierzehn christologische Quaestionen (Cod. Cus. 40, 144$^r$–146$^v$)." In Rudolf Haubst, *Die Christologie des Nikolaus von Kues.* Freiburg: Herder, 1956. Pp. 315–319.

# SELECT BIBLIOGRAPHY

*1.3 English Translations of Selected Sources*

*Dialogue about the Hidden God.* Translated by Thomas Merton. New York: Gray Bar Press, 1989. First published in *Lugano Review* 1, no. 5–6 (Summer 1966): 67–70.

*Of Learned Ignorance.* Translated by Germain Heron. New Haven: Yale University, 1954.

"On Learned Ignorance." Translated by Jasper Hopkins, *Nicholas of Cusa On Learned Ignorance: A Translation and an Appraisal of "De docta ignorantia."* 2nd ed. Minneapolis: Banning, 1985. Pp. 45–158.

"On Searching for God." Translated by William F. Wertz, Jr., *Toward a New Council of Florence: "On the Peace of Faith" and Other Works by Nicholas of Cusa.* Washington D.C.: Schiller Institute, 1993. Pp. 155–171.

"On Seeking God." Translated by Jasper Hopkins, *A Miscellany on Nicholas of Cusa.* Minneapolis: Banning, 1994. Pp. 139–158.

"On the Hidden God." Translated by Jasper Hopkins, *A Miscellany on Nicholas of Cusa.* Minneapolis: Banning, 1994. Pp. 131–137.

"On the Hidden God: A Dialogue of Two Men, the One a Gentile, the Other a Christian." Translated by William F. Wertz, Jr., *Toward a New Council of Florence: "On the Peace of Faith" and Other Works by Nicholas of Cusa.* Washington D.C.: Schiller Institute, 1993. Pp. 149–154.

"On the Summit of Vision." Translated by William F. Wertz, Jr., *Toward a New Council of Florence: "On the Peace of Faith" and Other Works by Nicholas of Cusa.* Washington D.C.: Schiller Institute, 1993. Pp. 561–574.

*The Single Eye: Entituled the Vision of God Wherein is Infolded the Mistery of Divine Presence.* Translated by Giles Randall. London: Printed for John Streater, 1646.

*The Vision of God.* Translated by Emma G. Salter. London: Dent, 1928.

*The Vision of God.* Translated by Jasper Hopkins, *Nicholas of Cusa's Dialectical Mysticism. Text, Translation and Interpretive Study of "De visione Dei."* Minneapolis: Banning, 1985. Pp. 107–269.

## 2. SECONDARY LITERATURE

### 2.1 Articles

Beierwaltes, Werner. "Cusanus and Eriugena." *Dionysius* 13 (1989): 115–152.

———. *"Deus oppositio oppositorum."* *Salzburger Jahrbuch für Philosophie* 8 (1964): 175–185.

———. "Visio facialis—Sehen ins Angesicht. Zur Coincidenz des endlichen und unendlichen Blicks bei Cusanus." MFCG 18 (1989): 91–124.

Biechler, James E. "Nicholas of Cusa and the End of the Conciliar Movement: A Humanist Crisis of Identity." *Church History* 44 (1975): 5–21.

Bond, H. Lawrence. "The Journey of the Soul to God in Nicholas of Cusa's *De ludo globi.*" In *Nicholas of Cusa in Search of God and Wisdom,* edited by Gerald Christianson and Thomas M. Izbicki. Leiden: Brill, 1991. Pp. 71–86.

———. "Nicholas of Cusa and the Reconstruction of Theology: The Centrality of Christology in the Coincidence of Opposites." In *Contemporary Reflections on the Medieval Christian Tradition,* edited by George H. Shriver. Durham, N.C.: Duke University, 1974. Pp. 81–94.

———. "Nicolaus Cusanus from Constantinople to 'Learned Ignorance.' The Historical Matrix for the Formation of the *De docta ignorantia.*" In *Nicholas of Cusa on Christ and the Church,* edited by Gerald

Christianson and Thomas M. Izbicki. Leiden: Brill, 1996. Pp. 135–163.

Bond, H. Lawrence, Gerald Christianson, and Thomas Izbicki. "Nicholas of Cusa: On Presidential Authority in a General Council." *Church History* 59 (1990): 19–34.

Boyle, Marjorie O'Rourke. "Cusanus at Sea: The Topicality of Illuminative Discourse." *Journal of Religion* 71 (Nov.–Apr. 1991): 180–201.

Casarella, Peter J. *"His Name Is Jesus:* Negative Theology and Christology in Two Writings of Nicholas of Cusa from 1440." In *Nicholas of Cusa on Christ and the Church,* edited by Gerald Christianson and Thomas M. Izbicki. Leiden: Brill, 1996. Pp. 281–308.

———. "Neues zu den Quellen der Cusanischen Mauer-Symbolik." MFCG 19 (1991): 273–286.

———. "Nicholas of Cusa and the Power of the Possible." *American Catholic Philosophical Quarterly* 64 (1990): 7–34.

Certeau, Michel de. "The Gaze of Nicholas of Cusa." *Diacritics* 17 (1987): 2–38.

Christianson, Gerald. "Nicholas of Cusa and the Presidency Debate at the Council." In *Nicholas of Cusa on Christ and the Church,* edited by Gerald Christianson and Thomas M. Izbicki. Leiden: Brill, 1996. Pp. 87–103.

Colomer, Eusebius. "Nikolaus von Kues und Heimeric van den Velde." MFCG 4 (1964): 198–213.

Cranz, F. Edward. "Cusanus, Luther, and the Mystical Tradition." In *The Pursuit of Holiness,* edited by Charles Trinkaus and Heiko A. Oberman. Leiden: Brill, 1974. Pp. 93–102.

———. "1100 A.D.: A Crisis for Us?" *De Litteris* (1982): 84–108.

———. "The Late Works of Nicholas of Cusa." In *Nicholas of Cusa in Search of God and Wisdom,* edited by Gerald Christianson and Thomas M. Izbicki. Leiden: Brill, 1991. Pp. 141–160.

Duclow, Donald F. "Nicholas of Cusa in the Margins of Meister Eckhart: Codex Cusanus 21." In *Nicholas of Cusa in Search of God and Wisdom,* edited by Gerald Christianson and Thomas M. Izbicki. Leiden: Brill, 1991. Pp. 57–69.

Duhem, Pierre. "Thierry de Chartres et Nicolaus de Cues." *Revue des sciences philosophiques et théologiques* 3 (July 1909): 525–531.

Dupré, Louis. "Introduction and Cusa's Major Works." *American Catholic Quarterly* 64 (Winter 1990): 1–6.

———. "The Mystical Theology of Nicholas of Cusa's *De visione Dei.*" In *Nicholas of Cusa on Christ and the Church,* edited by Gerald Christianson and Thomas M. Izbicki. Leiden: Brill, 1996. Pp. 205–220.

———. "Nature and Grace in Nicholas of Cusa's Mystical Philosophy." *American Catholic Philosophical Quarterly* 64 (1990): 153–170.

Dupré, Wilhelm. "Absolute Truth and Conjectural Insights." In *Nicholas of Cusa on Christ and the Church,* edited by Gerald Christianson and Thomas M. Izbicki. Leiden: Brill, 1996. Pp. 323–338.

Ehses, Stephan. "Der Reformentwurf des Kardinals Nikolaus Cusanus." *Historiches Jahrbuch* 32 (1911): 274–297.

Führer, M. L. "The Consolation of Contemplation in Nicholas of Cusa's *De visione Dei.*" In *Nicholas of Cusa on Christ and the Church,* edited by Gerald Christianson and Thomas M. Izbicki. Leiden: Brill, 1996. Pp. 221–240.

———. "Nicholas of Cusa and Albert the Great." In *Nicholas of Cusa in Search of God and Wisdom,* edited by Gerald Christianson and Thomas M. Izbicki. Leiden: Brill, 1991. Pp. 45–69.

Gadamer, Hans-Georg. "[Nicolaus von Cues in der Geschichte des Erkenntnisproblems] Epilog." MFCG 11 (1975): 275–280.

# SELECT BIBLIOGRAPHY

————. "Nikolaus von Kues in modernen Denken." In *Nicolò Cusano agli inizi del mondo moderno*. Florence: Sansoni, 1970. Pp. 39–48.

Hallauer, Hermann. "Eine Visitation des Nikolaus von Kues im Benediktinerinnenkloster Sonnenberg." MFCG 4 (1964): 104–119.

Haubst, Rudolf. "Die erkenntnistheoretische und mystische Bedeutung der 'Mauer der Koinzidenz.' " MFCG 18 (1989): 167–191.

————. "Nikolaus von Kues als Intepret und Verteidiger Meister Eckharts." In *Freiheit und Gelassenheit: Meister Eckhart Heute*, edited by Udo Kern. Munich: Kaiser, 1980. Pp. 75–96.

————. "Die Thomas- und Proklos-Exzerpte des 'Nicolaus Treverensis' in codicillus Straßburg 84." MFCG 1 (1961): 17–51.

————. "Vorwort zur deutschen Übersetzung." In Nikolaus von Kues, *De visione Dei. Das Sehen Gottes*, translated by Helmut Pfeiffer, 3-4. Vol. 3 of *Textauswahl in deutscher Übersetzung*. Trier: Institut für Cusanus-Forschung, 1985.

————. "Zum Fortleben Alberts des Grossen bei Heymerick von Kamp und Nikolaus von Kues." *Studia Albertina*, Supplement IV BGPThM (1952): 420–447.

————. "Zur Filiation der Handschriften von 'De visione Dei.' " MFCG 19 (1991): 143–153.

Imbach, Ruedi. "Le (Néo-)platonisme médiéval, Proclus latin et l'école Dominicaine allemande." *Revue de théologie et de philosophie* 110 (1978): 427–428.

Izbicki, Thomas M. "The Church in the Light of Learned Ignorance." *Medieval Philosophy and Theology* 3 (1993): 186–214.

————. "The Literature in English, 1989–1994." In *Nicholas of Cusa on Christ and the Church*, edited by Gerald Christianson and Thomas M. Izbicki. Leiden: Brill, 1996. Pp. 341–353.

# SELECT BIBLIOGRAPHY

————. "Nicholas of Cusa: The Literature in English through 1988." In *Nicholas of Cusa in Search of God and Wisdom*, edited by Gerald Christianson and Thomas M. Izbicki. Leiden: Brill, 1991. Pp. 259–281.

Krämer, Werner. "Der Beitrag des Nikolaus von Kues zum Unionskonzil mit der Ostkirche." MFCG 9 (1971): 34–52.

Lohr, Charles H. "Metaphysics." In *The Cambridge History of Renaissance Philosophy*, edited by Charles B. Schmitt et al. Cambridge: Cambridge University Press, 1988. Pp. 537–638.

————. "Ramón Lull und Nikolaus von Kues. Zu einem Strukturvergleich ihres Denkens." *Theologie und Philosophie* 56 (1981): 218–231.

Lossky, Vladmir. "Icons of Christ" and "The Saviour Acheiropoietos." In Leonid Ouspensky and Vladmir Lossky, *The Meaning of Icons*, translated by G. E. H. Palmer and E. Kadloubovsky. Crestwood, NY: St. Vladimir's Seminary, 1989. Pp. 69–72.

McTighe, Thomas P. "*Contingentia* and *Alteritas* in Cusa's Metaphysics." *American Catholic Philosophical Quarterly* 64 (1990): 55–71.

————. "Thierry of Chartres and Nicholas of Cusa's Epistemology." *Philosophie* 56 (1981): 218–231.

Mantese, Giovanni. "Ein notarielles Inventar von Büchern und Wertgegenständen aus dem Nachlass des Nikolaus von Kues." MFCG 2 (1962): 85–116.

Meister, Alois. "Die humanistischen Anfänge des Nikolaus von Cues." *Annalen des historischen Vereins für den Niederrhein* 42 (1896): 1–21.

Meuthen, Erich. "Die deutschen Legationsreise des Nikolaus von Kues 1451/1452." In *Lebenslehren und Weltentwürfe im Übergang vom Mittelalter zur Neuzeit: Politik-Bildung-Naturkunde-Theologie*, edited by Hartmut Boockmann, Bernd Moeller, and Karl Stackmann, revised by Ludger Grenzmann. Göttingen: Vandenhoeck & Ruprecht, 1989. Pp. 421–499.

349

# SELECT BIBLIOGRAPHY

———. "Neue Schlaglichter auf das Leben des Nikolaus von Kues." MFCG 4 (1964): 37–53.

———. "Nikolaus von Kues in der Entscheidung zwischen Konzil und Papst." MFCG 9 (1971): 19–33.

———. "Nikolaus von Kues und das Konzil von Basel." *Schweizer Rundschau* 63 (1964): 377–386.

———. "Peter von Erkelenz (ca. 1430)–1494." *Zeitschrift des Aachener Geschichtsvereins* 84/85 (1977/1978): 701–744.

———. "Die Pfründen des Cusanus." MFCG 2 (1962): 15–66.

Miller, Clyde Lee. "God's Presence: Some Cusan Proposals." In *Nicholas of Cusa on Christ and the Church*, edited by Gerald Christianson and Thomas M. Izbicki. Leiden: Brill, 1996. Pp. 241–250.

———. "The Icon and the Wall: *Visio* and *ratio* in Nicholas of Cusa's *De visione Dei*." *Proceedings of the American Catholic Philosophical Association* 64 (1990): 86–98.

———. "Nicholas of Cusa's *On Conjectures* (*De coniecturis*)." In *Nicholas of Cusa in Search of God and Wisdom*, edited by Gerald Christianson and Thomas M. Izbicki. Leiden: Brill, 1991. Pp. 119–140.

———. "Nicholas of Cusa's *The Vision of God*." In *An Introduction to the Medieval Mystics of Europe*, edited by Paul Szarmach. 293–312. Albany: State University of New York, 1984. Pp. 293–312.

Moran, Dermot. "Pantheism from John Scottus Eriugena to Nicholas of Cusa." *American Catholic Philosophical Quarterly* 64 (Winter, 1990): 131–152.

Murdoch, John E. "Infinity and Continuity." In *The Cambridge History of Later Medieval Philosophy*, edited by Norman Kretzmann et al. Cambridge: Cambridge University Press, 1982. Pp. 564–591.

# SELECT BIBLIOGRAPHY

Panofsky, E. *"Facies illa Rogeri maximi pictoris."* In *Late Classical and Mediaeval Studies in Honor of A. M. Friend, Jr.* Princeton: Princeton University, 1955. Pp. 392–400.

Pindl-Büchel, Theodor. "The Relationship between the Epistemologies of Ramon Lull and Nicholas of Cusa." *American Catholic Philosophical Quarterly* 64 (1990): 73–87.

Schmidt, Margot. "Nikolaus von Kues im Gespräch mit den Tegernseer Mönchen über Wesen und Sinn der Mystik." MFCG 18 (1989): 25–49.

Senger, Hans Gerhard. "Mystik als Theorie bei Nikolaus von Kues." In *Gnosis und Mystik in der Geschichte der Philosophie*, edited by Peter Koslowski. Zürich: Artemis, 1988. Pp. 111–134.

Stieber, Joachim W. "The 'Hercules of the Eugenians' at the Crossroads: Nicholas of Cusa's Decision for the Pope and against the Council in 1436/1437—Theological, Political, and Social Aspects." In *Nicholas of Cusa in Search of God and Wisdom*, edited by Gerald Christianson and Thomas M. Izbicki. Leiden: Brill, 1991. Pp. 221–255.

Sullivan, Donald. "Cusanus and Pastoral Renewal: The Reform of Popular Religion in the Germanies." In *Nicholas of Cusa on Christ and the Church*, edited by Gerald Christianson and Thomas M. Izbicki. Leiden: Brill, 1996. Pp. 165–174.

———. "Nicholas of Cusa as Reformer: The Papal Legation to the Germanies, 1451–1452." *Mediaeval Studies* 36 (1974): 382–428.

Tillinghast, Pardon E. "Nicholas of Cusa vs. Sigismund of Habsburg: An Attempt at Post-Conciliar Church Reform." *Church History* 36 (1967): 371–390.

Watanabe, Morimichi. "Nicholas of Cusa and the Reform of the Roman Curia." In *Humanity and Divinity in Renaissance and Reformation: Essays in Honor of Charles Trinkaus*, edited by John O'Malley, Thomas M. Izbicki, and Gerald Christianson. Leiden: Brill, 1993. Pp. 185–203.

———. "Nicholas of Cusa and the Tyrolese Monasteries: Reform and Resistance." *History of Political Thought* 7 (1986): 53–72.

———. "Nicolaus Cusanus, Monastic Reform in the Tyrol and the *De visione Dei*." In *Concordia discors: Studi su Niccolò Cusano e l'umanesimo europeo offerti a Giovanni Santinello*. Padua: Editrice Antenore, 1993. Pp. 181–197.

———. "The Origins of Modern Cusanus Research in Germany and the Foundation of the Heidelberg *Opera omnia*." In *Nicholas of Cusa in Search of God and Wisdom*, edited by Gerald Christianson and Thomas M. Izbicki. Leiden: Brill, 1991. Pp. 17–42.

Watanabe, Morimichi, and Thomas M. Izbicki. "*Nicholas of Cusa, A General Reform of the Church*." In *Nicholas of Cusa on Christ and the Church*, edited by Gerald Christianson and Thomas M. Izbicki. Leiden: Brill, 1996. Pp. 175–202.

### 2.2 Books

Baum, Wilhelm. *Nikolaus Cusanus in Tirol: Das Wirken des Philosophen und Reformators als Fürstbischof von Brixen*. Bozen: Athesia, 1983.

Beierwaltes, Werner. *Visio absoluta: Reflexion als Grundzug des göttlichen Prinzips bei Nicolaus Cusanus*. (HSB Jg. 1978, 1. Abh.) Heidelberg: Winter, 1978.

Brüntrup, Alfons. *Können und Sein. Der Zusammenhang der Spätschriften des Nikolaus von Kues*. (*Epimeleia. Beiträge zur Philosophie*, 23.) Munich: Pustet, 1973.

Buber, Martin. *Between Man and Man*. Translated by Ronald Gregor Smith. Boston: Beacon, 1955.

Cassirer, Ernst. *The Individual and the Cosmos in Renaissance Philosophy*. Translated by Mario Domandi. New York: Harper, 1963.

Christianson, Gerald. *Cesarini, the Conciliar Cardinal: The Basel Years, 1431–1438*. St. Ottilien: EOS, 1979.

# SELECT BIBLIOGRAPHY

Christianson, Gerald, and Thomas M. Izbicki, eds. *Nicholas of Cusa in Search of God and Wisdom*. (Studies in the History of Christian Thought, vol. XLV.) Leiden: Brill, 1991.

―――. *Nicholas of Cusa on Christ and the Church*. (Studies in the History of Christian Thought, vol. LXXI.) Leiden: Brill, 1996.

Colomer, Eusebio. *Nikolaus von Kues und Raimund Llull*. Berlin: De Gruyter, 1961.

Dangelmayr, Siegfried. *Gotteserkenntnis und Gottesbegriff in den philosophischen Schriften des Nikolaus von Kues*. Meisenheim am Glan: Hain, 1969.

Dupré, Louis. *Passage to Modernity: An Essay in the Hermeneutics of Nature and Culture*. New Haven: Yale University, 1993.

Gadamer, Hans-Georg. *Truth and Method*. 2nd rev. ed. Translated by Joel Weinsheimer and Donald G. Marshall. New York: Crossroad, 1989.

Haubst, Rudolf. *Das Bild des Einen und Dreieinen Gottes in der Welt nach Nikolaus von Kues*. (*Trier theologische Studien* Bd. 4.) Trier: Paulinus, 1952.

―――. *Die Christologie des Nikolaus von Kues*. Freiburg: Herder, 1956.

―――. *Streifzüge in die Cusanische Theologie*. (*Buchreihe der Cusanus-Gesellschaft*.) Münster: Aschendorff, 1991.

Heinz-Mohr, Gerd, and Willehad Paul Eckert, eds. *Das Werk des Nicolaus Cusanus*. 2nd ed. Köln: Wienand, 1963.

Hillgarth, J. N. *Ramon Lull and Lullism in Fourteenth-Century France*. Oxford: Clarendon, 1971.

Honecker, Martin. *Nikolaus von Cues und die griechische Sprache*. Vol. II of *Cusanus-Studien*. (HSB Jg. 1937–1938, 2. Abh.) Heidelberg: Winter, 1938.

# SELECT BIBLIOGRAPHY

Hopkins, Jasper. *A Concise Introduction to the Philosophy of Nicholas of Cusa.* 2nd ed. Minneapolis: University of Minnesota Press, 1980.

Jacobi, Klaus. *Die Methode der Cusanischen Philosophie.* Freiburg-Munich: Alber, 1969.

Jaspers, Karl. *Anselm and Nicholas of Cusa.* From *The Great Philosophers*, vol. II. Edited by Hannah Arendt and translated by Ralph Manheim. New York: Harcourt Brace Jovanovich, 1966.

Koch, Josef. *Die Ars coniecturalis des Nikolaus von Kues.* (*Arbeitsgemeinschaft für Forschung des Landes Nordrhein-Westfalen, Geisteswissenschaften*, Hft. 4.) Köln: Westdeutscher Verlag, 1956.

————. *Nikolaus von Cues und seine Umwelt.* (HSB Jg. 1944–1948, 2. Abh.) Heidelberg: Winter, 1948.

————. *Predigten. 7. Untersuchung über Datierung, Form, Sprache und Quellen. Kritisches Verzeichnis sämtlicher Predigten.* Vol. I of *Cusanus-Texte.* (HSB Jg. 1941–1942, 1. Abh.) Heidelberg: Winter, 1942.

Küng, Hans. *On Being a Christian.* Translated by Edward Quinn. New York: Doubleday, 1976.

Mahnke, Dietrich. *Unendliche Sphäre und Allmittelpunkt.* Halle: Niemeyer, 1937.

Marx, Jakob. *Geschichte des Armen-Hospitals zum h. Nikolaus zu Cues.* Trier: Paulinus, 1907.

————. *Verzeichnis der Handschriften-Sammlung des Hospitals zu Cues bei Bernkastel a. Mosel.* Trier: Hospital zu Cues, 1905.

Meier-Oeser, Stephan. *Die Präsenz des Vergessenen. Zur Rezeption der Philosophie des Nicolaus Cusanus vom 15. bis zum 18. Jahrhundert.* (Buchreihe der Cusanus-Gesellschaft, X.) Münster: Aschendorff, 1989.

Meuthen, Erich. *Die letzten Jahre des Nikolaus von Kues.* Köln: Westdeutscher Verlag, 1958.

# SELECT BIBLIOGRAPHY

———. *Nikolaus von Kues, 1401–1464: Skizze einer Biographie.* 7th ed. Münster: Aschendorff, 1992.

———. *Das Trierer Schisma von 1430 auf dem Basler Konzil: zur Lebensgeschichte des Nikolaus von Kues.* Münster: Aschendorff, 1973.

Oberman, Heiko. *The Dawn of the Reformation.* Edinburg: T. and T. Clark, 1986.

Offermann, Ulrich. *Christus-Wahrheit des Denkens. Eine Untersuchung zur Schrift "De docta ignorantia" des Nikolaus von Kues.* Münster: Aschendorff, 1991.

O'Malley, John W. *Praise and Blame in Renaissance Rome. Rhetoric, Doctrine, and Reform in the Sacred Orators of the Papal Court, c. 1450–1521.* Durham, N.C.: Duke University Press, 1979.

Pannenberg, Wolfhart. *Jesus-God and Man.* Translated by Lewis L. Wilkins and Duane A. Priebe. Philadelphia: Westminster, 1968.

Pralle, Ludwig. *Die Widerentdeckung des Tacitus. Ein Beitrag zur Geistesgeschichte Fuldas und zur Biographie des jungen Cusanus.* Fulda: Parzeller, 1952.

Senger, Hans Gerhard. *Die Philosophie des Nicolaus von Kues vor dem Jahre 1440. Untersuchungen zur Entwicklung einer Philosophie in der Frühzeit des Nikolaus (1430–1440).* (BGPThM NF 3.) Münster: Aschendorff, 1971.

Sigmund, Paul E. *Nicholas of Cusa and Medieval Political Thought.* Cambridge, Mass.: Harvard University, 1963.

Stinger, Charles L. *Humanism and the Church Fathers: Ambrogio Traversari (1336–1439) and Christian Antiquity in the Italian Renaissance.* Albany: State University of New York, 1977.

Tillich, Paul. *Systematic Theology.* Vols. I–III. Chicago: University of Chicago Press, 1951–1963.

# SELECT BIBLIOGRAPHY

Vansteenberghe, Edmond. *Le Cardinal Nicolas de Cues: L'action--la pensée.* Paris: Champion, 1920.

Wackerzapp, Herbert. *Der Einfluss Meister Eckharts auf die ertsen philosophischen Schriften des Nikolaus von Kues.* Edited by Josef Koch. (BGPThM 39, n. 3.) Münster: Aschendorff, 1962.

Watanabe, Morimichi. *The Political Ideas of Nicholas of Cusa with Special Reference to His De concordantia catholica.* Geneva: Librairie Droz, 1963.

Watts, Pauline Moffit. *Nicolaus Cusanus. A Fifteenth Century Vision of Man.* Leiden: Brill, 1982.

Zellinger, Eduard. *Cusanus-Konkordanz. Unter Zugrundelegung der philosophischen und der bedeutendsten theologischen Werke.* Munich: Hueber, 1960.

# INDEX TO INTRODUCTION

Aindorffer, Caspar, 32
Anselm, 15
*Apologia doctae ignorantiae*
  (Cusa), 6, 7, 31
*Apology of Learned Ignorance.*
  See *Apologia doctae
  ignorantiae* (Cusa)
Augustine, 29

Bessarion (archbishop of
  Nicaea), 5
Bovelles, Charles de, 15
Bregno, Andrea, 13
Bruno, Giordano, 15
Buber, Martin, 16
*Bursa Cusana*, 13
Bussi, Giovanni Andrea, 13, 16

Can-Is. See *Posse*
Carvajal, Juan de, 6
Cassirer, Ernst, 17
Cesarini, Giuliano (cardinal),
  4, 20
Christ: incarnational theology,
  35, 54–55; as *Posse*, 68;
  union of divine and human
  natures, 25, 26
Coincidence of opposites, 14,
  17, 18, 20–36, 44–46, 48,
55, 59, 65; declarative
function, 51–52;
descriptive function, 50–
56; evocative function,
49–50; iconographic
function, 51, 52–55;
incarnational theology
and, 54–55; as method, 22,
23, 38, 29–30; mystical
theology and, 48–55; as
remedy, 28; symbolic
language and, 52–54;
theological applications,
27–36; as unity, 27–28
*Compendium* (Cusa), 12, 57,
  59, 70
*Complicatio-explicatio*, 14, 15
Conciliarism, 3, 4, 5, 6, 14
Contemplation, 56–70
Cranz, Edward, 69–70
*Cribratio Alkorani* (Cusa), 11
Cusa, Nicholas of: attempted
  murder of, 9; bishop of
  Brixen, 6, 8–10; cardinal,
  6, 7; conciliarism and, 3,
  4, 5, 6, 14; death, 13; early
  life, 3–4; education, 4;
  importance of, 13–19;
  influence on later writers,

15; as metaphysician, 16, 17; ordination, 6; papal emissary, 6, 7–8. *See also* specific headings, e.g.: *De apice theoriae* (Cusa); Learned ignorance
Cusanus-Gesellschaft, 16
*Cusanus-Studien*, 16
*Cusanus-Texte*, 16

D'Étaples, Jacques LeFèvre, 15
*De aequalitate* (Cusa), 10
*De apice theoriae* (Cusa), 12, 56–70; *Memoriale*, 68, 69
*De arithmeticis complementis* (Cusa), 7
*De auctoritate praesidendi in concilio generali* (Cusa), 4
*De beryllo* (Cusa), 9–10, 69
*De concordantia catholica* (Cusa), 4
*De coniecturis* (Cusa), 7
*De dato patris luminum* (Cusa), 7, 59, 70
*De Deo abscondito* (Cusa), 7, 37–39, 43, 60
*De docta ignorantia* (Cusa), 7, 19–36, 45, 47, 51, 65. *See also* specific headings, e.g.: Learned ignorance
*De filiatione Dei* (Cusa), 7
*De genesi* (Cusa), 7
*De ludo globi* (Cusa), 12
*De mathematicis complementis* (Cusa), 12
*De non aliud* (Cusa), 12, 70
*De pace fidei* (Cusa), 9
*De possest* (Cusa), 10, 57–69, 70

*De principio* (Cusa), 10
*De quaerendo Deum* (Cusa), 7, 39–43
*De theologicis complementis* (Cusa), 9
*De transmutationibus geometricis* (Cusa), 7
*De venatione Dei* (Cusa), 12
*De visione Dei* (Cusa), 9, 18–19, 43–55, 59, 63, 70
*Dialogues de Deo abscondito*. See *De Deo abscondito* (Cusa)
*Dialogues on the Hidden God*. See *De Deo abscondito* (Cusa)
*Dialogus concludens Amedistarum errorem* (Cusa), 7
Dionysius the Areopagite. *See* Pseudo-Dionysius
*Docta ignorantia*. *See* Learned ignorance

Eckhart, Meister, 7, 17, 69
Eriugena, John Scotus, 36
Eugene IV (pope), 4–5, 21

Felix V (antipope), 6
Ferrara, council of (1438–1439), 5–6
Fulgentius, 36

Gadamer, Hans-Georg, 16
Gerson, Jean, 33

Heidelberg Academy, 16
Heimburg, Gregory, 9
Heymeric van den Velde, 4

*Idiota* (Cusa), 8, 59–60
Ignorance, 36–43, 51;
    illumined ignorance, 41.
    *See also* Learned ignorance
Incarnation, 35, 54–55
Infinite, 22, 26, 29, 30, 47–48

Jaspers, Karl, 17
Jesus Christ. *See* Christ
Jubilee year (1450), 7

Kues, foundation at, 10, 13
Küng, Hans, 16

Learned ignorance, 6, 18, 19–
    36, 65
Lewis, C. S., 16
Lohr, Charles, 16
Lull, Ramon, 4, 15
Luther, Martin, 17

Marcus Eugenicus (archbishop
    of Ephesus), 5
Martins, Ferdinand, 13
Mathematics, 22, 30, 47. *See
    also* Infinite
Maximum: absolute, 15, 19, 23,
    24–27, 34, 35; contracted,
    19, 23, 24–27
Meier-Oeser, Stephan, 15
Merton, Thomas, 16
Mystical theology, 43–55
*Mystical Theology, The* (Pseudo-
    Dionysius), 4, 33

Names of God, 38–41, 59
Negative theology, 33–34, 55,
    59, 66–67

Nicholas of Cusa. *See* Cusa,
    Nicholas of
Nicholas V (pope), 6, 7

Oberman, Heiko, 16
*On Can-Is. See De possest*
    (Cusa)
*On Conjectures. See De
    coniecturis* (Cusa)
*On Learned Ignorance. See De
    docta ignorantia* (Cusa)
*On "Possest." See De possest*
    (Cusa)
*On Seeking God. See De
    quaerendo Deum* (Cusa)
*On the Beryl. See De beryllo*
    (Cusa)
*On the Gift of the Father of
    Lights. See De dato patris
    luminum* (Cusa)
*On the Hidden God. See De Deo
    abscondito* (Cusa)
*On the Hunt for Wisdom*
    (Cusa), 70
*On the Not-Other. See De non
    aliud* (Cusa)
*On the Summit of
    Contemplation. See De
    apice theoriae* (Cusa)
*On the Vision of God. See De
    visione Dei* (Cusa)
Oresme, Nicole, 15

Pannenberg, Wolfhart, 16
Parentucelli, Tommaso, 6. *See
    also* Nicholas V (pope)
Peter Wymar of Erkelenz, 56,
    58, 59

# INDEXES

Piccolomini, Aeneas Sylvius, 4, 6, 9. *See also* Pius II (pope)
Pius II (pope), 9, 10, 12
Platonism, 16
Plethon, Georgius Gemistus, 5
*Posse*, 56–70
Pseudo-Augustine, 36
Pseudo-Dionysius, 4, 6, 7, 33

*Reformatio generalis* (Cusa), 10
*Reparatio kalendarii* (Cusa), 4
Römer, Johann, 13

Sánchez de Arévalo, Rodrigo, 7
Sigismund (duke of Austria), 7, 9, 10, 11, 12
Stuben, Verena von, 9

Thierry of Chartres, 4, 7, 15
Tillich, Paul, 17
Toscanelli, Paolo del Pozzo, 4, 13
Treverinsis, Nicolaus. *See* Cusa, Nicholas of
Trinity, 14, 15, 29, 30, 68, 69

Ulrich of Manderscheid, 4

Vincent of Aggsbach, 32–33

Waging, Bernard de, 15
Watanabe, Morimichi, 15
Wehlen, Simon von, 9
Wenck, Johannes, 7, 32
Wismayer, Leonard, 7, 9

# INDEX TO TEXTS

Anaxagoras, 140
Anselm, 102
*Antiquities* (Varro), 95
Aristotle, 88–89, 101, 109, 155
Augustine, 101, 113, 282, 283
Avicenna, 139

Boethius, 101

Can-Is. *See Posse*
Cesarini, Giuliano (cardinal): letter to, 205–6
Christ, 272–89; ascension into heaven, 188–91; born of Virgin Mary, 180–83; church and, 201–5; as consummation, 287–89; death, 183–86; faith in, 196–201; happiness and, 276–78; judge of living and dead, 191–96; resurrection, 186–88; union of divine and human nature, 272–76; Word of life, 284–87
Church, 201–5
Cicero, 125
Coincidence of opposites, 91–92, 252–56

Contemplation, 293–303
Creation, 137, 166–69

*De apice theoriae* (Cusa), 293–303; *Memoriale*, 300–303
*De coniecturis* (Cusa), 130, 142, 144, 155, 171, 172
*De Deo abscondito* (Cusa), 209–13
*De docta ignorantia* (Cusa), 87–206. *See also* specific headings, e.g.: Maximum; Trinity
*De visione Dei* (Cusa), 235–89
*Dialogues de Deo abscondito*. See *De Deo abscondito* (Cusa)
*Dialogues on the Hidden God.* See *De Deo abscondito* (Cusa)
Dionysius the Areopagite. *See* Pseudo-Dionysius
*Docta ignorantia. See* Learned ignorance

Epicureans, 101

Faith, 196–201
Firmicus Maternus, Julius, 124

# INDEXES

Hermes Trismegistus, 121, 124, 148
Hilary of Poitiers, 126

Ignorance. *See* Learned ignorance
Infinite, 88; attributes of infinite line, 102–12, 131; God as absolute infinity, 257–67; infinite sphere as metaphor for existence of God, 119–20; infinite triangle as metaphor for maximum trinity, 112–14

Jesus Christ. *See* Christ

Learned ignorance, 87–89, 127–206

Martianus Capella, 98
Mathematics, 100–106, 112–18, 128, 129, 154. *See also* Infinite
Maximum, 89–127; contracted, 94, 139, 145, 149, 154–55, 169–80
Music, 128–29
Mystical theology, 235–89
*Mystical Theology, The* (Pseudo-Dionysius), 107

Names of God, 121–25, 218, 220, 242
Negative theology, 125–26

*On Conjectures*. See *De coniecturis* (Cusa)

Parmenides, 120
Paul, 197, 217
Peripatetics, 101, 143, 148, 151, 152–53
Peter Wymar of Erkelenz, 293–300
Plato, 109, 133, 139
Platonists, 101, 145–46, 147, 150–54, 165, 171; use of mathematics, 101
*Posse*, 294–303
Providence, 118–19, 239–41
Pseudo-Dionysius, 107, 109, 112, 122, 126
Pythagoras, 95, 96, 98, 101

Resurrection, 186–88

Socrates, 88, 133, 139
Stoics, 148

Trinity, 98–100, 123, 144–46, 158, 267–72

Universals, 139, 143–44

Varro, Marcus, 95
Virgil, 165

# Other Volumes in This Series

**Julian of Norwich** • SHOWINGS

**Jacob Boehme** • THE WAY TO CHRIST

**Nahman of Bratslav** • THE TALES

**Gregory of Nyssa** • THE LIFE OF MOSES

**Bonaventure** • THE SOUL'S JOURNEY INTO GOD, THE TREE OF LIFE, AND THE LIFE OF ST. FRANCIS

**William Law** • A SERIOUS CALL TO DEVOUT AND HOLY LIFE, AND THE SPIRIT OF LOVE

**Abraham Isaac Kook** • THE LIGHTS OF PENITENCE, LIGHTS OF HOLINESS, THE MORAL PRINCIPLES, ESSAYS, AND POEMS

**Ibn 'Ata' Illah** • THE BOOK OF WISDOM AND KWAJA ABDULLAH

**Ansari** • INTIMATE CONVERSATIONS

**Johann Arndt** • TRUE CHRISTIANITY

**Richard of St. Victor** • THE TWELVE PATRIARCHS, THE MYSTICAL ARK, AND BOOK THREE OF THE TRINITY

**Origen** • AN EXHORTATION TO MARTYRDOM, PRAYER, AND SELECTED WORKS

**Catherine of Genoa** • PURGATION AND PURGATORY, THE SPIRITUAL DIALOGUE

**Native North American Spirituality of the Eastern Woodlands** • SACRED MYTHS, DREAMS, VISIONS, SPEECHES, HEALING FORMULAS, RITUALS AND CEREMONIALS

**Teresa of Avila** • THE INTERIOR CASTLE

**Apocalyptic Spirituality** • TREATISES AND LETTERS OF LACTANTIUS, ADSO OF MONTIER-EN-DER, JOACHIM OF FIORE, THE FRANCISCAN SPIRITUALS, SAVONAROLA

**Athanasius** • THE LIFE OF ANTONY, A LETTER TO MARCELLINUS

**Catherine of Siena** • THE DIALOGUE

**Sharafuddin Maneri** • THE HUNDRED LETTERS

**Martin Luther** • THEOLOGIA GERMANICA

**Native Mesoamerican Spirituality** • ANCIENT MYTHS, DISCOURSES, STORIES, DOCTRINES, HYMNS, POEMS FROM THE AZTEC, YUCATEC, QUICHE-MAYA AND OTHER SACRED TRADITIONS

**Symeon the New Theologian** • THE DISCOURSES

**Ibn Al'-Arabī** • THE BEZELS OF WISDOM

**Hadewijch** • THE COMPLETE WORKS

**Philo of Alexandria** • THE CONTEMPLATIVE LIFE, THE GIANTS, AND SELECTIONS

**George Herbert** • THE COUNTRY PARSON, THE TEMPLE

**Unknown** • THE CLOUD OF UNKNOWING

**John and Charles Wesley** • SELECTED WRITINGS AND HYMNS

**Meister Eckhart** • THE ESSENTIAL SERMONS, COMMENTARIES, TREATISES AND DEFENSE

Francisco de Osuna • THE THIRD SPIRITUAL ALPHABET
Jacopone da Todi • THE LAUDS
Fakhruddin 'Iraqi • DIVINE FLASHES
Menahem Nahum of Chernobyl • THE LIGHT OF THE EYES
Early Dominicans • SELECTED WRITINGS
John Climacus • THE LADDER OF DIVINE ASCENT
Francis and Clare • THE COMPLETE WORKS
Gregory Palamas • THE TRIADS
Pietists • SELECTED WRITINGS
The Shakers • TWO CENTURIES OF SPIRITUAL REFLECTION
Zohar • THE BOOK OF ENLIGHTENMENT
Luis de León • THE NAMES OF CHRIST
Quaker Spirituality • SELECTED WRITINGS
Emanuel Swedenborg • THE UNIVERSAL HUMAN AND SOUL-BODY INTERACTION
Augustine of Hippo • SELECTED WRITINGS
Safed Spirituality • RULES OF MYSTICAL PIETY, THE BEGINNING OF WISDOM
Maximus Confessor • SELECTED WRITINGS
John Cassian • CONFERENCES
Johannes Tauler • SERMONS
John Ruusbroec • THE SPIRITUAL ESPOUSALS AND OTHER WORKS
Ibn 'Abbād of Ronda • LETTERS ON THE SŪFĪ PATH
Angelus Silesius • THE CHERUBINIC WANDERER
The Early Kabbalah •
Meister Eckhart • TEACHER AND PREACHER
John of the Cross • SELECTED WRITINGS
Pseudo-Dionysius • THE COMPLETE WORKS
Bernard of Clairvaux • SELECTED WORKS
Devotio Moderna • BASIC WRITINGS
The Pursuit of Wisdom • AND OTHER WORKS BY THE AUTHOR OF THE
   CLOUD OF UNKNOWING
Richard Rolle • THE ENGLISH WRITINGS
Francis de Sales, Jane de Chantal • LETTERS OF SPIRITUAL DIRECTION
Albert and Thomas • SELECTED WRITINGS
Robert Bellarmine • SPIRITUAL WRITINGS
Nicodemos of the Holy Mountain • A HANDBOOK OF SPIRITUAL COUNSEL
Henry Suso • THE EXEMPLAR, WITH TWO GERMAN SERMONS
Bérulle and the French School • SELECTED WRITINGS
The Talmud • SELECTED WRITINGS
Ephrem the Syrian • HYMNS
Hildegard of Bingen • SCIVIAS
Birgitta of Sweden • LIFE AND SELECTED REVELATIONS
John Donne • SELECTIONS FROM DIVINE POEMS, SERMONS, DEVOTIONS AND
   PRAYERS

Jeremy Taylor • SELECTED WORKS
Walter Hilton • SCALE OF PERFECTION
Ignatius of Loyola • SPIRITUAL EXERCISES AND SELECTED WORKS
Anchoritic Spirituality • ANCRENE WISSE AND ASSOCIATED WORKS
Nizam ad-din Awliya • MORALS FOR THE HEART
Pseudo-Macarius • THE FIFTY SPIRITUAL HOMILIES AND THE GREAT LETTER
Gertrude of Helfta • THE HERALD OF DIVINE LOVE
Angela of Foligno • COMPLETE WORKS
Margaret Ebner • MAJOR WORKS
Marguerite Porete • THE MIRROR OF SIMPLE SOULS
John Henry Newman • SELECTED SERMONS
Early Anabaptist Spirituality • SELECTED WRITINGS
Elijah Benamozegh • ISRAEL AND HUMANITY
The Classic Midrash • TANNAITIC COMMENTARIES ON THE BIBLE
Vincent de Paul and Louise de Marillac • RULES, CONFERENCES AND
   WRITINGS
Isaiah Horowitz • THE GENERATIONS OF ADAM
Early Islamic Mysticism • SUFI, QUR'AN, MI'RAJ, POETIC AND THEOLOGICAL
   WRITINGS
Theatine Spirituality • SELECTED WRITINGS
Carthusian Spirituality • THE WRITINGS OF HUGH OF BALMA AND
   GUIGO DE PONTE